SELECTIONS

FROM THE CORRESPONDENCE

OF

THEODORE ROOSEVELT

AND

HENRY CABOT LODGE

1884–1918

VOLUME I

SELECTIONS
FROM THE CORRESPONDENCE
OF
THEODORE ROOSEVELT
AND
HENRY CABOT LODGE
1884–1918

Edited by
Henry Cabot Lodge
and
Charles F. Redmond

VOLUME I

DA CAPO PRESS · NEW YORK · 1971

A Da Capo Press Reprint Edition

This Da Capo Press edition of
Selections from the Correspondence of Theodore
Roosevelt and Henry Cabot Lodge, 1884-1918,
is an unabridged republication of the first
edition published in New York and London in 1925.
It is reprinted by special arrangement with
Charles Scribner's Sons.

Library of Congress Catalog Card Number 72-146156

SBN 306-70129-4

Published by Da Capo Press, Inc.
A Subsidiary of Plenum Publishing Corporation
227 West 17th Street, New York, N.Y. 10011
All Rights Reserved

Manufactured in the United States of America

SELECTIONS
FROM THE CORRESPONDENCE
OF
THEODORE ROOSEVELT
AND
HENRY CABOT LODGE
1884–1918

From a photograph copyright by Pirie Mac Donald

Theodore Roosevelt

SELECTIONS

FROM THE CORRESPONDENCE

OF

THEODORE ROOSEVELT

AND

HENRY CABOT LODGE

1884–1918

VOLUME I

CHARLES SCRIBNER'S SONS

NEW YORK · LONDON

1925

PREFACE

THE letters in these volumes are selections from a correspondence between Theodore Roosevelt and the editor of the selections, which extended from May, 1884, to December, 1918. It is a continuous correspondence during that time, with no intermissions except at the periods when the writers of the letters were both living in the same city. I have ventured to make and to publish these selections because the correspondence has seemed to me of large and general interest. There is much of it which is concerned, as is to be expected, with public affairs because we were both in public life for many years together; but the correspondence as a whole is very general in character and the letters deal with all sorts of topics relating to our families and friends, with literature and the life of the time, as well as with the many other subjects in which we had a common interest. The letters of Colonel Roosevelt, apart from their historical importance, have as it seems to me a peculiar value as showing during a long period of years the widely varied interests which engaged his attention, and in that way they throw light upon one of the greatest and most remarkable men who has ever played a large part and exercised a powerful influence in the history of the United States.

I have only to add that these letters never would have been selected, edited, or published if the editor had not had throughout the kind approval as well as the wise counsel and sympathetic aid of Mrs. Roosevelt. It is not possible for me to express my debt to her, which is but one of many affectionate kindnesses which I have owed to her during a friendship that has lasted now for years.

During the past summer illness prevented my continuing for a time the work involved in editing the letters. I had completed them through 1909. Beyond that point I had read the letters but had not as yet attempted to edit or arrange them. Fortunately my secretary, Charles F. Redmond, had been my assistant in all the work I had done on the letters and was entirely familiar with them and with the subjects. He was therefore able to go on with those which had not been fully edited and arranged and my obligation to him, which I wish here to acknowledge to the fullest extent, has been very great indeed.

I am also very deeply indebted to my friend of many years, Charles G. Washburn, of Worcester, a classmate and devoted friend and admirer of Theodore Roosevelt, in regard to whom he has written a most admirable book. He read all the letters of the later years, from 1910 to 1918, a period in our political history with which he was extremely familiar. I had therefore the benefit of his judgment before sending the letters of these later years to the press and the amount of work and anxiety which he saved me and the help which he gave me I find it difficult to express. I can only say that I am very grateful to him for aid of the most efficient kind at a moment when I much needed it.

H. C. L.

SELECTIONS
FROM THE CORRESPONDENCE
OF
THEODORE ROOSEVELT
AND
HENRY CABOT LODGE
1884–1918

SELECTIONS FROM THE CORRESPONDENCE OF THEODORE ROOSEVELT AND HENRY CABOT LODGE

1884

ALBANY,
May 5th, [1884.]

My dear Mr. Lodge,

Curiously enough I had just begun a letter to you when I received yours. I wish to, in turn, congratulate you upon *your* success,* which, by the way, is of a far more solid and enduring kind than is mine. The result of the Utica convention was largely an accident; chance threw in our way an opportunity such as will never occur again; and I determined to use it for every ounce it was worth.

Unquestionably, Blaine is our greatest danger; for I fear lest, if he come too near success, the bread-and-butter brigade from the south will leave Arthur and go over to him. We who stand against both *must* be organized, and, moreover, must select our candidate with the greatest care. I have a plan which I would like to talk to you about. I do not believe New York can by any possibility be held solid; our delegation will split into three, and we will do more than I believe we can if we unite any two of the parts.

Can you not come on to New York on Saturday the 16th; and stay with me, at 6 West 57th St? We are breaking up house, so you will have to excuse very barren accommodations. On Saturday I hope to have a number of the independent delegates meet, and should like you to see them. I will then go on with you to Washington with pleasure. On Thursday I go down to New York to stay till Monday; so write me there (6 West 57th St.)

Very truly yours,

THEODORE ROOSEVELT.

* My election as delegate at large from Massachusetts to the Republican National Convention at Chicago.

1

6 West 57th St.,
NEW YORK,
May 10th, '84.

Dear Mr. Lodge,

I shall expect you on Saturday evening; if you are able to come by an earlier train come round to Delmonico's where there will be an informal, and strictly private meeting of some of the "Edmunds"* delegates from New York. I shall be able to tell you pretty well how things stand in this State; and I shall with pleasure go on to Washington † with you.

Yours always,   THEODORE ROOSEVELT.

NEW YORK,
May 25th, [1884.]

Dear Lodge,

Many thanks for your kind note. Putnam ‡ is a trump, but on politics—oh, heavens! Some of the papers have had a very amusing account of an imaginary dinner we gave to Edmunds, at which he treated us with ferocious disdain, and made us leave his presence in crestfallen wrath—this being advanced as an explanation of our alleged conduct in endeavoring to "sell him out" for Lincoln. § Truly, the liar is abroad in the land! Also the crank.

I have written to the western Edmunds men, and to the Vermonters as you wished.   Most truly,

THEODORE ROOSEVELT.

NEW YORK,
May 26th, [1884.]

Dear Lodge,

For Heaven's sake don't let the Massachusetts delegation commit any such act of suicidal folly as (from panic merely)

---

* George Franklin Edmunds—then a Republican Senator from Vermont.

† We went to Washington soon after this note was written. We saw many interesting people, leaders in politics—many Senators; but made little effective headway. There was plenty of support visible for Blaine and for Arthur and abundant hostility to each of them. There seemed to be practically no support for Edmunds.

‡ George Haven Putnam of New York, distinguished and well known publisher and author.

§ Robert Lincoln, Secretary of War.

supporting Arthur would be. Arthur is the very weakest candidate we could nominate though, as you know, I regard Blaine as even less desirable, on account of his decidedly mottled record. Arthur could not carry New York, Ohio or Indiana; he would be beaten out of sight.

I agree with you that Blaine is still the most dangerous man; but he has lost strength, and will not have more than three hundred votes, if as many. I have tried my best to make the *Times* attack him; and I think it will now but they regard Arthur as much more formidable; *one reason they attack Arthur so much more than Blaine is because they have heard that the Massachusetts men are merely Arthur delegates in disguise.* Now, in trying to avoid the Blaine devil, don't take a premature plunge into the Arthur deep sea; I think we can keep clear of both; if we go to either we are lost.

Yours,   THEODORE ROOSEVELT.

LITTLE MISSOURI,
June 17th, [1884.]*

My dear Lodge,

Having been off on a four days hunt after antelope I have but just received your telegram. The despatch to the *Post* was simply a flat denial of the authority of my alleged interview, which some newspaper correspondent has made up out of the whole cloth. I am absolutely ignorant of what has been said or done since the convention, as I have been away from all newspapers for ten days.

I hope soon to be back when I will see you and decide with you as to what we can do. I think Dakotah is my hold for this autumn.   Yours always,   THEODORE ROOSEVELT.

LITTLE MISSOURI,
June 18th, '84.

My dear Lodge,

I have just received your long and welcome letter; my brief note of yesterday was sent before I had received it. I

* This was after the Convention had been held and Blaine and Logan nominated. Roosevelt had gone West to his ranch immediately after the Convention adjourned. I had returned to Massachusetts.

am now writing under difficulties, being in the cattlemen's hut, and having just spent thirteen hours in the saddle.

The St. Paul "Interview" was absolutely without foundation in fact; I had not spoken a dozen words to any reporter; my telegrams to the "Post" merely contained an explicit denial of its authenticity.

I allowed myself to be interviewed in St. Paul for the purpose of giving a rap to the *Post*; but to my regret the cream of the interview does not seem to have been copied in the Eastern papers. I thought I would touch up Godkin* and Sedgwick† a little.

You are pursuing precisely the proper course; do not answer any assaults unless it is imperatively necessary; keep on good terms with the machine, and put in every ounce, to win. Certainly the Independents have little cause to congratulate themselves on a candidate of Cleveland's moral character; with Barnum‡ to manage his canvass, and Hendricks§ to carry behind. The veto of the Tenure-of-Office Bill was inexcusable; I have written a letter to a fellow Assemblyman (Hubbell) about it, which I think will be published shortly in the *Tribune*. I shall be east about a week after you get this letter, and shall write you immediately, as I wish to see you at once; I am very anxious you should take no steps hastily, for I do not know a man in the country whose future I regard as so promising as is yours; and I would not for anything have you do a single thing that could hurt it, unless it was a question of principle, when of course I should not advise you to hesitate for a moment.

With warmest regards to Mrs. Lodge, believe me,

Always yours,   THEODORE ROOSEVELT.

P. S.—I have not seen a newspaper since I left Chicago.

---

* E. L. Godkin—editor of the New York *Nation*.

† Arthur Sedgwick—on the staff of *The Nation*.

‡ William Barnum had been Senator from Connecticut. At this time he was Chairman of the Democratic National Committee.

§ Thomas A. Hendricks—then aspiring to the Democratic nomination for Vice-President.

422 Madison Ave.,
NEW YORK,
July 28th, '84.

My dear Lodge,

I was very glad indeed to hear from you; Mrs. Lodge and yourself *must* make us a visit next winter; my sister is as anxious as I am to have you.

I did not have a chance to see either Sedgwick or Godkin; I wrote Putnam and incidentally asked him to give my compliments to either or both of the gentlemen named, and to tell them from me that I thought they were suffering just at present from a species of moral myopia, complicated with intellectual strabismus. Most of my friends seem surprised to find that I have not developed hoofs and horns; the independents are rapidly cultivating the belief that the Utica Convention was really gotten up in the interest of Blaine; and that you and I are, with Elkins,* his chief advisers.

I have received shoals of letters, pathetic and abusive, to which I have replied with vivacity or ferocity, according to the circumstances of the case.

The bolt is very large among the dudes and the Germans; how large the corresponding bolt among the labouring men is I can not now tell.

Keep straight on; get out of the committee as soon as it is in decent working order; don't answer any attacks, and work every line for success.

Remember me most warmly to Mrs. Lodge.

Always your friend,
THEODORE ROOSEVELT.

LITTLE MISSOURI,
DAKOTAH,
Aug. 12th, '84.

My dear Lodge,

I was very glad to hear from you, and was greatly amused over the slip from the *Advertiser;* you know that the Boston Independents circulated through New York the idea that I was a misguided weakling, who would have liked to be honest, but who was held in moral thralldom by the unscrupulous

* Stephen B. Elkins—afterward a Republican Senator from West Virginia.

machine-manipulator of Nahant.* Unless I get caught by some accident in the Bighorn I shall be on hand to do what I can, on the stump or otherwise. By the way, if Cleveland does not remove Davidson, the miscarriage of Justice will be, though less in degree, even greater in kind, than was the case with the Star Route thieves, and the only possible explanation will be that Cleveland is willing to pardon malfeasance in office on the part of a public official, in consideration of political service rendered him by the latter. I say this deliberately, and after careful thought. It must be remembered that the previous trial and acquittal of Davidson has no bearing whatever on the case, for he was indicted on a number of very trivial points, none of which were even alluded to in our report; while none of the counts on which we ask his removal were touched upon in the indictment, which would almost seem to have been so carelessly drawn up as to ensure Davidson's acquittal and a resulting effect on the public mind in his favor.

If the Sheriff is acquitted, you are welcome to use the above as you see fit—quoting it entire, as coming from me if you choose. Between ourselves, the indictment was drawn up by the District Attorney, a county Democrat, one of Cleveland's appointees, so as to ensure Davidson's acquittal. It was ridiculous on its face. I have rarely been more pleased by anything than I was by your pleasant words of friendship for me; for two or three years I have felt that you were one of "the" very few men whom I really desired to know as a *friend;* and I have never been able to work so well with any body before.

I agree with you heartily in thinking that, unless very good cause—more than we now know—can be shown, we can take part in no bolt; but I do not think we need take any *active* part in the campaign, and before you decide to do so, old fellow, I wish you would think the whole matter over very seriously. It is impossible for me to say that I consider Blaine and Logan as fit nominees, or proper persons to fill the offices of President and Vice President—and unless the Democratic nominees are hopelessly bad I should not think it probable

* A sea-coast town in Massachusetts where I have a summer place.

that I would take any part whatever in the campaign—indeed I may be in Dakotah on election day.

In a day or two I start out, with two hunters, six riding ponies and a canvas topped "prairie schooner" for the Bighorn Mountains. You would be amused to see me, in my broad sombrero hat, fringed and beaded buckskin shirt, horse hide chaparajos or riding trousers, and cowhide boots, with braided bridle and silver spurs. I have always liked "horse and rifle," and being, like yourself, "ein echter Amerikaner," prefer that description of sport which needs a buckskin shirt to that whose votaries adopt the red coat. A buffalo is nobler game than an anise seed bag, the Anglomaniacs to the contrary notwithstanding.

Do write me once or twice again; I am very anxious to hear how things go with you. Remember me most warmly to your wife.

Always yours,
THEODORE ROOSEVELT.

POWDER RIVER, MONTANA,
Aug. 24th, 1884.

My dear Lodge,

You must pardon the paper and general appearance of this letter, as I am writing out in camp, a hundred miles or so from any house; and indeed whether this letter is, or is not, ever delivered depends partly on Providence, and partly on the good will of an equally inscrutable personage, either a cowboy or a horse thief, whom we have just met, and who has volunteered to post it—my men are watching him with anything but friendly eyes, as they think he is going to try to steal our ponies. (To guard against this possibility he is to sleep between my foreman and myself—delectable bed-fellow he'll prove, doubtless.)

I have no particular excuse for writing, beyond the fact that I would give a good deal to have a talk with you over political matters, just now. I heartily enjoy this life, with its perfect freedom, for I am very fond of hunting, and there are few sensations I prefer to that of galloping over these rolling, limitless prairies, rifle in hand, or winding my way among the barren, fantastic and grimly picturesque deserts of the so-called Bad Lands; and yet I can not help wishing I could be battling along with you, and I can not regret enough the unfortunate turn in political affairs that has practically debarred me from taking any part in the fray. I have received fifty different requests to speak in various places—among others, to open the campaign in Vermont and Minnesota. I am glad I am not at home; I get so angry with the "mugwumps," and get to have such scorn and contempt for them, that I know I would soon be betrayed into taking some step against them, and in favor of Blaine, much more decided than I really ought to take. At any rate I can oppose Cleveland with a very clear conscience. I wonder what he will do about Davidson.

By the way, did I tell you about my cowboys reading and in large part comprehending, your "Studies in History"? My foreman handed the book back to me today, after reading the "Puritan Pepys," remarking meditatively, and with, certainly, very great justice, that early Puritanism "must have been darned rough on the kids." He evidently sympathized keenly with the feelings of the poor little "examples of original sin."

I do not at all agree with *The Atlantic Monthly* critic in thinking that the volume would have been better if you had omitted the three essays dealing more especially with English subjects. Puritanism left if anything a more lasting impress upon America than upon England; the history of its rise, and especially of its fall, has quite as direct a bearing upon the development of New England as a province, and afterwards of the United States as a nation, as it has upon the development of latter-day Britain. Cobbett's* visit to America gives us a vivid glimpse of a very curious phase of our early national existence, while a close and accurate knowledge of the England in which the younger Fox* played so prominent a part is absolutely essential to the students of American affairs. Your view

---

* "William Cobbett" and "The Early Days of Fox": essays in the volume referred to.

of George III is certainly a novel one; I think it very true, as regards the moral side of his character; but do you not think he *was* a stupid man, in spite of his low, treacherous cunning? Have you had time yet to read Lecky's History of England in the 18th Century? (You've been pretty busy in politics for the last year or two, or I would not ask the question.) I have a good deal of admiration for his account of the Revolutionary war.

Now, for a little criticism on a wholly trivial point. Do you not think you do Cornwallis a great injustice in lumping him with the British imbeciles who commanded with him in that war? His long campaign in the southern states, in which he marched and countermarched from Virginia to Georgia through the midst of a bitterly hostile population, and in the course of which he again and again defeated in the open field superior forces of American troops, led by our best commanders, and often largely composed of the excellent continental soldiery— this campaign, I think, was certainly creditable to him; and his being hemmed in and forced to surrender to greatly superior forces at Yorktown was entirely Clinton's fault, and not at all his own.* I believe Washington was, not even excepting Lincoln, the very greatest man of modern times; and a great general, of the Fabian order, too, but on the battle field I doubt if he equalled any one of half a dozen of the Union and Rebel chiefs who fought in the great Civil War.

Sometimes I think that your diagnosis of the Whig party under Walpole would apply pretty well to the Republican party, and to the condition of public opinion that rendered Blaine's nomination possible; but I regard reformation as being quite as impossible to expect from the Democrats as it would have been in England to expect it from the Jacobites; all the good elements have their greatly preponderant representation in the Republican Party. Excuse this rambling scrawl. Remember me to Mrs. Lodge.

Always Yours,

THEODORE ROOSEVELT.

---

* His judgment about Cornwallis was correct. At a later time in writing of our Revolutionary War I think I followed it quite closely.

New York,
Nov. 7th, '84.*

Dear old fellow,

I just did not have the heart to write you before. It is simply cruel; and I do not dare trust myself at present to speak to an Independent on the subject; I wrote an open letter to Godkin but I tore it up afterwards; we must not act rashly.

Of course there seems no use of saying anything in the way of consolation; and probably you feel as if your career had ended; that is *not so :* you have certainly received a severe blow; but you would be astonished to know the hold you have on the party at large; not a man in New York have I seen (Republicans I mean, of course) who does not feel the most bitter indignation at your defeat. They will never forget you and come back in time you must and will.

Now a word of advice; don't let the Independents see you express any chagrin; be, as I know you will be, courageous, dignified, and above all *good tempered*; make no attacks at present; at any rate write me first. This is merely a check; it is in no sense a final defeat; and say nothing, even to the fools who hurt you, without cool thought.

I wish I could be with you. It may be some comfort to know that the Independents draw no distinction between your defeat and my retirement. You have a hold on the party that I can not have; and beyond question you will in time take the stand you deserve in public life.

Here everything is at sixes and sevens. I shall be happy if we get clear without bloodshed; thanks to the cursed pharisaical fools and knaves who have betrayed us.

Remember that your wife and yourself have promised to visit us this winter.   Always your friend,

THEODORE ROOSEVELT.

* This letter refers to my defeat for Congress owing to the defection of Republicans who were against Blaine. The fight had been a severe one. Out of a total poll, Democratic and Republican, of 30,027 votes, Mr. Lovering received 15,146 and I 14,881—a majority for Mr. Lovering of 265.

At this point it seems not unsuitable to give a brief account, more continuous than is possible in contemporary letters, of the position taken by Theodore Roosevelt and by me following the Blaine nomination.

After Theodore and I announced that we intended to support Blaine and Logan, nominated in the Chicago Republican Convention at Chicago, we were savagely attacked and were misrepresented in every possible way by some of those Republicans, with many of whom we had been closely associated, who had decided to bolt the Republican nominees for President and Vice President. There was one charge constantly made at the time, and kept up in a desultory way for some years, which I think ought properly to be disposed of here in connection with these letters. That charge was that Roosevelt had been prevented from bolting Blaine by my evil and unfortunate influence. It would be enough to say that such a thing was in itself as false as it was absurd, for no man ever lived who could have influenced, still less controlled, Theodore Roosevelt on such a question as this. But the matter is serious enough to warrant a more thorough and detailed denial.

When we met in New York in May, 1884, we discussed thoroughly the coming convention and the conflict before us. We both agreed that, as a matter of simple honesty and good faith, should we enter the Convention expecting others to support our candidate if fairly nominated we were absolutely bound to support the nominee of the Convention whoever he might be. There was no argument between us upon this question because we were entirely agreed that there was no other course. We made no secret of this position but spoke of it freely to all our friends, some of whom later seemed to have forgotten what we had said before the Convention met. I recall very well one case which was an example of many others. During the first visit to New York referred to in the opening letters Theodore and I called one morning upon Mr. Godkin, the editor of *The Nation*. We went to his office. Mr. Godkin was very hostile to Blaine and we discussed all phases of the situation. Early in the conversation we said: "Of course if we go to the Convention and Blaine is nominated we shall have to support him." "I quite understand," said Mr. Godkin, "but Blaine's defeat is so important that I think you ought, indeed it is your duty, to go to the Convention because there is a chance of stopping him at that point." This conversation, I was led to believe by articles in *The Nation* subsequently escaped Mr. Godkin's recollection.

After the Convention adjourned it was Roosevelt's intention to go West, remain there and take no part in the campaign. Later he changed his mind, came home and spoke in my District and I think elsewhere. The allusions in the letters to the "Committee" refer to the Republican State Committee of Massachusetts of which I was Chairman, and we discussed the wisdom of my resigning, but came finally to the conclusion that to resign would be a mistake and put me in the most pathetic of all attitudes, that of half-doing what it was my duty to do if I was going to support the party and run as a candidate for Congress on the Republican ticket, which should be done either thoroughly or not at all. I give here the speeches made by Roosevelt in Massachusetts, of which only newspaper reports exist and which have not, I think, been hitherto reprinted. They show the position we took at the time:

(*Boston Daily Advertiser, October 21, 1884*)

ROOSEVELT'S VIEWS

He Addresses a Republican Rally in Malden

CRITICISMS OF GOVERNOR CLEVELAND—HIS OWN CLAIMS TO INDEPENDENCE—SPEECHES BY THE GOVERNOR AND MR. LODGE.

The Republicans of Malden held a well-attended rally last evening in the skating rink. The speakers were escorted to the hall by the Blaine and Logan Battalion of Malden and the Lodge Cadets. Henry E. Turner, Jr., called the meeting to order and the Hon. Elisha S. Converse was made president. Governor Robinson rehearsed some of the arguments which he presented at the Faneuil Hall meeting on Saturday and Mr. Lodge made substantially the same statement of his views which he is making in every town in the sixth congressional district. Mr. Theodore Roosevelt made the first speech which he has made before a New England audience, and the clear and candid presentation which he made of his reasons for supporting Blaine and Logan surprised the audience, as much as the singularly youthful figure of the speaker. The meeting was not at all enthusiastic in general, but the hearty applause which greeted Mr. Lodge and Mr. Roosevelt showed that those young reformers still have a strong hold upon the people.

Mr. Lodge's speech was attentively listened to. At its conclusion Deacon Converse presented Mr. Theodore Roosevelt of New York, who received the most hearty greeting of the evening. Mr. Roosevelt said, when quiet had been restored:—

"*Gentlemen :—*The cordiality and warmth with which you have greeted me would prove to me, if it were necessary to be proved, that a Massachusetts audience will always cordially welcome a Republican from another State. (Applause.) The reason that I have come here tonight was because after carefully looking over the whole field I thought that in no way could I do better service to the Republican party than by coming here and doing what I could to procure the presence in Congress of a Republican like Henry Cabot Lodge. (Great applause.) Now, generally when you send a representative for the first time to the halls of the National Legislature, you send him there with the expectation that he will earn a national reputation. You rarely send him there because he has already earned one, and yet that is the case in this instance. I have had the pleasure upon more than one occasion of working shoulder to shoulder with Mr. Lodge, for what we deemed to be the best interests of the Republican party,—notably at the great convention at Chicago; and there it would certainly have been a flattering thing for you, his constituents, it certainly must have been a flattering thing for the State of Massachusetts, to see how he as one of our representatives,—indeed, as he was there considered, as her especial representative,—to see how he was looked upon by all of our fellow-Republicans from the rest of the Union. I had the pleasure of seeing him rise in his place in the convention, when the younger heads decided that they would try conclusions with the older ones, when we won one little victory, and it certainly would have been a pleasant thing to you to see that your representative was so widely known and so widely respected. It is a good thing for a district to be able to say that they send a representative to Congress who is not only popular in that district, who is not only spoken of there as being a good man, but is considered to be a representative American all over the country. (Applause.)

"Now gentlemen, I am going to bore you a little, and only a short while—for I realize that you must be anxious to get away—about national issues. Luckily, after what has been said to-night, it is needless for me to say that it is a question of parties, not a question of men. There has been a certain amount of talk that if you have a good man he is all right, no matter what the party behind him. Now in 1864 nobody that I know of questioned the moral character of George B. McClellan, and yet no disaster suffered by the Federal Armies during the long war for the Union would have begun to equal in importance the terrible disaster that it would have been to have McClellan elected as President. Then again four years later a fellow-citizen of mine, Mr. Seymour of New York, was chosen by the democracy as their standard bearer. He was of blameless private life, of the most unsullied character in public life; yet his election would have meant the undoing of everything that had been done by the most lavish expenditure of our blood and our treasure. It seems to me that everyone in his senses must recognize that the man is not everything, that the man is not even so much, but that the party is most of all. Now we have heard some talk that would seem to imply that we are electing an irresponsible autocrat to rule over us; and were we to choose a dictator I grant you most freely that it would be wise to choose that dictator purely with reference to himself; but we are merely choosing a servant of the people. We are choosing a man who will have to be a servant of the party that elects him. We all know the old proverb, 'Like master like man.' Nowhere does that proverb apply with greater force than in politics. The public servant must obey and must be like the party that he serves. The Republican President must represent the wishes of those who have nominated and who will elect him. Now, Mr. Blaine was nominated much against the wishes of many of us, against my wishes and against my efforts. He was nominated fairly and honorably because the delegates at the Chicago convention fairly represented the sentiment of the great Republican States. (Applause.) He was nominated because those whom Abraham Lincoln, in one of his quaint, homely phrases that meant so much, called 'the plain people,' wished to see him as their President. He was nominated against the wishes of the most intellectual, and the most virtuous and honorable men of the great seaboard cities, but he was nominated fairly and honorably, because those who represent the bone and the sinew of the Republican Party, those who have constituted the main strength of that party, wished it, and I for one am quite content to abide by the decision of the plain people. (Applause.)

"Now, I had intended to say a little about the Southern question tonight. I might not have objected to gleaning where one man has reaped, but where one has reaped and the other has gleaned there is but short stubble left for me. I will merely point out one fact. The last Democratic President that was elected was Mr. Buchanan—famed as facing both ways. Mr. Buchanan was elected by the votes of the solid South. The white votes of the South then represented not only their own numerical power, but in addition to that, by a provision of the Constitution, three-fifths of the dark-skinned Americans whom they held in bondage and who had no voice in that election. We have freed the slaves, but the one effect upon a national contest of their manumission has been that the Southern white vote has been swelled, not only to the extent of three-fifths, but to the extent of all the blacks in the Southern States. That has been the sole difference between the vote as it then stood and the vote as it now stands. In other words, the democracy play this game to rule the Union with loaded dice.

"Now there is one thing that I am perhaps better able to tell you than one of your own orators even can tell you, and that is I can speak to you of Governor Cleveland's career. I have not been in politics a long time, but Governor Cleveland's public career is still shorter. (Laughter and applause.) Now I want to speak, before coming to that, one word to our good friends, the eclectics. (Laughter and applause.) Now, mind you, I have a very high respect for the eclectics. They do try to choose out of the best, I have no doubt, and I have no question that the bulk of them are actuated by thoroughly honest motives in the course they have taken, although I think that by their course they have been brought into doing things and approving men in a manner that they cannot but heartily regret when the sober second thought comes to them. Now these gentlemen have had a good deal to say about how very right, and very proper and very conscientious they are, with a strong impression conveyed abroad that we are not quite what we ought to be, because we do not altogether share their views. Now, as I said the other night, I do not at all object to their considering themselves the salt of the earth, but I must insist that the entire rest of the world has some virtue in it. Now, these gentlemen, very few of them profess to have gone completely over to the Democratic party. They say the Democratic party is all that it has been described to be in times past, but they have nominated Grover Cleveland, and he will resist all the evil tendencies in the party and hold them back by his own personal courage.

"Now, gentlemen, I am going for a very few minutes to ask you to go over Governor Cleveland's past career. I do not think he is a demagogue; I do think he is a Democratic politician. Now, in the first place, it is necessary for me to say that in his personal relations with me he has always been most courteous and most considerate. He has been a good Governor for a Democrat, but there has been nothing whatever in his past career to warrant us in saying that he will be able to resist the pressure of his party, that he will have the power to resist the almost incalculable pressure that will be brought to bear upon him if he is elected. Now he came in upon an enormous wave of popular approval in New York; or to speak more accurately, I should say, an enormous wave of popular disap-

proval of the Republican candidacy. I have been in the legislature three years; that comprises practically all of my public
life. For two years Governor Cleveland has been governor.
That comprises practically all his public life. His career can
be roughly divided into two parts—first of all, his actions prior
to the first of last March, when he was not talked about as the
Democratic candidate; secondly, his actions after the first of
March, and his actions after that were widely different from
his actions before. He has done some very good things during
his career as governor. For instance, he recommended to the
first legislature, which was Democratic, that it should take in
hand and execute certain reforms. That legislature failed to
adopt these reforms, but the next legislature—which was
Republican—took them up and put them through. Then the
governor approved part of them—those that did not bear too
harshly on the Democratic organization. You know, gentlemen,
in New York we have a Democratic party which comprises
nearly—not quite, but nearly—half of the voting population
of the State. We have the good fortune to have the Democrats divided into two factions. There is but one point upon
which I sympathize with Tammany Hall, and that is its
thorough detestation of the regular democracy. I agree with
the regular democracy, too, in the way in which it looks upon
Tammany Hall. Now, we had several bills that bore upon
Tammany Hall. The Governor signed those most unflinch-
ingly—with reckless heroism. Then we had several that
affected the county democracy and the leader of the county democracy—my esteemed fellow-citizen, Mr. Hubert O. Thompson—and those measures came to an untimely end. There
were several measures I would like to allude to. The first
measure, and one that has been but little alluded to in this
campaign, was to build a great aqueduct in New York. It
was put through the first legislature, the Democratic legislature, in a manner that was simply scandalous. We were, all
of us, under the rule of the previous question, denied our right
to express our dissent from the bill. It was savagely denounced
in the independent press of New York—the same papers that
are supporting Mr. Cleveland now,—as an outrageous scandal.

But members of the county democracy—lawyers—appeared to argue in favor of the bill and the bill was signed. That was the first measure. Last winter we passed a number of bills with the object of reforming the government of New York City, which certainly stands sadly in need of it. One of those bills—the most important perhaps—was the aldermanic bill. That bore heavily upon the Republicans and Tammany Hall and was signed. To round out the principle of that bill we passed the so-called tenure-of-office bill. At present the mayor, after his successor has been elected, appoints his subordinates who are to hold office through the terms of his successors and the successor's successor. In other words, instead of our being able to judge the mayor by the acts of his subordinates, we have to complain if the present commissioner of public works does not suit, of a mayor who went out of office before the mayor who went before this mayor went out of office. We merely proposed to make all subordinate officers go out of office at the same time as the mayor. We proposed to put into practice the same system under which our neighboring city of Brooklyn has done so well. That matter, however, affected Mr. Hubert Thompson. At that time it became evident that Mr. Cleveland might be nominated for the presidency. We cannot say that it was because of this, but it looked as though it was, because the Governor vetoed it and the reasons which he gave appeared very weak indeed. At the same time a committee of which I was chairman brought specific charges against the sheriff of the county. Among other things, we charged him with having procured under fraudulent vouchers, fraudulently sworn to, thousands of dollars. These vouchers charged for more than twenty thousand prisoners that were transported according to the account, the defense being that the clerks had during the year made twenty thousand clerical errors."

(*Boston Daily Advertiser, October 22, 1884*)

HELPING TO ELECT MR. LODGE

THEODORE ROOSEVELT AGAIN ON THE STUMP AT
MELROSE—AN ADDRESS BY LODGE

The Republican rally in the Town Hall, Melrose, last evening was well attended, and the speakers seemed to express sentiments congenial to the larger portion of the audience. Before the meeting the speakers were given an informal reception at the residence of the Hon. Daniel W Gooch. Mr. Albert Hocking called to order in the hall and Mr. Gooch was made president. The first speaker was Mr. Henry Cabot Lodge, who was received with uproarious enthusiasm.

Mr. Theodore Roosevelt of New York was received with tumultuous applause. His remarks were in the main the same as those made at Malden Monday evening, and they were closely listened to throughout and often applauded. He spoke in warm praise of Mr. Lodge and said he considered his chances of election excellent. "For him," said Mr. Roosevelt, "I can ask the votes not only of Republicans but of all independents who are true independents. We do full justice to their motives, and we feel that they will do all they can for him who has been one of the most conspicuous examples of independent republicanism." The speaker compared Mr. Lodge with Mayor Low of Brooklyn. "These young men, and those like them, should be kept in politics. Adequate cause and the proper occasion should be chosen for leaving a party."

"We may feel confident that the best of our Irish citizens will henceforth be found with the Republican party. We are responsible to no one but ourselves. The rest of the world must let us go our own way. I maintain all my faith in American institutions. We insist that the many shall govern themselves. The mass of the American people are honest, and have chosen their own candidate. I am glad that I have cast in my lot with the very great majority of the Republican Party. I believe the Republican Party will again score a victory in November."

(*Boston Daily Advertiser, October 29, 1884*)

PARTY RALLIES

MR. ROOSEVELT AND MR. BEARD AT WINCHESTER.

ROOSEVELT REPLIES TO JOSIAH QUINCY; AN INTRODUCTORY AD-
DRESS BY MR. A. R. COFFIN—THE READING INDEPENDENTS

The Republicans of Winchester held a largely attended
rally at the Lyceum Hall last evening, at which speeches were
made by Mr. A. W. Beard of Boston and Mr. Theodore Roosevelt of New York. At quarter of eight the speakers came upon
the platform and were greeted with applause. The meeting
was called to order by Mr. J. F. Dwinell, and the Hon. A. B.
Coffin was chosen to preside.

Previous to the speaking the audience was favored with
campaign songs, finely rendered by the Hawthorne Quartette
of Boston. Upon taking the chair, Mr. Coffin spoke briefly,
paying tributes to Governor Robinson, Henry Cabot Lodge,
the Hon. John D. Long, the Hon. A. A. Ranney and Colonel
Allen. He held that the Republicans were *all* independents,
and that for every independent who this year voted for Cleveland there would be 500 just as independent who would vote
for Blaine and Logan. (Applause.) Mr. Coffin introduced as
the first speaker of the evening Mr. Theodore Roosevelt of
New York. Mr. Roosevelt was received with great applause
and three cheers, and after quiet had been restored spoke as
follows:—

"*Gentlemen and Ladies :*—I must thank you very warmly for
the warmth of your reception. I always like to speak before a
New England audience, and yet a New England audience is
always a little bit formidable, and more especially so when it
is composed very nearly half, as this is, of the ladies in New
England. Now, before coming down to the real business of my
speech, I am going to ask your permission to tell a short story
that has a direct bearing upon the first part of it. It is something that is attributed to a famous Boston literary man, I
believe Mr. Richard Grant White, who was on one occasion
requested to write a series of twelve articles on the English

language; and he occupied the first of them in telling what he was going to say in the other eleven, and he occupied the other eleven in answering the attacks that were made upon the first. (Laughter.) Now I do not intend to occupy the rest of the time that I have got to speak before New England audiences in answering the attacks made upon my first efforts, but I am going to ask your patience while I respond to just one or two points that have been raised in reference to my last speeches. In the first place, a very good personal friend of mine, Mr. Josiah Quincy, at the independent meeting in Boston, saw fit to devote most of his speech to criticising what I had said, which I did not mind at all, and then to criticising what he thought I had said, to which I did strongly object. I know very well that Mr. Quincy intended to tell the truth, but his efforts were singularly unsuccessful. (Laughter.) He quoted me as saying that Mr. Blaine was nominated against the wishes of all wise and honorable men. Now I said just the reverse; so that the statement is lacking in the important detail of being true. Then he stated that I had been a candidate for re-election to the Assembly, and that owing to the success of my fellow-townsman, Mr. Jacob Hess, I was beaten. Now, as it happened, I was offered a re-nomination for the Assembly, and I refused it; I was offered a nomination for Congress, and I refused that. So *that* statement was also a trifle inaccurate. He then stated that I had denied that I was a member of the Cobden Club and had spoken in favor of protection. Now I had not alluded to either the Cobden Club or protection in my speech. Mr. Quincy's speeches do not penetrate to New York, so that my sole knowledge of them is gained from a scrap cut from the Boston *Herald*. Now, either the Boston *Herald* has failed to report accurately Mr. Quincy, or else Mr. Quincy has been afflicted with mental strabismus, which means that he is almost cross-eyed. (Laughter and applause.) And if the accuracy of Mr. Quincy's statements in regard to the campaign in general is to be gauged by the accuracy of his statements in regard to my speech in particular, Mr. Quincy's utterances at present must be taken in a purely Pickwickian sense. I think I have finished Mr. Quincy.

"Now, another small point, I said when I was last here that I had been informed by the president of the Young Men's Republican Club of Brooklyn, which is composed of the independents of the Republican party, that only 112 out of 2600 members, that is not much more than four per cent, had resigned their membership because they could not vote for Blaine and Logan. I see in one or two Boston papers that some member of the club has written here that there was not 112, but 352 who had resigned. So I inquired about that when I was on in New York of the president of the Young Men's Republican Club. This gentleman, you know, bolted from the club because, upon moral reasons, his sense of propriety was shocked when it came to supporting Mr. Blaine and Mr. Logan. But his sense of propriety grew a little bit elastic when he came to take some subsequent actions, because he sent out a circular to members of the club stating that their names had been put down as being men who were going to bolt Blaine and Logan, and if he did not hear from them to the contrary, he should so consider it. Well, you all know how a circular like that is answered. It is not answered at all. Nobody takes the trouble to write back; and all those who did not reply went to swell the 352 members who were supposed to have bolted. Now my authority in this matter is the records of the club: 112 members as it was then, 120 members as it is now, have left the club, and for each member that has left four have come in. (Applause.) The club is stronger numerically and is more influential than it ever has been at any time previous to this in its history."

The speaker then paid a tribute to Henry Cabot Lodge, to the Republican candidates for the presidency and vice-presidency, and compared the records of the Republican and Democratic parties, repeating substantially the remarks which he made in his Malden speech. He also dwelt briefly upon Governor Cleveland's record, rehearsing also his statements made at Malden in regard to that matter. Continuing he said: "There is one point which I think has scarcely been dwelt upon sufficiently in this campaign, and that is the national judiciary. The next President runs a chance of having to appoint four

judges of the Supreme Court. We all know that there have
been, from the beginning of the formation of our Republic,
two judicial schools,—one, that of the 'loose constructionists,'
— the school of Marshall and Story, the men who believed that
we were one nation, that the National Government was the
supreme power,—the school to which the most of our greatest
politicians (using the term politician in its proper sense) have
belonged, the school to which Washington, Hamilton, Lincoln, and Seward all belonged; that is one school. Then there
is the other, of which Chief-Justice Taney stands fairly as the
most prominent representative, who belonged to those who were
the 'strict constructionists,' so-called. His decisions, if followed
out, would have changed us from a mighty and prosperous
nation into a confederation of petty and wrangling republics.
He was the judge who announced from the bench that the black
man had no rights that the white man was bound to respect.
Now, certainly I cannot help thinking that every Republican,
that every independent ought to feel that it is for the advantage of the nation that the next four judges to be chosen should
belong to the school of Marshall and Story, the Federalists,
and not to the school of Taney, the Democrat. (Applause.)
Our opponents say to us that this is a matter of ancient history,
that that question does not come up now, that the question of
centralization or decentralization does not come up before the
judges now. It is not true. When it came to rechartering our
national banks, the Democrats strongly opposed the measures
because they held that they were not constitutional. When it
came to passing a law to prevent the spread of pleuro-pneumonia among the great cattle herds that cover the prairies of
the West, the Democrats opposed it upon the same ground.
Now I want to have a bench that will decide, should the question ever come before them, that the national banks are constitutional, that the law by which they are created and extended
is constitutional, that the law providing for the suppression of
pleuro-pneumonia and of kindred diseases by the National
Government should be held constitutional. Issues like that
are not decided in a day. They are not decided in 20 years.
It is a question of national growth, and the same fight that has

been going on for the last half century or more will continue
to go on for some time longer.

"Now there is one word more that I wish to say: I think that
we are all very apt to take a pessimistic view of the times that
are present with us. We are always hearing praises of the good
old times; we hear nothing but abuse of the times in which we
now live. And yet, I believe, if you take the last 24 years, that
future historians will hold it to be the heroic period of American history. (Applause.) There never has been a time that the
nation has striven so hard, has suffered so much and gained
so much. There never has been a time that so much good has
been done and that so much bad has been undone as in the
past 24 years, and it has been done by the Republican Party.
(Applause.) Again our friends tell us that this is all ancient
history. Now the other day, at a meeting in one of your towns,
I think it was in Melrose, we walked under a banner that had
been used in 1860 and had on it the words 'Lincoln and Hamlin.' I suppose that that represented the deeds of ancient
history. Certainly I would prefer to act with a party that has
a record of which it is proud, rather than to act with a party
which has a record of which all honest men must be ashamed.
We are asked to forget all that has been in the past; we are
asked to trust the promises of the Democracy for what it will
do in the future rather than to judge it by what it has done in
the past. Certainly, if one of us in private life were requested
to hire a servant, and were told that he had committed homi-
cide in 1860, robbed a bank in 1864, committed burglary in
1868, and had been a sneak thief in 1872, we would not be
prepossessed in his favor. (Laughter.) I think I put that
statement mildly (renewed laughter and applause): and that
is precisely what these gentlemen ask us to do with the Democratic party. They say, 'We acknowledge that it is very
largely composed of the same men that it formerly was; we
acknowledge that it is the party that tried to destroy the
Union, to keep slavery in existence, that opposed the national
banks, that has committed about every sin that it was capable
of committing for the last 25 years, but it says it is going to be
good, and we ask you to believe it.' I think I should like to

see them bring forth fruits first before I believe it. I have detained you longer than I ought. Let me simply say in conclusion that I am delighted that I remained where by inheritance and education I feel I belong with the Republican Party." (Applause and cries of "Good.")

In looking over my correspondence recently I found in a memorandum written by Roosevelt, a copy of a letter to some one else, which had no general relation whatever to the Blaine campaign, but happened to contain—though I had forgotten it—so direct and final a statement as to our attitude at that time that I give it here:

(Extracts from Memorandum of Theodore Roosevelt, dated February 10, 1908)

Altho I had met Cabot Lodge once or twice in the Porcellian Club, I never really knew him until the spring of 1884, when we came together in connection with the effort to prevent Blaine's nomination for President. We both took the same view, namely: that if possible Blaine should not be nominated, but that if nominated we would support him.

From that time on he was my closest friend, personally, politically, and in every other way, and occupied toward me a relation that no other man has ever occupied or ever will occupy. We have not always agreed, but our subjects of disagreement have been of but little weight compared to the matters upon which we did agree. For the past twenty-four years I have discussed almost every move I have made in politics with him, provided he was at hand and it was possible for me to discuss it; and as regards many matters of policy and appointment, it would be quite impossible for me now to say whether it was he or I who first suggested the appointment I made or the course that I followed.

NEW YORK,
Nov. 11th, '84.

Dear Cabot,

I am awfully sorry, but I shall in all probability be unable to get back from the west until Xmas; can you not appoint some time in January or February when Mrs. Lodge and yourself can come to stay with us? Any time will suit us; but you *must* come. I really long to have a chance of talking with you.

I was very glad to receive your letter; and I can not say how glad I have been to hear from all sides of the gallant front you showed in defeat. That the blow is a serious one I do not pretend to deny; that it is necessarily fatal however I am far from admitting. The Republican party in Massachusetts will not break up; it will remain the dominant party of the State; and it will feel thoroughly that it owes its success in the immediate past more to you than to any other one man, and that you have sacrificed yourself to save it; your hold upon it—a hold gained not by one service, but by a long course of services performed during a considerable space of time—is very strong; and the party will, I think, next put you in a position where you can receive its vote throughout the State.

Of course it may be that we have had our day; it is far more likely that this is true in my case than in yours, for I have no hold on the party managers in New York. Blaine's nomination meant to me pretty sure political death if I supported him; this I realized entirely, and went in with my eyes open. I have won again and again; finally chance placed me where I was sure to lose whatever I did; and I will balance the last against the first. I have stood a great deal; and now that the throw has been against me, I shall certainly not complain. I have not believed and do not believe that I shall ever be likely to come back into political life; we fought a good winning fight when our friends the Independents were backing us; and we have both of us, when circumstances turned them against us, fought the losing fight grimly out to the end. What we have been cannot be taken from us; what we are is due to the folly of others and to no fault of ours.

By the way, R. R. Bowker* tackled me the other day; and I think I made mince meat of him. Last night I lectured before the 19th Century Club. Now, old fellow, I think the end with you is not yet reached; at least you have done the

* Then commonly known as "the original mugwump."

right thing, and have done it manfully and bravely and in spite of the pressure brought to bear on you; you have been really independent.

With warmest regards to Mrs. Lodge, I am, as ever

Your friend,

THEODORE ROOSEVELT.

LITTLE MISSOURI,
Nov. 23rd, 1884.

Dear Cabot:

Many thanks for the scraps; I wish you would tell Mr. Matthews that I am greatly obliged to him.

I was very much pleased with your address; it was temperate and dignified and not in the least hypocritical.

I rode fifteen miles last night, the thermometer being 20 degrees below zero, bringing in a buck, after missing two others. My cattle are looking well—and in fact the Statesman (?) of the past has been merged, alas, I fear for good, into the cowboy of the present.

Warmest regards to Mrs. Lodge.

Yours always,

THEODORE ROOSEVELT.

1885

422 Madison Ave.,
NEW YORK,
Mar. 8th, '85. .

Dear Cabot:

I have just sent my last roll of manuscript to the printer, and so have a little leisure time. I am very much pleased with the first volume of Hamilton*; it is gotten up in just the proper style; the preface reads admirably. Altogether it is a piece of work with which you have a genuine right to be satisfied.

In a fortnight I shall go out West; my book† will be **out**

---

* My edition of Hamilton's works.   † "Hunting Trips of a Ranchman."

before I return. The pictures will be excellent—as for the
reading matter, I am a little doubtful.

Certainly in politics we have reached a stage that can best
be described as the Apotheosis of the Unknown; Cleveland's
cabinet is respectable, except the two New York secretaries,
one of whom has nothing to commend him, and the other
everything that should disqualify him. Lt. Gov. Hill has kept
in Davidson; with the adroitness that has of late years marked
all the operations of the Cleveland-Manning machine he published his letter refusing to turn him out at the time of the
inauguration when every one's attention was so taken up with
the latter that very little hostile criticism was made. Of
course the ultra "Independents" (heavens! what a misnomer)
highly approve of it. I wonder if Thompson* will get anything?

Every now and then I meet an Independent who, taking it
for granted that you and I were actuated by selfish motives,
points out how much better for ourselves we would have done
to have bolted. I always surprise him by saying that we have
always been very well aware of that fact, and knew perfectly
well that we had been pretty effectually killed as soon as
Blaine was nominated. If our consciences would have permitted
it I have not the slightest doubt that by bolting we could have
done an immense amount for ourselves, and would have won a
commanding position—at the cost, perfectly trivial in true
Mugwump eyes, of black treachery to all our warmest and
truest supporters and also at the cost of stultifying ourselves
as regards all of our previous declarations in respect to the
Democracy.

The other night I spoke at the Harvard dinner; got along
very fairly, the rest of the company being mugwump however.
My wrath still burns hot against Godkin.

Remember me most warmly to Mrs. Lodge.

Faithfully yours,
THEODORE ROOSEVELT.

* Hubert O. Thompson—prominent New York politician and leader of the
County Democracy.

422 Madison Ave.,
New York,
Mar. 30th, '85.

My dear Cabot:

I was very glad to receive your letter, and the clipping from the *Advertiser*, which I had not seen; I am delighted that you are pleased with the article.

Yesterday I went out with the Meadowbrook hounds for the first time; the field was about twenty-five strong and the run lasted nearly twelve miles; I got along very well and was in at the death with the first three or four, receiving one of the "pads." But it will be many a long day before I try to take a horse over a 3 foot six hurdle without stirrups. *

Of course you must stay with me when you come on for the Irving dinner; I did not intend to go to it but I will as you are going; how long can you stay with me then? Let me know the time of your arrival soon.

With warm regards to Mrs. Lodge and the three immortal minor Lodges, I am

Yours,
Theodore Roosevelt.

Medora,
Dakota,
May 15th, 1885.

Dear Cabot:

I was delighted to see your familiar handwriting again; many thanks for the newspaper clipping; there is no need to remind me of my promised visit to you, for you may be sure I shall not forget it. As yet, however, I cannot tell the exact date when I will be in Boston. By the way, some kind friend sent me a criticism from *Life* on my *Century* article, and on myself, which was marked by all the broad intelligence and good humor so preeminently characteristic of the latter day mugwump. In fact it was quite Godkinesque—two parts imbecility and one part bad temper.

I have had hard work, and a good deal of fun since I came out here. Tomorrow I start for the roundup; and I have just come in from taking a thousand head of cattle up on the trail.

---

* An overflattering allusion to something I had done.

The weather was very bad and I had my hands full, working night and day, and being able to take off my clothes but once during the week I was out.

The river has been very high recently and I have had on two or three occasions to swim my horse across it; a new experience to me. Otherwise I have done little that is exciting in the way of horsemanship; as you know I am no horseman, and I can not ride an unbroken horse with any comfort. The other day I lunched with the Marquis de Mores, a French cavalry officer; he has hunted all through France, but he told me he never saw in Europe such stiff jumping as we have on the Meadowbrook hunt.

Cleveland is "spindling" wonderfully; Higgins has been repeated *ad nauseam*. I am afraid Evarts is too old*; I doubt if we are able to do much with him.

Remember me most warmly to Mrs. Lodge.

Yours,   THEODORE ROOSEVELT.

(Writ in a cowcamp; I fear that my caligraphy harmonizes with the environment.)

LITTLE MISSOURI,
June 5th, '85.

Dear Cabot,

A cowboy from "down river" has just come up to the roundup, and brought me my mail; with your letter in it. I am writing on the ground; so my naturally good handwriting will not show to its usual advantage.

I have been three weeks on the roundup and have worked as hard as any of the cowboys; but I have enjoyed it greatly. Yesterday I was eighteen hours in the saddle—from 4 A.M. to 10 P.M.—having a half hour each for dinner and tea. I can now do cowboy work pretty well.

Toronto† must be a dandy; I wish I could pick up one as good. That is, if he is gentle. You are all off about my horsemanship; as you would say if you saw me now. Almost all of our horses on the ranch being young, I had to include in my

---

* As a candidate for the Presidency.   † A hunter belonging to me.

string three that were but partially broken; and I have had some fine circuses with them. One of them had never been saddled but once before, and he proved vicious, and besides bucking, kept falling over backwards with me; finally he caught me, giving me an awful slam, from which my left arm has by no means recovered. Another bucked me off going down hill; but I think I have cured him, for I put him through a desperate course of sprouts when I got on again. The third I nearly lost in swimming him across a swollen creek, where the flood had carried down a good deal of drift timber. However, I got him through all right in the end, after a regular ducking. Twice one of my old horses turned a somersault while galloping after cattle; once in a prairie dog town, and once while trying to prevent the herd from stampeding in a storm at night. I tell you, I like gentle and well broken horses if I am out for pleasure, and I do not get on any other, unless, as in this case, from sheer necessity.

Vilas* seems to be a perfect ass; his circular was really phenomenal; I should think it would awaken even the grovelling imbecility of the Independent mind to a sense of the true state of affairs.

Bayard,† however, seems at least to appreciate Hamilton; — I should think the elder Bayards would turn in their graves over most of his speeches.

Warmest regards to Mrs. Lodge.

Yours,

THEO. ROOSEVELT.

MEDORA,
DAKOTA,
June 23rd, '85.

Dear Cabot,

Just a line to blow off steam on one or two points. The roundup is swinging over from the east to the west divide; I rode in to get my mail and must leave at once. We are working pretty hard. Yesterday I was in the saddle at 2 A.M., and except for two very hasty meals, after each of which I took a

---

* William F. Vilas—then Postmaster General.
† Thomas F. Bayard—then Secretary of State.

fresh horse, did not stop working till 8:15 P.M.; and was up at half past three this morning. The eight hour law does not apply to cowboys.

Mayor Grace wants me to take the position of President of the Board of Health, from which he is just trying to oust Shaler; I don't know what to do about it.

Your article on Black vs. Veazie was first rate. I have just picked up a copy of *Harpers Weekly* containing an elaborate effort to excite the Prohibitionists against the Republicans and praising them up. *The Nation* is in the same strain. More absolute moral dishonesty could not be found; it is discouraging to see men claiming to stand as the representatives of enlightenment and disinterestedness acting in a manner that is really scoundrelly. It is impossible that they are not hypocrites; by no chance can their motives be good. The Prohibitionists have always been their pet horror.

They have very, very seriously injured the cause of Civil Service Reform. The Brooklyn Postmaster is a dandy.

Yours,

T. R.

SAGAMORE HILL
SYOSSET STATION, L. I.
OYSTER BAY P. O.

Sept. 30th, '85.

Dear Cabot,

I am glad we drew blood. We are right; and I shall not draw back a handsbreadth from the position we took on the southern question.

I am awfully sorry to say that owing to some infernal races, the hunt requested me to put our meet off till the 24th; and we could not well refuse. Now do you care to come then? Or to keep to your original date? Just whichever you please. In either event, there will be two or three weeks in the neighborhood; and you shall have Frank,* and follow them, and between times we'll ride the polo ponies.

Give my warmest regards to Mrs. Lodge.

Yours always,

THEODORE ROOSEVELT.

* The name of his hunter.

OYSTER BAY, L. I.,
Oct. 7th, '85.

Dear Cabot,

I had already carefully read and admired your platform. It was in all respects an admirable piece of work; you deserve, and I am glad to see receive, the highest credit for it. It is a really statesmanlike document; a fine piece of political writing, and just what we needed at this time. The illustrations in the *Globe* were very funny. The only paper here that did not endorse it without reserve was the *Post*, which had a laboured attack on Hoar* and yourself.

I was glad to read of the applause with which you were greeted; it shows the deep hold you have on the party. In every way your reappearance in politics was one upon which you are to be congratulated.

I honestly believe I shall see you in the United States Senate, but meanwhile *don't* run in that damned congressional district again.

Last Thursday I hunted, and never knew the old horse go better. I kept in the same field with the hounds almost the whole time, and was second in at the death; ahead of the huntsman and master. The polo ponies are in fine shape, and ready to scuttle all round Christendom with us. The London *Athenaeum* just gave mean exceedingly complimentary review.

Always yours,
THEODORE ROOSEVELT.

SAGAMORE HILL
SYOSSET STATION, L. I.
OYSTER BAY P. O.

Dear Cabot, Oct. 25th, 1885.

The "pleasant and gentle feat of arms at Ashby-de-la-Zouche" was a trifle compared to the meet here yesterday.

I can not say how I, and indeed all of us, wished that your self and spouse were here; I know you would have enjoyed it. The weather was glorious, and everything went off without

* Senator George F. Hoar of Massachusetts.

a hitch; the entire neighborhood turned out in drags, tandems, etc. The field was only about 35 in number, mostly in red; but at least 25 were as hard riding men, mounted on as good hunters, as are to be found on either side the Atlantic; every crack rider of the Meadowbrook and Essex clubs was here, each mounted on his very best horse, and each bound to force the pace from start to finish. The country was too stiff for any timid rider to turn out.

We opened over a succession of small fields with fences by actual measurement from 4 feet 6 to five feet, and the fun grew fast and furious very rapidly. The run was for ten miles with one check, over the country you saw. Douglas* took my sister's mare out to school her; at the third fence she turned a couple of handsprings and literally "knocked him silly," and took half the skin off his face; he rode along the roads the rest of the way. A great many men had falls, and about half way through I came to grief. Frank† is stiff and the company was altogether too good for him; I had pounded the old fellow along pretty well up with the first rank, but he was nearly done out. Then we came to a five foot fence, stiffer than iron, that staggered the best; my old horse, completely blown, struck the top rail, didn't make an effort to recover, and rolled over on me among a lot of stones. I cut my face to pieces and broke my left arm (which accounts for my super-ordinarily erratic hand writing). After that I fell behind, as with one hand I could not always make Frank take his fences the first time; however three or four miles farther on a turn in the line enabled me again to catch up, and I was in at the death, not a hundred yards behind the first half dozen. I looked pretty gay, with one arm dangling, and my face and clothes like the walls of a slaughter house. I guess my hunting is over for this season, as my arm will be in splints for a month or six weeks; anyhow Frank is shut up, gone both before and behind. I have had my money's worth out of him however, not to mention a healthy variety of experiences on and off his back.

The *Post* of course pitched into my Brooklyn speech, as waving the bloody shirt, and talked its usual idiotic claptrap

* His brother-in-law, Douglas Robinson.   † His horse.

about it; the speech took well, however, and went well in the West.

With warmest regards to Madame, I am

Your crippled friend,

THEODORE ROOSEVELT.

SAGAMORE HILL

Dear Cabot,   Oct. 26th, '85.

I never held any such conversation as that attributed to me in the *Record;* I never spoke of Cleveland's administration as I am quoted as speaking; I have all along insisted that Mr. Davenport's* election would be in no sense either an endorsement or a rebuke of the Administration. You can make what use of this you choose.

SAGAMORE HILL

Dear old Cabot,   Oct. 30th, '85.

It was very good of you and your wife to write even before you heard from me. You needn't feel in the least melancholy about me; I viewed the affair from the first as mainly comic in character. Now I can dress myself all right, and do about everything but ride and row; all I minded was missing the rest of the hunting season—and I question if Frank would carry me much longer at the pace at which I care to go. My face will not be scarred except across the nose—which however will not be handsome. The accident did not keep me in five minutes. I rode straight through the rest of the hunt—the arm hurt very little and indeed I did not know it was actually broken until after going about six fields, when the bones slipped up past each other—went out to dinner that night.

Douglas nearly had concussion of the brain; he did not intend to follow but the mare went so beautifully at and over the first fence that he thought she was a natural hunter.

* Ira Davenport: well known as a Member of Congress. He was defeated for Governor of New York.

A couple of days ago I walked over the course we went and measured the jumps, having now plenty of time on my hands. We opened over a 4 foot 6 in. fence, then took a 4 foot 2, then a double, 4 foot 7 and 4 foot 1, where Douglas fell, then a 4 foot 11, which was as high as any we had. Where I fell was only 4 feet 8; still, that is a big jump in the hunting field, much bigger than in the club after dinner. When riding with one hand I did not have any very high fences, though I went over about 20; every very big one about always had the top rail taken off somewhere by one of the men in front. I think I had nothing higher than 4 feet 3, and half of them down almost to 3 feet 6. Old Frank was blown or he would not have fallen. Ralph* must be a dandy; but I don't like a horse that gets too hot in the hunting field; Toronto is more my kind.

I wouldn't mind the broken arm a bit if I was engaged in some work, so that I was occupied; I wish I had got started in the Mexican war; but I am afraid my bolt is shot, in literature as well as politics. At any rate, yours isn't.

I don't grudge the broken arm a bit; I would willingly pay it for the fun I have had on Frank. I have hunted him just eight times; seven times I have been in at the death, and three times took the brush, over a very stiff country and against very hard riders. I am always willing to pay the piper when I have had a good dance; and every now and then I like to drink the wine of life with brandy in it.

Yours always,
THEODORE ROOSEVELT.

422 Madison Ave.,
NEW YORK,
Dec. 21st, '85.

Dear Cabot,

Gilder† took to the idea kindly. He wants about seven thousand words from you; and he would like your manuscript and more especially the photographs you intend to send him as

---

* One of my horses.
† Richard Watson Gilder—then editor of the *Century Magazine*.

soon as possible. I guess you can keep the manuscript until you come on, and then we will go over the two pieces together.*

I can not say how I enjoyed *all* the entertainments at your house; I don't think I ever took more pleasure in anything. It was really delightful to meet such a set of men; I had always wished to make the acquaintance of the very ones whom I met at lunch and dinner.

Remember me particularly to Theologian Sargent†; I can never sufficiently admire the singularly happy manner in which he was able to combine the most fervent orthodoxy of sentiment with lurid profanity of expression.

With very best wishes, I am

Always yours,

THEODORE ROOSEVELT.

1886

NEW YORK,
Feb. 7th, '86.

Dear old Cabot,

I really can not say how I have missed you and your "cara sposa." Tell the latter why I was not able to see her off; the infernal doctor had to see me before eleven o'clock. I only hope you both enjoyed your visit one half as much as we enjoyed having you here. I feel really blue when I think that it will be some nine months before I see you again; I trust that you won't entirely forget your somewhat happy-go-lucky friend during that time. Anything connected with your visit makes me rather pensive.

I feel a little appalled over the Benton‡; I have not the least idea whether I shall make a flat failure of it or not. However I will do my best and trust to luck for the result. I will be delighted when I get settled down to work of some sort again. Not even the charm of Mrs. Z. would make me content to pass another purely "society" winter. To be a man of the world is *not* my strong point.

* This refers to two articles we wrote about hunting.
† Lucius M. Sargent of Boston, one of my most intimate friends.
‡ His "Thomas H. Benton" for the American Statesmen series.

I suppose you will soon get to work at the Washington.* Important and useful though the *Advertiser* is, do not let it distract you from the work that will have real and lasting value.

Always yours,

THEODORE ROOSEVELT.

ELKHORN RANCH,
MEDORA, DAKOTA,
Mar. 27th, '86.

Dear Cabot,

I thought the article on [Gouverneur] Morris admirable in every way; one of your crack pieces. Some of the sentences were so thoroughly characteristic of you that I laughed aloud when I read them. One of my men, Sewall (a descendant of the Judge, by the way) read it with as much interest as I did, and talked it over afterwards as intelligently as any one could.

I have written the first chapter of the Benton; so at any rate I have made a start. Writing is horribly hard work to me; and I make slow progress. I have got some good ideas in the first chapter, but I am not sure they are worked up rightly; my style is very rough and I do not like a certain lack of sequitur that I do not seem able to get rid of.

At present we are all snowed up by a blizzard; as soon as it lightens up I shall start down the river with two of my men in a boat we have built while indoors, after some horsethieves who took our boat the other night to get out of the county with; but they have such a start we have very little chance of catching them. I shall take Matthew Arnold along; I have had no chance at all to read it as yet.

Have you begun on your Washington yet? And do you really intend to run for Congress this fall?

Give my warmest love to Nannie†; and remember me to everybody else, including "Commander" Luce‡; I hope he has forgiven me for having dubbed him by that infernal title.

Goodbye, old fellow.

Yours,

T. R.

---

* My "George Washington" for the American Statesmen series.   † My wife.
‡ My brother-in-law J. D. H. Luce—son of Rear Admiral S. B. Luce, U. S. N.

ELKHORN RANCH,
MEDORA, DAKOTA,
April 16th, 1886.

Dear Cabot,

I think the Harvard speech a first rate one (bar the allusion to me; did you see the N. Y. *Herald* on this latter point?); and was also greatly pleased with the editorials on Dawes* and Indiana Civil Service Reform—especially the latter. Black must be quite a pill for the civil service people, by the way; what perverse lunatics the mugwumps are anyway. The St. Paul *Pioneer Press*, a very liberal paper, had a stinging article on them the other day. Your Hamilton† is a work which was most assuredly well worth doing.

I got the three horsethieves in fine style. My two Maine men and I ran down the river three days in our boat and then came on their camp by surprise. As they knew there was no other boat on the river but the one they had taken and as they had not thought of our building another they were taken completely unawares, one with his rifle on the ground, and the others with their's on their shoulders; so there was no fight, nor any need of pluck on our part. We simply crept noiselessly up and rising when only a few yards distant covered them with the cocked rifles while I told them to throw up their hands. They saw that we had the drop on them completely and I guess they also saw that we surely meant shooting if they hesitated, and so their hands went up at once. We kept them with us nearly a week, being caught in an ice jam; then we came to a ranch where I got a wagon, and I sent my two men on down stream with the boat, while I took the three captives overland a two days journey to a town where I could give them to the Sheriff. I was pretty sleepy when I got there as I had to keep awake at night a good deal in guarding, and we had gotten out of food, and the cold had been intense.

The other day I presided over the meeting of the Little Missouri Stockmen here, preserving the most rigid parliamentary decorum; I go as our representative to the great Montana Stockmeeting in a day or two.

---

* Senator Henry L. Dawes of Massachusetts.
† My edition of the works of Alexander Hamilton.

Can you tell me if President Harrison was born in Virginia*? I have no means of finding out here. I hope he was; it gives me a good sentence for Benton.

I am as brown and as tough as a hickory nut now.

Yours always,

T. R.

ELKHORN RANCH,
MEDORA, DAKOTA,
May 20th, '86.

Dear Cabot,

I have got the Benton about half through; if I could work at it without interruption for a fortnight I could send Morse† the manuscript; but tomorrow I leave for the roundup, and henceforth I will have to snatch a day or two whenever I can, until the end of June. I have really become interested in it; but I can not tell whether what I have done is worth anything or not.

I have had to study your Webster‡ pretty carefully; do you [know] I am inclined to agree with Corinne§ and like it even better than the Hamilton? Benton is not as good a subject; let alone the treatment it will have.

I find that since my departure from New York I have won what a Milesian would call a posthumous political victory. I had carefully arranged all the details of the ticket and the fight generally before I left; but at the last moment they found they had to put me on for President, as the only hope of carrying the district—and I was elected. I am really sorry, for I can not spend the time necessary to take much personal part in politics now.

If things go well I may make a long bear hunting trip in the north Rockies this fall, and of course in a trip like that it is almost impossible to make even an approximate guess at the time when I can return.

This spring I have done enough antelope shooting to keep

* He was born in Ohio. His grandfather William Henry was born in Virginia.
† John T. Morse, Jr., of Boston—editor of the American Statesmen series.
‡ My biography of Webster in the American Statesmen series.
§ His younger sister, Mrs. Douglas Robinson.

the ranch in venison. Really, I enjoy this life; with books, guns and horses, and this free, open air existence, it would be singular if I did not.

I received a hasty note from Gilder the other day bespeaking our account of my horsethief hunt for *The Century*. I don't know whether to write it or not.

Give my best love to Nannie. Goodbye, old fellow; send me any important editorial in the *Advertiser*.

Yours always,   T. R.

ELKHORN RANCH,
MEDORA, DAKOTA,
June 7th, '86.

Dear Cabot,

I wonder if your friendship will stand a very serious strain. I have pretty nearly finished Benton, mainly evolving him from my inner consciousness; but when he leaves the Senate in 1850 I have nothing whatever to go by; and, being by nature both a timid and, on occasions, by choice a truthful man, I would prefer to have some foundation of fact, no matter how slender, on which to build the airy and arabesque superstructure of my fancy—especially as I am writing a history. Now I hesitate to give him a wholly fictitious date of death and to invent all of the work of his later years. Would it be too infernal a nuisance for you to hire some one on the *Advertiser* (of course at my expense) to look up, in a biographical dictionary or elsewhere, his life after he left the Senate in 1850? He was elected once to Congress; who beat him when he ran the second time? What was the issue? Who beat him, and why, when he ran for Governor of Missouri? and the date of his death? I hate to trouble you; don't do it if it is any bother; but the Bad Lands have much fewer books than Boston has. As soon as I can get these dates I can send Morse the manuscript. (Have a copyist write them out and let him send them to me.)

I have been on the round-up for a fortnight, almost steadily. When we started, there were sixty men in the saddle who splashed across the shallow ford of the river; every one a bold rider, and every one on a good horse. It has been great fun; but hard work—fourteen to sixteen hours every day. Breakfast comes at three; and I am pretty sleepy, all the time.

Where (page and exact words would be appreciated) do you speak of Jackson's financial antics being like those of a monkey with a watch?*

In your Webster I notice you quote Browning's "Love Among the Ruins"; that has always been one of my favorite poems. But what made him write such infernal nonsense, as, for example, "Another Way of Love"? That intellectual prank can't be even parsed, much less understood. It isn't obscure; it's unintelligible. When he writes some such sentence as "Inflamable red Giotto qualifies potatoes," while I confess I don't understand it, I also humbly admit he may use the words in a poetic sense which my coarse nature can't grasp; but when he uses qualifying words that qualify nothing, a predicate with no object, and sentences, or alleged sentences that are fortunate if they have one of the three parts I was taught to consider indispensable when I studied grammar—why then I rebel.

However I am getting on. Tell Nannie I am going to make a serious study of the gentleman from Avon; it is bad enough to be caught when she quotes the Bab Ballads or Dickens, with her impassive face—but to be caught with Shakespeare is too much. Ask her, too, if you, Cabot, still grow noisy and injured over the pleasant game of "Louisa"†—or "Susannah" or "Anna Maria," or whatever or whichever the name of the thing is. Does she remember the time she refused to run down Cooper's Bluff?‡ Nobody who heard her would ever again have accused her of possessing a timid or irresolute character.

Yours ever,

T. R.

---

* I used the expression but have not been able to find it. I had thought it was in my "Daniel Webster."

† A game named in honor of my wife's youngest sister. It was invented as I remember by her uncle, Professor Benjamin Peirce, the distinguished mathematician.

‡ At "Sagamore Hill," the Roosevelt place on Long Island.

ELKHORN RANCH,
MEDORA, DAKOTA,
June 19th, '86.

Dear Cabot,

You are an old trump. The information is just what I want.

Seriously, and joking aside, of course I shall not send the manuscript to Morse until I have carefully gone over it in New York or Boston; but I wanted to get it so far done that a week's hard work when I get East near the Public Libraries would finish it. There is much filling in to be done everywhere, but especially in the last chapter; and I wanted to get the skeleton out. I will, after writing a few pages more, lay the thing aside till the fall.

I wrote to Mrs. Fremont; [she] did not even write a reply, but sent a newspaper cutting saying she was herself preparing a sketch of Benton's life, to be added to Fremont's book.

You need not delude yourself with the idea that you have escaped my advent in the fall; I will surely be on.

Your articles on civil service reform were very good; your new editor is unquestionably a very able man; his handling of Bayard and of the *Herald's* tariff utterances was very good indeed.

My ranch house looks like an Indian camp now as the other day, when we were out of fresh meat, I shot two elk and some antelope, and the flesh is drying in strips all about.

Yours always,
THEODORE ROOSEVELT.

SAGAMORE HILL

My dear Cabot,   July 25th, '86.

Both of the books you sent me yielded me very valuable information; indeed I am greatly obliged to you.

You have genuine cause to be satisfied with Anderson's remarks*; so has Dacre Bush,† for that matter. The photo-

---

* Edward Anderson of Cincinnati. He was the first I think to take instantaneous photographs of horses in motion, at all gaits, trained in the *manège* and jumping fences.

† Dacre Bush was an old friend and classmate of mine who had taken some admirable photographs of horses jumping fences. My contribution was riding the horses at the jump.

graphs are excellent, much the best of the kind I have ever seen. I am going to take them out west to show them to the cowboys.

I am anxious for you to try my horse Sagamore. I know you will like him. He is in character a curious compound of Ralph and Toronto; quiet as a mouse to get on and off of, or while trotting on the road, and a very safe fencer, although hard to sit; but a hot devil if there is any chance of a horse passing him and he sees a fence in front. He is not well bitted, and turns round like a buggy; the other day I started to turn him in a narrow lane, and the second he was half round he pricked up his ears and jumped over the fence—a four foot post and rails! He nearly got me off. He is very fond of jumping.

I was amused at a remark of Stanley Mortimer's which was repeated to me. He was explaining who I was to somebody whom he had told that I was a member of the hunt; and, to localize me, said that I was a man who "wrote," and being asked what, responded with some hesitation that he believed I "wrote speeches." Thank heaven he did not think I wrote poems, at any rate.

I leave for Dakota in a week; I shall see Douglas on Wednesday, in re hunting.

Yours always,

THEODORE ROOSEVELT.

ELKHORN RANCH,
MEDORA, DAKOTA,
Aug. 10th, '86.

Dear Cabot,

Just a line, to make a request.

I have written on to Secretary Endicott offering to try to raise some companies of horse riflemen out here in the event of trouble with Mexico. Will you telegraph me at once if war becomes inevitable? Out here things are so much behind hand that I might not hear the news for a week. I haven't the least idea there will be any trouble; but as my chance of doing anything in the future worth doing seems to grow continually smaller I intend to grasp at every opportunity that turns up.

I think there is some good fighting stuff among these harum-scarum roughriders out here; whether I can bring it out is another matter. All the boys were delighted with your photographs—except the one in which you left the saddle,* which they spotted at once. They send a very cordial invitation to come out here; though they don't approve of bobtailed horses.

I sent the Benton ms. on to Morse yesterday; I hope it is decent, but lately I have been troubled with dreadful misgivings.

Remember me particularly to Nannie and tell her that the opening lines of "Childe Harold to the dark tower came" (in Browning, I mean) now always excite pensive memories in my gentle soul.

Always yours,
THEODORE ROOSEVELT.

ELKHORN RANCH,
MEDORA, DAKOTA,
Aug. 20th, '86.

Dear Cabot,

I am glad I did not see the unholy glee of Nannie and yourself over Childe Roland's new synonym (there, the Gods have certainly deserted me; I don't know how *that's* spelt even); Childe is always in my mind associated with "Harold" or "of Elle." My youth was an unlettered one.

I couldn't insure the Benton in the express office here, so sent it on trust; I haven't heard whether it turned up safely or not; I hope so for I would not rewrite it for a good deal.

I wrote as regards Mexico *qua* cowboy, not *qua* statesman; I know little of the question, but conclude Bayard is wrong, for otherwise it would be phenomenal; he ought to be idolized by the mugwumps. If a war had come off I would surely have had behind me as utterly reckless a set of desperados, as ever sat in the saddle.

* They did not mean that I "came off," but that I did not sit close going over the jump.

It is no use saying that I would like a chance at something I thought I could really do; at present I see nothing whatever ahead. However, there is the hunting in the fall, at any rate.

Tomorrow I start with Merrifield for the Rockies after problematic bear and visionary white goat; so I will not have a chance to write again as I will not come back till about October 1st when I start at once for home.

When do you begin at [the] Washington? How ridiculous to have Clay in two volumes *; just like that Dutchman to go off on such a tangent.

I guess the gentle mugwumps will feel their hair curl when they look at some of the sentences in Benton.

Always yours, old fellow,

T. R.

SAGAMORE HILL

Oct. 10th, '86.

Dear Cabot,

I killed three white goats, also elk, deer, etc., and had some good coursing with the greyhounds after foxes and jack rabbits.

I got back here day before yesterday; yesterday I took Sagamore out after the hounds, and he kept me right in the first flight till the death; I have never been on as good a horse. Poor old Elliott † broke his collar bone the third time he was out with the hounds; so did Winty Rutherford; and Herbert broke his leg. I am happy to say we now try to get easier country.

I won in my primary contest. I was asked to take part in the Maine and Ohio campaigns; but could not, for I have an awful amount of work to do here.

I am afraid that I can not possibly get away now for more than a day or two; now tell me frankly, are you really able to give me a mount for one run on Toronto? I do want to see your country; but remember, I am no rider, and if you think I can hurt the horse I don't want to ride; but I will come on for a day or two anyhow, if you wish me. Can I come on some

* Written by Carl Schurz for the American Statesmen series.
† His brother.

day between the 18th and the 26th? I will come on in the
night train and go straight out to Nahant, so as to be there
early in the morning, if you will tell me what train to take.

Have you any idea when my Benton will be out?

Give my best love to Nannie.

Of course if there is any earthly thing I can do to help you
in your campaign I will be only too glad to do it. I do hope
you beat Andrew* out of sight; is it possible that the rank and
file democrats will support him?

Yours always,

THEODORE ROOSEVELT.

SAGAMORE HILL

Dear Cabot, Oct. 17th, '86.

Just two hours after writing you my last card, I was visited
by a succession of the influential Republicans of the city to
entreat me to take the nomination for Mayor. With the most
genuine reluctance I finally accepted. It is of course a perfectly
hopeless contest, the chance for success being so very small
that it may be left out of account. But they want to get a
united Republican party in this city and to make a good record
before the people; I am at the head of an unexceptionable
ticket. They seemed to think that my name would be the
strongest they could get, and were most urgent for me to run;
and I did not well see how I could refuse.

If I make a good run it will not hurt me; but it will if I
make a bad one, as is very likely. Many of the decent Republicans are panicky over George,† whose canvass is not at all
dangerous, being mainly wind; if the panic grows thousands
of my supporters will go to Hewitt for fear George may be
elected—a perfectly groundless emotion. The *Evening Post* is
for Hewitt and is harping vigorously on this string. So it is
quite on the cards that I will be most hopelessly defeated. All

* John F. Andrew, son of Governor Andrew, an old and good friend of mine,
and also a friend of Roosevelt. He had bolted Blaine and was running on the
Democratic ticket.

† Henry George.

that I hope for, at the best, is to make a good run and get out the Republican vote; you see I have over forty thousand majority against me. If I could have kept out I would never have been in the contest.

We have the horse show here on the 3rd, 4th and 5th of November; can not you come on to me then? I will be in hopeless confusion; but I would like to see you for twenty-four hours at any rate—and as much more as you can give. I hate to give up my visit to you.

Always yours,

T. R.

Write me a line how your own private contest is progressing.

UNIVERSITY CLUB
MADISON SQUARE

Dear Cabot,   Oct. 20th, '86.

Though up to my ears in work (I had a hundred letters in this morning's mail) I must answer you. You don't know how I wish I could see you; half an hour's talk with you would make me feel like a different man—for it is horrible work to run such a canvass as this.

I would give anything if you could only be elected; of course I can not tell about your chances but do you know I can not help having a feeling you will be successful. How I hope for it! The *Herald,* Col. Codman & Co. *must* of necessity be dishonest in their attitude towards you. If I could only be where I could work for you and against—oh, how heartily against! — Andrew!

The Independents here are as bitter against me as in Boston against you. The *Times* supports me heartily; *Harpers* and *Puck* are against me; and the *Evening Post* assails me with its usual virulent and lying malignity.

This must not be spoken outside; but in reality, not only is there not the slightest chance of my election, but there is at least an even chance of my suffering a very unusually heavy and damaging defeat; I was most reluctant to run; but all the prominent party leaders came to me, and put it on the score of absolute duty to the party; and I did not see how I could refuse. The George vote will be very large, but how large no one can tell; nor can we say if there will or will not be many Republicans in his ranks. The *Post* and *Harpers* are working up the scare over him so effectively that undoubtedly thousands of my should-be supporters will leave me and vote for Hewitt to beat him. If at this time the decent so-called Republicans would stand by me I would have a good chance of winning; as it is, if the Hewitt stampede grows strong I will be most disastrously defeated. The men who for years have howled for the Republicans to give them a decent ticket now when they have one, knife it in a body. In all probability this campaign means my final and definite retirement as an available candidate; but at least I have a better party standing than ever before, and my position there is assured.

I *must* see you and Nannie soon. Best luck, old fellow.

Always faithfully yours,   T. R.

UNIVERSITY CLUB
MADISON SQUARE

689 Madison Avenue,
Nov. 1st, 1886.

Dear Cabot,

I have written Nannie telling her that on Saturday next I sail for England to marry Edith Carow. The chief reason I was so especially disappointed at not seeing you both this fall was because I wished to tell you in person. You know, old fellow, you and Nannie are more to me than any one else but my own immediate family. The engagement is not to be announced, nor a soul told, until the 8th.

I only pray you may succeed. Here, I have but little chance. I have made a rattling canvass, with heavy inroads on the Democratic vote; but the "timid good" are for Hewitt. Godkin, White and various others of the "better element" have acted with unscrupulous meanness and a low, partisan dishonesty and untruthfulness which would disgrace the veriest

machine heelers. May Providence in due season give me a chance to get even with some of them!
Yours always,
THEODORE ROOSEVELT.

(Telegram.)

New York,
　To Henry Cabot Lodge,
　　Boston.
Nov. 2, 1886.

Am more delighted than I can say.* Do come on Thursday. Am badly defeated. Worse even than I feared.
THEODORE ROOSEVELT.

I went on immediately after this telegram was received and was with him and his sister until they sailed for Europe a day or two later. Roosevelt had made a fine and very telling campaign and was in excellent spirits in all ways and very happy in his approaching marriage.

LONDON,
Nov. 22d, '86.

Dear Cabot,

I have had very good fun here. I brought no letters and wrote no one I was coming, holding myself stiffly aloof; and, perhaps in consequence, I have been treated like a prince. I have been put down at the Athenaeum and the other swell clubs, have been dined and lunched every day, and have had countless invitations to go down into the country and hunt or shoot. I have really enjoyed meeting some of the men—as Goschen, Shaw, Lefevre, John Morley, Bryce (who wished to be remembered to you, and was especially complimentary about your Hamilton) and others. Lord North and Lord Carnarven were also pleasant.

I had one very good day with the Essex hounds, including an hour's sharp run. It was totally different from our Long Island draghunting; there was infinitely more head work

---

* I had been elected to Congress. The total Democratic and Republican vote was 26,262. Lovering 12,767 and Lodge 13,495—majority for Lodge 728.

needed by the men and more cleverness by the horses, but there was not any of our high jumping or breakneck galloping. My horse was a good one but his wind gave out and we came two tremendous croppers; but the ground was so soft I was hardly even jarred and I kept my reins tight, so as to be over again as soon as the horse was up. The field was a couple of hundred strong. But the country was so blind that I could not ride my own line at all, and followed the master or one of the two or three in the first flight all the time. The horses I saw would not, I believe, face our high timber at all; but ours would do quite as badly at first here; they would go straight into the ditches on the far sides of the hedges. I hate jumping through bull-finches.

I am to be married on Dec. 2d. Edith sends her warmest remembrance to you and Nannie, and says that you two at any rate must try to like her.

Remember to send me a copy of the Benton, if not too much trouble.

Yours always,

T. R.

1887

Paris,
Feb. 15th, '87.

Dear Cabot,

I am delighted that you are pleased with the Benton; you can easily imagine how pleased I was with your letter. If I write another historical work of any kind—and my dream is to make one such that will be my *magnum opus*—I shall certainly take more time and do it carefully and thoroughly, so as to avoid the roughness and interruption of the Benton. Of course from its very nature if it attracts criticism at all it will be savagely attacked. It was not written to please those political and literary hermaphrodites the mugwumps.

I wish them joy of Dawes. Hiscock* is a good man—and a politician too.

By the way, don't you think Lowell has rather fallen off?

---

* Frank Hiscock—then a Republican senator from New York.

Of course he is a great writer; but there seemed to me to be a good deal of rather thin matter, or else of wrong headedness; in certain of his "Essays" just out. But of course there was much that was admirable; and I especially liked the address on Wordsworth; and, saving your presence, don't you think that much of it might apply to Browning? Not that I would compare the two.

A former friend and political supporter of mine, Harold Frederic, is writing a serial in the *Scribner's* which I like very much; it is worth reading—"Seth's Brother's Wife" is the name. Thank Heaven Henry James is now an avowedly British novelist.

I have regarded with much dispassionate enjoyment the Corrigan-McGlynn-George-Davitt-Papal controversy. May each vanquish all the others! It is one of those few contests in which *any* result is for the good.

When will the Washington be ready?

Was the Senate wise in rejecting that amiable colored Democrat Matthews?   Yours always,   THEODORE ROOSEVELT.

LONDON,
Mar. 7th, '87.

Dear Cabot,

In Paris we dined at the Jays, and there, to our great delight, met Bigelow*; and the following evening (our last before coming here) dined with him at a restaurant. He was most charming; but, Cabot, *why* did you not tell me he was an esoteric Buddhist? I would then have been spared some frantic floundering when the subject of religion happened to be broached. I'll tell you about it in full when we meet.

In Paris I went for two or three days to one of the riding schools, just to see what they did; and I was struck by the fact that they really did teach one something, instead of doing as at Dickels and most of our American so-called schools. The first thing I did was to spend half an hour riding without

---

* Dr. William Sturgis Bigelow of Boston, a lifelong friend of mine who became one of Theodore's most intimate friends.

stirrups, on a different horse each day; then jumping, etc., followed.

Here we have had a lovely time, as usual, and have met the very pleasantest people, social, political and literary. I have been greatly interested in the debates in the House of Commons, a dozen different members whom I know have taken me round there. Some of them I have met at dinner; among others Chamberlain; who impressed me very greatly by his keenness, readiness and force, and who by the way was thoroughly the gentleman; and Trevelyan* who was simply the most delightful dinner companion imaginable. Lord Spencer and Forster were also very interesting. I also went out a little among the Bohemians, of the Savage Club, etc., once dining with some of the Parnellites and sitting by Healy whom I really liked. Next week we dine out to meet, among others, Lords Hartington and Charles Beresford—different enough, but each in his own way worth seeing.

I have been hunting in Essex and Norfolk; in a day or two I shall see some hunting in Warwickshire, where we are going to spend a short time with the Norths—I wanted Edith to see a really first class English country house; but isn't it funny to think of a rabid American like myself having every courtesy extended him by Lord North? Edith, thank Heaven, feels as I do, and is even more intensely anti-anglomaniac; and I really think our utter indifference, and our standing sharply on our dignity, have been among the main causes that have procured us so hospitable a reception.

As for the hunting it is lovely; one is often six or eight hours in the saddle. But the jumping does not begin to be as stiff as on Long Island; a five bar gate which all of our American horses would hop over without thinking will here not be attempted by more than four or five men out of a field of perhaps two hundred. The brooks even are flinched by the great majority. But on the other hand there is infinitely more headwork and knowledge of the country required; I personally never attempt to do anything more than follow some one else.

* Sir George Otto Trevelyan.

And the oxers and bullfinches though rare are most formidable. I wish I could have hunted with the Quorn or Pytchely; but I knew no one there, and preferred to hunt from my friend's houses rather than go off all alone on a hired hack in a strange country where I knew no one. Best love to Nannie.

Yours,   T. R.

ELKHORN RANCH,
MEDORA, DAKOTA, April 20th, '87.

Dear Cabot,

I was delighted to receive your two letters.

Your speech was admirable. Massachusetts is *the* important State; and with the present infernal mugwumpian squint in the public eye you must organize from now on to carry it. You were right in beginning the campaign now. I am not on the ground; but after Rhode Island I feel nervous. I hope Andrew may be buried out of sight.

I hate speech making and never feel confident of my ability to do more than make a few pointed remarks in debate. However, I suppose I shall have to do my best at the Federal Club; I shall certainly take a hack at the estimable Godkin.

Well, we have had a perfect smashup all through the cattle country of the northwest. The losses are crippling. For the first time I have been utterly unable to enjoy a visit to my ranch. I shall be glad to get home.

The scrap of paper you enclosed me contains some excellent ideas, which I shall try to use.

Give my love to Nannie and remember we are looking forward to seeing you both in June.

I must be off, now, down the river; so goodbye.

Yours ever,   T. R.

689 Madison Ave.,
May 15th, 1887.

Dear Cabot,

The Anti-saloon people are harmless enough. I shall deliver a very *short* address.

I have just sent the *Tribune* the last clause of my unhappy Federal Club speech in full; I will give the mugwumps something to howl over. I am in for war to the knife with the whole crew. Am having a most absurd correspondence with Tyler of Richmond.*

We have a jolly rowboat at Sagamore Hill now, all ready for you and Nannie. Sagamore the horse will just be in good condition for you. The Morrises† won't let me see the old gentleman's papers at any price; so I am in rather a quandary. Morse wants me to write the life anyhow.

Yours ever,

T. R.

SAGAMORE HILL

Dear Cabot, May 20th, '87.

I am so very sorry Nannie had such a fall; from your first letter I did not realize that it was anything serious. Tell her how sorry I am. Sagamore will be in beautiful shape for you; do you care for rowing? You must come, if you possibly can.

As for us, we have been settling down, and have worked at the house like a couple of dusty, not to say grimy, beavers.

I drew blood from the mugwumps, surely; the *Post* has devoted an editorial to me about every day; and I got a neat little side hit at Godkin the other day, coupling him with Dorsey in a way he doesn't like. But now I rather wish I had sailed for him at the dinner anyhow. How I despise the lying hypocrite!

I shall gladly avail myself of the chance to look over the Pickering letters; I don't feel very confident about the Morris.

How goes it with the Washington? You know you can work at it down here.

Give my best love to Nannie; I do hope she is all right now.

Ever yours,   THEODORE ROOSEVELT.

* Relating as I remember to President John Tyler.

† Gouverneur Morris's descendants. Roosevelt was writing the life of Morris for the American Statesmen series.

SAGAMORE HILL

June 11th, '87.

Dear Cabot,

We are all just too sorry that you two can not come; and even more sorry that Nannie should still be suffering from the effects of her fall.

Well, it can't be helped; and you shall ride Sagamore some other time.

Last Saturday Edith and I spent the whole day in our boat, rowing over to a great marsh, filled with lagoons and curious winding channels, through which the tide runs like a mill race; we took Browning and the Matthew Arnold you gave me along. By the way she is very fond of your favorite, Clough. I only care for a few of his pieces—"Qua cursum," "Christ is Not Risen," etc. Did you see in the last *Century* a most scathing review of Lord Wolseley's article on Lee? If that flatulent conqueror of half armed savages chance to read it, it will just make his hair curl. What a fool he is! For him to criticise Grant and Lee is like old Tippecanoe Harrison criticising Wellington and Napoleon.

My life will be most uneventful this summer. Let me know how the Washington gets on.

Yours ever,

T. R.

SAGAMORE HILL

June 23d, '87.

Dear Cabot,

I first saw your speech while at the Jays; it was pointed out to me in the *Post*, with, mirabile dictu, some sentences of qualified praise, though with the usual covert sneer.

It was a *very* good speech; and it was just the chance you wanted—or rather that I wanted for you. It was thoroughly dignified and that fact gave its utterances of good will a genuine ring to them, that mugwump hysteria lacks. It is in every way a speech you can be proud of.

Spring Rice* stayed here a week. Once, not being an over good rider, he let the polo pony Caution run off with him.

* Afterwards Sir Cecil Spring Rice, British Ambassador at Washington during the War with Germany.

On rejoining us he remarked, with his quiet, cool little manner: "I never met a pony that had such a thorough command over its rider," as his only comment.

Do you know, I can not help thinking John Jay more deserving to have a place in the Statesmen Series than Morris, though the last is so much more amusing. Jay left a mark that the other did not; and in fact it is only Morris' criticisms on the French that give him his especial prominence. However, I would far rather write about him than about Jay, as far as my own feelings go.

Both my wife and sister send you all their best love. Indeed if I can I will be on in the fall, if only for a day's hunting; now and then I let Sagamore hop sedately over a small fence.

When will the Washington be published?

I am so very glad Nannie is so much better. How I wish I could see you both!

Yours ever,
T. R.

Sagamore Hill
June 28th, '87.

Gracious Heavens, Cabot, do you really think I want to change that entertaining scamp Morris for dear, dull, respectable old Jay? Not much. I think the latter had a good deal more influence on the country, but the other is twice as good a character to write about—besides, I have him nearly quarter finished. I only hope I haven't given Morse the idea I wanted to change; he couldn't drag me into doing it.

Really I suppose the two lives cover so much the same ground that it is hardly necessary to have both in the series.

Your "Confederate" speech* was most excellent, as I told you; there were several reasons why I was particularly glad you made it.

By the way is it possible for me to get at the full reports (only as regards population, descent, families, etc.) of the last Mass. census? And what number of *MacMillan's Magazine*

---

* A speech I made in Faneuil Hall at a dinner of Grand Army men to Confederate Veterans.

had an article on Morris? By the way I shall, I fear, have to crib a good many of your observations on the latter in *The Atlantic*—with proper acknowledgments, of course. I wish that article was in with your other "Studies in History."

Best love to Nannie.

Yours ever, T. R.

SAGAMORE HILL

Aug. 20th, '87.

Dear Cabot,

Not only do I never wish to glean where you have reaped, but hereafter I shall be careful not to reap where you have gleaned; I have a wild desire to incorporate bodily in my book about half your article on Morris. I now have only about a fortnight's work left. I am in a great quandary over the Pickering papers. Are they published? For reasons that you know, September is the very month I can not leave here. If not published, would there be any way I could have the letters *from* Morris copied and sent me? Could you tell me some person or firm to whom I could write to have it done?

Oh, how I loathe the mugwumps. The Administration's record on Civil Service Reform is disgraceful; but all the mugwump papers are squirming round it with sneaking dishonesty. Curtis* spoke well at the conference; but, went back on it in his paper. Still, the Civil Service Reform publications are doing moderately honest work. What made Ames† sign the soldiers exemption bill? I was both sorry and angry at it. Will it not hurt his chance for this year?

If I get an opportunity I am going to sail in to the mugwumps with a sword dipped in vitriol this year. I hate hypocrites.

I am looking forward to visiting you next winter; I would give anything if I could arrange to come this fall.

Won't you have to work pretty hard to get through your Washington in time? I was glad you enjoyed Bar Harbour. We are going to try to get up a polo club here for next summer.

Ever yours, T. R.

* George William Curtis.   † Governor Ames of Massachusetts.

SAGAMORE HILL
SYOSSET STATION, L. I.
OYSTER BAY P. O.

Dear Cabot,   Sept. 5th, '87.

It was very good of you indeed to take so much trouble over the Pickering papers; it greatly relieved me.

I sent off the Morris to Houghton & Mifflin yesterday. The work was not as congenial to me as the Life of Benton. I don't know whether I have done well or not. However I think I struck one or two good ideas. I laid into him savagely for his conduct in 1812–15; when, I am sorry to say, some of my worthy forefathers still continued much of the same mind with him.

Won't you find it very difficult to get the Washington through now before Congressional work begins?

If I possibly can, I am going to visit Austin Wadsworth* while you and Nannie are there; say about the 16th or 18th of October. Sagamore is fit as a fiddle. Frank Underhill has two new Geneseo horses besides Lady Golightly. One of them, the Don, bucked his brother-in-law off yesterday. They jump like deer.

Elliott† writes me that, of all people in the world, he and Anna have fraternised with Browning!

We have been having tennis matches down here; in the doubles I was given a first class partner who won in spite of me. I have turned my share of the "cup" into a new Winchester rifle that I have been longing for.

Has Spring Rice been to see you? Best love to Nannie.

Yours ever,
THEODORE ROOSEVELT.

SAGAMORE HILL
Dear Cabot,   Sept. 11th, '87.

While I have waded into the Pickering-Morris wing pretty fiercely, I have been careful to give full credit to the moderates,

---

* A life-long friend of ours who had a place and a pack of hounds at Geneseo, N. Y.

† His brother.

or "Union Federalists," under Cabot. My own people were also Federalists; of course they were merely of the rank and file.

Are you going to Philadelphia to the dinner? I could not accept. Where will you stay in New York? The trains on Sunday go at such hopeless hours that I do not know whether I can get in. If things go all right here I shall go to Geneseo if even only for two or three days; but, oh, my too, too modest friend, after such a jump as that you took with Ralph why taunt me by a pretense of *my* riding anywhere near you? I shall follow you like Peter—afar off.

Of course I have read your life of Cabot; Henry Adams' book I do not know.

I envy you your hunting. Here we have not yet begun; and indeed it is so far off and the arrangements are so inconvenient that I expect to get very little this season. If we start a polo club I shall sell Sagamore and get two ponies. You must be riding with a recklessness *very* shocking in parent and statesman.

Do you see how the Newport cads have taken up the Duke of Marlborough?

Yours ever,
T. R.

1888

689 MADISON AVENUE

Jan. 15th, '88.

Dear Cabot,

I have been waiting to see if I could not find your full interview; but somehow I have missed it, and have seen nothing but extracts from and condensations of it. Judging from these I should say that you simply told the exact truth—that Blaine is the choice of the bulk of the Republicans, that his name alone awakens enthusiasm, and, by inference, that he would poll most votes. It is unfortunate, but it is true. Of course the mugwumps don't like it; truth they abhor.

I am glad you liked my Lamar resolutions. Whitelaw Reid insisted on trying to carry through his abolition of whiskey tax scheme, in the Union League Club; so I made a minority report of one, and after a hard fight beat him. I do hope the Republican party can steer clear of becoming a mere party of reaction. To pass a dependent pension bill and try to abolish the total tax on whiskey are not symptoms of advance.

I am delighted you introduced your Civil Service extension bill; it is on just such questions as that that we can make *part* of our fight.

Choate will be with us in the next campaign. He views Blaine's nomination precisely as we do. Seth Low is preparing to bolt. I will give you some points about Ashbel P. Fitch when we meet.

I will write you at once when I find out the time I can come on to Washington.

Best love to Nannie.

Yours ever,
T. R.

689 Madison Avenue

Dear Cabot,   Jan. 17th, '88.

Can I come to you on the 27th?

I think your attitude on the Thebe-Carlisle case* perfectly proper; the only proper one in fact.

I am very glad to hear what you say about the Republican attitude in Congress towards the whiskey tax.

My minority report to the Union League Club, not being printed beforehand, was suppressed by our ultra-protectionist Committee—although mind you I had all the intelligent protectionists with me.

I advocated taking off the tax on tobacco and sugar and spirits used in the arts; and the employment of part of the surplus in building a navy and providing adequate coast defence. Whiskey I believe *should* be taxed.

Anent the tariff, I stated that both the Republican party and the country at large were definitely committed to a policy of protection; that any reversal of the policy at the present

---

* George H. Thebe, Labor candidate, was contesting the right of Speaker Carlisle to his seat. I took the ground that he ought not to be voted out on a technicality, but should be given a hearing.

time would be in the highest degree unwise; but that we certainly should not declare that the maintenance of the present tariff unchanged with all its anomalies was a point to which every other interest and issue should be subordinated.

Then I pitched into the Morrison bill as being ludicrous in conception and futile in execution; and made a savage onslaught on Cleveland and Carlisle—for I did not wish the mugwump papers to regard my attitude as in any way one of alliance with them.

I will tell you all about Low when we meet.

Give my best love to Nannie; Edith is so sorry she cannot come.

Yours ever,   T. R.

[New York]   1888, Jan. 22.

Dear Cabot—

These are my Union League Club remarks. I will drop you a line later to tell you the train I come by on Friday.

You have made your mark in the Thebe-Carlisle case. I doubt if any other new Congressman has ever so early taken such a prominent position; it was a great chance and you took it.

Yours,   T. R.

It will be a very nice dinner on Saturday.

Mr. President:

I did not originally intend to speak to-night in reference to the report of your Committee; for I have been unable lately to attend the meetings of the Committee; and I have a very high regard for the gentlemen who have signed the report, both personally and politically, and dislike to differ from men with whom I usually agree. But as I am a member of the Committee, and as so much public attention has been attracted to the report, I feel that perhaps it is only proper that I should state to you the reasons why I cannot agree to it in its entirety.

That the Internal Revenue system is in many ways an objectionable one I admit, and I heartily concur in the recommendation to take the tax off tobacco. But I emphatically disbelieve in taking it off of spirits. It is a rudimentary axiom of political economy to raise revenue when practicable by a tax on mere luxuries and superfluities; and if there is a single article that it is right to tax, it is whiskey. The people who drink and sell liquor are of all others those who should be made to contribute in every possible way to pay the running expenses of the State, for there can be no hardship involved in paying heavily for the use of what is at best a luxury, and frequently a pernicious luxury. The very fact that the third party, prohibitionists, have declared in favor of removing the tax should make us set our faces against it; for experience has invariably shown that these same third party prohibitionists, are the most valuable allies the liquor sellers possess and are the consistent opponents of every rational scheme for dealing with the liquor question.

The Republican party, and the Republican party alone, has hitherto shown itself capable of grappling with the financial and business difficulties of the country, and I believe that its future will not belie its past. The question of the surplus must be met fairly and intelligently. The tax should be taken off tobacco and sugar. That is our first duty. In the next place, the possession of the surplus deprives us of all excuse for not attending to certain pressing national needs. It is a disgrace to us as a nation that we should have no war ships worthy of the name, and that our rich sea-board cities should lie at the mercy of any piratical descent from a hostile power. We are actually at the mercy of a tenth rate country like Chili. Now we have ample means wherewith to prepare a navy capable of upholding the honor of the nation and a system of coast defence adequate to our needs. He is both a poor patriot and a short sighted economist who longer opposes our doing so.

In the next place, we should meet the tariff question. The Republican party, and the country at large as well, is definitely committed to the policy of protection; and unquestionably any reversal of that policy at present would do harm and produce widespread suffering. But for the Republican party to announce that the inequalities and anomalies in the present tariff must not be touched, and that the high tariff is in itself something to which every other interest must yield, and to which every other issue must be subordinated, would be in my opinion a serious mistake. I think that there should be a prudent and intelligent revision of the tariff on the lines indicated by the declarations of the last National Republican Convention and the official utterances of the last Republican President. I further believe that the Republican party is alone capable of making such a revision; the last attempt of democracy to do so, under the guidance of Mr. Morrison was as ludicrous in conception as it was futile and contemptible in execution.

Moreover, I do not think it wise to make our next fight purely on one issue, and that the issue of our opponents choosing, albeit as regards that, I think it not improbable that Mr. Cleveland can be beaten on the very points he has himself raised. The Republican party stands for other things in addition to protection. It stands for the national idea, for honest money, and for any honest civil service. I do not wonder that Mr. Cleveland in his last message forbore to touch on such points as these. An allusion to the first would come with bad grace from a President who has appointed to represent us at foreign capitals such avowed traitors as Keilly and Jackson. As for the other two, Mr. Cleveland evidently thought it worth while to ensure an identity in policy and utterance on the tariff between himself and Mr. Carlisle, but equally evidently he did not think it worth his while to try to prevent the committee on coinage being handed over to the apostle of the dishonest dollar, or to protest against the Chairmanship of the Committee on Civil Service Reform being given to the man who had introduced the bill to repeal the Civil Service Act. Nor indeed would such a protest have been taken seriously, coming from the President who wrote the Fellows letter; who appointed Higgins, Thomas, Raisin and a host of their kind; who has made Senator Gorman the chief of his kitchen cabinet; who has retained Garland as his chief legal adviser; who has connived at the utter degradation and prostitution of the public service in Maryland and Indiana, and under whom the old spoils doctrine of "a clean sweep" among faithful public servants for merely partisan reasons has been applied almost throughout the country with a thoroughness that would have done no discredit to Andrew Jackson. Doubtless President Cleveland meant to make good his original pledges concerning the civil service; doubtless no one regrets more than he himself his inability to stand up against the pressure of the spoilsmen within his own party; but the fact remains that he has signally failed thus to make good his pledges; that his acts have been absolutely at variance with his words; that hardly ever has an Administration been more false to its promises on any subject than the Administration has shown itself to be on the question of civil service reform.

When we can make a telling fight on so many issues the President fears to raise, it seems wise to do so, in addition to meeting him promptly on the one point he actually has raised. Above all, do not meet him on this question in a way that will tend to give the impression that the Republican party is willing to subordinate all its other principles and all other considerations of public policy, to the single end of preserving untouched the present tariff, in its bad as well as in its good features. Let us make the next fight on the broad ground of Republicanism, with all, and not part merely, of what the name implies.

THEODORE ROOSEVELT.

689 MADISON AVENUE

Feb. 2d, '88.

Dear Cabot,

I suppose I need hardly say how I enjoyed my visit; they were four as pleasant days as I ever spent. I was very glad indeed to see some of my old political friends again; I was able to make real progress in mapping out my book-work; and above all, I enjoyed so much seeing Nannie and yourself.

I have just corrected the last galley proofs of the Morris. Did you see how Goldwin Smith pitched into Morse and myself? But I thought it on the whole a very complimentary review of the series.

I am really delighted with your Washington; or at least

with the three extracts you read me. I had been a little afraid
of it; but I think you have been more than successful. It
looked to me as if it was going to be the best thing you had
done yet.

With best love to Nannie, I am

Ever yours,
T. R.

P. S.   Edith and Bamie* both send love.

689 Madison Ave.,
NEW YORK,
Mar. 15th, '88.

Dear Cabot,

We had great fun in the blizzard. Bamie was at Tuxedo,
with Elliott, Anna, and an assorted supply of dudes; they
started home, and spent from Monday morning to Wednesday
afternoon snowed up at the pleasing town of Paterson.

I am awfully obliged to you for what you did about Louis
Butterfield; it was a great kindness. Best love to Nannie.

At breakfast today, I received a telegram from Mrs. Selmes
with advice, in a tone of subdued irony, in reference to weather-
ing the blizzard.

Yours ever,
THEODORE ROOSEVELT.

SAGAMORE HILL,
OYSTER BAY, LONG ISLAND, N. Y.,
April 7th, '88.

Dear old Cabot,

When do you come through New York on your way to Boston? I suppose not for some time; let me know, and I will
come in for the day to see you.

Voorhees is a disgrace to the Senate, as well as to the Demo-
cratic-Mugwump party of which he is a member. In fact, I
am not particularly fond of Ingalls either. Of course the mugwump papers confine all their abuse to the latter. For rank,
mendacious dishonesty they certainly beat the world. I was
amused to see the *Times* drag me in neck and crop to the
Wilson speech, to couple me with you as a turncoat on the

* His older sister Anna—now Mrs. W. S. Cowles.

question of machine politics. They use words with such utter looseness of meaning that it is impossible to attach any exact significance to them. I am awfully afraid we are going to have Blaine again; I wish it could be Gresham—or Harrison or any other really first rate man.

I am pegging away, rather slowly at the *magnum opus;* and go over each chapter as soon as written to decapitate the King Charleses.*

Are things still going perfectly smoothly in your district? Best love to Nannie.

Yours, T. R.

SAGAMORE HILL
SYOSSET STATION, L. I.
OYSTER BAY P. O.

Dear Cabot,   April 15th, '88.

I fairly shouted over your letter; Edith says she keenly sympathises with the reference to Mr. Dick, but "if you only knew what she had made me leave out, you would be genuinely grateful."

At any rate, if you debit me with Lee, you should certainly credit me with Jefferson Davis. Oh, you bigoted New Englander! Because, when I slash into all the rest of the country, I occasionally venture on a timid and hesitating criticism of the northeast, I am held up as a ruthless iconoclast! Do you think I dealt any more gently with the New Yorkers? or that the admirers of Jefferson, or the adherents of the southern separatist school will feel any very profound gratitude to me?

I do wish I could see you. By the way, to my utter surprise, *The Nation* just gave me a long and favorable review of the Benton. I am really very much absorbed in my new book. I have not the least idea whether it will be worth anything or not.

With best love to Nannie.

Yours ever, T. R.

If on your way back to Boston you all can stop here, good; if not, I will come in and meet you in N. Y. It struck me as

* See "Mr. Dick" in "David Copperfield."

an outrage to submit to the bullying of the southerners about the direct tax bill.

"THE HOMESTEAD,"
GENESEO, LIVINGSTON COUNTY, N. Y.,
July 11th, 1888.

Dear Mr. Lodge:—

I did not feel as much inclined to thank you for Nannie's picture until I saw the slanderous photographs they have of her up here. Now I think that you sent one wonderfully good and am accordingly thankful.

I hope you will try to come to us again. I cannot say how we enjoyed your visit and how very glad I shall be if you can manage to repeat it.

This pen is not like a whip lash, but has every other possible bad quality.

Theodore is tramping up and down talking politics to Mr. Wadsworth.

Sincerely yours,
EDITH K. ROOSEVELT.

Dear Cabot,

I have made Edith stop so as to write a line or two myself. Douglas and Corinne come to visit O. B.* about the 22d—in a week—to stay a fortnight; he brings two ponies (by the way "polo gives you lots of exercise"); can't you get on to see us while they are with us? We would have such fun. I do wish you and Nannie were here; we have been loudly wishing for you every day. The sports were great fun; of course a Carey, on the inevitable "Patchen" won most of the prizes. We have been having a simply delightful time. On Sunday afternoon I went out for a quiet horseback stroll with three Careys and Arthur Clark; as you may imagine, I had to do some tall jumping. Not having been over a fence since last October, I sat pretty loose in the saddle; to the uproarious delight of the Careys; finally, after going over some big timber, my horse bolted at a fence, stopped short, and then bucked over, while I literally sat on its ears and used my legs as a throat latch. As I wriggled back into the saddle I thought my com-

* Oyster Bay.

panions would have rolled off their horses and they howled till it sounded like a boiler factory.

Yours ever, T. R.

SAGAMORE HILL,
OYSTER BAY, LONG ISLAND, N. Y.,
July 14th, '88.

Dear Cabot,

Edith and I are delighted at the prospect of your visiting us; come at any time; only let us know as far ahead as you can, so as to arrange things (not household arrangements, but with Douglas, Elliott, etc.). I am going to make you play polo on one of my ponies. Douglas and Corinne will be down, and perhaps Elliott and Anna; either at Aunt Annie's house or here. We will shoot, play tennis, ride—do anything.

If you could only have been at Geneseo! I rode Archie* one day; he is the best saddle horse of them all, but on that day his forefeet were tender and he would jump nothing of any size. I also rode the Deacon.* He is a much pleasanter horse to sit over large fences than Black Friar,* but I doubt if he is as safe a jumper, and I should hate to ride him in a hunt on account of his pulling. Black Friar pulls too, but I can always master him, and though rough, he is a high and safe jumper. Being out of practice he sometimes refused.

I am myself more and more encouraged over the political prospects. We have got back only a small percentage of the mugwumps, but many of the real Independents; of course we lose the office holders and some of the Blaine Irishmen, as well as some excellent men on the whiskey question (which I think it unwise to have put in the platform, whatever we did in Congress—it is an ugly cry to meet) but the bulk of the temperance people are with us, and we are undoubtedly making enormous gains on the tariff question. Both here and in Geneseo the country politicians seem very confident. But of course it is as yet guesswork.

Yours, T. R.

* A hunter belonging to Austin Wadsworth.

SAGAMORE HILL,
OYSTER BAY, LONG ISLAND, N. Y.,
Aug. 12th, '88.

Dear Cabot,

It was delightful to get your letter. Edith sends you and Nannie her love; I always thought it nonsense for you to call her Mrs. Roosevelt; it was the very greatest pleasure to me to find that she had taken such a fancy to you, and had enjoyed your visit as much as I had.

I am glad Morse may take the Franklin in hand, and feel much complimented that he likes my books. I continue greatly absorbed in my new work *; but it goes very slowly; I am only half way through the first volume. I shall try my best not to hurry it, nor make it scamp work.

We have had great fun here with the polo. When Douglas came down we organized a four—he and I, Thorpe, and a man named Farr—and Elliott brought over a Meadowbrook team (himself, Frank Appleton, Dick Richardson and Carroll) to play us. We whipped them finely, six goals to one (made by Elliott). At the very end, while busily engaged in riding Elliott out, I got a tumble that knocked me senseless. I was all right in an hour, and perfectly recovered in three or four days. So if you and Nannie wish us to come to Washington next winter, we will accept now. Edith has been saying just today how much she wished to go to you there. But in September I shall be out West. (I start Sunday or Monday.) I am coming back in October to take part in the canvass; it is very difficult to prophesy in politics, and I am afraid I may take too rosy a view, but I can't help thinking things look better here than I have seen them since Garfield's run. It really looks very bright; and unless we have some check I believe we shall win.

How does Nannie like Mahaffy's books about Greece?

I presume you only want the White and Indian losses in Washington's time; I send you today (having marked on the inside of the cover the pages at which you will need to look) Smith's narrative; it contains the fairest account of the Indian fights; but, I think, it if anything exaggerates the dispro-

* "The Winning of the West."

portion of loss against us. But never until Jackson's time did we succeed in inflicting as much loss as we suffered. Bear in mind however that in *men* (not women and children) the figures are not nearly so adverse to us.

I wish you could see West and Alfred* playing polo!

Yours, T. R.

SAGAMORE HILL,
OYSTER BAY, LONG ISLAND, N. Y.,
Aug. 20th, '88.

Dear Cabot,

Herewith I send you a copy of the "American Pioneer"; I don't know whether you have it or not; on pp. 51, 315, and 351 are accounts by participants in Wayne's battle. If you can, please return the volume prior to October 1st.

Mann Butler in his history of K'y—the most trustworthy of the western state histories—says Wayne had 1600 Regulars and 1600 K'y volunteers; the figures probably represent a minimum. In the "History of the Late War," a Kentucky book (written by Robt. R. McAfee, Lt. Gov. of K'y; but in the printed edition without any name on the title page), there are given some intercepted letters of the British agent McKee, in which he puts the numbers of the Indians at 1000; this was just before the battle. Some friendly southern Indians with Wayne's army gave this same estimate, as reported in the Knoxville *Gazette* shortly afterwards.

McMaster's account of Wayne's campaign is most characteristic; he starts him off with elaborate detail, and then evidently forgets all about him; I never could find that he ever made any more than an allusion to his victory. If all of McMaster's chapters were changed round promiscuously it would not, I am confident, injure the thread of his narrative in the least. He has put much novel matter in a brilliant, attractive way; but his work is utterly disconnected, and even his researches are the reverse of exhaustive. Moreover he has fallen off. In fact all he has done is to provide *material* for history.

* His cousins, West and Alfred Roosevelt.

I am off tomorrow for the West; and return early in October for campaign work. I saw Quay, Dudley and our own men the other day, to offer my services; they seem very hopeful. But New York politics are "mighty onsartin." Seth Low and Ashbel P. Fitch (I like to give him his middle letter) are our chief losses; I doubt if they control a dozen votes.

Edith sends her best love to Nannie and you.

Yours, T. R.

SAGAMORE HILL,
OYSTER BAY, LONG ISLAND, N. Y.,
Oct. 19th, '88.

Dear Cabot,

Many thanks for the books. We were delighted to hear of your easy canvass; I think the permanence of your position in politics now is well assured by the very fact of the hard fight you had at first. As for the rest of Massachusetts, I am especially interested in seeing Higginson* beaten. Here I am now acting as a kind of stop-gap orator.

Of late years I have been out in my political prophecies on two or three different occasions, so I have some hesitancy in trying my hand again; but I can't help thinking that this time we have our foes on the hip.

I hear of, and *see*, on every side defections from the Democratic ranks; but I know of very few indeed on our side who have followed Seth Low and Ashbel P. Fitch—the latter however, will I am afraid be reelected as a Democrat. This county, usually 1500 Democratic, will I think be nearly a stand off (I find my coachman, as well as various Democratic laymen, are going to vote Republican, for the first time). The *silent*—much the largest—mugwump vote is with us this year. Our State Committee honestly believe a tidal wave has come in our favor; Quay is much more cautious; but even he told me today he thought we should win. On all sides I hear of huge workingmen's clubs that are out in our favor. Hill has a tremendous pull among the workingmen however, for

* Thomas Wentworth Higginson, running on the Democratic ticket.

some inexplicable reason; he is as bad as Tweed, though more careful; but Miller* is making an admirable fight.

Of course we are bound to lose some Blaine Irishmen—I think only a few—and some Germans on the liquor question; but it certainly looks as if these losses would be made good many times over.

Edith and I had immense fun on our campaigning tour in the West; I'll tell you all about it: I am just hungry to see you and Nannie again.

Yours ever, T. R.

SAGAMORE HILL,
OYSTER BAY, LONG ISLAND, N. Y.,
Dec. 16th, 1888.

Dear Cabot,

The enclosed note from Merriam, the Governor-elect of Minnesota, seems to me very satisfactory. Show it to Reed. Do you think he, or you, should write Merriam? The *Tribune* wouldn't print the part of my short speech at the Federal Club in which I backed Tom Reed.

I also enclose a letter from my dear old uncle, Capt. Jas. D. Bulloch.† It explains itself. He wishes to know if he is entitled to a pension as a veteran of the Mexican war. Would it bother you too much to have your secretary or somebody find out about it? It is literally everything to him.

Yours, T. R.

SAGAMORE HILL,
OYSTER BAY, LONG ISLAND, N. Y.,
Dec. 27th, [1888].

Dear Cabot,

Dana's ‡ letter was simply delicious; do you notice that those fellows have a regular dialect? I can tell the Professional Civil Service Reformer—who never really does anything for

---

* Warner Miller.

† Capt. Bulloch—ex-Confederate—served in the Navy and as Commissioner of the Confederate States in England.

‡ Richard H. Dana, of Cambridge, Mass.

what he calls "the Reform"—if I can see two sentences of any of his speeches or writings.

I fairly chuckled with delight over your answer; I do hope he reads it aloud to the surviving vice-presidents of his body. I wish it could be published; I think it would "brace up" the "reformers" themselves in a very healthy manner.

Speaking quite dispassionately I believe we who have really worked hard to take the civil service from politics have been far more hurt than helped by the loud-mouthed advocates of the cause during the past few years.

As for Godkin I have long believed him to be a malignant and dishonest liar; I am not surprised at aught he does.

Yours,   T. R.

Do get the Washington off your hands.

1889

689 MADISON AVENUE

Mar. 25th, '89.

Dear old Cabot,

You are certainly the most loyal friend that ever breathed. Edith and I were more touched than I can say over your letter; all the more so from its absolutely unexpected nature. I hope you will tell Blaine how much I appreciate his kind expressions.*

I would have particularly liked to have been in Washington, in an official position, while you were in Congress; we would have had a very good time; and so I would have been glad to have been appointed. But aside from this feeling—and of course the pleasure one feels in having one's services recognized — it is a good deal better for me to stay where I am. I would like above all things to go into politics; but in this part of the State that seems impossible, especially with such a number of very wealthy competitors. So I have made up my mind that I will go in especially for literature, simply taking the part

* This refers to my urging Roosevelt's appointment as Assistant Secretary of State. It resulted in his appointment as Civil Service Commissioner.

in politics that a decent man should. I am going to keep my residence in the city because I have more hold here.

I was much amused the other day at an editorial in the *Times* about your Winchester system*; it was fairly complimentary though of course it's mugwump mind felt a certain suspicion of the affair. Whitridge,† by the way, has apparently suffered a change of heart; he spoke with bitter contempt of the futility of the average reformer, the other evening, and casually mentioned that he regarded you as the most promising young man in America! I fairly gaped at him.

Give my best love to Nannie, from both Edith and myself, and with the very heartiest thanks, old fellow, I am

Ever your friend,
THEODORE ROOSEVELT.

689 MADISON AVENUE

Dear Cabot,   Mar. 27th, 1889.

I will call on Grant tomorrow. I don't know at all whether Rosy will or will not stay.

The appointment of Lincoln‡ is admirable. Rice§—well, less admirable. Reid and Halstead are individually good appointments, though I am utterly against editors being given political positions, as a principle.

I am glad that the Railway Mail Service has been changed as it has been; but I hope there won't be a sweep of the fourth class postmasters. Your post office methods are the proper ones—wait until the incumbent's term has expired, and fill his place with the man the majority of the Republicans think best fitted.

I dined with Whitney¶ last night. He is evidently thoroughly familiar with your career. I was rather surprised to see how well he understood it.

Yours ever,   T. R.

---

* Choosing a postmaster by a general vote of all Republican voters.
† Frederick Whitridge of New York.
‡ Robert Lincoln, Minister to Great Britain.
§ Allen Thorndike Rice, Minister to Russia.
¶ I suppose William C. Whitney, Secretary of the Navy in Cleveland's first administration.

HOUSE OF REPRESENTATIVES
WASHINGTON

March 29th [?], 1889.

Dear Theodore:

Many thanks for your letters; both gave me great pleasure especially the first. I had a little talk with the President about you and he spoke very pleasantly but he is a reserved person. I met Reed today. He said he had been waiting to see me because he wanted to talk to the President about you and said all kinds of pleasant things and went there and then to the White House but the Cabinet was meeting and so he goes again. He is a loyal friend and as true as steel. I have spoken to Walker Blaine* about Butterfield and will look after him. Blaine told me that Evarts had spoken to him about you saying you should have handsome recognition and be brought into public life again. I tell you these things because I know you will like to hear them. I am harassed to death and if this accursed patronage does not kill me politically and destroy my health and temper nothing will. It is simply awful.

Love to all.

Yrs.,

H. C. L.

689 MADISON AVENUE

Mar. 30th, 1889.

Dear Cabot,

I am really pleased to hear about Tom Reed; I value his friendship.

We are threatened with a real calamity here, for I learn that Harrison thinks of making an ordinary ward politician, Van Cott, a Platt henchman, postmaster; a horrible contrast to Pearson. It would be an awful black eye to the party here; a criminal blunder. Platt seems to have a ring in the President's nose as regards New York. I feel very uneasy over it; have put in a strong counter plea.

Good bye, old fellow; curse patronage—but neither that nor anything else will kill you.

Yours, T. R.

* Solicitor of the Department of State under his father, who had just been appointed Secretary of State.

689 Madison Avenue
Dear Cabot,   April 4th, 1889.

I am awfully glad you are coming for the celebration*; what day will you be here? I have tickets for you for everything. We have asked the Tom Reeds to dinner.

I am very anxious to talk to you. I am really concerned at what you say of the difficulties you have over the patronage; but I have not much fear that it will hurt you seriously; the clamor is deafening, but it is curious how it dies away.

I enclose a letter to Bay.†
                                        Yours ever, T. R.

                                        689 Madison Ave.,
                                        New York,
Dear Cabot,   April, 1889.

I hope you will be here on Saturday the 27th; Ernest Crosby, our "high license" man, and a first rate fellow, will be here to dinner, and perhaps Choate; do come; I want to see and talk with you dreadfully. I do hope the President will appoint good civil service commissioners; I am very much discontented with him so far; in this state he has deliberately built up a Platt machine.
                                        Yours, T. R.

                                        1211 Conn. Ave.,
                                        [Washington, D. C.]
Dear Nannie and Cabot,‡   June 12th, 1889.

When I reached here Tuesday morning I found my room all ready, and a very nice breakfast waiting for me. Martha seems a very good woman; she cooks well, keeps my room in order and doesn't bother me. (By the way, I gave her Nan-

---

* One hundredth anniversary of the Government of the United States.
† My eldest son—George Cabot Lodge.
‡ He had been appointed Civil Service Commissioner and came to Washington to take office. He was living in my house.

nie's note.) Everything is as comfortable as possible; you have no idea of the difference it makes, coming here instead of to a hotel; and I *am* fully aware of what I owe you, Edith to the contrary notwithstanding.

Of course I feel a little homesick at being away from Edith and the children; but I have my hands fairly full of work. On Sunday we leave for a ten days' trip through some western postoffices; I guess there is a Cleveland hold-over at Milwaukee who will stand some overhauling.

I called on the Blaines, and on Quay; then my (two) visiting cards gave out, and I must wait until Edith sends me some more. I also called on Billy Wharton,* and we arranged to dine together for the next two or three evenings, until I go west—tonight I dine at the Thompsons. †

Tell Bay to brace up and study all he knows how, and we'll have a great trip to the Little Missouri. If there is any point of his equipment about which he needs information let him write me at once. I called on Walker Blaine to see about Butterfield, and I think he will be all right. Let Cabot be sure to write some time to Governor Merriam of Minnesota about Tom Reed; I will do so too—or rather I will see him when I go out in the fall.

Goodbye; I shall keep you informed from time to time how things are going on.   Yours ever,

THEODORE ROOSEVELT.

P. S.   To Cabot; don't write about Bishop Potter until you have read his piece; it was really not what *he* said, but what the mugwumps interpreted it to mean, together with a certain lack of wisdom in choosing the time and place for utterance, that made the remarks unfortunate. They were unwise in part; but they also contained some truth; and there are far more serious offenders than Bishop Potter.

---

* William F. Wharton of Boston—Assistant Secretary of State.

† Ex-Governor Hugh Thompson of South Carolina, a member of the Civil Service Commission, a most admirable man. He became a close friend of Roosevelt.

UNITED STATES
CIVIL SERVICE COMMISSION,
WASHINGTON, D. C.

Dear Cabot,   June 24th, 1889.

Well, here I am back again, to routine work, and heat, and, as a relief, pleasant dinners with the equally lonely Wharton. We had only a week's trip but we stirred things up well; the President has made a great mistake in appointing a well-meaning, weak old fellow in Indianapolis, but I think we have administered a galvanic shock that will reinforce his virtue for the future. Cleveland's postmaster at Milwaukee is about as thorough paced a scoundrel as I ever saw—an oily-Gammon, church-going specimen. We gave him a neat hoist. The Chicago postmaster is a trump; a really good fellow (Republican). At Grand Rapids, the redoubtable Congressman Belknap turned up as meek as a lamb and we fraternized most amicably. The West knows much less about civil service reform than the East, and there will be a row next winter; nevertheless some of their papers are very strong on the subject. I enclose an editorial from the Chicago *Tribune*.

I haven't seen my book * at all; but I know yours † is out for I saw a three column review, of the most appreciative order, in the N. Y. *Tribune*. It was written very intelligently and really seemed to appreciate pretty well the magnitude of the work you had accomplished. All that it needed to make it perfectly truthful was to have summed up by stating that it was *the* life of the greatest of all Americans. It is no small triumph to have written such a book as that.

Best love to Nannie.

Yours, T. R.

UNITED STATES
CIVIL SERVICE COMMISSION,
WASHINGTON, D.C.

Dear Cabot,   June 29th, 1889.

Tell Nannie I have called on all the people whose names she gave me, and virtue has had its reward. The Hitts ‡ had me to dinner (where I met Blaine and Phelps), Linden Kent drives

* "The Winning of the West."   † My "George Washington."
‡ Robert R. Hitt, distinguished Member of Congress from Illinois.

me out to the country club this evening and last evening I dined with the Herberts,* who were very pleasant; I am sworn friends with Billy Wharton and usually dine with him at Welckers. There we usually growl over our respective griefs. Blaine, and Walker B. do not treat him with the consideration that is his due; Walker usurps all the most pleasant and honorable part of his duties. As for me, I am having a hard row to hoe. I have made this Commission a living force, and in consequence the outcry among the spoilsmen has become furious; it has evidently frightened both the President and Halford † a little. They have shown symptoms of telling me that the law should be rigidly enforced where people will stand it, and gingerly handled elsewhere. But I answered militantly; that as long as I was responsible the law should be enforced up to the handle *every where;* fearlessly and honestly. I am a great believer in practical politics; but when my duty is to enforce a law, that law is surely going to be enforced, without fear or favor. I am perfectly willing to be turned out—or legislated out—but while in I mean business. As a matter of fact I believe, I have strengthened the administration by showing, in striking contrast to the facts under Cleveland, that there was no humbug in the law now. All the Chicago and Milwaukee papers are backing me up heartily. The Indiana men are very angry—even Browne‡ has gone back on his previous record. It is disheartening to see such folly; but it's only effect on me personally is to make me more doggedly resolute than ever to insist on exact and full justice.

I still have not seen your Washington; it must be awaiting me at Sagamore Hill.

Yours,   T. R.

SAGAMORE HILL,
OYSTER BAY, LONG ISLAND, N. Y.,
July 1st, '89.

Dear Cabot,

I was delighted to receive your letter, and need hardly say how much pleased I was with your opinion of my book. You

---

* Michael Herbert and his wife. He was the Secretary at the British Legation.
† E. W. Halford, the President's Secretary.
‡ Thomas McClelland Browne, Congressman from Indiana.

must certainly see the *Tribune* review; it is written with real appreciation; it is headed "A Brilliant Work." I have now read your book carefully through, and can only reiterate what I have already said as to its worth. It is head and shoulders above what you have already done; and it is *the* life of Washington. You have now reached what I am still struggling for; a *uniformly* excellent style. The contrast between your description of Virginian society in this book and in your "History of the Colonies," is so great as to be almost amusing. Moreover, though you have no absolutely new material, your chapter on "Washington as a party man" (I am thankful you took that exact title; it acts as a mordant to set the picture) is in reality as absolutely new as if based on mss. never before unearthed. It is a great work.

I was glad to hear from you in approval of my western trip, when I made "a slam among the post offices." I have been seriously annoyed at the mugwump praises, for fear they would discredit me with well-meaning but narrow Republicans, and for the last week my party friends in Washington have evidently felt a little shakey. This has no effect on me whatever; I took the first opportunity to make a slash at the Port Huron man especially to show that I was resolutely bent on following out my course to the very end. Even Halford, however, says he is alarmed at the feeling against the law in the West; but as I told him, it had far better be repealed than allowed to remain as under Cleveland a non-enforced humbug. If you get the chance do dwell on the fact that it is to Harrison's credit, all that we are doing in enforcing the law. I am part of the Administration; if I do good work it redounds to the credit of the Administration. This needs to be insisted on; both for the sake of the mugwumps and for the sake of Harrison himself.

How fortunate it is that I did not get the Assistant Secy'ship of State! I could have done nothing there; whereas now I have been a real force, and think I have helped the cause of good government and of the party.

Best love to Nannie.

T. R.

SAGAMORE HILL,
OYSTER BAY, LONG ISLAND, N. Y.,
July 6th, '89.

You blessed but jaundiced sage,

Your letters were so very gloomy that they made me quite regain my spirits. Edith thoroughly agrees with you about interviews; so I cry peccavi and will assume a statesmanlike reserve of manner whenever reporters come near me. Seriously, I was only led into saying as much by the not unnatural desire to hit back at the western politicians who were hitting at me.

I did not mean to worry you about Wharton. I told him that he *must* keep his position for three years; that as long as possible he must avoid a collision, and, if necessary to have it, must temper firmness with great diplomacy and smiling good manners.

I had an extremely good letter from Col. Clapp,* which I shall show to Halford and the President. I have no idea that I shall be asked to resign, and it would need really treacherous treatment to make me do so of my own accord. As far as I can see at present all that the Commission will do before October will be to finish the fight with the Milwaukee Postmaster and try to get one in Grand Rapids indicted (both are Democrats); and I may have a single "interview" on the practical character of our examinations just before leaving, in July or August, for the West. (Let me know as soon as possible about Bay.) So you see the Commission will relapse nearly into the much desired condition of innocuous desuetude.

As for the reformers of the professional sort attacking you, why their praise and blame are equally valueless. What is the Washington *Star?* I never even heard of it. If it is not better than the Washington *Post* it is vile indeed. I am case-hardened; the praise I am now receiving from the mugwumps excites in me mere good-natured amusement. Your book has permanent value; your work in Congress for the country has permanent value; your children's children will feel honored to bear your name;—you can snap your fingers at the snarling host of little yelpers, whose lies are predestined to rot in forgotten obscurity.

Best love to Nannie.

Yours,
T. R.

* Col. William W. Clapp, editor of *The Boston Journal.*

UNITED STATES
CIVIL SERVICE COMMISSION,
WASHINGTON, D. C.

July 11th, 1889.

Dear Cabot,

I read your speech with great care; I did not write you about it before because I wished to write a little at length. I think it so good as to be worth keeping in permanent form. Keep an accurate copy; it must go in, if it ever becomes necessary to publish a volume of "letters and speeches" of a distinguished, etc., etc. You took Bishop Potter's sermon exactly right, laying stress on just the proper points—the time chosen to deliver it, the application made by the mugwumps, and the failure to see that one has as much right to use Benedict Arnold as Washington as a sample public man of a century back; and yet you did not rebel at proper criticism. Moreover your whole speech was in tone and style that of a trained scholar who was also a trained politician—using the word in its proper meaning. I wonder whether it did not occur to our mugwump friends that it was an honor to the community to have in Congress a man capable of making such a speech.

Your remarks about indiscriminate, abusive criticism of course go to my heart; I am going to try to drag in something of the sort into my volume on N. Y.* for Freeman's series if I ever write it. I regard this dishonest jealousy of decent men on the part of people who claim to be good, and this wholesale abuse, as two of the most potent forces for evil now existent in our nation. The foul and coarse abuse of an avowed partisan, willing to hurt the nation for the sake of personal or party gain, is bad enough; but it receives the final touch when steeped in the mendacious hypocrisy of the mugwump, the mis-called Independent. If the Civil Service Reform papers do not make much of your address, it can only be because they care less for reforming civil service than for gratifying their malignant personal jealousies and animosities, at any cost to good government. I do not know when I have read a clearer, stronger, terser argument on behalf of the reform than that in your speech. It was in all ways admirable.

* A history of New York City.

I am glad your Washington sold so well; but I have never had a doubt as to the reception. In fact, in both literature and politics, you have attained a really wonderful position; in literature you have won it both with educated critics and with the general reading public, and in politics you have the confidence of the great body of decent American citizens who are neither silly nor vicious, who form part of neither the mugwumps nor the mob.

As for me, I have come back to my work. I saw Wharton for a moment; and the Commission had a very satisfactory interview with the President. The old boy is with us,—which was rather a relief to learn definitely. Wanamaker* has been as outrageously disagreeable as he could possibly be; and he hinted at so much that when the President telegraphed for us yesterday we thought it looked like a row. But as a matter of fact he has, if not supported us against Wanamaker, at least not supported Wanamaker against us; and when we are guaranteed a fair field I am quite able to handle [him] by myself. We have done our best to get on smoothly with him; but he is an ill-conditioned creature. He seems to be the only one of the Cabinet who wants to pitch into us; Porter† (who will keep his census out of our grip) is the best of friends with me; and I get along well with the absurd Tanner. It has been a great and genuine satisfaction to feel that the President is with us. The Indianapolis business gave him an awful wrench, but he has swallowed the medicine, and in his talk with us today did not express the least dissatisfaction with any of our deeds or utterances.

By the way, about interviewing, I really say very little; but I can't help answering a question now and then, and it promptly comes out as an interview. I was rather glad that *Puck* pitched into me; the chorus of mugwump praise was growing too loud. The attack was purely by innuendo and indirection, and was therefore in true mugwump style.

How about Bay? I hope he will come out with me whether

* John Wanamaker—then Postmaster-General.
† Robert Porter, Chief of the Census.

ae passes or not; it will do him good and it would be a great disappointment to him not to go.

During the hot weather we shall have comparatively little ;o do; it is pretty dreary to sizzle here, day after day, doing routine work that the good Lyman* is quite competent to attend to by himself; and I shall take my six weeks in the West with a light heart and a clear conscience. I shall start about August 6th.

Give my best love to Nannie, and tell her it is everything or me to have 1211 as a home.

Yours ever, T. R.

I guess from what the Prex says I will stay in unless knocked on the head by Congress—but I do wish he would give us a *ittle* more active support; in this Milwaukee case Wanamaker 'rom pure spite will not interfere to prevent the (Democratic) Postmaster from turning out the subordinate who gave us the nformation.

UNITED STATES
CIVIL SERVICE COMMISSION,
WASHINGTON, D. C.

July 17, '89.

Dear Cabot,

Read the enclosed letter to Bay (I can't spell it Ba— it sounds too lamb-like, and he is *not* a lamb) and give it to him or not as you see fit.

Clapp is a trump, through and through; how I wish we had his like in New York journalism!

Life's admiration of Scotch-Irish "liberalism" was delicious; I chuckled over it. Tom Reed's letter was excellent and very characteristic. But I don't know about sending him my book. A lot of small authors have pestered me with booklets recently — mostly poems; and I don't want any one to despise me as I despise them for sending me their own productions. What do you think about it? You certainly have reason to be proud of such letters from men like Bancroft, Winthrop and Howells.

Tomorrow we get out our report in the Milwaukee case;

---

* Charles Lyman—then President of the Civil Service Commission.

in it I hit Paul between the eyes. He's a regular oily Gammon. When we meet I'll tell you how Wanamaker has done. He opposes us so much that we have to go cautiously. For instance, they (Bonaparte,* etc.) have wished us to investigate the Baltimore Post Office; it is doubtless bad; but Wanamaker antagonizes what we do so freely that I shall try to have them get his department to investigate it instead; then he'll be hot for it. I mean to avoid a quarrel with him; both for the sake of the reform and of the party; but every now and then he intrudes too much, and I have to hit him a clip.

Tomorrow evening I have Wharton, Batcheller and Halford to dinner.

Yours always, T. R.

UNITED STATES
CIVIL SERVICE COMMISSION,
WASHINGTON, D. C.

July 28th, '89.

Dear Cabot,

I laid the case before the Commission; the charges against Saltonstall fell through. About the matter of removals, we are rather in a quandary; Wanamaker has laid before us the case of Brown of Baltimore. He has discharged 356 men out of 367; of course they have been replaced by democrats. Now, such a state of things is an outrage; a man acting in that way can pretty well nullify the whole Civil Service Law, for none but favorites will come forward to take the examinations in such an office.

I do wish the President would give me a little active, even if only verbal encouragement; it is a dead weight to stagger under, without a particle of sympathy from any one of our leaders here, except old Proctor.† I am a little weary over the case of the Milwaukee Postmaster; he has a strong pull, and the President has slumbered on his case over a week; if he is not dismissed, as we recommend, it will be a black eye for the Commission, and practically an announcement that here-

* Charles Bonaparte—afterward Secretary of the Navy in Roosevelt's Cabinet.
† Redfield Proctor, then Secretary of War.

after no man need fear dismissal for violating the law; for if Paul has not violated it, then it can by no possibility be violated.

The Putnams write me that the first edition of my book is nearly sold; so I suppose it is doing fairly well.

Look in the Sunday *Tribune;* I think it will contain a short skit by me on that demented mugwump Fiske.* I saw a Boston *Herald* article; and then met their correspondent and, unless I am in error, somewhat electrified him.

The Indiana Civil Service *Chronicle* quotes your 4th of July speech with much approbation.

The other day I wasted a dollar and a half on Swinburne's new volume of poems—but threw it away when I at last came to a sonnet addressed to "Our Lady of Laughter" Nell Gwynn, and containing the rather startling assurance that the virtuous Nell was one whom "neither court nor stage could taint." I cannot countenance idiocy beyond a certain point.

Yours, T. R.

UNITED STATES
CIVIL SERVICE COMMISSION,
WASHINGTON, D. C.

Dear Cabot,   August 1st, '89.

I am glad you liked the skit on Fiske; Mr. Dick, having proved applicable to me at your hands, I thought might be used as a weapon by me in turn. I am now varying matters by a thrust at that arch-spoilsman Frank Hatton; who devoted editorial after editorial to me.

Today I caught a glimpse of the President, and repeated to him the parable of the backwoodsman and the bear. You remember that the prayer of the backwoodsman was "Oh Lord, help me kill that bar; and if you don't help me, oh Lord, don't help the bar." Hitherto I have been perfectly contented if the President would preserve an impartial neutrality between me and the bear, but now, as regards Postmaster Paul of Milwaukee, the President *must* help somebody,

* John Fiske the philosopher and historian.

and I hope it won't be the bear. I guess he'll stand by us all right; but the old fellow always wants to half-do a thing.

I shall leave for the Rockies on Monday evening, if before that I can settle what may be an ugly fight with the Treasury Department; Windom has let a Port Huron collector cut up some fearful antics; I hope he will now make him undo all his deviltry; otherwise, we shall be forced to make a square stand up fight of it; which will be very bad, for the President will almost certainly back Windom, while if he does it is certain to discredit the Administration. I have put Batcheller on Windom, and he will, I am certain, do all he can to have the mischief undone; for he sees that the law has been shamefully violated.

As for Wanamaker he and I are sworn friends; but he will be a little put out soon; he wishes me to recommend the Baltimore Postmaster's removal for making a clean sweep, and yet not to make it a precedent.

I saw McKinley the other day; and explained to him that I was supporting Reed; he was as pleasant as possible—probably because he considered my support worthless.

Don't be disappointed if I fail to get you the elk horns; I can take but a short trip this year, and am especially hot for bear, who haven't any horns.

Yours, T. R.

SAGAMORE HILL,
OYSTER BAY, LONG ISLAND, N. Y.,
August 4th, '89.

Dear Cabot,

Just after writing you I received your note. I was very much pleased indeed with the Plymouth speech; particularly so. It has exactly the tone I like to see you take; the fearlessness that dares to point out an evil and yet the high patriotism that makes one sure of America, and of the ultimate triumph of good; above all, the *pointing out how to remedy* the evil—not mere cold criticism. I shall write a letter to the *Journal*, I think. It is a *very* good paper.

Yours ever, T. R.

ST. PAUL,
Aug. 8th, '89.

Dear Cabot,

I saw Governor Merriam this morning; he is all straight
for Reed, but of course I don't know, and he doesn't know,
what he will be able to accomplish. On my way back he is to
have two of the Congressmen to meet me at dinner. He was
exceedingly pleasant.

Did you see in *Belford's Magazine* an ode to Grover Cleveland by Edgar Fawcett? written in stern remonstrance of the
folly of the people of this "tax-wrung" land, who refused to
vote for the "high, pure" (I think these were the adjectives)
Grover? The poem itself, the place where it appeared, the man
who wrote it, and the man to whom it was written, taken
altogether formed the most delicious combination I have yet
encountered.

Harrison in the Milwaukee Postmaster business followed
his usual course of trying to hold the scales even between
myself and the bear. He accepted Paul's resignation on the
one hand, and notified him on the other that if he hadn't
resigned he would have been removed. It was a golden chance
to take a good stand; and it has been lost. It is absolutely
impossible for any man to deserve removal more than Paul
did. I suppose a half-and-half, boneless policy, may be safe;
I hope so, most sincerely; but it is neither ennobling nor
inspiring.

Best love to Nannie.

Yours,
T. R.

MONTANA CLUB,
HELENA, MONTANA,
Aug. 28th, '89.

Dear Cabot,

Having finished my month off, I am now on my way home.
By Jupiter, I feel well; I have had a hard but a very successful trip—moose, bear, elk, etc.; one bear nearly got me—and
never was in better condition. So now for work again.

They have all received me like a prince here in Helena; I

wish to Heaven I could take off my coat and go into the campaign for the next three weeks; I get along pretty well with a Rocky Mountain audience. It is nip and tuck here; I think we have lost the governorship, which is of no great moment, but there is at least an even chance for the Congressman and legislature. In Washington our party has been split in bad shape; but a great effort is being made to heal the breach.

I wish Tom Reed could have come out here on the stump; I know it would have strengthened him with the northwestern members.

I just saw *The Nation* with its long reviews of the Washington—unless I am mistaken they were written by Everett. It seemed to me that they contained the sincerest of all tributes, that unwillingly extorted from an enemy; their length acknowledged the importance of the book, and their hostility on certain points was most genuine flattery.

Write me to Oyster Bay until the 20th; then Washington. Best love to Nannie.

Yours, T. R.

Is Sullivan* really going to run for Congress? I think it is the most exquisite bit of humor if he does.

SAGAMORE HILL,
OYSTER BAY, LONG ISLAND, N. Y.,
Sept. 18th, '89.

Dear Cabot,

I have just learned of Miss Davis'† marriage; I am heartily glad at the good news, and am particularly pleased that I already know the groom. Will you forward the enclosed letter?

The *Courier* comment on you was delicious. By the way, *The Congregationalist*, in criticising my book, startled but pleased me the other day by regretting that it did not possess the same sustained charm and interest as, of all things in the world, my "War of 1812"!

---

* I suppose he means John L. the prize fighter.
† Mrs. Lodge's sister—married to Brooks Adams, son of Charles Francis Adams.

I do wish I could see you now; I have much to talk over with you; especially I wished to speak about the very ugly signs that are appearing not only in the west but in the middle states of determined Republican hostility to the Civil Service Law; I believe we have very stormy times ahead in Congress, and fear that a numerous body of Republican congressmen will join in refusing appropriations. However, whether we are knocked on the head or not, I am glad I took the office. But even with so much that I wish to say, I do not see how I can go to Boston now.

I am very sorry, for I very greatly desire to talk the situation over with you. I wrote Tom Reed in full after my visit to St. Paul; I think I got in some fair work for him.

Tell Nannie how pleased I am about the marriage.

Yours ever, T. R.

UNITED STATES·
CIVIL SERVICE COMMISSION,
WASHINGTON, D. C.

Dear Cabot, Sept. 26th, '89.

I congratulate you heartily on your excellent platform.* From the somewhat meagre accounts I have seen it would seem that in the Beard matter you were victorious over Hoar. I do not know if you took any active share in the fight between Brackett and Crapo. The latter would seem to me to be the better man. In New York (where I have been having a little effective correspondence with Depew) we also got a good platform and a clean ticket. I don't know whether it has much chance of winning or not.

Do you know if Tom Reed ever got the letter I wrote him from St. Paul? Best love to Nannie.

Yours in great haste, T. R.

P. S. Is there any chance of Brackett's not pulling through?

* Massachusetts State Republican platform.

UNITED STATES
CIVIL SERVICE COMMISSION,
WASHINGTON, D. C.

Sept. 27th, '89.

Dear Cabot,

I wrote you as soon as I saw the results of your work; and I have just received your letter written before the convention. I have already told you how admirable I thought the platform; and apparently you scored a complete victory in the Beard matter. To an outsider Crapo would seem a better nominee than Brackett. Do you think there is any danger of Russell's election? I would mortally hate to see a mugwump triumph— especially in view of the usual mugwump lying that is now going on, notably in the *Times* and *Post*, about the N. Y. Republican convention's civil service plank. As a matter of fact that plank is as explicit as possible, for it makes special reference to the C. S. plank in the national platform, endorsing it without reservation.

The *Advertiser* articles were admirable.

Thank Heaven I have Thompson for a colleague. Lyman is a good, honest, hardworking man, very familiar with the law; but he is also the most intolerably slow of all the men who ever adored red tape.

I was particularly pleased at Howells selecting the two points he did to lay stress on in his review of your Washington. I wrote him a note of thanks for what he said about my book. Edmund Kirke has made an assault of fairly hysterical rage upon me through the New York *Sun*. I do wish I could see you. Will you be on here shortly after the election?

Yours,   T. R.

UNITED STATES
CIVIL SERVICE COMMISSION,
WASHINGTON, D. C.

Sept. 28th, 1889.

Dear Cabot,

I have received the *Globe* which was very bright—I was especially amused with the picture of the "Resoluter"—and the *Journal* and *Advertiser* which certainly do back you up most handsomely. It is worth while being a "scholar in politics" when it enables one to produce a platform that calls forth hearty applause all over the Union, whereas ordinary platforms are hardly heeded. The Philadelphia *Press* had a peculiarly strong editorial in favor of your plank on the Civil Service question.

I breakfasted with Halford today; he was most enthusiastic about you and especially Nannie. I will probably call on the President this afternoon. I am very sorry the latter removed Silas Burt—I suppose Platt and Hiscock "laid down on him."

Yours, T. R.

UNITED STATES
CIVIL SERVICE COMMISSION,
WASHINGTON, D. C.

Dear Cabot,   Oct. 8th, '89.

I have time for but a line, for we are just closing the office. The town is jammed with a huge "re-union" of Knights Templar, all clad in cheap finery and prancing solemnly through the streets in processions huge and vast. All their wives and daughters have come too, and the hotels swarm so one can hardly get a meal; they all look very serious, and sheepishly proud of their gaudy appearance, and altogether are having a very characteristic American holiday.

I will give you full particulars of the Lyman matter when we meet. I am delighted Tom Reed is in the territories.

It made my blood boil when I read Curtis' speech. I strongly admire your attacking them fair and square; of course do it with the discrimination which I especially complain of them for not showing. Show the great harm they do by pretending to be independent, and foully slandering decent men in a spirit of shameless partisanship. Treat Curtis courteously; but point out that he and his friends so far from being independents are the bitterest—and many of them the most unscrupulous—of partisans; they belong to a bitter Democratic faction, none the less bitterly democratic because it happens to be at odds with another faction. My hands are tied by my position here; otherwise I should be at their throats in a moment—while not hesitating to acknowledge that there is much the Administration has done of which I do not in the least approve.

Best love to Nannie.

Yours, T. R.

SAGAMORE HILL,
OYSTER BAY, LONG ISLAND, N. Y.,
Oct. 17th, '89.

Dear Cabot,

I have carefully read through your speech; and I like it much. It has drawn blood; the *Times* had a long editorial thereon—in which by the way it admitted that you had fully cleared yourself as regards the Navy Yard charges.

But I think you can do still better on the same subject; I hope you will carefully prepare yourself and make one more, and even stronger—much stronger—attack on the base hypocrisy and insincerity of the mugwumps, at some opportune time in the present campaign. Make it when the speech will be printed in full.

I hate to seem to urge you into a fight which I can not share; but you know well I am fairly straining at the leash in my eagerness to be in the fray myself; and I am certain that a telling attack on the mugwumps helps you greatly, with your party and with the people at large. They hate you bitterly; and I fully believe that from the stand point of mere policy it will pay you to pitch into them. I owe them a debt of gratitude; for their utterly unjust and hypocritical malevolence has quite reconciled me to the Administration, of which, as you know, I only lukewarmly approved. Dwell on the fact that they are the most dangerous foes of the reform.

The *Evening Post* speaks of the democratic victory in Indianapolis as a "wholesome mugwump triumph"; point out that it was a victory for the ballot-box stuffer Sim Coy, whom the democrats nominated while his hair was still short from his 18 months in prison—and whom therefore the mugwumps elected. Point out with additional emphasis the inexcusable partisanship of Curtis' speech, its utter hypocrisy and injustice, as shown by his backing up the non-civil service reform platform of the Massachusetts democrats. Take President Eliot's words wherein he disposes of the "independent" nonsense, and shows a man ought to be a party man, and point out the ridiculous position in which this leaves his fellow mugwumps; and show how ridiculously he himself now stands towards civil service reform, ballot reform, high license, and the like. Above all show the utter hypocrisy of the mugwump newspapers of N. Y. and Boston (name them); instance the way they treated Russell and Burnett* on Civil Service Reform, and how quiet they kept while Collins and Cleveland stuffed your Navy Yard. Speak courteously of Curtis and Eliot; less so of the *Post*, etc., and use towards all the most bitingly severe language you can muster. Make your points as clear as possible; and thrust the steel well home. It is foolish to show mercy.

I will be here a fortnight more, to read to Edith, etc. Love to Nannie.

Yours, T. R.

SAGAMORE HILL,
OYSTER BAY, LONG ISLAND, N. Y.,
Oct. 19th, '89.

Dear Cabot,

Perhaps, if the mugwumps are showing signs of repentance, you might as well wait a short while before hitting them again. I am glad the *Record* is to print an abstract of your speech— but the *Record* has been most unfair and partisan in its *relative* attitude to the Republicans as compared to the Democrats.

As I told you I liked your speech very much; yet I want you some time to do even a little better, by elaborating it more, so as to show at length the essential injustice and insincerity of the mugwump position.

I will meet Dodge in New York (say at the Union League

* John E. Russell and Edward Burnett, Democratic Congressmen from Massachusetts.

Club, 39th St. and 5th Ave.) any day next week; but let him
write me *at least* three or four days before hand. I regard
Saltonstall as an honest, brave, old puzzlehead; the best of
tools for politicians. But I hope I won't have to attack him
myself; it will be *very* awkward for me. Of course, excellent
though Thompson is (and I can not be glad enough he is my
colleague) I hardly dare trust him in such work. As for Lyman,
he is utterly useless; I wish I had one more good Republican
on the Commission: Lyman is utterly out of place as a Commissioner; I wish to heaven he were off. If I only had an
honest, intelligent and fearless Republican colleague, who
would never be partisan, but whom I could trust for just such
work as this!

Yours ever, T. R.

SAGAMORE HILL,
OYSTER BAY, LONG ISLAND, N. Y.,
Oct. 27th, '89.

Dear Cabot,

Yesterday I picked up *The Atlantic* and saw that both your
book and mine were reviewed therein. I thought the reviewer
utterly failed to do justice to your book; Howells, on the
contrary, really grasped what it meant, in last month's *Harper's*. The man who reviewed my book however evidently
knew the subject, and one or two of his hits were perfectly
justifiable (others were not). I had no idea that any of the
Haldimand mss. were in any printed collection of documents;
and I failed to find the traces of the concerted movement against
us in the West which he shows was planned by the British.
Still, I think his article as a whole rather showed that my book
was of some weight.

I go on to Washington on Wednesday, and will return next
Sunday to see Kermit christened. I have been writing out a
rough draft of our C. S. report; I want to make it incisive and
to the point, and to keep Lyman from filling it with statistical
tables and making it totally unreadable. With Thompson's
help I hope to succeed.

I saw Dodge; but except as to the character of two members of the local board he made no charge whatever; and of course I must have something more than mere suspicion to go on. Tell me about Hall and Flatley.

Yours ever,

T. R.

THE UNION LEAGUE CLUB

Dear Cabot,   Oct. 30th, '89.

Last evening the Crugers invited me over to dine with Hiscock; and tonight I dine with ex-Senator Miller. Hiscock remarked that the New York delegation were "practically solid" for Reed; and he said that he thought we stood an excellent chance of electing our State ticket—he is the first politican who has told me so. Miller is, naturally, in a bitterly angry and contemptuous mood towards the Administration; as for the election he says that no human being can forecast the result; if the Cleveland men are not curs they will stand aloof, and if [they] do we may very well win.

The man who criticised me in *The Atlantic* knew a good deal of the subject*; I don't suppose any author sets a true value on his work; but I felt that he did not give me sufficient credit for the many things I had done, while he made one or two points—and failed signally in trying to make one or two others against me. On the whole I thought he was a hostile critic; and therefore the grudging praise that was unwillingly extorted from him was all the more valuable. I have finished my controversy with Kirke; in my last letter I put the knife into him up to the hilt.

What funnily varied lives we do lead, Cabot! We touch two or three little worlds, each profoundly ignorant of the others. Our literary friends have but a vague knowledge of our actual political work; and a goodly number of our sporting and social acquaintances know us only as men of good family, one of whom rides hard to hounds, while the other hunts big game in the Rockies.

* "The Winning of the West."

Can I come pretty often to dinner while in Washington before Edith comes?

You *must* beat Russell. It would be gall and wormwood to have him elected.

Love to Nannie.

Yours,   T. R.

1890

UNITED STATES
CIVIL SERVICE COMMISSION,
WASHINGTON, D. C.

May, 1890.
Dear Cabot,   Monday.

Can you stop at the office tomorrow on your way to the house to see Governor Thompson? If not, let him know when and where he can see you during the day. He wishes to see you about the report; as I am now going away. It is very important that the present Commission be given an absolutely clean bill of health by a majority of the Committee whatever a minority do. I don't want a compromise verdict, even to get all to sign. We have done absolutely the straight thing throughout and the Committee is in honor bound to do so too, and stand by us. Do see Greenhalge and Butterworth or Lehlbach.* The *Post* [Washington] has done all it can to hurt the reform; a verdict against us is a verdict against the reform and against decency.

I wish the Boston *Journal* I sent you could be given to Halford or the President.

Yours,   T. R.

UNITES STATES
CIVIL SERVICE COMMISSION,
WASHINGTON, D. C.

Dear Cabot,   May 9th, '90.

The enclosed is from the best paper in Ohio, the Cleveland *Leader*.

I wonder whether the Philadelphia *Press* reference to the

* All members of the House.

Dudley case was not due to Wanamaker's connection with it? To me the proposition that it is right to protect a government witness who is being persecuted for telling the truth seems so self evident that it is with difficulty I can dismiss it patiently. This Commission has been able to do effective work because we *have* waged war on wrongdoers; and to do this effectively we must protect our witnesses. To accomplish anything we had to be aggressive; and to be aggressive usually implies taking punishment.

I saw the President yesterday and had a long talk with him; I will tell you about it when we meet. The conclusion of the talk was rather colorless, as usual. Heavens, how I like positive men!

Send back the enclosed slip; I want to keep it.

We had a very pleasant dinner at the Davises last night.

I hope you and Nannie are enjoying yourselves.

The *Times*, by the way, has certainly treated you fairly about the Civil Service debate—much better than the *Tribune*, on that point!

Yours in haste,
THEODORE ROOSEVELT.

SAGAMORE HILL

Dear Cabot,   July 31st, '90.

Both Edith and I were exceedingly interested in the Higginson* pamphlet; it struck a high note, and one arose feeling better for having read it. It was tolerant without being weak, and it was charitable without being maudlin. I am glad to have seen it.

Next Monday I go back to Washington, to be there nearly three weeks. When do you go there?

Douglas has been spending a week here, and we have had some great fun with the polo—my head, by the way, getting cut open again in one game, but not badly. Ferguson is beginning to play very well. Edith and I have had some lovely rows on the bay, taking our lunch and books with us.

* Major Henry Lee Higginson.

Get the last *Lippincott;* Rudyard Kipling has a story in it which I think one of his best.

My Chautauqua speech went off well; but there was no regular report of it.

Politically here we seem in about a normal condition; which I fear, in a non-presidential year, means a good chance for the Democrats. But we ought to hold our own with the Congressmen.

Best Love to Nannie.

Yours, T. R.

WASHINGTON, D. C.
Aug. 23rd, '90.

Dear Cabot,

From all I can glean in the papers you did well in Maine, and I congratulate you. But I really regret much that you were not here while Bryce* was. It was only for two days, but I contrived to let him see a good deal in that time. Each morning I breakfasted alone with him and his wife—a bright, pleasant woman. One day we lunched in the Speaker's room, with the Hitts; the next day he lunched with John Andrew to meet a number of the House Democrats—including Rogers† and others of the ilk. One evening the Hitts gave them a dinner, asking among others Ingalls, Carlisle, Gibson, Wheeler, Bingham and Adams—mixed.

The next night I had Bryce to a dinner of representative Republicans—Hoar, Hawley, Saunders, Jones of Nevada, who is the most amusing storyteller I ever met, Reed, McKinley, Butterworth, Cannon, Hitt and McKenna of California. They are an able set of men, and Bryce thoroughly appreciated them. He grasped at once the distinction between these men who *do* things, and the others who only think or talk about how they ought to be done. I think his visit here will be a needed anti-septic; for he now goes to visit Godkin

---

* James Bryce—afterward British Ambassador at Washington.
† John Henry Rogers, Member from Arkansas.

and Eliot! He ended his letter of thanks, when he left, "I won't let myself be captured by excessive mugwumpery after your warnings." So you see I did good missionary work.

I hate to leave my work here now. The P. M. G. has refused us any detail of clerks and it is almost—indeed quite—impossible to get the papers marked for the new places without them; so we shall fall behind, and there will be a row which I hate to leave Lyman to face. Oh, Heaven, if the President had a little backbone, and if the Senators did not have flannel legs! Write me to O. B.

Love to Nannie.

Yours, T. R.

SAGAMORE HILL,
OYSTER BAY, LONG ISLAND, N. Y.,
Aug. 27th, '90.

Dear Cabot,

I have sent your letter to Bryce; I do hope he is not engaged already, and can visit you.* He is a man of such good common sense that I do not wish him to see only the mugwumps here; I wish him really to understand American life. I think he really enjoyed and understood what he saw at Washington.

Clapp of the *Journal* is a trump; I am really touched by the way he has stood by me this winter. By the way did you see that poor Walter Howe was drowned. He was a disinterested and upright public servant, and one of the most useful citizens New York had. I greatly regret his loss.

I told the Longmans Green people that you would probably have the "Boston"† for them about the beginning of December. Get the cursed thing off your hands.

I did not leave enough of Grosvenor‡ to be put in a coal scuttle. Before I was half way through he took refuge in what he called his "constitutional right" not to be questioned else-

---

* Mr. and Mrs. Bryce came to Nahant and stayed with us for a few days; I think just at this time.

† Longmans' series of "Historic Towns."

‡ General Grosvenor, Member of Congress from Ohio.

where for what he had said in the House. The Committee fairly screamed with laughter.

You have evidently done well in Maine.*

Yours ever, T. R.

MEDORA,
Sept. 23d, '90.

Dear Cabot,

I have just reached here, our party having separated after a really lovely two weeks in the Yellowstone Park. The scenery is certainly most wonderful and beautiful, and we all enjoyed it to the full.

Almost the first person I saw on getting here was Bay, rugged, hearty and healthy; he had killed three antelope, and had not had his clothes off since I left; so he is thoroughly happy.

The Governor has just sent me a copy of Grosvenor's attack on me in my absence. He is a liar and a coward, and as soon as I get back I shall write him an open letter telling him so.

I enclose a letter from Jas. R. Gilmore (Edmund Kirke) and my answer; it relates to the new cyclopedia. I am surprised at his writing me on any subject, after our correspondence in the *Sun*; and I hardly think I care to answer him. Don't you think it best to leave it unanswered? If so, destroy my letter; otherwise send it back to me.

I wired Reed† a line of congratulation on his victory. Maine has done gloriously. Your speech was really admirable; I think it the best you have ever done. The touch about the *Post* was delicious. I do wish I could take part in the campaign this year.

Show Nannie this about Bay.

Yours ever, T. R.

---

* We, the Republicans, did well in Maine that year but nowhere else at the General Election two months later.

† This was just after Reed's reform of the Rules of the House.

MEDORA,
Sept. 23d, '90.

Dear Cabot,

Just after writing you my letter, five minutes ago, the mail came in with yours of the 19th, and the paper containing Greenhalge's speech and the platform. Both of them are admirable. Massachusetts is certainly well to the front. Heavens, how I wish we could win this year! The great point is, shall our Congress legislate or not—shall our Congress be a real legislative body, or an assembly on the Polish order. This is even a more important question than that of any particular piece of legislation, vital though the latter may be. I would give a great deal to be allowed to make just one speech about it. I see that Kilgore, Cummings and others violently forced their way out the other day; I think it very unfortunate they are not fined at least five hundred dollars a head.

I think I shall have to skin Grosvenor again.

To my amusement Bay's hunter, an old buffalo hunter named Mason, turns out to be an intense Republican and warm admirer of yours; a very staunch supporter of the election bill. He is a really intelligent old fellow. Bay likes him; is enjoying himself thoroughly, and is growing continually more hardy.

Thank you greatly for what you did in the Grosvenor matter.

Yours ever,   T. R.

ELKHORN RANCH,
Oct. 4th, '90.

Dear Cabot,

I was very glad indeed to get your letter. I shall adopt your advice about Gilmore and send him a letter modelled à la John Hay and yourself. I guess you're right about Grosvenor, too; nothing that he can say behind my back can alter the fact that he ran away when brought to face me.

I am very anxious to talk over politics with you. I think I'll have to give the Bennett law a boost in Wisconsin—it will probably prove fatal to it, but one of the reporters who was last year in Washington, a very good fellow, is now editing a paper out there and wants me to write him a piece, which I can do without trenching on politics proper.

Bay is in excellent health, hardy and stout; I think I may say he is enjoying himself thoroughly. He has recently killed a blacktail doe, and a number of ducks; and was up all night with us fighting a prairie fire—a less simple operation than it sounds. We shall start home about a week hence.

Ever yours,
T. R.

1820 Jefferson Place,
WASHINGTON, D. C.,
Oct. 22d, '90.

Dear Cabot,

Just after sending you my note yesterday I received your letter enclosed in one from Edith. It contained just what I wished to hear about you. Of course take just as much care as if Everett were a formidable foe; but I can not help believing you will even increase your majority against him. Your reception in Music Hall must indeed have pleased you.

Foulke* is here. He is going to pitch into Wanamaker strong in a few days—my withers are unwrung. Foulke is a very good fellow. I find he is with us on the election bill; and I will relate to you an amusing dialogue he had with one of your opponents in Boston, in which, to the unspeakable horror of the mugwump, he admitted that you had faults, but called on your foe, as an honest man, to admit that Cleveland's were much worse, and his good qualities less conspicuous. Foulke also thinks Reed all sound. He is weak on the McKinley bill— but I can easily forgive him that. If I can get my article on the Bennett law I'll send it to you.

Here things are much as usual. I had a very short and cold interview with the President. His one anxiety is *not* to have anything [to do] with us or the Civil Service Law.

Love to Nannie.

Yours,
T. R.

* William Dudley Foulke.

1820 Jefferson Place,
WASHINGTON, D. C.,
Oct. 23d, '90.

Dear Cabot,

I was very much pleased with your speech wherein you used up, first the youthful Williams, and then the hoary Schurz. The former must be insufferable. I do hope he is beaten. I really hardly understand his audacity in prolonging a "lobby" discussion, after Russell's connection with it, and his own speech concerning him.

I have not received any copy of my letter to the Wisconsin *State Journal*, but I know it has been published because the Washington *Post* had a paragraph telling about my "ringing appeal" to the Wisconsin Republicans.

Here I am having a small scuffle over some Republican Clubs of office holders. They do no good and give the opposition something to cry about; but it is needless to say Harrison shuffles uneasily round and is silent when I speak to him about them.

Ask Bay if he still remembers the night we spent fighting the prairie fire.

Yours,   T. R.

P. S. Everett can not be a very serious opponent.

1820 Jefferson Place,
WASHINGTON, D. C.,
Oct. 26th. [1890.]

Dear Cabot,

You are now in the closing days of the campaign; so don't take a minute to answer this.

Edith and the children arrived yesterday; by the way, Henry Adams sent her a gift copy of his History.

I am surprised and indignant rather than alarmed to hear that money has been sent down to beat you—for I know they can not possibly succeed. The New York and Western papers all speak of you as the central figure in the Massachusetts fight this year.

Good luck, old fellow.

Yours ever,   T. R.

P. S. The enclosed letter explains itself; I have just received it. They wish very much to have you speak at the Marquette Club. I really think it would be worth your while. You would be speaking to all the West. It is a first class Republican Club, of the best kind. I guess they would like to hear from you about Ballot-Reform, as that is what you are now identified with. I think it would be worth your while going. This year *I* have nothing to say; *you* have.

> 1820 Jefferson Place,
> WASHINGTON,
> Nov. 10th, '90.

Dear Cabot,

I have felt too down hearted over the election to write you since; and besides there seemed really nothing to say. Well, at any rate you showed yourself stronger than your party by running ahead of your ticket, as far as I can judge by the return. The overwhelming nature of the disaster is due entirely to the McKinley bill; as you know I never liked that measure. There were some other features of the election which I wish to discuss with you; especially some insight I got during the last two months into the way things were looked at at home.

The Democratic majority will run wild; and Andrew, Hoar* & Co. will have a fine time keeping pace with the capers of the [Farmers] Alliance men of the West and Southwest.

Now, finish your "Boston" and get it off your hands; and let me know the day and train you arrive.

Love to Nannie.

Yours,   T. R.

* Sherman Hoar, Congressman from Massachusetts.

1891

UNITED STATES
CIVIL SERVICE COMMISSION,
WASHINGTON, D. C.

William Potts, Esq.,　　　　　February 13, 1891.
18 *Wall Street, New York.*

My dear Potts: I do not think I can possibly get on for the 19th. I have got to speak in New Haven anyhow on the 18th, which I bitterly regret, for in the present crisis I do not want to be away from Washington. We are in danger of being starved by having our entire appropriation cut off. I do wish that our Massachusetts men would attend with proper severity to Congressmen Cogswell, O'Neil, and Walker.

In great haste,　　　Yours sincerely,

THEODORE ROOSEVELT.

P. S. Thanks to the magnificent pluck and leadership of Lodge, McComas and Butterworth, the cleverness of Dingley, the fight has been won since the above was written. Boatner, and Dockery and Clements, Democrats, aided in a subordinate way. The *Tribune* and *Times* have had equally unjust and partisan accounts of the matter. I do wish our Association would take strong ground for the gentlemen named above and also for Moore of N. H., Lehlbach of N. J., Greenhalge of Massachusetts and Tracey of New York. Besides the men given at the foot of this letter, the Association ought to attack by name Payson of Illinois, Cannon of Illinois, Cogswell and Walker of Massachusetts, and Grosvenor of Ohio (Republicans).

SAGAMORE HILL,
OYSTER BAY, LONG ISLAND, N. Y.,
Dear Cabot,　　　　　June 8th, '91.

Many thanks for sending the paper containing your New Bedford speech. I thought it admirable in every way. You made a very strong summing up of what the Republican party should stand for. What a foolish article McAdoo* wrote about

---

* William McAdoo of New Jersey, Congressman and Asst. Secretary of the Navy.

immigration—though he was sound on the main point. The *Tribune* has come out practically against any kind of restriction; of course that alien organ the *Evening Post* already occupied this position. The newspapers in fact are showing the usual cowardice produced by the approach of a presidential election.

I can not make out from the papers what the Massachusetts Legislature has done about redistricting. Apparently the timid and foolish element got the upper hand. How does it leave your district?

I am now carrying on a fight with the "hustlers" in our local assembly association; I shall smash them; they have brought a series of wild charges against the local board of examiners, and now fail to advance an iota of proof.

I am going to get your "Boston" tomorrow, as I hear it is out; I was told by a friend just back from England that Green * was greatly pleased with it.

Speck † has been spending a week here; he is learning polo with German solemnity and thoroughness.

Give my best love to Nannie. Edith sends love.

Yours,   THEODORE ROOSEVELT.

UNITED STATES
CIVIL SERVICE COMMISSION,
WASHINGTON, D. C.

Hon. H. C. Lodge, Nahant, Mass.   June 15, 1891.

Dear Cabot: Do let me know a little bit about your new district. Are you all right? That is the thing that I have been mainly worried over. I cannot yet get a full idea of what the inside of the business has been, either on the Democratic or Republican side. Do let me know a little about it. I presume that a number of our brethren have been weak-kneed, as they usually are. It does seem to me, however, as though some of the elect on the other side have been having a parrot and monkey time too, for which praised be a merciful Providence.

* John Richard Green, the English historian.

† Baron Speck von Sternberg, attached to the German Legation, afterwards Ambassador from Germany.

Did you write the editorial in the Boston *Journal*? It struck me as one of the most deliciously humorous things of its kind that I had recently seen. I cannot help hoping that Brother Quincy will play the rest of the brethren some unholy tricks from time to time; they need it; it will do them good. And it will do him good to be found out.

Assistant Postmaster-General Bell apparently made a very good speech the other day. At least it was so reported in the Boston *Journal*. He spoke mighty sensibly. I am glad to hear that he did so.

I have carried my fight in New York through to a successful conclusion, I believe, although some skirmishing yet remains to be done. What especially delighted me was the evident feeling of the Republican association, the people who are investigating the case, that I was a good Republican, and a man whom they could trust and tie to. I think that that is going to come out all right. Certainly they cannot but see that we throw open the doors to every inquiry, and allow every responsible party to find out everything that has been done.

Day before yesterday I saw Douglas's Orange team get an awful thrashing at Polo at the hands of the Meadowbrook men. I was out there, and to my immense amusement the dudes treated me with profound and elaborate courtesy. I have just read through your "Boston." It is certainly an excellent piece of work. It is one of which I think you have legitimate reason to feel proud. You do not want to do any more booklets, of course, any more than I do. But this particular booklet will be a credit to you. I think you have every right to feel fully satisfied with it. And as regards style, it is as good as anything that you have done.

Give my best love to Nannie.

Ever yours,
Theodore Roosevelt.

P. S. By the way, isn't your use of "condign" on p. 219 unwarranted? "condign punishment" implies merited punishment, does it not?* Look it up in the dictionary.

---

* He was right—"condign" in this connection means merited or suitable.

I enclose a delicious letter of Tom Reed's; send it back when you have read it.

Did you receive my last note?

The Nation condemned my book for its provincial Americanism.

UNITED STATES
CIVIL SERVICE COMMISSION,
WASHINGTON, D. C.

June 19th, '91.

Dear Cabot,

Your two letters reached me almost together. It was funny our copies of Reed's amusing letters crossing one another.

Springy* has been paying your "Boston" an evidently sincere meed of praise by reading it all through in two days, from beginning to end; he considers it very interesting and called my attention to various points as he read. Sensible, appreciative boy, Springy—very. He is much worked up at present over the excessive iniquity of American diplomacy. By the way, there *has* been some queer work of some sort over the Behring Sea matter; but we seem to have come out of it very well. Wharton has had his suspicions, and he talks very freely at rare intervals; but he is not in the confidence of the Administration and really knows very little more about it than every one does.

Beard's letter was very good. I shall devote a little spare time to him in our next annual report, showing the small number of dismissals and resignations, and saying that this is clear proof of honest enforcement of the law. Can you not have copies sent me of the extracts from Saltonstall's letters. I particularly wish them.

I am glad Hayes† advised you not to run for Governor. You don't wish that position. Washington is your place; and let it get abroad quietly, that you are to make the run for United States Senator.

Now, for a piece of social news, which will be of interest to

* Cecil Spring Rice.
† Elihu B. Hayes—one of my very warm supporters. He was Mayor of Lynn, Mass., and a conspicuous member of the legislature.

Nannie, as she ought to know of the more noted entertainments in high diplomatic and administrative circles. On Wednesday and Thursday evenings of this week I gave two dinners, assisted by Springy, with nice colored Millie as cook and waitress. First dinner. Guests, the British Minister* and the Secretary of War.† Bill of fare, crabs, chicken and rice, cherries, claret and tea. (Neither guest died; and I think Proctor, who is a good native American, hungered for pie, in addition.) Springy nervous and fidgety; I, with my best air of oriental courtesy, and a tendency to orate only held in check by the memory of the jeers of my wife and intimate friend. 2nd Dinner. Guests, the Secretary of the Navy‡ and the British Minister, who was laboriously polite and good but somewhat heavy in grappling with the novelty of the situation. Bill of fare, chops and rice, *pâté de foie gras*, raspberries, claret and tea. (Guests still survive.) Springy still nervous. Tracy in great form, very amusing and entertaining.

I'll bet they were dinners new to Sir Julian's experience, but both the Secretaries enjoyed them.

Yours, T. R.

UNITED STATES
CIVIL SERVICE COMMISSION,
WASHINGTON, D. C.

Hon. H. C. Lodge, Nahant, Mass.　　　　June 26, 1891.

Dear Cabot: I have been thinking over your request for me to speak in Massachusetts this fall, and I consulted Governor Thompson and Wharton.

I do not think I ought to go. I think it would be merely frittering away what I may be able to accomplish by speaking in Massachusetts in the congressional and Presidential contest a year hence. This year there is nothing particular to be gained, as far as I can see, by my appearance. You are not running, and there is no President in question and no Congress; and I would certainly weaken whatever good effect

* Sir Julian Pauncefote.
† Redfield Proctor—soon afterward Senator from Vermont.
‡ General B. F. Tracy.

would be produced by appearing next year. Remember, that when I speak I have got to make up my mind that unfavorable comment upon me, and therefore upon the Commission, will follow, and I have to weaken myself a certain amount, with the already overwhelming Democratic majority in the next House. I am perfectly willing to do this for an object, but it does not seem worth while doing it unless there is an object. The Governor is strongly against my going; he thinks it will have a very bad effect and Wharton also strongly advises against it. Of course, if you make a dead point of it, I will come. Meanwhile, cannot you come down to Oyster Bay between the 13th and 19th? That will be polo week, and it might amuse you to see it. We should very much like to have you. Come at any rate, even if only for a day or two.

Yours ever,

THEODORE ROOSEVELT.

P. S. Love to Nannie. I have turned into an anglo-maniac here and play tennis at the British Legation every afternoon. Play it very badly, too. Springy feels fairly venomous over American politics and social life just at present. He is a dear, and I soothe him. Have you seen Brander Matthews' clever little article on Briticisms and Americanisms in the July *Harper?*

UNITED STATES
CIVIL SERVICE COMMISSION,
WASHINGTON, D. C.

Dear Old Cabot,   June 29th, 1891.

Your letter made me feel really downhearted. You have certainly been treated with the basest ingratitude* by what ought to be, but emphatically is not, the best element in the community. You have had a most honorable and successful career in the House; at the worst I would take one or two terms more therein; and if you are elected to the Senate, you draw one of the great prizes of American politics. In your position it was absolutely inevitable for you to be bitterly

* This refers to my defeat for re-election as an Overseer of Harvard.

attacked by the Harvard College "educated" crowd. They have been all wrong for the last seven years; and they were bound in order to justify themselves, to assail the best man who took the opposite view. This attitude is radically false. Take what is happening now, for instance. They hate, or profess to hate, Tammany above all other things, yet Tammany is recognized as the corner stone of the northern democracy everywhere outside of New England, and the three "reform" candidates for speaker, Mills, Crisp, and MacMillan, are all to appear before Tammany on July 4th, to try for favors! Yet the mugwump papers will have no comment on this, no explanation as to what it really means, no exposure as to the attitude of the Speakership candidates whom they have extolled as the apostles of purity.

As for their praise of me, it is I am sorry to say a measure and sign of the fact that my career is over, and that though as I firmly believe I have done a good work—the best work I could do—yet that in doing it I have spent and exhausted my influence with the party and country. I am at the end of my career, such as it is; you may be but at the beginning of yours, and you have already had a most honorable one.

My task for the past two years has been simple. I have only had to battle for a good law; and though this meant drawing down on me the bitter animosities of the men who in New York, at least, control politics, it was easy to perform creditably, and offered no obstacles in the way of being misunderstood or misrepresented by men of standing and intelligence. A much harder, and much greater, task is the work of an organization, of a party in Congress. Had I been in Congress I should now be as bitterly assailed as you. I often have a regret that I am not in with you, Reed, and others in doing the real work; the work that is not too much in advance of the people—though I don't wish to be understood as regretting what I have been working at; on the contrary I am proud of it. There is an unexpectedly wise sentence about the necessity of being a good party man to do effective work in this month's Atlantic, in the review of Houghton's life.

By the way, to my utter surprise, I thought Schurz's article on Lincoln in the June *Atlantic* very good; if you see Morse tell him that if Schurz can write a whole volume in that tone he could do the Lincoln for the series very well.

Yours always,

THEODORE ROOSEVELT.

UNITED STATES
CIVIL SERVICE COMMISSION,
WASHINGTON, D. C.

July 1st, '91.

Dear Cabot,

Yesterday Springy and I moved over to 1721 where we are just as comfortable as possible, and are excellently taken care of by nice black Martha; and we think very gratefully of our absent host and hostess.

When we went to bed last night Springy performed a delicious feat. We went upstairs in the dark, and did not light the gas. I turned into my room; and noticed that, as I undressed, I did not hear anything of Springy. Soon however I heard my name called from the flight above; and then followed demands to know where *I* was, and where *he* was, and where our bedrooms were; and when I had answered these questions and lit the light Springy came paddling downstairs dressed à la Lady Godiva, with his clothes, shoes, etc., clasped in his arms. He had dreamily walked up one extra flight, undressed and started to get into bed; when it occurred to him as odd that the bed had no sheets. He couldn't find any matches, and began to feel that there was a mystery somewhere; and so he became vocal, and when I answered him from below he at first felt as if I had gone down to live in the cellar.

I have been here pretty steadily so far, save for ten days, when I was in New York, taking advantage of the 21st Dist. investigation. But I don't think I shall have to be here very much during the rest of the summer; probably only for a week or so at a time, and with a fortnight's intermission.

We saw the President today, about some changes in the rules. Having promulgated the Indiana rules he will do nothing else, and will not even consider changes to which there is no opposition, and which would merely simplify and expedite business; throughout the interview he was of course as disagreeable and suspicious of manner as well might be.

Things don't look very well for Wanamaker. I doubt if he did anything criminal; but he has, according to his usual practice, indulged in needless lying, thanks to his sloppy mindedness; and this may make it ugly for him. Did you see how our old friend Grosvenor lied and got caught, and fell in consequence?

During these two months the British Legation has really been a great comfort to me; I have played tennis there, or rowed on the river with Springy and Johnstone, every afternoon; and I have dined there two or three times a week as a rule.

Best love to Nannie; and Constance* and Bay and John.*

Yours, T. R.

UNITED STATES
CIVIL SERVICE COMMISSION,
WASHINGTON, D. C.

Hon. H. C. Lodge, Nahant, Mass.   July 22, 1891.

Dear Cabot: Here I am back again at work, and there is mighty little work to do. I am now at work on the annual report. I am going to put in a good deal of matter that I cannot relieve myself of in any other way.

I wrote to both Clapp and O'Meara, as you requested, and received exceedingly nice letters in return. I am very glad you gave me a hint in the matter.

Our polo team did very much better than I had any idea they would. Having a heavy handicap they beat Essex. making three goals which stood them six to the good, and in the finals with Morristown were only beaten by a quarter of a goal,—that is, by a knockout for safety. Next year, Heaven

* My daughter and my younger son.

willing I intend to be on the team myself, and do my own part.

Here I have been greeted warmly by Springy, still lame but no longer on crutches. Martha takes excellent care of me, as usual. Please tell Nannie this.

I need scarcely tell you what a great comfort it is to me that I am in your house, and not staying around at some dreary hotel in this hot weather. Naturally I am a little homesick for Oyster Bay, and as there seems to be very little to be done here I shall soon go back to it. I do not object in the least to staying here to work just as hard as can possibly be, but when there is nothing to be done, literally, then I hate to stay. However, I am getting off most of my report,—my annual report, and my Baltimore report is pretty nearly ready. In fact, all the work that can be done has been done. If the President would only act a little differently there is a whole raft of work which we could do, and which I should very much like to do. However, I cannot complain.

Best love to Nannie.
                  Yours very cordially,
                      THEODORE ROOSEVELT.

P. S. The President actually refuses to consider the changes in the rules which are necessary to enable us to do our work effectively. He has never given us one ounce of real backing. He won't see us, or consider any method for improving the service, even when it in no way touches a politician. It is horribly disheartening to work under such a Chief. However, the very fact that he takes so little interest gives me a free hand to do some things; and I know well that in life one must do the best one can with the implements at hand, and not bemoan the lack of ideal ones.

Foster* is doing his best in the Keystone Bank affair. Foster has also chosen two admirable men to investigate the seal fisheries. On the other hand, in truckling to the foreign vote he has chosen pretty poor sticks to investigate the all important problem of the immigrants who come here from Europe.

* Charles Foster of Ohio, Secretary of the Treasury.

SAGAMORE HILL,
OYSTER BAY, LONG ISLAND, N. Y.,
Aug. 13th, '91.

Dear Cabot,

As I telegraphed Nannie, Edith has a little daughter, and both are doing very well.

Bamie has come home; and sends her best love to you two. Edith particularly sent her love to you today.

I thought the *Sun's* article on you very good. It nearly gave the *Evening Post* a spasm. What is the trouble with Walker and Cogswell? They certainly, seen from a distance, look like a couple of first class idiots.

I don't like Erhardt's removal at all. Fassett is a good fellow, but a mere mouthpiece of Platt. It looks like trouble ahead for me in my official capacity. Erhardt has stood straight for the law.

Well, I do hope you win in Massachusetts this Fall. Did I tell you I had such pleasant letters from Clapp and O'Meara?

Yours ever, T. R.

SAGAMORE HILL
October 10th, '91.

Dear Cabot,

First about Constance.* I hope she got my telegram from Medora. I was simply dumbfounded; but I was delighted too, especially after I had made inquiries and had heard through Katy Griswold and others nothing but the warmest praise for Gardner. I really love Constance; and I firmly believe that no girl, and no man, can be so happy alone as if happily married; but I also feel what a dreadful thing an unhappy marriage is; and so I could not rest until I had begun to find out all I could of Constance's lover. As for him, I can quite honestly say that he has won the sweetest young girl I know; I do not know of another such still open to winning. Now I can really say I believe all will be well with them; and I know I need not say how heartily I wish them well, and how Edith and I sympathize with them. There is no other such happiness

* My daughter had just become engaged to Augustus Peabody Gardner.

on earth as there is for a true lover, and a sweet, fair girl beloved.

I am just back from my hunt. Tell Bay I shot nine elk. One of the heads is for you; not an unusual head at all, I am sorry to say; simply an ordinary "stag of twelve," what the old books call a "royal." Bob, whom I left out in the wilds, was having even better luck. When I left he had got on the trail of a bear; I think he will get it. I got into splendid trim physically by the end of my hunt.

Now, as to yourself. In the first place, your *Century* article,* from what I see and hear, has undoubtedly been a ten strike. I have again read and reread it, and I think it of very great and lasting value.

I also read carefully your speech in which you touched upon the civil service record of the Administration. It was *more* than good; and I was especially pleased at the points you brought out from my Baltimore Report. I should think that speech would have drawn blood. Lord, how I do hope you win in Massachusetts! If you take part in a joint debate do if possible *make* your opponent discuss the Democratic attitude on silver, take the aggressive with him, and, most emphatically we ought to win in New York too.

As usual, I come back to rumors of my own removal, immediately after the elections. The *Sun*, *World* and *Times* all contain accounts that Wanamaker has had "special agents" at work on the Baltimore P. O. and intends to "prove the falsity" of my report. Now that fool Wanamaker is quite capable of trying this, for his sloppy mind will not enable him to see that his case is weak; if he does try it I shall certainly lay him out as completely as I have already done twice; so he will gain nothing by it, but he may involve me against my will, in such a muss that the President will have to turn me out simply because he can't turn out Wanamaker. If only the President would take me into confidence in any way! Now, really, I can't help feeling that I might make one speech in Massachusetts and one here this Fall; I broached this at the White House before leaving for the West; but it was frowned

* "The Distribution of Ability in the United States."

on—at least that was the amount of it. If only they would back me up, and then let me act publicly, on the stump, as a Republican! But they won't do either, and seem to regard me with a curious mixture of suspicion and treacherous dislike.

There! I intended *not* to bore you with my complaints in the midst of your absorbing struggle—but I've been and done it, and feel better, too. At any rate I shall be with you next year, on the stump, if you wish me. I don't suppose I really shall be turned out; and we'll have two more winters in Washington together.

Do bring up the silver issue in your joint debates. If they attack you in any way hit back without mercy. Show them no quarter; if they attack your record on any point, not only show what your record really is but take their records and pick them to pieces.

Give my warmest love to Nannie and Constance.

Yours ever, T. R.

TELEGRAM*

NAHANT,
Dated NEW YORK   Oct. 25, 1891.
To Hon. Henry Cabot Lodge, Nahant, Mass.

Hearty congratulations. We are all more than proud of your canvass.

THEODORE ROOSEVELT.

UNITED STATES
CIVIL SERVICE COMMISSION,
WASHINGTON, D. C.

Hon. H. C. Lodge, Nahant, Mass.   October 29, 1891.

Dear Cabot: I have this letter typewritten, so that you shall read it as easily and as quickly as possible. Of course don't answer it.

I have read your speeches in the Boston *Journal's* report of the joint debate, and I may say with perfect frankness and sincerity that I read them with a glow of pride in you. I think

---

* Refers to my joint debate with John E. Russell.

that your peroration, the last five minutes of your second speech, is as fine as anything I know in oratory. Governor Thompson told me that he himself was thrilled when he read it. After I had read your speeches, and then reread them, I gave them to the Governor, and when he was through sent them around to Wharton, so you see your particular friends here know what you are doing. Tom Reed spent a night with us at New York, and was delightful. He spoke with very great admiration of the splendid canvass you are making.

By the way, I was much amused the other day to see in the *Evening Post*, in a review of Andrew Lang's new collection of Lyrics, the statement that it compared very unfavorably with Mr. H. C. Lodge's similar collection! I am very anxious to see you and talk over many things, literary and otherwise. I enclose you three funny cuts of yourself that may amuse you, and an article in the New York *World* apropos of my having written a letter concerning the New York canvass. I am rather pleased with the latter editorial; it prevents there being any doubt as to my position. The *Times* had a similar one, but of course very courteous in tone.

Best love to Nannie, and thank her very warmly for having written me.

Yours always,

THEODORE ROOSEVELT.

(Editorial Referred to in the Preceding Letter.)

MR. ROOSEVELT'S MISSION *

Civil Service Commissioner Roosevelt has disclosed what he is here for.

It is not to secure respect for the law which he is sworn to execute, nor to prevent the blackmailing of public servants by their official superiors. It is not even to repeat threadbare homilies on civil-service reform.

Mr. Roosevelt is here to help promote the election of Boss Platt's Mr. Fassett—the associate of Quay and Dudley in the

* From the New York *World*. Interesting when we compare it with the subsequent career of the man whom the *World* thus assailed.

Republican National campaign of boodle and bribery in 1888, and the eulogist of these pilloried rascals when a prudent regard for public opinion finally drove them from the Committee last winter.

Mr. Roosevelt has written a letter in Fassett's behalf stuffed full of lies and misrepresentations.

And this while every Federal employee in this city has received a circular demanding that tribute be paid for party purposes to a political committee of which Postmaster Van Cott and Collector Hendricks are members.

Mr. Roosevelt has not a word to say of this open and defiant violation of the law. He is here to aid the men who are trampling it under foot.

The Democratic House should refuse to vote one dollar to pay the expenses of the Civil Service Commission while this ranting young humbug is a member of it. He has made the very name of reform redolent of hypocrisy.

1892

UNITED STATES
CIVIL SERVICE COMMISSION,
WASHINGTON, D. C.

Dear Cabot,   May 13th, '92.

Good; your letter to E. is admirable. On reaching the office I found several newspaper men to whom I refused to say a word; and several of Wanamaker's papers (the Baltimore *American,* for instance) containing accounts of his testimony. I am keeping cool; but, I confess, with difficulty. Elkins has just telephoned me that he wishes to see me at four this p. m. I shall drop in later to see you; on your return from your ride. Do ask Hopkins* to drop in to see me. Ask him if he can't get in tomorrow, between 11 and 12 if possible; but let him telephone me now, and appoint his own hour.

Yours, T. R.

* Albert J. Hopkins, Member of the House; afterward Senator from Illinois.

SAGAMORE HILL,
July 15th, '92.

Dear Old Cabot,

You have been a trump all through the business, as you always are; no man not on the Committee could do anything.

My team came off better at polo than I had hoped; the second Meadowbrooks beat us, but only 2¼ goals. I made two goals myself. Douglas's team whipped the crack Westchester team finely, and then went to pieces in a game with Morristown and lost by half a goal. I tell you, a corpulent middle-aged literary man finds a stiff polo match rather good exercise!

Edith is probably going back to Washington with me on Monday, for a few days. I do wish you were to be there; but you can do far more at home. As for your feeling depressed, why that is all nonsense. Stay in politics; get to the Senate if you can (and I think you will); if not, take two or three more terms in the House; an honorable career, not too short, in Congress is something of which to be always proud. Moreover, it gives you a right, and a power, to draw historical lessons which is no mean part of your historical equipment. From every point of view your political career is useful; and it has been already of great service to you.

Best love to Nannie and The Bride.

Yours,   T. R.

UNITED STATES
CIVIL SERVICE COMMISSION,
WASHINGTON, D. C.

July 27th, '92.

Dear Cabot,

I had seen Adams' ridiculous article. I enclose the data you request; also the 7th Report which deals with the removals in the classified service. We have no means of knowing what they are in the unclassified—where however the amount is that both sides have removed about everybody.

Frankly I think the record pretty bad for both Cleveland and Harrison, and it is rather Walrus and Carpenter work choosing between the records of the two parties, as far as civil service reform is concerned. In the classified service Cleveland made more extensions than Harrison; but on the other hand Tracy has made an admirable start in the Navy Yards—but it is only a start, not permanent, and can not be until put under us. Cleveland had a much worse Commission; but Harrison has not sustained his Commission at all, and has allowed Wanamaker to put a premium upon the clearest violations of the law—in which the Republican members of the C. S. Committee have sustained him. So I really think it about a stand off here. We have put much more of a stop to political assessments; but the offices have been used for political purposes more shamefully and openly than even under the last Administration. In the first term of the 51st Congress we did better, and in the second worse, than in any term of the 49th or 50th.

Altogether I am by no means pleased with what our party, at both the White House and the Capitol, has done about Civil Service Reform. You are the one conspicuous Republican leader who has done his whole duty—and very much more than his whole duty—by the reform in the last three years.

I leave Washington tomorrow and start west from Oyster Bay on August 1st or 2nd. I have just written an article on the foreign policy of this Administration, where it is much sounder than on Civil Service Reform.

Edith and I have really had a pleasant time here in spite of the heat. I play tennis with Wharton at the Legation, on most afternoons; hitherto we have come out exactly even on sets, so it is good fun.

Best love to Nannie.

Yours ever, T. R.

SAGAMORE HILL,
OYSTER BAY, LONG ISLAND, N. Y.,
Sept. 25th, '92.

Dear Cabot,

Even in the West I saw by the occasional notices in the papers that you were getting the Republican machine into fine condition in Massachusetts, and that everyone recognized the fact that *your* hand was on the throttle. I can not help believing that you will win the Senatorship this time; if for any cause you fail, why it merely puts you in better shape for the struggle two years hence. Of course you are looking with double care after your congressional fences.

Although I had read your Homeric article* in ms., I have actually reread it twice since it appeared in print. I think it one of the very best essays, both in style and matter, I have ever read, by anyone on any subject.

Here, on my return after a month's tedious but important tour among the Indian reservations and schools, I find all very well; Edith and I have been taking long rides on the polo ponies. Bamie is absorbed in her World's Fair work; Elliot F. Shepard has just made a most scurrilous and indecent attack, in his paper, on her and her associates, by name. She, and my uncles, are very desirous I should not respond, for fear he will go on attacking her; and I am in a perfect quandary over the matter. He ought, by rights, to be horse-whipped.

The Farmers' Alliance is giving our people serious concern in Kansas, Nebraska and South Dakota; and ditto, the Germans in Illinois and Wisconsin. I feel like making a crusade against the latter. I wish the cholera would result in a permanent quarantine against most immigrants!

I passed a very pleasant three weeks on my ranch, and on the trip south to Deadwood, shooting three or four deer and antelope—one deer from the ranch verandah! In Deadwood I was enthusiastically received, and opened the Republican campaign by speaking to a really large audience in the fearful local opera house. Did you see my article on our Foreign Policy in the *Independent*? I enclose a very nice letter from Admiral Brown, thanking me for it. Please return this.

I have now got to plunge into the very disagreeable business of fighting political assessments.

Give my best love to Nannie. How is Constance?

Yours always,   T. R.

* "As to certain accepted Heroes."

UNITED STATES
CIVIL SERVICE COMMISSION,
WASHINGTON, D. C.

Dear Cabot,   Sept. 30th, '92.

The enclosed from the *Sun* amused Edith and me greatly; I send it to you for fear you may not get it. I suppose Everett will be an easy victim; but don't take any chances! The mugwumps seriously talk of carrying Massachusetts for Cleveland and Russell; it is not possible, is it? I don't know what to say of the chances in New York; the Democratic tariff plank has helped us much, but no one can prophesy *how* much; and Hill and Tammany seem to be fairly in harness for Cleveland.

Is Billy Wharton going to run against John Andrew? Let me know; and drop me a line as to your own chances—for which I care a hundred times more than for Harrison.

Yours, T. R.

WASHINGTON,
Dear Cabot,   Oct. 11th, '92.

Nor shall I ever write again for *The Cosmopolitan*. The hitch comes in with Walker, who has deprived Howells of control. I don't know when my Repplier article will come out—I shall take it away from them if they do not publish it soon. My Parkman article, two months after Howells, having asked for it, had accepted it with thanks, was returned by Walker, on the ground that the subject was not one in which his readers took any interest.

I do wish I could be with you! Although I am being worked up to the hilt here, I often feel as though I can hardly keep away from you in such a canvass as this. At any rate I shall speak to the point at the meeting on November 5th. But do you know, I feel sure you are going to win—I wouldn't say this if I thought you were overconfident.

As for the general prospects, I don't know what to say. We have an excellent fighting chance; but I think the odds are a little against us. Hill and Tammany seem to be pulling straight for Cleveland in New York; and it would be comic, were it not outrageous, to see how anxious the mugwumps are to let them have everything, if they'll only help Cleveland. The mugwump attitude towards an anti-Tammany city ticket is an excellent comment on the sincerity of their attacks on Republican "partisanship" in local affairs.

In Wisconsin and Illinois we are suffering for our good deeds; the movement among the Lutheran and Catholic Germans against us is most formidable; and it means a landslide, unless the latent Americanism in native Democrats is awakened—and though this may be, I hardly dare hope for it.

In Kansas, Nebraska and South Dakota the Alliance will give us a terribly narrow struggle. Still, in all these States, the old party feeling is strong, even among the German Lutherans and the wild Farmers' Alliance cranks; and I guess we'll carry them at the last, but by uncomfortably close majorities or pluralities. Halford is very hopeful as to the general result, and is sure that the drift is all our way.

Last night I dined at the Secretary's of State to meet Egan. Tracy, Rusk and Miller—also Wanamaker, who was rendered very uncomfortable by my presence.

By the Lord, I shall make a straightout party speech on the 5th! I'll cut for blood.

Best love to Nannie.   Yours, T. R.

SAGAMORE HILL,
OYSTER BAY, LONG ISLAND, N. Y.,
Oct. 16th, '92.

Dear Cabot,

I thought your civil service speech *excellent;* unanswerable; the showing was really better than I thought. I have sent it to the Governor. I have just come back from an absurd, though useful, "Indian" conference at Lake Mohonk; I will tell you about one or two of the incidents when we meet. By the way, I hope some of your Boston papers noticed the smashing we gave one section of the "Independent" manifesto; after I had roundly denounced it as an "outrageous slander" I found that one of the signers, Stimson, was sitting within ten feet of me.

Without yet being very hopeful, I think our chances have improved. The general sympathy for Harrison, because of his wife's illness, is helping him. But the general apathy is very great.

Shall I see you at the meeting on the 5th? *Very* warm love to Nannie from Edith and myself.

Yours, T. R.

OYSTER BAY,
Oct. 18th, '92.

Dear Cabot,

Have just received your note about the Indian paragraph of the Independent address.

Did not the *Journal* contain what I (and Morgan too) said about it at Mohonk? Green, the Worcester Postmaster, who was present, telegraphed it at once. If it has not appeared, will you have your secretary tell the *Journal* to have their correspondent call on me in Washington (where I go tomorrow). I will give them an interview straight from the shoulder; and I would like also to give them a statement about political assessments. I wish to say that I know these went on more extensively under the Democrats in 1888, and that the difference is that *we* have put them down; and it is our *action*, contrasted with the Democratic *inaction*, that makes the difference. To use a coarse illustration, the boil was worse under the Cleveland people; with us it is not so bad, *and we have lanced it;* whereat the idiots yell as if it was the lancing, not the boil—the cure, not the disease—which reflected discredit on the people who did it! Moreover, even Wanamaker has acted promptly, and very· creditably, on our letter calling attention to the attempt to use the postmasters for political purposes. All of which I will be delighted to say; tell the *Journal* to telegraph on for the interview at once.

Yours, T. R.

P. S. You certainly did use them up in the Wolsey matter. I never had so much as heard of Theodore *S.* Wolsey, the present man.

SAGAMORE HILL,
OYSTER BAY, LONG ISLAND, N. Y.,
Nov. 10th, '92.

Dear Cabot,

Well, as to the general result I am disappointed but not surprised, save as to the size of the majority in New York. I had given Leupp my figures, which were 70,000 against us in N. Y. City and 18,000 in Brooklyn. I knew the West was very shaky; and I never could see what were the facts which made our people confident there and in N. Y.

The ray of bright light is your success in Massachusetts. I can't get full returns here. Apparently Russell wins by a small majority, worse luck; but this can not affect your success with the general ticket, and leaving them but three Congressmen. Thank heaven for Williams' defeat. How large was your majority over Everett? I believe that this gives you the Senatorship practically without further struggle; and I am glad, as it has turned out, that you did run, and once more carry your district, and whip a mugwump hero. If you had not done it, it would always have been said that you did not dare try. Your foot is on their necks. But how it galls to see the self-complacent triumph of our foes! I only hope Hill does not prove the residuary legatee of this success. I shall go to Washington Monday. When do you come?

Best love to Nannie.

Yours, T. R.

P. S. Trumbull, of Chili, has written me about my article. I shall speedily answer him. I can't get the least help from Wharton in the matter.

UNITED STATES
CIVIL SERVICE COMMISSION,
WASHINGTON, D. C.

November 16, 1892.

Hon. H. C. Lodge, 31 Beacon Street, Boston, Mass.

Dear Cabot: Your predictions about the result in Massachusetts, made in your various letters to me, were fulfilled with curious exactness. You said that Harrison would get between twenty and thirty thousand majority, and that your own majority would be between two and three thousand, and that you would elect all but three, or possibly four, Congressmen; while all you said about the governorship was that you thought it would be very close, with a good chance of defeating Russell. As for our national committee, I could not help thinking that they were simply determined not to look the danger in the face. In Illinois, Kansas, and South Dakota the straws were so numerous that I could not help seeing them myself as I went about among the people and politicians in those States; and I thought that they were all wrong in basing hopes upon the N. Y. registration, because they entirely failed to take account of the change of population. Of course the registration is lighter below Fourteenth Street because each year a greater percentage of the tenement house population moves north. But as you say, I think this means trouble of an acute kind to the business interests of the country, and especially to the West, during the next four years. I rather hope that the Democrats get complete control of the Senate. I want to see them have full responsibility for their actions. Let them meddle with the tariff just as much as they wish, and let them get into the wrangle over the finances which is bound to come. I must say I contemplate the possibility of Hill's election with great horror. He is a most dangerous man, and now he is only the more dangerous because it is being knocked into his wicked head that he cannot succeed in running national politics with the same transparently open vileness that he has displayed in running New York politics. I had, of course, at once thought of Reed myself, and shall write to him at once as you suggest. Thank heavens he was perfectly loyal in this campaign and fought hard in it. I saw Blaine the other day, and he is a broken and used up man. I cannot see, judging from all the facts in my possession, how you can possibly be beaten for the senatorship. I regard it as yours, but I am very glad you do not intend to relax an effort, and that you yourself will see personally every man during the next fortnight. Barrett is so tricky a specimen that I wish to see you with a clear majority, not merely of the caucus, but of the whole legislature. I do not see why Crapo continues to hang on in the contest. It is a great comfort to me at any rate to see the smash that has come upon the mugwumps, or, more properly, the new mugwump-Democratic leaders, especially Williams, in Massachusetts. You certainly have done them up. Russell is the only one left. I suppose Quincy has had senatorial aspirations, but it is evident that he will have to wait many a long year yet before he can so much as think about them. In New York of course the silly better element is fatuous in its shortsighted delight and is utterly unmoved by the possibility of having Sheehan or Croker put in the Senate. I read an article in the New York *Nation* the other day so foolish, so malignant, so deliberately mendacious, and so exultant that it fairly made me writhe to think of the incalculable harm to decency that scoundrelly paper, edited by its scoundrelly chief, Godkin, has done. Early next week I shall go back to New York and get Edith, returning on December 1st; so I fear I shall not see Nannie until you come.

Yours, T. R.

1893

WASHINGTON,
Jan. 4th, '93.

Dear old Cabot,

Edith and I are too pleased for anything,* and eagerly awaiting your arrival to find out all the details. As soon as your telegram arrived I tore round to Nannie, for mutual congratulations. Of course I was very sure of the result; but the prize was so great that I felt nervous!

Well, I am glad of your triumph, first, for your own sake, next, for the sake of honest government, and because of the premium thus put upon integrity, ability, industry, and a high standard of public morality, and last, because of the way the worst elements, at the two extremes of the political scale, will gnash their teeth over the result. I shall buy the *Evening Post* for the next day or two.

Hail, friend! Love from Edith; best regards to your mother.

Yours, T. R.

* This refers to my election to the Senate.

WASHINGTON,
June 8th, '93.

Dear Cabot,

Very many thanks for the check; your only return for this act of gratuitous virtue will be the receipt of a splendid copy of the great "Book of the Boone and Crockett,"* wherein your name goes down to posterity as that of a mighty man with horse or rifle. Seriously, you were very good to send the check.

I did feel pretty melancholy when you left. But I have had an immense amount of work to do at the office; and in the evenings I have dined out with some of the people still in town. The real loneliness here will only begin a little later. I go back to O. B. day after tomorrow (from whence I shall write Nannie); but I have to spend four hot and dirty days in the cars immediately after, going to and from Chicago; and three more a week later, going to and from Groton. I hope I can make the time to take a day with you on this last trip.

Do you know I was really greatly pleased with your Washington† article in the *St. Nicholas;* I read it through with genuine interest and pleasure.

Yours, T. R.

SAGAMORE HILL,
Aug. 28th, '93.

Dear Cabot,

I will write Clement‡ at once; though I fear he may shy off at this second call upon him. It is worth the trial anyhow, however.

On p. 213 and following of Vol. II of Sheridan you will see what he says as to Seward's refusal to allow him to take measures which would overawe the French or materially hasten their departure from Mexico.

What a superb speech Reed's was! I do not suppose that the Republicans here would allow me to go; if they only would I should certainly be a Reed delegate at the next national convention.

* Club founded by Roosevelt.   † "City of Washington."
‡ E. H. Clement, editor of the Boston *Transcript.*

"What comforteth it a man if he have with him the better" (the meaning of this word in original uncertain—some translators make it 'fool') "sentiment of the country and loseth his own deestrick?"

(Proverbs CCCXXXIII, 91.)

Yours, sadly, T. R.

689 MADISON AVENUE

Thursday,
[November 15th,] 1893.

Dear old Cabot,

Late yesterday afternoon I saw about Lucius'* death, in the *Transcript;* I at once called on your mother, but she was out (she wrote me such a dear letter afterwards; do thank her most warmly for me) and I had no time to come again, while it was too late for me to break the different engagements which had been made especially for me; otherwise I should of course have stayed over. I need not say how distressed Edith and I are; she sends you her warm love, and so does Bamie; it is such a real tragedy; and we know what a fine, loyal fellow he was, and how much he was to you. Do you think you will stop here on your way back? Give my love to Nannie. If you think it right, will you send a few flowers from me to Mrs. Sargent? I enclose my card.

Good-bye, old fellow.

Yours always, T. R.

1894

SAGAMORE HILL,
OYSTER BAY, LONG ISLAND, N. Y.,
Sept. 2d, '94.

Dear Cabot,

I directed the *Star* containing my interview to be sent to you; it was given to the United Press too. I saw an extract of it which rather angered me because it made me couple Senator Cockerell with you; I had merely brought him in by

* Lucius Sargent, one of my most intimate and beloved friends, greatly liked by Roosevelt. His death came from a fall in the hunting field.

saying that he too should receive credit, being chairman of the sub-committee to which the amendment was referred. I started the interview with a flourish for you!

The Lancaster P. O. case flatted out, as I was sure it would after I had found that Brosius was weakening; and moreover the other side was about as bad as the postmaster.

I finished all the odds and ends of work at Washington, and on Thursday start for the west; I shall return about the first of October.

The drift is all our way! The Democratic congressional committee is still hopelessly at odds as to whether they must make the campaign for or against the Gorman bill. But I wish I felt a little surer of our carrying the next house. I *think* we shall get it by a narrow margin; but I am far from sure. We shall gain but three or four seats in the south, while in the Rocky Mountain States, the Dakotas, etc., the revolt against the Democrats, while it will utterly destroy *them*, may result merely in the election of populists. This would leave us only the northeast and middle west, and we will have to carry these overwhelmingly to win without assistance elsewhere.

I read the close of an article by Edward Atkinson in *The Forum*, assailing our regular army as useless; and this less than two months after the Chicago strike. I *must* go for that prattling creature soon; I mean just to dress him down incidentally in the course of an article.

I send you back the Kidd;* I wrote a very voluminous review of him when I once got started. Springy was very nice in Washington during the last fortnight I was there.

Edith sends you her love; give mine to Nannie and the boys—also Constance if she is at hand. The children seem all right; Kermit seems to be rather on the mend.

Yours always, T. R.

* Benjamin Kidd's "Social Evolution," which was at that time attracting a great deal of well-deserved attention.

SAGAMORE HILL,
OYSTER BAY, LONG ISLAND, N. Y.,
Sept. 30th, '94.

Dear Cabot,

I spent only two weeks at the ranch. The cattle are not doing particularly well; the drought has been very severe on everything. However, except for feeling a little blue, I passed a delightful fortnight, all the time in the open; and feel as rugged as a bull moose. Tell Bay I shot five antelope—only one a doe—and a fine white tail buck, too.

Is it true that Barrett* was nominated? Bourke Cockran told me so. I hope not. I came on from Chicago with Clarence King.

I believe we will whip Hill readily; but he was the strongest man they could nominate. It will be a great misfortune if he wins; but I don't think he can. I hear all around that the working men intend to vote "for the policy of a full dinner pail," as one of them in the village told my friend and coachman, Hall. It looks as if Quigg† might be run for Mayor; he will have some great elements of strength, but I don't know whether we can get him taken seriously enough.

West of the Mississippi the populists will give us trouble; but I think you are right about our carrying the next house; what I have seen in the west and east and heard from the south makes me feel so.

Edith sends you both her best love; tell Nannie I have something delicious to tell her when we meet.

Yours always,
THEODORE ROOSEVELT.

SAGAMORE HILL,
OYSTER BAY, LONG ISLAND, N. Y.,
Oct. 2nd, '94.

Dear Cabot,

Your letter has just followed me from Medora (my health improved so rapidly that I returned, in my normal anaemic state, sooner than my medical advisers dared hope). It contained exactly the kinds of news I wished to hear. I have

* William E. Barrett of Massachusetts.
† Lemuel E. Quigg—then a member of Congress from New York.

written Hayes. I sincerely hope Barrett will continue to behave well; we can only wait and see. Everett's end was as childishly undignified as his whole career in Congress; what a poor, timid, learned buffoon it is!

I liked your speech. When I get at Atkinson I am going to treat him, as well as I can, with a mixture of contempt and ferocity—"solemn prattler" is one expression I have already picked out. He is a fine archtype for our Calico School men; with his gospel of mean and foolish baseness.

All the drift I see is for Morton* against Hill; it seems to me that we are going to win hands down; but I am always uneasy about Hill's hold over the lowest elements; the liquor vote, and all its dependent votes, he will get solid.

To my distress, Mr. Wolcott writes Edith that Storer† was defeated for the renomination. I suppose it was the A. P. A.

What a good thing Breckinridge's defeat was!

It is delightful to see Bamie‡; and just as strongly American and Republican as ever.

Ever yours, T. R.

OYSTER BAY, L. I.,
Oct. 8th, '94.

Dear Cabot,

I enclose Hayes' letter, as you may like to see it. Personally I think no good can be done with such a movement as the A. P. A. About Nov. 8th I have to perform one of my usual dreary feats by speaking one evening at Groton and one at Harvard, the latter on Civil Service Reform; it will be a flying visit, and my speeches being in the evening I can't get down to Nahant; but can't you get up to Boston for lunch one day? and I'd like to see Hayes.

I go to Washington tomorrow, and Edith and Bamie take the children to Vermont for a fortnight.

---

* Levi P. Morton—Vice-President under Harrison; afterward Governor of New York.

† Bellamy Storer, then a Congressman from Cincinnati.

‡ She had been in London with her cousin, James Roosevelt, Secretary of the American Embassy.

In politics, it does seem to me that we shall beat Hill this time; all the signs are that way; and my only uneasiness is that Hill's strength has always laid in those bottom strata about which we really know so very little. Austin Wadsworth I find has somewhat the same uneasiness; I met him the other day. Morton is a perfectly good candidate, but has no personal strength whatever before the people; he will merely get the party vote, plus the "reform" element which is against Hill, and that all-important class of unknown size—the determining element in the problem—the man with the dinner pail who wants to down the Democratic party. We have a fair chance of carrying our Mayor, unless the Democrats unite on a strong man. When we meet I'll tell you my own experience in the mayoralty matter; I simply had not the funds to run.

Yours, T. R.

UNITED STATES
CIVIL SERVICE COMMISSION,
WASHINGTON, D. C.

October 11, 1894.

Hon. H. C. Lodge, Nahant, Mass.

Dear Cabot: It is awfully good of you to send me the clippings containing the account of the convention. I think the platform admirable. I wish we had as good a one here in New York. We may possibly be hurt a little by the fact that our men were timid about taking any action one way or the other that would seem to recognize the trouble caused by the A. P. A. Your two planks, the school plank and the one following, are simply admirable. The result will be that the A. P. A.'s won't cut any figure at all. You were indeed received as usual, and as I have always seen you received at every meeting I have been to in Massachusetts. The Barrett business can't hurt you personally one ounce. I like your speech greatly, and I like Senator Hoar's greatly.

I have seen Storer since coming back here. He takes his defeat very well. Of course he minds it much. He is just as sweet and good as ever.

In New York I have great hopes, not only for the governor-ship, but that we shall put a Republican in as mayor. I don't however, regard it as the certainty that some people do. Morton does not arouse any enthusiasm, and it is curious to see how bitter the anti-Platt feeling is. It is not so much anything that Platt does, but the fact that he is unwise enough to say things attacking reformers, and making a show of bossism, which sets many people against him. The professional re-formers in the city are loudest against him, but they are not really the ones that hurt. It is the farmers in the country and the men in the small cities, who have a vague idea that they want to be against him because he is a boss, and who have a queer distrust of the machine, so often irrational, which is, I am inclined to think, a real marked attribute of the Republican party. Hill will have much more money than Morton, while Morton will have the name of having more money than Hill, and this is against us. Moreover Platt is no organizer of vic-tory at the polls, while Hill's machine work will be done to perfection, and he has a real pull on the worst elements in our party. Nevertheless, there is a very decided bolt against him among the best people of his own party, and what is infinitely more important, the drift is unmistakably our way. He has to swim against a tidal wave, not with it, this time. I think we shall down him, but I am not so dead sure as I would like to be.

Strong, our candidate for mayor, is a good man, and Tam-many is weak. On the other hand Tammany has also nomi-nated a good man, and a great many Democrats will support him against a man who, like Strong, is a good fellow, but one of whom they know nothing in connection with public life.

If I get on to Boston on the 9th to speak at Harvard I do hope you can get into town and I can see you.

Always yours,

THEODORE ROOSEVELT.

UNITED STATES
CIVIL SERVICE COMMISSION,
WASHINGTON, D. C.

Hon. H. C. Lodge, Nahant, Mass.   October 16, 1894.

Dear Cabot: I don't like to be over sanguine, and I have been trying hard to keep in mind what an able organizer Hill is, what a personal hold he has in the lower ranks, and what a resolute fight he is making, but I can't help getting more and more sanguine as the days go by. The stars in their courses fight for us. I regard Tammany's nomination for mayor as weak. I believe that we will elect Morton, and I am actually inclined to think we will elect Strong too, as mayor. I should not be a bit surprised if we gave a tremendous majority. I have just seen McKee of the Congressional Committee. He has hopes of carrying the next House by a narrow margin, but he feels disturbed over the far western States. Of course we wish to have a majority of the States in the next House. McKee thinks we can get it if we can get some kind of help financially from the East for these Western States where they are down in absolute penury. One of our men who has just come back from a tour there tells me he doesn't think anything can save the Republicans. He believes Waite will capture Colorado and the Populists overwhelm everything out there. I am inclined to think the latter view is probably true. Still McKee is hopeful, but he does need money. Do you think any of your Boston people, as this is a year you will have very little expense for your own state, will be able to help those Westerners out?

I come on to Groton on November 8th—Thursday. On Friday the 9th I shall be in Boston. Can't we arrange to meet then?

Give my best love to Nannie.

Yours always,

THEODORE ROOSEVELT.

UNITED STATES
CIVIL SERVICE COMMISSION,
WASHINGTON, D. C.

Hon. H. C. Lodge, Nahant, Mass.   October 27, 1894.

Dear Cabot: I thought Sewall's [speech] more than good. It fired my blood to read it. I am not very keen about the tariff business myself, having, as you know, a tinge of economic agnosticism in me, but our foreign policy is, to me, of an importance which is difficult to overestimate. There is one comfort about my not being in the mayoralty race this year. I could not talk against the Democracy on the subject on which I feel deepest, our foreign relations, while I was running for mayor. I am surprised all the time to receive new proofs that every man even every Southerner who lives outside the country, has gotten to have a perfect hatred and contempt for Cleveland's administration because of its base betrayal of our interests abroad. I do wish our Republicans would go in avowedly to annex Hawaii and build an oceanic canal with the money of Uncle Sam.

Harry Davis* is just leaving. He was with me again the other day, and I read him a couple of pages of an article I am trying to compose for *The Forum*, these pages having reference to Edward Atkinson. I have a large vocabulary I should like to use on that person, and I have only used about half. Harry, who is of a ferocious temperament, much approved of my expressions. I shall show them to you to see if you think them too strong. One of the mildest of them is a pet sentence in which I state that he combines the imagination of a green grocer with the heart of a Bengalee baboo.

Always yours,

THEODORE ROOSEVELT.

P. S.—I am writing a note to the editor of the *Atlantic* about a piece by Henry Childs Merwin in defence of Tammany, in which he says the Civil Service Law in the departments at Washington was under Harrison and is now under Cleveland

---

* My brother-in-law Rear-Admiral Charles Henry Davis, second of the name in the Navy.

"a mere mockery," quoting Carlisle and you as authorities. If not too much trouble send me what you really said, as I am going to rap him.

689 Madison Avenue,
December 1st, 1894.

Dear Cabot,

It seems to me that this brutal stupidity and cowardice of Gresham in the matter of the surrender of the two Japanese calls for the most decided and prompt action. I think there is a great chance for you at once, on Monday, to demand all the papers for the Senate. If possible I wish he could be impeached. It has indicated our course in Chili with dramatic completeness. I shall arrive Monday evening.

Yours, T. R.

1895

UNITED STATES
CIVIL SERVICE COMMISSION,
WASHINGTON, D. C.

February 19, 1895.*

Hon. H. C. Lodge, Senate Chamber, Washington, D. C.

Dear Cabot: In reference to what Senator Hale was saying about our fish-culturist examination I enclose you herewith a copy of the fish-culturist questions which form the chief subject in the examination, which the Arkansas man passed and in which the Maine man failed. You did not tell me the name of the Maine man but the only one from Maine who failed at that time was Daniel H. B. Hooper. Will you find out from Hale if this is the man he means? If not get him to give you the name and I will look it up. The same questions were asked of both Robinson and Hooper and we simply used the questions the Fish Commission asked us to. The Commissioner of Fish and Fisheries has been very well satisfied with the results of the examination as he says he is now able to be sure that he does

---

* I print this and a few other similar letters to show the extreme thoroughness with which Roosevelt defended and fought for Civil Service reform and the classified service.

not have shoved on him some man whom he may find out to
be incompetent. It was at his earnest request that we had the
examination at all. Please show the list of questions to Hale
because it really does seem to me that they are questions of a
kind that ought to be easily answered by an applicant for such
a position. I am not an expert in such matters but the questions
do look fairly practical.   Faithfully yours,
                                        THEODORE ROOSEVELT.

                        UNITED STATES
                CIVIL SERVICE COMMISSION,
                    WASHINGTON, D. C.
                                        February 28, 1895.
Senator H. C. Lodge, Senate Chamber, Washington, D. C.

   Dear Cabot: Do remember to make the fight for Doyle's*
appropriation and publish that list. Point out the fact that
Breckinridge made the point of order against Doyle, and did
not dare to make it against Thurber, the President's Secretary,
against Hamlin and Curtis and Assistant Postmaster General
Jones, and all the others; and find out if Gorman and his
crowd will vote in the face of those figures to knock out Doyle.
I see Gorman prophesies a great deficit, but it is an infamy to
cut down battleships when they actually pass that cursed
sugar bounty.   Yours,
                                THEODORE ROOSEVELT.

                        UNITED STATES
                CIVIL SERVICE COMMISSION,
                    WASHINGTON, D. C.
                                        April 3, 1895.
Hon. Henry Cabot Lodge, Hotel Brunswick, New York, N. Y.

   Dear Cabot: I received a strong appeal from Douglas to take
the Police Commissionership if offered me. I do not know that
there is much need of discussing the matter now, for I suppose
the Mayor has settled on somebody else. A week ago he would
have offered it to me if I had been willing to take it. Still, I
wish you would see Douglas and talk the matter over with

---

* John T. Doyle, Secretary of Civil Service Commission.

him and talk the matter over with Strong too. The average New Yorker of course wishes me to take it very much. I don't feel much like it myself, but of course I realize that it is a different kind of position from that of Street Cleaning Commissioner, and one I could perhaps afford to be identified with.

Murray* writes me that there is nothing in the talk of my being Chairman of the Commission. You know as well as I do, and indeed I think you feel as much as I do, the arguments for and against my being Police Commissioner. You are on the ground, and do talk it over with Douglas and the Mayor; it is an important thing for me and if I ought to take it I must do so soon. It is very puzzling!

Faithfully yours,

THEODORE ROOSEVELT.

689 Madison Avenue,
Sunday midnight,
[May 12th, 1895.]

Dear Cabot,

Edith and I must send a line just to wish you many happy returns of the day, and to give our best love to Nannie; you can not imagine how dreadfully homesick we feel for you both; and how I wish I could see you to talk over my difficulties! They are parochial, but pressing. I am in a very wearing and harassing work; it is terribly hard to know what is best and wisest to do. I enclose a nice note from Quigg (send it back). At the Union League and Republican clubs my course seems to be heartily approved. As you supposed, Parkhurst is strongly Republican on national issues.

I had a very nice call on your mother. I told her I was so glad you were going abroad, for the recreation; whereupon she answered, "Yes, my dear, and for his education; he is *very* young, and was a mere boy when he was last abroad." So I shall often think of you two tender young grandparents toddling round Europe to improve your juvenile minds. We just love her.

Yours, T. R.

* Joe Murray, an active Republican politician and devoted follower and friend of Roosevelt in his district.

POLICE DEPARTMENT
PRESIDENT'S OFFICE
CITY OF NEW YORK.
May 18, 1895.

Hon. Henry Cabot Lodge, 1765 Massachusetts Ave., Washington, D. C.

Dear Cabot: I should have written you earlier, but I have had more work on my hands than you can imagine; on an average I have not left this office until after six, and once I left it after eight. I hope in a fortnight when I have grown warm in the collar I shall be able to get through my work quicker.

It is absorbingly interesting; but you need not have the slightest fear about my losing my interest in National Politics. If the Re-organization Bill had only gone through, I would have had this force completely remodeled in six months; and after that time, though I should have been interested in it, and would have been very glad to have the work in default of any other, yet its great interest for me would have gone. As it is now, I shall have a lively and far from pleasant interest in the work all summer, for the difficulties in getting a good force are immeasurably increased and the result will necessarily be far more imperfect and the process much slower.

We shall have to try to get this legislation next year, which again will keep me interested through the winter. If we don't get it next year the chances are, we shall not get it at all, and in any event by the time we do get it, if it is two years hence, most of the work will be done in some shape or other; if we do get it, three months at that time will enable us to finish the whole affair. So that in a couple of years or less I shall have finished the work here for which I am specially fitted, and in which I take a special interest. After that there will remain only the ordinary problems of decent administration in the Department, which will be already in good running order. I shall then be quite ready to take up a new job, if I think I can do it better, or can accomplish more in it. While, if nothing offers itself, I shall continue to do my work here; by that time all the big problems here will be disposed of one way or the other, and I can put my hand on other things.

For the next six months I am going to be absorbed in the work here and under a terrific strain; I have got to move against the scandals in this Department, if my work is to be at all thorough; but my hands have been tied in a large measure, thanks to the action of the legislature.

I shall not neglect the political side, you may be sure. With Quigg, Brookfield and some of the others, I shall keep in close touch. I shall do my best to keep out of faction fighting, but it will be difficult, for its perfectly astounding to see how Platt succeeds in identifying himself with the worst men and the worst forces in every struggle, so that a decent man *must* oppose him.

I wrote to Ainsworth* in a very hearty and friendly way. I won't be able to do as much on the political side as I should wish, because I am so completely absorbed by the work and struggle here, but I shall do what I can, you may rest assured.

Edith is distinctly better; the children are well.

Give my best love to Nannie. You cannot imagine how I miss her and you; and Edith is as homesick for you both as I am. Really, I have hardly seen her and the children, I have been so busy.

Ever yours,

THEODORE ROOSEVELT.

P. S. I think I shall move against [Inspector] Byrnes at once. I thoroughly distrust him, and cannot do any thorough work while he remains. It will be a very hard fight, and I have no idea how it will come out.

POLICE DEPARTMENT
PRESIDENT'S OFFICE
CITY OF NEW YORK

May 21st, 1895.

Hon. Henry Cabot Lodge, 1765 Massachusetts Ave., Washington, D. C.

Dear Cabot: Brander Matthews told me yesterday that he thought it would help our book† if we had at the end a brief

* General Ainsworth, U. S. A. War Department.

† "Hero Tales from American History" which Roosevelt and I wrote together.

chronology, giving the chief dates in the U. S. History; and also a list of authorities; that is, books of reference for each chapter. These two could be put in a short list at the end of the volume.

For Washington we could refer to your Life and for Lincoln to Morse's Life, for Clark and Boone to my "Winning of the West," and for the "Armstrong Privateer," "The Cruise of the Wasp," and the Battle of New Orleans, to my "War of 1812," etc.

He says this would give it a much better chance among school teachers and principals of academies. I don't know whether there is anything in this idea; if there is, do you think you could prepare the two supplemental pages? which would be about all there is necessary.

By the way, in spite of my absorption here, I have time to flame with indignation over the antics of the administration in foreign affairs. Great Britain's conduct about the seals is infamous. We should at once take her action as a proof that she has abrogated the treaty and should ourselves treat it as abrogated, and seize all Canadian sealers as pirates.

Yours always,
THEODORE ROOSEVELT.

689 Madison Ave.,
NEW YORK,
May 23rd, '95.

Dear Cabot,

The enclosed explains itself; I don't think the suggestion particularly good. They have pictures for all the articles save three, two of which are among yours; can you tell them where to get portraits of Gouverneur Morris and J. Q. Adams?

I shall dine with you as a matter of course at the Brunswick on Tuesday the 28th; unless that infernal Republican Club, which has been vacillating as to its date, chooses that night. I don't think it will, and even if it does, I guess I can dine with you first, rather early, and you can then come up with me. I'll get in to see you as early as possible.

You may have seen that I have already begun to move about the elections business. The Chairman of the Republican Committee has written me a most grateful letter about it.

Atkinson sent me his speech!

The work is very hard, and is going to continue so for some months at least.

As for Byrnes, I feel we ought to act quickly for reasons I will tell you in full.

Best love to Nannie. I am hungrily looking forward to seeing you both.

Yours, T. R.

POLICE DEPARTMENT
PRESIDENT'S OFFICE
CITY OF NEW YORK.

June 5th, 1895.

Hon. Henry Cabot Lodge, Nahant, Mass.

Dear Cabot: By Jove, that speech of Holmes'* was fine; I wish he could make Edward Atkinson learn it by heart and force him to repeat it forwards and backwards every time he makes a peace oration.

Scribner's took my Civil Service article and promised to put it in the September number, and paid me One Hundred and Seventy-five ($175.00) Dollars. *The North American Review* has taken my article on Kidd. I will get a copy of the current number today and go through your Venezuela article carefully.

Harry White† spent last night with me at Sagamore (he sails for Europe today), and told me your article was admirable. I lunched with him the other day to meet Smalley,‡ and could not resist chaffing the latter a little about his attitude about Bayard.

I have written a warm letter of congratulation to Greenhalge upon his veto of the Veterans bill. It was a plucky thing to do.

* Oliver Wendell Holmes;—afterward appointed to the Supreme Court by Roosevelt. The speech was about the Civil War and the men who fought in it.
† Henry White, the diplomatist.
‡ George W. Smalley, journalist. In this year he became American correspondent of the London *Times*.

To my great amusement our old friend Raines* called on me the other day to explain that he was a much abused and misunderstood man, and to ask me to draw up a drastic Civil Service Reform bill for him to introduce at the next Session of the Legislature. The good gentleman is slightly nervous about his seat.

This State shows very strong symptoms of going in good earnest for Morton; and Harry White told me that there is an immense amount of talk about Morton in the West. I am a great deal annoyed and alarmed to find that there is a very widespread feeling among good solid Republicans here that Tom Reed has straddled the financial issue, and they are very luke-warm about him in consequence. I do wish he had taken the opportunity to come out straight and strong against free silver; I think it would have nominated him without a doubt; as it is the matter is very doubtful indeed; but I hope that when he becomes Speaker we can get the boom on. I wish you would, if you think it best, write to him that the feeling among sound money people is so strong that I believe, aside from its being right, it would also be in the highest degree expedient to come out in the most emphatic manner against free coinage. He can't keep the Silver fanatics with him, and undoubtedly the sound money men at present feel that he is luke-warm in the matter, and is trying to play politics for the Silver vote. Of course, I know that this is an utterly mistaken idea; and the few men whom I can reach I can generally convince of their error, but most of them I can't reach, and the feeling exists.

My work here is as absorbing as ever. I have been only two nights in the country.

The Republicans and the Good Government Club people are standing by me with enthusiasm, and though I shall not be able to accomplish all I could wish, still, I shall do a good deal. The *Sun* is very amusing about me. I think Uncle Jim† is gnashing his teeth because the *Tribune* and the *Sun* have both

---

* Tom Raines, New York State Assemblyman and Senator—author of the well known Raines Law.

† Mr. James Roosevelt—member of the Park Board.

been bewailing the fact that I cannot be President of the Park Board for twenty-four hours, so as to put that "mismanaged department" in good working order.

Give my best love to Nannie. I am so anxious to see you both, and am looking forward to my night at Nahant.

Ever yours,

THEODORE ROOSEVELT.

P. S. I have just read your article; and it is admirable; the most convincing showing of what England has done; if only our people will heed it!

SAGAMORE HILL,
OYSTER BAY, LONG ISLAND, N. Y.,
June 16th, '95.

Dear Cabot,

Tell Nannie that Jessie* is now very much at home, and such a very nice dog; accompanies us on our walks, sits with us in the evening, and is beloved by the children. Archie is much fascinated by her red tongue, when she lies still and pants; and crawls up and tries to grab it.

I shall be on for our class dinner on the 25th. On the 26th I am to be Marshal under Roger Wolcott†; and I'll go home with you to Nahant; on the afternoon of the 27th I ought to start back for New York. I made another night patrol. I am beginning to get the department pretty well in hand, though I have a vast amount of work before me yet. I am rather amused at the way I have become for the moment rather a prominent personage; but I am not deceived, and neither must you be; there is nothing permanent in my hold, politically. But I hope I shall be able to make my weight count in the delegate choosing next Spring; and I am very well pleased to be doing a needful piece of work in rather good shape.

Nannie's note to Edith was so sweet. Edith will stay over night to meet you two when you come on.

Yours always, T. R.

At commencement we can meet at the Porc.‡

* A dog we gave them.
† Then Lieutenant-Governor, afterward Governor, of Massachusetts.
‡ The Porcellian Club of Harvard.

SAGAMORE HILL,
OYSTER BAY, LONG ISLAND, N. Y.,
July 14th, '95.

Dear Cabot,

For good or ill I have made an upset in New York politics; and, with true parochialism, the average New Yorker regards the tariff, silver, and presidential nominees as all secondary to the Excise question.*

It is an awkward and ugly fight; yet I am sure I am right in my position, and I think there is an even chance of our winning on it. Hill has written a long letter, with a labored attack on me and on my position, picturing me as "indulging in a champagne dinner at the Union League Club" while I deny the poor man his beer. Clarkson,† quite needlessly, came to Hill's assistance, in an interview in which he assailed me for aiding the democrats by my "puritanism," and compared me to the Iowa Prohibitionists. The Goo-Goos,‡ and all the German leaders, backed ferociously by the *Staats-Zeitung*, the *World* and the *Morning Journal*, and also by Platt's paper, the *Advertiser*, have attacked me. The *Evening Post* flinched characteristically; but has finally been driven to support me. All the churches however have rallied round me enthusiastically. I am going to assail Hill with heart and soul at a German City Reform Club Tuesday; and I shall not flinch one handsbreadth from my position. Their last move, and a momentarily embarrassing one, has been, through various lawyers, to revive various obsolete blue laws, and bring the cases before the magistrates. Parker§ is proving an invaluable ally; and we shall win on the main point. The blue law business is puzzling; but I think I am working out even a solution to that. Meanwhile I have, for once, absolutely enforced the law in New York, which has always been deemed impossible.

I receive all kinds of clippings from outside papers, among them one from a paper of yours, the Springfield *Union*, with an editorial on me as a scholar and statesman, in which it

---

* Enforcement of the State Excise Law.

† James S. Clarkson of Iowa, 1st Assistant Postmaster General under Harrison, moved to New York. In 1902 he was appointed Surveyor of that port by President Roosevelt.

‡ The cant name for the Good Government Club.

§ Andrew D. Parker, one of Roosevelt's colleagues on the Police Commission.

says I am like Salisbury and Rosebery in England, or Lodge *and Everett* in America! Intelligent editor; very.

Cornell made a very poor showing at Henley.

I am at work as hard as ever, or harder, and see no chance of a let up; and my own work is so absorbing that I don't keep as well posted as I should in outside matters. The silver craze is certainly subsiding.

Give my warmest love to Nannie; and remember me to Bay and John.

One comic feature of the situation here is that recently several persons supposed to look like me have been followed at night by very unfriendly mobs! However I've never encountered anything unpleasant myself on my midnight patrols.

Yours always, T. R.

P. S. The other day there was an Irish riot against the Orange parade in Boston. Friday was the anniversary of the Boyne battle, and the Orangemen paraded here. There had been some uneasiness because of the Boston riot; so I had all the reserves in the stations with their night sticks, and sent a double number with the parade, under Inspector McCullough, who is of protestant Irish blood; and instructed him that the word was to be "clubs" if there was the slightest disturbance or attempt to interfere with the procession. It went off as quietly as a Sunday school meeting!

This has been a very egoistic letter. Edith sends you both her love, and says she wishes she were with you. I should wish it too, if I had time enough to wish anything. Do write me all about the people you meet, and particularly the Whites; to whom remember me very warmly. They are among the few people whom I really wish to see again.

Edith is well; she is going to ride Diamond soon; that veteran polo pony is now a saddle horse for her sister Emily Carow. I shall write Harry* as soon as the *Montgomery* comes to harbor, and try to get him out here.

The children are in fine health. Archie crawls up to Jessie and kisses her muddy nose, and Jessie licks his face; which

* Rear-Admiral, then Captain, C. H. Davis.

seems symptomatic of rather untidy affection. I have bought Ted a Flobert rifle and am teaching him how to shoot. The Boone and Crockett gave Willie Chanler and Von Höhnel a dinner, which was one of the pleasantest I ever went to.

The only exercise I get is to ride to and from the station on a bicycle when I don't pass the night in Town.

Have you met Bryce and Balfour, Morley and Lang?*

Yours, T. R.

POLICE DEPARTMENT
PRESIDENT'S OFFICE
CITY OF NEW YORK

July 20th, 1895.

Hon. Henry Cabot Lodge, c/o J. S. Morgan & Co., Bankers, London, England.

Dear Cabot: While you are engaged in a round of reckless dissipation with the English aristocracy, I intend, from time to time, to inflict on you accounts of the work we hot and groveling practical politicians of the baser sort are doing as our summer work in New York.

Two or three nights a week I have to stay in town; Sunday I spend in the country; the other days I ride to and from the station on my bicycle, leaving my house at half past seven in the morning, spending a perfect whirl of eight hours in New York, and returning just in time for a short play with the children before I get dressed for supper.

I have never been engaged in a more savage fight. Senator Hill thinks he sees in my actions a chance to strike the keynote for the Democratic campaign this fall. He has accordingly written a long letter against me and my conduct to the Local Democracy. I responded in a speech, of which I enclose a copy from a hostile paper; will you send it back to me? It produced me the following telegram from Senator Hoar:

"WORCESTER, MASS.,
July 18, 1895.

"Your speech is the best speech that has been made on this continent for thirty years. I am glad to know that there is a man behind it worthy of the speech.   GEORGE F. HOAR."

* As it happened I saw them all in London.

That was pretty good for the old man, was it not? I was really greatly flattered. I have had letters from all over the country backing me up, and even in New York City here, I believe there is a very strong feeling for me; but of course the outcry against me at the moment is tremendous. The *World*, *Herald*, *Sun*, *Journal* and *Advertiser* are shrieking with rage; and the *Staats-Zeitung* is fairly epileptic; the *Press* stands by me nobly. The *Tribune* and *Times* more tepidly; the *Evening Post* has been afraid of its life, and has taken refuge in editorials that are so colorless as to be comical. P. S. The *Post* has now suddenly changed and is howling in my favor; and the *Tribune* is strengthening considerably. However, I don't care a snap of my finger; my position is impregnable; and I am going to fight no matter what the opposition is.

Parker is proving himself an exceedingly efficient ally, and I get on well with both my other colleagues.

Carl Schurz has written me an agonizing letter to enforce the law against soda-water as much as beer. I wrote him back that I would tackle the soda-water in time, but nothing could make me relax my grip on the liquor sellers.

Tell me about the Whites; and the different people whom you have met.

Give my best love to Nannie.

Yours always,
THEODORE ROOSEVELT.

LONDON,
July 24, 1895.

Dear Theodore:

I have been trying every day since we got here to find time to sit down to write to you but I have been so constantly occupied that I really have not seemed to have a moment. Today comes your letter which it was so good of you to write in the midst of your press of work that I, who am only amusing myself, feel smitten with a sense of my shortcomings. My dear boy, you can never be egotistic to me. I wanted to hear about you and your work and Edith and the children more than anything else. Smalley writes to the *Times* about you very often and of course very well and in cordial sympathy. In the *Morning Post* too the other day was a column and a half from another correspondent, an Englishman, all about the Police. There were some silly things in it but he stated that altho' New York politics were "parochial"—his very word—the question was exciting great attention and that you and Mayor Strong were working a great reform. So you see your fame spreads far. You are perfectly right in your position. I am as clear on that point as ever. How can Clarkson be so foolish? Platt of course thinks you are going to wreck the party and squirms. On the other hand Depew whom I saw said you were doing capitally. He stands for a certain class of opinion. You are not going to wreck the party. You are right and they will rally to the standard and to *you*. I welcome the conflict with Hill. That is a piece of real good fortune and will help you and the party both. Once more in my opinion you are doing rightly, wisely and splendidly and building up a reputation and establishing a leadership from which I expect great fruits.

Altho' only amusing ourselves we have been very busy every moment and we seem to have been gone months instead of two weeks. Everyone has been most kind and we have been lunched and dined and taken about without intermission. The dissolution of Parliament swept all the political leaders out of town and down to the constituencies so that I have not yet seen Harcourt or Balfour or Bryce or Morley. But I am going to stay until the opening of Parliament and they will all be back before that and I shall see them all. We are to dine with the Curzons on Friday to meet the Asquiths and I lunch with Balfour next Monday unless something breaks. Meantime we have passed a Sunday at Birmingham with the Chamberlains. He and I had much talk and he tells me that the new government considers it part of their policy to have an international conference and do something for silver. This coming from him who was regarded as an out and out gold man is significant. I had lots of politics from him and he is very much at the top of the tree at present. I have lunched at Lady Jeune's and am going there for a Sunday. We met Lecky and Mr. Buckle the chief editor of the *Times* at a lunch at Lady Londonderry's.

Our host and hostess were most hospitable and cordial and asked these men to meet me and I was very glad to meet Buckle and Lecky. I have lunched at the Fergusons with Lang and today Nannie and I lunched with the Langs at their own house—no one but themselves which is the really pleasant way of seeing people. He is a most interesting man. We met Lord Peel at Mrs. Dugdale's. I like him as you do. The politicians having all left town the Whites had a different set at their dinner which they gave for us. It was really a very perfect dinner and very handsome. I was glad to see once the people they had. The Duke and Duchess of Devonshire—the Duke of Sutherland—Lord and Lady Cowper—she very agreeable, and so ·on, and then Sir Frederick Leighton and Mrs. Humphrey Ward whom I took in, who is pleasanter a good deal than her books. I sat next to and talked with the Duke of Devonshire after dinner. The pleasantest dinner I have been to was last night at Lord Gray's. He is most pleasant and so too was Lord Lansdowne who was there—who has been as you know Governor General of Canada and Viceroy of India. I had a long talk with him and the whole dinner was lively and pleasant. I am more than ever impressed with the vast difference between the Englishman who has travelled and governed abroad and those who have not. Many of the latter are apt to be insular and self-absorbed and stiff as a rule while the former are almost always agreeable and well worth meeting. Lord Lansdowne struck me too as a man of much quiet ability. In the way of big things we have been to a reception at Stafford House and to the Shah's reception to the Prince of Wales, good only as sights. But I have given you more than enough of this. The Whites have been devoted to us and done everything you can imagine. I shall surely give them your message which will please them. They really have a very good place here and are very popular. They know everybody and have at their house not merely titles but the cleverest men of all sorts. The Fergusons, Mrs. Dugdale, the indefatigable Frewen, have all been devoted to us too and done everything. And of course dear Bamie is like one of our own and there is no end to her kindness. She is looking and is remarkably well. Everyone knows Bamie and she and Capt. Cowles* seem to do all that is done. We had a glimpse of Douglas and Corinne but they went off to the country at once as Corinne was really wretchedly. If you are wearied out with these small details of society turn it over to Edith. She and I love Belles Lettres and have other weak tastes in common and this is all written as much for her as for you.

Best love to Edith and the chicks. Do write when you can get a chance.

The thing that has most impressed me here is the growth of the United States—you feel it here better than at home—and oh, how glad I am to be an American! How much better—and then we are so much more interesting and amusing as a people. I have been watching the elections, been to the polling places in London and have collected a lot of material for an article which will make our Anglo-Americans sit up. I have a million things to say to you. No letter can hold them. So good night.

Yours, H. C. L.

Bimetallism played a good deal of a part in the election—was strongly pushed and they have a majority of the house. I have been to two dinners of bimetallist silverites.

POLICE DEPARTMENT
PRESIDENT'S OFFICE
CITY OF NEW YORK

July 30th, 1895.

Hon. Henry Cabot Lodge, c/o J. S. Morgan & Co., Bankers, London, England.

Dear Cabot: It certainly looks to me as if the silver sentiment was very much on the wane. From the standpoint of policy and expediency I regret more and more all the time that Tom Reed did not make a strong anti-free coinage speech when he voted for the Gold Bonds. Had he done so, and come out in a ringing speech as the champion of sound money, there would not now be the slightest opposition to him in New York.

---

* Then naval *attaché* at the American Embassy. He subsequently married Miss Roosevelt.

As things actually are the Morton movement bids fair to be serious.

When I get at the table with a man I can always explain to him at full length that Reed is a fearless champion of sound money; and I can usually, after some length of time, show him that I am speaking the truth; but Reed's attitude ought not to need explanation. I am not criticizing what he did. Speaking from a purely academic standpoint, I think it was right; but as regards New York State events have shown that it was a blunder. We may be able to offset the effects later; I think we shall; but we have now a doubtful fight, whereas, under other circumstances victory would have come without an effort.

All of the best men (I do not mean Mugwumps, I mean Republicans) have gotten the idea firmly fixed in their heads that Reed tried to straddle the Silver Question. When I meet one of them, I can gradually pick the idea *out* of his head; but there are nine hundred and ninety-nine that I do not meet.

Extraordinary though it seems, I do believe that Cleveland is planning for a third term, and that he *may* be nominated: I think we should beat him if he was; but I am by no means sure that he would not give us a good deal of a fight. People are crazy over him; though I think it is more our kind of people than the "masses."

At the Presidential election all the Southern States are going to go Democratic, no matter what they think about silver. With Cleveland up we should have a terrific struggle in the North East, unless we make our fight so uncompromising against free silver as to deprive us of all chances with the Rocky Mountain States.

However, this is the alarmist view of the situation. In spite of the subsidence of the silver craze, and of the hidebound allegiance of the silver Democrats to the Democratic party, I cannot help thinking there will be much trouble for the Democratic leaders on the financial question; and they have to fear a bolt in their own ranks. *We* only have to fear the Rocky Mountain States.

Our own conventions, from Iowa east, are coming out all

right on the financial issue; and the good crops bid fair to knock the life out of the Populists; so that I think the chances, looked at dispassionately, are considerably in our favor.

I enclose you Harry's letter; it is so characteristic. I have asked him out for next Sunday as Smalley, Florence Lockwood and Grant LaFarge are coming out.

Yours always,

THEODORE ROOSEVELT.

P. S.—The excise, or rather Sunday-closing, fight is as bitter as ever; but I think matters are beginning to look better for us. Edith and the children are well.

ARLINGTON MANOR,
NEWBURY,

August 3, 1895.

Dear Theodore :

Your letter of the 20th came two days ago and I was delighted to get it and hear further of your doings. I had already read a bad report of your speech in the *Sun* and was especially glad to get a good report which I have read with the greatest care and interest. It is a very strong speech and admirably put. It is entirely unanswerable. No successful assault on your position is possible, and I have faith to believe that it must and will win in the end. Hoar's telegram was capital. He is sound and eminently right-minded as I always told you. In saying that it was the best speech made in thirty years he has very carelessly overlooked some of the utterances of his colleague during that period but otherwise I have no fault to find with it. I quite agree that there is a man behind the speech. I really envy you the work you are doing—it is so full of effectiveness and importance. I don't wonder you are receiving letters from all over the country for you are doing brilliantly. You are making a great place and reputation for yourself which will lead surely to even better things. Remember too that apart from the great principle of enforcing all laws there is a very large and powerful body of Republicans in the State who will stand by you and behind you because you are enforcing that particular law. This may be a narrow view but it is of the greatest political importance. You handled Hill in fine style.

Since I wrote you I have seen many people of interest. I have lunched and dined with Balfour who is, I think, the most attractive man I have met. The Curzons gave us a dinner where we met the Asquiths, Matthews, (Home Secretary in the last Conservative ministry)—Thomas Hardy the novelist who was charming and Alfred Milner the Egyptian and Treasury man, remarkably agreeable. I think I told you that I had already met Lecky at a lunch Lady Londonderry gave us— but he is shy and twists his legs so that altho' he is very gentle and pleasant as well as clever, it is hard to get much out of him; then the Asquiths gave us a dinner where we met Rosebery who was most cordial and pleasant and who asked us to Dalmeny to stay which was very civil and I wish we could go —Haldane was there also—a very amusing clever man and Lord and Lady Ribblesdale who are extremely pleasant people. I think on the whole it was the pleasantest dinner and the pleasantest set we have had in London. Then we went down to Malwood and passed a day and night there with the Harcourts. Sir William has as you know a reputation for sharpness and rough manners but in his own house I must say that no man could have been more charming and I had a great deal of interesting talk with him. At this moment I am staying over Sunday with the Jeunes. Nannie has remained in London and I think has chosen the better part which sounds ungrateful but I have come to the conclusion that I do not care for English house-parties. Lady Jeune and Sir Francis are of course most pleasant and Judge Daly of our native land who is here is as you know a good old fellow and always agreeable. Du Chaillu was also there with Judge Daly. Du Chaillu is most interesting, vivacious and full of his adventures and travel. But the miscellaneous assortment of British youths and maidens who are here some titled and some not are a weariness to me. Lady Somerset's son who is here is very intelligent and so is at least one other untitled one whose name I do not know—but the rest!

Rockhill* is in London and went to call on Bayard who received him very cordially and on parting said: "Now is there anything I can do for you? Let me see, I will give you my number at the Cooperative Stores and I tell you, I will give you my card and write your name on it and then if you get into trouble with the police they will know you."

It is Sunday morning and I should be in bed. Best love to Edith.

Ever yours,   H. C. L.

Bamie is coming home with us Nov. 16, which is delightful. Godkin I hear is in London, which may account for the improved attitude of the *Post.*†

POLICE DEPARTMENT
PRESIDENT'S OFFICE
CITY OF NEW YORK

August 8th, 1895.

Hon. H. C. Lodge, c/o J. S. Morgan & Co., Bankers, London, England.

Dear Cabot: Your letter was delightful. Edith and I read and re-read it. It gave just exactly what we wanted to know. We want to hear about *all* your dinners, exactly whom you meet there, and how you like them. We want to know where you go, what you see and whose houses you stay at. Make your next letter even more full of details. Tell us something about Bay and John too.

I earnestly hope that the Conservatives will do something for international bi-metalism; it would help us out greatly. One good thing they will accomplish will be to shut the mouths of the silly fools who have been denouncing our strongest anti-free silver people, because they are also international bimetalists.

* W. W. Rockhill—distinguished orientalist and diplomat.
† The New York *Evening Post.*

I am thankful to say that the Missouri Democrats have come out for free silver. The Iowa Democrats have repudiated it.

I am going to write an article on the Republican side of the issue of the next Presidential campaign for the November *Century*. Your beloved fellow patriot, Governor Russell, is to take the Democratic side. I should have preferred a somewhat worthier opponent; but I was glad to have a chance of making my own party position clear. Anyhow my article on Tom Reed will come out in the December *Forum* too. I am very fortunate in the fact that at present almost all of the men who attack me are Democrats; and though I am administering this law in an absolutely non-partisan way; yet the Republicans appreciate that I am their most effective champion; and my support among the Republicans (and decent people generally) is very strong, but there is a very serious defection from us among the Germans.

I am just as busy as ever; but after this I am going to try to get Saturday off, as I shall not be able to take any regular holiday this year.

Edith, of course, persists in regarding me as a frail invalid needing constant attention; and when I spend a night or two in town she sometimes comes in and spends it with me. In one way, however, I think this does her good because she gets away from the children, and usually spends a quiet day in the Society Library.

I have just had a beautiful time at the Catholic Total Abstinence Silver Jubilee. A Democratic State Senator named O'Sullivan dragged politics into the affair and attacked Mayor Strong and myself. I followed and went for him red-handed, and never in my life did I receive such an ovation. I enclose the account in the *World*, which, you may be sure, did not color things in my behalf.

Edith has great fun driving the two ponies, which are in fine feather and she and her sister are soon to begin riding. I have not had my leg across a horse since I last rode Gladstone.* I guess my riding and shooting days are pretty well over. Indeed for the last three months about all of my time

* A hunter of mine.

has been taken up with the Police Department; but I find it very interesting.

Best love to Nannie.   Always yours,

THEODORE ROOSEVELT.

P. S.—To our great regret Harry Davis could not come out for Sunday. Smalley was as pleasant as possible. Grant La-Farge is really a good deal of a fellow.

POLICE DEPARTMENT
PRESIDENT'S OFFICE
CITY OF NEW YORK

Dear Cabot,   Aug. 9th, '95.

My secretary is doubtful whether she enclosed the clipping, so I enclose a couple, from unfavorable papers. The *Press* and *Tribune* of course whooped me up. You see O'Sullivan was before fellow-Catholics and Democrats too, mostly; but I downed him, and never in my life have I been received with such enthusiasm. I had sent my speech to the papers before-hand, and so they did not report my attacks on O'Sullivan; I hit him as I never hit anyone before in a debate, and he literally broke down and sobbed after the close of the meeting. He is supposed to be the second Bourke Cockran of Tammany. Hayes wrote me a rapturous letter from Lynn about the affair.

Pardon my egotism!

Yours,   T. R.

LONDON,
Dear Theodore: August 10, 1895.

We have been away since Monday up in Warwickshire at Warwick and Stratford and on our way home at Oxford, very delightful days. Thus it comes that I have only just received your letter of the 30th. I know the truth of what you say about Reed. In Boston there was something of it among the Mug-wumps but they do not count and it existed nowhere else. I fancy it is strong only in New York City. He spoke as he felt at the time and quite honestly and the idea of his straddling is very unjust but still there it is and I know how you meet it. We must trust to the future to set this right and I think we shall. I hear that Reed and Morton both are growing in the West and McKinley and Harrison are losing ground—I see also very strong interviews from Hale and Frye for Reed which will stiffen things wonderfully. Until he gets the Speakership and Congress meets we cannot really judge. As to Cleveland I have no sort of fear of him in the North East. He is not strong with the people.

If the Republicans were to declare for free silver he would have standing but they won't and he will be nowhere. I think him the weakest man that can be put up. We should beat him to death on the third term issue and need make no other point. The sentiment of the country is against third terms and sentiments cannot be reasoned with. They will not nominate Cleveland. I wish they would. Now as to the general situation. The Democrats will either declare for free silver or they will not. If they do we shall beat them surely on a sharp fight and beat them badly on that issue. If they do not and I do not think they will stand on the same ground as ourselves on silver then we shall whip the life out of them on the tariff, foreign policy and general incompetency.

The situation seems to me very clear and I see no escape from it unless we blunder beyond belief in Congress or there should be another frightful panic to upset everything. I may be all wrong but putting aside details which will not affect the national voting it seems to me that we must win and more or less easily.

I enclose a letter from Smalley to the *Times* and a long editorial which appeared this morning. You may not have seen them and they will serve to show how far your candle throws its beams—a remarkable distance as I think. I do not understand the allusion to Grant.* I have been out of the way of papers and Smalley says nothing of it. Is it possible that he has gone so far and stops now for want of breath? It seems

* Frederick Dent Grant—a colleague of Roosevelt's on the Police Commission.

incredible. Even if he is under political influence one would think the veriest dolt would see that it was altogether too late to try to conciliate and that the only possible safety is in forging straight ahead. By the way, Smalley, whose despatches are invaluable to us here is making one error because he has not yet seen people enough I suppose—I wish you would set him straight. He keeps saying that there is no general interest in the Monroe doctrine, that only a few jingos talk about Venezuela, that there is no real objection among our people to England's going there, that the Irish brogue can be read in every line about Trinidad, etc., etc. Do explain to him that a majority of the U. S. Senate, including your humble servant, who have no touch of Irish brogue feel very strongly on these matters. So do the great majority of the American people and Congress will act upon their feelings. His despatches have properly great weight here—they are quoted on every side and the tone he takes on these points can only encourage England in a policy which will surely lead to trouble if persisted in. He ought to discourage British aggressiveness which our people dislike. I do not want to recommend my own writings but it would do no harm if he would read my piece on Venezuela. I find it has been read here and noted. When you see him take time from the police to set him straight on these points and on American feeling. It is important he should not go wrong and he is doing most admirable work in every other direction.

You are all right—keep right on. Talk as little as possible, except when you make a set speech which always helps. I am surprised to see how well you have got into the public mind Tammany's purpose in the land. Your position is absolutely right and impregnable and is bound to win. If they make it an issue you will carry the State with you if not the city. I am more proud than I can say of the magnificent fight you have made and the brilliant work you have done and are doing. You have forged to the front tremendously in a very short time.

We are off to the Continent a week from today. I shall see Ronald* Monday and am to meet the Speaker and Birrell I believe at dinner on Wednesday. Bryce is still away. Morley

* Ronald Ferguson—now Lord Novar.

is beaten and not coming back. With these two exceptions I have seen pretty much all the most interesting men and seen them simply and pleasantly. It has been a delightful month and well worth while. Harry's letter was delicious. Do not on any account show Smalley what I have written but put it to him with your own Oriental tact.

They have given John* a preliminary certificate which is unlooked for good fortune and ought to ensure his getting in next year.

Yours ever, H. C. L.

August 11.

Smalley's despatch this morning explains about Grant and that the division is healed which I am glad to see. He also at length shows how public opinion is swinging to your side and gives an account of your meeting the Catholics and your reply to O'Sullivan; how I should like to have seen it. If the Republican party will only have the sense to back you up on the broad ground of enforcement of the law they will sweep things. They should make your policy their own. But you are bound to win. As people understand it they are coming and must come to your position.

Yours, H. C. L.

POLICE DEPARTMENT
PRESIDENT'S OFFICE
CITY OF NEW YORK

Dear Cabot: August 22, 1895.

I have found that I cannot do my work and go in and out every day. The work is of a very exhausting kind and the amount in mere quantity is very great. When I am in town I usually stay in my office from half past eight or nine until seven or half past seven o'clock. On the other hand Saturday is a half holiday and all of the City Departments close at twelve

---

* My younger son.

o'clock; so when possible I intend hereafter to try to take Saturday and Sunday off in the country and during the rest of the week to stay in town, perhaps going out in the country for Wednesday or Thursday night and coming back by the morning train. I have had to do this for two or three weeks and as I said Edith usually spends two of the nights with me; on the other nights I have to speak or do something of the kind, so that I am kept busy enough. Anyhow I have no time to feel melancholy or desolate. Indeed I have heartily enjoyed this last three months and a half. Last Sunday I spent in town with Jacob Riis driving and walking about for nine hours to see for ourselves exactly how the Excise law was enforced. I had no idea how complete our success was; not four percent of the saloons were open and these were doing business with the greatest secrecy and to a most limited extent. We have really won a great triumph so far; of course we cannot let up on the strain at all.

I have now begun to think that we ought not to have the saloons open on Sunday and that all we need in the way of changing the Law is to alter certain of its provisions so as to make it easier to enforce. But publicly I have resolutely declined to take any position except to say that I stood squarely on the plank of honestly enforcing the Law. The *World* and *Journal* nearly have epilepsy over me; there are very few crimes which they do not accuse me of committing; and they are united in portraying me as spending my Sundays drinking heavily in the Union League Club.

I see no chance for a let up in my work for the next three or four months; but I feel as strong and well as possible. I think that next winter I shall have a great deal to bother me as regards the Legislature and ourselves; and also on the question of presidential delegates. I think that by May my hands will be tolerably free and I can then enter unhampered into the presidential campaign.

A big game-seeking Englishman came to me with a letter of introduction the other day and said much of an editorial in the London *Times*; it also contained a letter from Smalley—the date was August 10th. If it would not bother you in the least

I wish you would send me a copy of that date; but don't do it if it is the least bother.

Smalley was really very pleasant the night he spent at my house; but he is all wrong about foreign affairs and about Bayard too. In my article in the November *Century* I shall take very strong ground on Foreign Affairs. I am really very glad they asked me to present the Republican side.

Be sure to tell me of all your further experiences and about the interesting people you meet. If I was not having such a good time as Police Commissioner I should be awfully sorry that Edith and I were not abroad too and going around with Nannie and yourself.

I do not at all like the way the *Defender** keeps breaking things in the races. She is a fast boat but fragile. I hope the *Valkyrie* does not carry off the Cup for that cad Dunraven.

Best love to Nannie.   Yours always,

THEODORE ROOSEVELT.

P. S.—Anecdote for Nannie.

Ted (who now begins to ride and swim quite decently and to shoot a Flobert rifle) the other day looked meditatively at his scarred little bare legs and remarked "How much browner and harder my legs are than other parts of me—my stomach for instance."

POLICE DEPARTMENT
PRESIDENT'S OFFICE
CITY OF NEW YORK

Dear Cabot:—   August 27th, 1895.

I have just received your letter with the clipping from the London *Times;* they greatly interested me.

I cannot judge of the effect of our action on politics. The bulk of the Republican party are enthusiastically with us. We have surprising support from quarters that I did not expect. The crowded east-side audiences of Second Avenue and Avenue "A" greet me with an enthusiasm I never anticipated. Of

* The American champion yacht.

course there is much hostility shown too; but the wonder is that I should have so strong a following among them.

I have spoken again and again in packed halls on the East-side during the summer with the temperature at boiling point, both as regards the weather and the audience. It has been in some respects like a campaign. Generally, I have been interrupted, and frequently some speaker has jumped up and at my request very often has taken the platform to speak against me; but I have never failed to carry the house with me at the end.

Joe Murray and the Counsel of the Excise Board (a very honest little East-side Jew) are in ecstasies, and insist that my course is making a big gain for the Republican party in the very districts that were hostile to us. All the respectable people and almost all of our own leaders who were at first very doubtful about my course now heartily support me. I am inclined on the whole to think that it will have a good effect upon the Republican party, from a political standpoint. At any rate it was the only one I could possibly follow. But we are not in a satisfactory condition altogether in this State, thanks primarily to Platt and what he represents. He acquiesced in turning down three Senators who had done most of his dirty work last year; and now two of them are running as Independent Candidates. On the other hand he renominated Raines; there is a big bolt from him. Moreover, he is trying to make us run a straight ticket in this City, which will alienate all the decent people and will be perfectly futile.

Quigg is heart and soul for him again at bottom, though keeping on good terms with me; as indeed Platt, himself, I believe, is. So the outlook is not very favorable; yet, I cannot help thinking that the drift is so much our way that we shall win anyhow. If we do not it may possibly have a good effect by preventing any overconfidence in the Presidential contest. If we keep the legislature, even though Tammany gets the City, we shall have held our own.

As regards my own action, I have one consolation. If I had not done anything and had not enforced the Excise Law, we would probably have been beaten anyhow; and we would have had no offset in the shape of having done our duty. Now we have gained something tangible; and I do not think we have impaired our chances of victory in the least. There was risk either way; and only one way leads toward honesty.

In my *Century* article I worked in a paragraph smashing between the eyes the gold bugs for their attitude toward Reed on the bond business. I took the tone of speaking about it incidentally, simply to show the folly of the men whom the free silver fanatics had driven into an opposite fanaticism quite as extreme; and in half a dozen sentences showed Reed's consistency, and unflinching support of sound money. I think you will like the article.

Smalley will write a Jeremiad over it as the work of a Jingo. I have spoken to him as plainly as mortal can and told him, not only that my own feeling, but also the general sentiment of the country was rather hostile to England and was very strong in support of the Monroe Doctrine; but he does not meet the men who share our views. He told me he did not believe there were many men of high standing that felt as I did; I instanced you, and he promptly asserted that you were an exception; a most charming and attractive man; but a mono-maniac on foreign policy.

I shall write him at length, at once, again. I shall not quote your letter. He read your piece on Venezuela; but it only caused him pain.

I really envy you meeting all the men you have met in such a delightful way. They have certainly treated you well.

As I said before I think that my action on the whole will help the Republican party, even though it may not avert a Tammany victory here; it would only be a chance if we averted such a victory any way. But you must not be under any delusion as to the effect of my actions upon me personally. I have undoubtedly strengthened myself with the rank and file of our party. I have administered this office so far with what I may call marked success; but I have done so by incurring bitter enmity. I have not in any way increased my grip on the party machinery. In other words, my victory here does not leave me with any opening. It leads nowhere.

For the moment the Good Government Club people and their ilk regard me as a hero; and the bulk of the Republican party are very strongly with me; but such feeling, as you know well, is very evanescent. I have not any permanent hold; it is simply a sporadic feat; and at the end all I shall gain is a chance, and probably a remote chance, of being put into some similar place, in the very unlikely event of our side again winning another such municipal victory. Don't think from this that I feel blue, for I do not. I have thoroughly enjoyed this work and I feel that it is honorable and creditable; I have been far too busy to waste a thought on the future; but I do not want *you* to get false ideas about the position. You look at my deeds through rosy glasses;—no one else shares your view.

I am delighted to hear that John has his preliminary certificate. I do not believe there will be any further trouble.

Give my best love to Nannie.

Yours always,

THEODORE ROOSEVELT.

HOTEL DES DEUX MONDES,
PARIS,
Aug. 31, 1895.

Dear Theodore :

I am glad that I have known you long and loved you well and that you are a person of a loyal disposition for you are rushing so rapidly to the front that the day is not far distant when you will come into a large kingdom and by that time I shall probably be a back number and I shall expect you to look after me and give me a slice. It is true that your performance has come at a fortunate [time] when you had no rivals in the public attention except large strawberries and sea-serpents. Nevertheless you have done well after all deductions and seem to be the "Man of the Month" as Washburn wrote me with enthusiasm, speaking of *The Review of Reviews*. By the way Stead tried to land me in London, but I have a great prejudice against him and eluded him. Seriously I am over-joyed at the way things are working. You are not only doing splendidly but public opinion and Republican opinion are swinging steadily to your side. How can it be otherwise when you are so absolutely and simply right. The Catholic meeting was not only a great personal triumph,—quite deserved by the way,—but most significant of the trend of opinion. Your speech was capital. I read the *World* account, which your secretary did not forget, with the greatest interest. It was all admirable. Your opponents Hill and O'Sullivan have been very good to give you such opportunities of which you have taken full advantage. If the Republicans only stand to their guns they will win and on your issue and then your political position is made. That Senatorship is getting well into sight, my dear boy.

Balfour in the House the other day gave little encouragement for action on Bi-metallism but I think it will come. I think I was in London a week after I last wrote. I saw the opening of Parliament very pleasantly and was much interested. Crisp turned up—Bayard had allowed him—the Speaker of our House, to dine down there all alone with merely a ticket—very characteristic. Luckily he met me and I introduced him to Harry White who took charge of him and bore him in to see the Speaker and Balfour and I presented him to Chamberlain and all was well. But there is an instance why the Whites succeed and Bayard and your esteemed cousin are nowhere. During the week we met the Speaker at a dinner also Canon Wilberforce—Sir Alfred Lyall—Haldane again and Spencer Walpole. Then another night dined with Mrs. Dugdale just to meet her brother Sir George Trevelyan with whom I had a long and very interesting talk and liked him much. Afterwards we all went over with Sidney Buxton and had tea on the terrace—very picturesque at night. Nannie and Buxton looked into the House and heard Balfour finish a speech and Asquith begin one. During the week we saw the Harcourts again at dinner and more of Balfour who is one of the few men about whom I feel a real regret that I cannot see him constantly.

Two weeks ago tomorrow we left England and travelled through Normandy—Amiens—Rouen—Caen—Bayeux—Coutances—Mont St. Michel—Vitré—Le Mans—Chartres and

Paris where I found your letters awaiting me. I do not know
when I have enjoyed anything so much as the last ten days in
Normandy. I am not sure as to your views on architecture.
Perhaps you regard it as you do Belle Lettres—but I am very
fond of it and hungry after such a long interval to look on some.
In Normandy is the best Norman and Gothic building in the
world—the splendid material and artistic result of the ages of
faith—beautiful and absorbing to study beyond words. Then
that corner is crowded with history. Men have fought and
prayed and lived there for a good many years and some great
men and great fighters. It was all very fine.

I had a most successful time in England and now it is over
I look back on it with great pleasure. It was a good experience
to have. We shall stay here a while and then travel through
the South of France back here again and so home.

Harry White took Bay up to Scotland and gave him a week's
shooting. Bay got his hand in pretty soon and found the birds
very easy after our prairie chickens and the wild duck and
killed abundant brace and enjoyed himself. Henry Adams has
been with us all the time and is the most delightful of travelling
companions.

We are all well. Give my best love to Edith.

I am glad she is looking after you properly—you need it.
Write when you can.

Ever yrs., H. C. L.

PARIS,
Sept. 3rd, 1895.

Dear Theodore:

Just after I had mailed my last letter to you came yours of
Aug. 22nd, and I hasten to answer it not only because it was
most welcome but because I want to tell you that I sent you
the Smalley letter and the editorial from the *Times* the very
day after they appeared—i. e. the 11th mailed probably the
12th and I cannot understand why you have not received them
and the long letter that went with them. I shall be disgusted
if they are lost. I wrote you from Lady Jeune's the 4th Aug.—
mailed the letter and again just a week later one sending the

clippings. Let me know whether you received both. This is my second letter from Paris.

I do not wonder at Edith's anxiety. You are having a very hard summer and will miss your health trip so pray take [care] of yourself and be reasonable. Your success in closing is great. The action of the liquor dealers which I have seen in the papers is another good point for you as it seems to me. How wise has been the policy of not expressing an opinion on the merits of the law. Actual experience inclines you to believe in the law. Now you are free. I cannot see that you have made any mistake so far. I am glad you are going to do that article. Bear down on the point that they have left us with a monthly deficit which has stimulated all our financial troubles and that the Republican surplus against which they cried out kept us all right. Also the abandonment everywhere of *Laissez faire* as an immutable principle. You need no suggestions on Foreign affairs. In your present state of brilliant conspicuousness our book* ought to sell like hot cakes.

[The remainder of this letter is missing.]

POLICE DEPARTMENT
OF THE CITY OF NEW YORK

300 Mulberry Street,
Dear Cabot,   NEW YORK, Sept. —, 1895.

I did not suppose that Ted had kept much of an eye on the Yacht race; but it appears that he had, for, entirely of his own notion, he has just christened the new pig "Sulky Dunraven."

The other day I went up to the New York Athletic Club meeting, in my official capacity to preserve order, and incidentally to see the Americans whip the English in every one of the eleven events; and in six of them to win the second place.

The fight is on here now in earnest. I am greatly angered at the course of the Republican State Convention. They were

* "Hero Tales from American History."

too cowardly to endorse our action in.enforcing the law; and the Democrats were too cowardly to condemn it. Both sides shuffled on the Excise question. The Platt machine people are wholly impossible; they actually proposed to make no mention whatever of the one question which was engrossing the whole attention of the Committee to the exclusion of every other.

Warner Miller saved us from absolutely hopeless defeat by putting in a Sunday resolution; but even this resolution was ill drawn and ill considered. The Democratic resolution was just as ambiguous; but it is much more carefully drawn, and therefore on the whole rather better than ours, for their Committee on Resolutions carefully repudiated the proposition of Hill and Perry Belmont to attack us for our enforcement of the Law. If our Convention had had any sense it would have hailed with delight the issue given by Hill as to the honest enforcement of the Law, and would have made this the first plank in their platform. Had they done so, we should have swept this State as it has never been swept before. Now, the fight is doubtful, though, I think we shall win, and if we can only make the party managers, even at this late day take our ground and fight straight for the honest enforcement of the Law, we can win with a good majority.

The irritating feature in the conduct of machine leaders is, its utter fatuity. They cannot placate the liquor men in the least. They will not win a brewer or saloonkeeper to our side, but they will succeed in rendering a great mass of men who would have turned to us lukewarm, or even hostile.

Dr. Parkhurst is back and full of fight. He is a very good fellow. Joe Murray under stress of opposition has developed into an anti-saloon man of a ferocity which makes my attitude toward the liquor men seem one of timid subserviency.

From now on I shall have but little time to myself until after election. I don't have enough time to myself even to envy Nannie and you your trip through Southern France and Spain. Edith and I still fairly revel in your letters.

Always yours,

THEODORE ROOSEVELT.

POLICE DEPARTMENT
PRESIDENT'S OFFICE
CITY OF NEW YORK

Dear Cabot: Sept. —, 1895.

I have just received your two letters from France. Yes, I
received the clippings right after I sent you the letter asking
you to get them for me.

Edith and I have enjoyed your letters immensely. I am
sorry to say she seems to sympathize with your view as to my
probable failure to appreciate the splendid architecture of the
Norman Cathedral towns. In this she is wrong. The great
Cathedrals have always possessed as much fascination for me
as for those who know far more about architecture than I do.

I envy you your trip both in England and in France. How
I wish we could have been abroad at the same time.

Like yourself, I was a little nervous about the *Defender.*
Edith and I went down to see the first race on the Police Patrol
Boat; and at its finish I was not nervous in the least. In a
very low wind and in smooth waters the two boats were nearly
equal; but when there was a sea on the *Defender* was the
better boat; and as soon as the wind rose her superiority
became very marked. Her second race was a really wonderful
feat, thanks to Dunraven's fouling her (when he tried a piece
of sharp practice and attempted to bluff the Yankee Captain,
who would not be bluffed), the *Defender* was never able·
to make use of her large head sails at all; but although crippled
she was beaten by only forty-seven seconds. This second race
proved that the *Valkyrie* had not a chance. Dunraven
then funked; it was a clear case of showing the white feather.
His talk about the excursion boats was all nonsense; they
bothered one boat as much as the other. They did not interfere seriously with either of the boats. And in the third race,
which he abandoned, they did not interfere at all. They had
no effect whatever on the result of either race.

He has shown himself a poor sportsman; he has sulked and
flinched.

I am very much touched by your persistence in far over-
estimating the position I hold; but you really make me a

little uneasy for I do not want you to get false ideas of my standing. I undoubtedly have a strong hold on the imagination of decent people; and I have the courageous and enthusiastic support of the men who make up the back-bone of the Republican party; but I have no hold whatever on the people who run the Republican machine.

Platt's influence is simply poisonous. I cannot go in with him; no honest man of sincerity can. Yet, his influence is very great; he has completely overthrown the Brookfield people. At the Primaries, my own Assembly District we held, although after a close vote; but elsewhere throughout the city the Platt people generally triumphed. He can gain victories over Republicans in Primaries and Conventions; but he cannot gain victories against Democrats; and he has no hold on the rank and file of the Republican party. On the contrary they are reluctant to vote for any man whom he controls. The Platt men carry the other Assembly Districts in my Congressional District.

At present, I do not see how I can get to the National Convention as a delegate. The Platt people will probably control the District. Moreover, in my own Assembly District there are:

Chauncey Depew,	Gen'l. Sam Thomas,
Joseph Choate,	Mayor Strong, and
Anson G. McCook,	Brookfield.

All of these are men of note; and all of them, excepting probably Choate and Strong, will be among the many candidates for Delegates for the presidential Convention. The shrewdest among them are, I think, McKinley men; and the decent people are all embittered against Platt, so that it would be very difficult to make them join with his people, even merely to send two Reed Delegates. I shall try to fix up some arrangement by which I can go with another Reed man, whether the latter be for Platt or Brookfield; but just at this moment I don't see my way clear to success.

The absolute cowardice and dishonesty of the Platt people who now control our Republican State politics, was shown at the Republican State Convention.

This summer, I have, as you know, been careful to identify myself in every way with the Republicans. Hill has attacked me violently as a Republican; and I have made an equally savage counter-attack upon him. He has made me the arch foe of the Democracy. The Clergy of all denominations are standing by me with the utmost enthusiasm.

Hill has committed the Democracy to attacking me and my course; and also to attacking the principle of closing the saloons on Sunday. Not only common honesty; but every consideration of expediency, indicated to the Republicans to follow the opposite policy to the one pursued by the Democrats; yet, the Platt people prepared a platform from which every allusion to the Excise matter was struck out, and in the Committee on Resolutions they voted down even a resolution endorsing our course in honestly enforcing the law. If the platform had gone through in this shape I would have been absolutely debarred from saying a word for the party; and what is much more important, we would have been beaten overwhelmingly, for the excise issue is the main issue in our State. Warner Miller, however, made a bold fight in open convention and got in a plank, which while not very satisfactory, still does give us a chance of success and enables me to support the party. This was done in spite of every effort of the Platt people; but the union of the Brookfield people with the country Republicans who are afraid of church-going voters proved irresistible on this one point.

I bore you with this account of our rather parochial politics just so that you may understand that I seriously mean what I say when I tell you that I have no real hold on the party machinery here, and cannot under the present circumstances get such a hold without sacrificing my self-respect. The chance for future political preference for me is just about such a chance as that of lightning striking. In the meanwhile, however, I have certainly accomplished a great deal in my present position; and I have what is, perhaps, as great a satisfaction as any man can have, the knowledge of having performed a difficult and important work well. It would be mock modesty for me not to say this. But it would be self-deception if I thought that I had gained a permanent position, or opened any future career. However, I have had a thoroughly enjoyable time, and I am over-joyed that I took the position.

Give my warm love to Nannie. Tell me a little about Bay's plans.

Yours always,

THEODORE ROOSEVELT.

PARIS,
Sept. 12, 1895.

Dear Theodore:

Your letter of Aug. 27th came more than a week ago and I was especially glad to get it and to hear about Grant and to understand the situation fully. You have managed very well I think and got through that particular difficulty wonderfully well on the whole. I think all will go well politically if Platt will only have the sense to make your issue a party one—but he is singularly lacking in political sense of the large kind. I see by a dispatch in the *Herald* that he has carried all the primaries and that Quigg has resigned. I am surprised at what you say about Quigg going back to Platt. Perhaps he can make him take a sensible view of your fight. Why don't you run for Congress in Quigg's place? The Platt crowd would be delighted to have you do it I should think, and it would be a great opening, but perhaps you would not feel it right to leave the commission so soon. I am glad you put in the bit about Reed and the gold bugs. I am astonished that Smalley judges the situation so ill. Apropos of feeling on that matter I think I wrote you that Eustis* gave me a breakfast and among other things talked foreign affairs. He wants the canal, immediate possession of Hawaii and Cuba, assertion of the Monroe Doctrine and vigor generally. He is a Democrat and a Cleveland appointee. Then I met Ben Cable of Illinois on the street and he said that he hoped that our party would declare most strongly for a vigorous foreign policy and he was going to try to get the Democratic National Convention to do the same,—that on this we ought all to be united. He is a Democrat and a Cleve-

* Mr. James Eustis, American Ambassador to France. He had represented Louisiana in the Senate where I had served with him.

land man. How idle to suppose that the people do not feel as we do. However, Smalley will learn better when Congress meets and we must keep with him for he is all right in the main and a stanch friend to you. I am under no delusion about you. You have won a following, a big one and great reputation. You only need to use these advantages politically—in party matters you can force the machine to give you what you want. In my opinion they will be only too glad to support you. You are too dangerous and too strong for them to fight you profitably. Storer whom I have seen here several times shares my "rosy delusions" about you. He thinks we shall lose Ohio and the Senator on account of Foraker. It is a natural view for him to take, but it will be hard to lose that Senatorship. It looks as if we should get Kentucky.

The weather here for the past ten days has been intensely hot but I have amused myself very well with art and architecture. I am especially fond of the latter and love to study it. It is one of my little weaknesses like my fondness for Belles Lettres which I share with Edith but which I fear does not appeal to your more masculine understanding. We go to Tours for a week among the chateaux of the Loire next Sunday and then into southern France and to Spain.

P. S.—By the way I hear of your family here—Blanche Roosevelt (Bamie's cousin, I believe) was in the bank the day I was there and trying to borrow money on a book she was about to write. John Munroe tells me that Cornelius* owes him twenty thousand dollars—able man Cornelius—J. M. hopes to get it from what Frank left Cornelius but did not seem to [feel] sure.

I got the August *Scribner's* and read your article with pleasure and gratitude. I cannot see why Burlingame put it in the *"Fiction* Number"—that is all right for your writings on Natural History and Western adventure—even your history perhaps, but it seems singularly unfit to group an article which contains such allusions to me under that title.

H. C. L.

---

* Cornelius Roosevelt—son of Weir Roosevelt, first cousin of Theodore—Blanche Roosevelt was an actress, I believe—no relation at all. This Post Script is all chaff.

PARIS,
Sept. 22, 1895.

Dear Theodore:

We are just back from a week at Tours in the Loire Country, among the chateaux and castles. It is full of beauty and interest architectural and historical and we have enjoyed it immensely. We expect to start for Spain on Tuesday or Wednesday next.

While I was at Tours I saw Smalley's account of the New York convention. I do not know whether it would have been politically shrewder to declare for Local Option or not but as S. says they have certainly taken a "manly stand." It is a great triumph for you to be so sustained by your party. Being given to "delusions" I expected it. Now I am going to give you some earnest advice. Your party has made your fight theirs. You must lead it. You owe it to them and to yourself and must win. Do not fail to go on the stump—not through the city where it is needless but through the State where your strength is and where the masses of Republicans are with you. They must see you and get to know you. I regard this as of the utmost importance. I can judge of your standing and reputation better than you and I am a fair judge of political forces. The same political forces which compelled the convention to take your issue will compel them if rightly handled to take you. You have, thanks to your wisdom and good sense, no personal quarrel with the machine and you have a great chance to take the leadership of powerful and controlling elements of the party which can put you in the Senate. You do not realize how you have impressed the popular imagination and that means getting what you want. I am no dreamer either about you or myself. You have a more difficult machine in New York than I had in Massachusetts but then you have a more brilliant and conspicuous position and success than I to go upon. There are to be two Republican Senators from New York soon—one very soon. There is a good chance for you to get the first one if you put yourself at the head of the element which forced your issue on the convention. I do not say you are to be President tomorrow. I do not say it will be —I am sure that it may and can be. I do say that the Senate which is better is well within reach. Stump the State. Get to know the people and insist everywhere on the vital importance of electing a Republican Legislature to choose a Republican Senator. Make speeches for all the State Senators and Assemblymen in their districts that you properly can support and get to know the Assemblymen and Senators. They are as absolutely controlled by a *strong enough* public opinion as members of a convention. You will pardon all this advice but I am sure I am right as I was about your taking this place. My intense interest and belief in you do not mislead me, but the underestimate you always make of your own political position and weight may mislead you.

I received some time since a letter from Cushman Davis* dated August 10th. He is given to rosy delusions and here is what he says. "I see that Theodorus Pacificus is soothing Hill and his followers in New York with characteristic suavity. Seriously, he is aiding the cause of municipal reform everywhere. The corruption in New York presents itself throughout the country even in small cities." Last night I found here a letter from Hayes—another visionary person—but an excellent judge all the same of popular feeling. He says "Mr. Roosevelt is today the most conspicuous figure in American public life. He would make a more popular candidate for President than any man in the country." And then he goes on about you very interestingly and of his delight in your work for two pages. If you were like most men I should not repeat these things to you but you so underrate your political strength that I fear you will neglect to use it and so miss the opportunity which will give you a big place in national politics. Your course is exactly right in your work; I have not a suggestion to make, but you ought to use your success to establish a leadership in the party which will send you to the Senate where you belong. There, my lecture is over. I only ask that you should follow my advice after showing what I have said to Edith who has a proper confidence in my opinion.

Love from all.

Ever yrs., H. C. L.

The Yacht race had a miserable ending but I must say Dunraven has behaved like a baby.

* Then Senator from Minnesota.

300 Mulberry Street,
Dear Cabot,   NEW YORK, October [3rd], 1895.

Things are so hopelessly mixed so far as politics are concerned and matters have gone so much away from our local
stand point, that it has become almost amusing.

First, as a piece of irrelevant information, I had a chance at
the Civil Service dinner the other day to hit Godkin and his
local Civil Service Reform colleagues square between the eyes.
Godkin was not present. He will not come to dinners where I
am; but his colleagues were present, and I included him
specifically by name. I explained that they were utterly inefficient; that they grossly mismanaged the law; and that I
would have been quite unable to get good material for the
Police if I had been kept under them; and that our own Civil
Service Board was ten times as effective, and really did rule
out all questions of politics, while theirs did not.

It was not an important matter, but I enjoyed it nevertheless.

The country Republicans and all the decent church-going
Republicans are very strongly in my favor. The Platt machine
people, especially in this City, are on the verge of open war
with me. I have never alluded to Platt or any of his henchmen
in any speech this summer.

I have made a warfare on the Democracy, which I could
very easily do, as it was controlled by Hill and Tammany. I
have even kept out of factional fighting between the Brookfield and Platt people. The truth simply is, that they will not
pardon me for having administered this office honestly and
fearlessly. Lauterbach, the Chairman of the Republican
County Committee, the other day gave out an authorized
interview as Chairman, in which he stated that the Republican
Party was not in any way responsible for Rooseveltism; and
that there was but one Republican, and that was Grant, on
the Police Board. I am having just about such a time as you
would have if Barrett and Elijah Morse* had complete control of the Republican Party in Massachusetts.

* Member of Congress, inventor of "Rising Sun Stove Polish."

I receive from all over the State requests from Church bodies and non-partisan bodies to speak before them; but these requests I refuse. If I speak at all outside of the city I want to speak to Republican meetings.

My work here in this office is so very engrossing and exhausting that I have had very little time to go into outside politics; but I am making my fight in the strongest way as a Republican, and I do feel a little irritated at the way the machine men ignore what I have done.

I may make one speech outside the State at the Republican Club of Massachusetts. Tom Reed has asked them to ask me. If he goes I shall have to.

Don't think I lack interest in the lovely time you and Nannie are having. Edith and I talk over often your trip through the Loire country and in Spain; but literally I am being driven to death by the work here and the responsibility.

The Republican machine men have been loudly demanding a straight ticket; and those prize idiots, the Goo-Goos, have just played into their hands by capering off and nominating an independent ticket of their own. The ticket is of excellent gentlemen, many of them good Republicans; but whom the Republican Party won't accept, and who cannot possibly be elected.

The result of this is that there actually is no single clear cut issue before the people. No party has dared either to attack me or champion me; and they all dodge the Excise Question. I am speaking almost every night with houses jammed and packed with people wherever I go; but all I can do is to stand up for the Republican State ticket, and ferociously denounce Tammany and the State Democracy.

The cowardice and rascality of the machine Republicans; and the flaming idiocy of the "better element" have been comic, and also disheartening.

Another most annoying thing has been in connection with our book. The *Century* people have deliberately suppressed our signatures to the different pieces, so there is nothing to show which of us wrote them. I have written them that the information must be promptly supplied in the form of an extra leaflet put into each book; and that the change must be made in the table of contents itself before a single other volume is printed.

The enclosed from the *Century* will show that the mistake is being rectified.

Just at this point I received your most welcome letter of the 22nd, ult. It gave me just the advice I needed to have. I think you are quite right, I shall call on the State Committee and see if I cannot go out in some of the Country districts; but I have already been told that the State Committee, which simply registers Platt's decrees has issued a mandate that I am not to be asked to speak; and that they will not allow the regular Republican local Committees to ask me to speak if it can be prevented.

As for my being a United States Senator, I have, as I wrote you, just about as much chance of being Czar of Russia.

Things in this city look badly; but I cannot help feeling that we shall carry the State.

Always yours,

THEODORE ROOSEVELT.

689 MADISON AVENUE

Dear Cabot,   Oct. 11th, '95.

Another note, to be filled full of my own interest in these parochial politics!

I can't help writing you, for I literally have no one here to whom to unburden myself; I make acquaintances very easily, but there are only one or two people in the world, outside of my own family, whom I deem friends or for whom I really care.

Well, at least the greatest dangers are past. I am in line with my party; we have nominated a fusion ticket locally; and I can give both that and the State Ticket hearty support. But the attitude of the Germans has caused a regular panic among our people, from Platt to Strong; and they have all run away from the issue, with the result, of course, that they have not helped themselves in the least, and have immensely strengthened the enemy. Strong has actually been endeavoring to make me let up on the saloon, and impliedly threatened to try to turn me out if I refused! It is needless to say that I told him I would not let up one particle; and would not resign either. The Republican County Convention came within one ace of passing a resolution, which went through their committee of Resolutions, disavowing all responsibility for me, and stating that the Republican party had nothing to do with me. Two or three of my friends, by threatening a bolt, stopped this; but neither the Republicans nor their local allies made any allusion to our work, or dared even to say they believed all laws should be enforced. Tammany, fortunately, is less reticent, and they have attacked me by name, and denounced me for enforcing the law in a "severe and unintelligent" manner. It is almost comic to see the shifts of our State and City party managers in keeping me off the platform; it is at times a little difficult for them, for when they let me go on, I attract more of an audience, and receive more applause, three times over, than any other speaker.

I have no real standing among the party managers, of either side; and I have too much support from the cranks. But at any rate I shall go right on in the course I am pursuing.

Yours, T. R.

MADRID,
Oct. 13th.

Dear Theodore:

We got here night before last after two weeks travelling through the south of France and consequent separation from all letters. Here we found a large collection and among them two from you to my great delight. They were undated but I gather from the postmarks were written about Sept. 25th. You have long ere this received my letter from Paris anent the Convention. After reading the report of the Convention in the *Tribune* and what you say I see no reason looking on as I am from a distance to change my opinion. You evidently expected more and probably had reason to do so. But I think you are too much disappointed and do not, being in the thick

of it realize how much you won. I knew Platt would seek to
ignore the issue and I was in very great anxiety lest he should
succeed. Therefore when the Convention declared for the
maintenance of the Sunday law, the precise point in issue, it
seemed and seems to me a very great victory indeed. Of course
I agree with every word you say about Platt. Of course you
cannot go in with him. I never for a moment meant to imply
that you could. But I do believe that you have forces behind
you in the party which may enable you to force his hand just
as he was forced on the resolution. The chance is certainly
there and you have never made a personal fight with the
machine which would make it life or death to beat you if you
show yourself as I believe you will so strong with the masses,
that they must in prudence accept you, little as the machine
would like it. I sincerely hope you will win, but Smalley's
despatches indicate to me great difficulties in the City from
Platt on one side and the impracticable and hasty good government clubs on the other.

I see Cleveland and his crowd have backed down in Kentucky
most contemptibly and that they are all going in to elect free
silver candidates and "save the State from negro domination." Yet I suppose people in New York and Boston are
still pointing to Cleveland as the noble champion of sound
money. A letter from John Hay to Henry Adams (who left
us in Paris to return home) showed that the McKinley people
were very much alarmed; thought that Quay's victory assured
Penn. to Reed and that N. Y. would follow. I cannot understand the people you speak of in New York being for McK.
I believe Platt has the one virtue of being against an Ohio
candidate. But on these things I am guessing in the dark. I
was very glad to hear what you said about Dunraven; it confirmed my own view. Bay, about whom you ask me means to
live in Paris to study modern languages for a year at the Sor-
bonne and then come home and set to work. I think he will
profit by the study. He is absorbed in the art and architecture
which we have been seeing and sits about absentmindedly a
good deal and then writes. He has written a good deal of verse.
What he will come to I cannot guess. He is struggling for

utterance and when he gets command of his instrument we shall know whether he has anything to say. He has not shown me much of what he has been writing but one thing quite a long poem he has shown. It was suggested by Canterbury and is the *apologia pro vita sua* of Fitzurse giving his view of the killing of Becket. It seems to me quite good. He is working it over and I am going to bring it home for you to see. It is very different from anything of his you have seen—dramatic and narrative.

It seems rather a comedown to drop from your life of activity and work to the travelling of a holiday maker. But the last two weeks we have greatly enjoyed. We left the land of the great Norman Gothic and came to that of the Romanesque churches and of the remains of Rome at Nimes and Orange and Arles. There are two of the latter finer in their way than anything in Italy. One is the theatre at Orange. It strikes you hard to come out into the quiet square and see the back wall of that theatre. "Back-wall" does not sound imposing does it? But this wall is 118 feet high and 330 long and thirteen feet thick and goes right up unsustained to the sky line—plumb and true as the day it was built. You pass through it and there is the auditorium of the theatre cut out of the solid rock of the hill. This was a little provincial theatre, mind you. On the hill above, the castle of the Prince of Orange has crumbled to a few shapeless ruins but the theatre stands. Then the Pont du Gard at Nimes—three tiers of noble arches—one above the other framing earth and sky—160 feet above the beautiful gorge and 880 feet span—built by Agrippa 1900 years ago —no cement and the whole held merely by the weight and the adjustment of the stones and it is as true and solid as when it was first raised. Great building primarily, an imposing architectural effect too. Bay and I scrambled up to the top which was steep enough to have given you a moment's pleasure and went into the water way—7–8 feet high. The sides of huge rough monoliths torn from the mountain side—roofed with flat monoliths on which "men might march on nor be pressed —twelve abreast"— Behind, a tunnel driven through the mountain. Behind again, the way went along a ledge—across a small gorge and through the mountain. And all for what? To bring water 25 miles to the little provincial city of Nimes. I think I felt the force, the might of Rome more that afternoon than ever. Such a prodigality of strength that could use such means for such ends. The Maison Carreé at Nimes is a gem. Then we saw Aigues Mortes and Carcassonne. You would have enjoyed those. Two perfect walled mediæval towns with all their towers and defences perfect and Carcassonne was the wonder of its own time. They are great experiences. The Pyrenees are fine and we came over them into this poverty stricken country. From France here a great deal of savage scenery but for the habitation of civilized man for 2500 years an inconceivable picture. You never saw such desolate dreary plains and here and there a dying town. Even Madrid is bleak and cheerless. The people repel one, looking at the general effect of them seen by a traveller which is an important point of view. They seem sullen and indifferent. The manners you meet and notice are cold and rude. They are beaten, broken and out of the race and are proud and know it. They depress and repel me like their landscape. But the gallery is magnificent. As John Hay says in his "Castilian Days": "It is Eclipse first and the rest nowhere." There is one room which contains more perfect specimens of more great masters than I ever saw within four walls. I longed for Edith as I sat there yesterday.

Hannis Taylor has been to call; he is very pleasant, and very kindly insists on dining us. I do not want society when sightseeing. This is intolerable this letter—"It shall to the barber's with your beard"—Goodbye. Best love to Edith. I am longing now for home whither we soon turn our footsteps. I am beginning to be restless and anxious to be back. I love that great land of mine across the sea so much better than anything else.

Yrs., H. C. L.

Smalley I see has found out that there is something in Venezuela!

POLICE DEPARTMENT
OF THE CITY OF NEW YORK

300 Mulberry Street,
NEW YORK, Oct. 18th, 1895.

Dear Cabot:

You are doomed to read another letter filled with parochial politics. One danger at least I have surmounted; I met the Mayor fair and square on the Excise question; and I told him no matter what he did or what stand he took, I would not alter my course a particle; and that I should make it clear that the entire responsibility for the split between us on this issue rested with him. He was terribly angry; but when he found I would not change, and the crisis came, he was more afraid of me than of all the Germans who were pushing him from behind; and he said he would do nothing until after election. I care very little what he does after election.

The Republican machine has acted as badly toward me as it possibly can. The Platt people really seem bent on making me refuse to vote the fusion ticket. Lauterbach, the Chairman of our City campaign Committee, has not only read me out of the party, but Grant as well, stating that Murray and Kerwin were excellent Republicans, and were turned out for the sake of two men who are not Republicans at all. He has fully stated this again and again. The State and City Committees have resolutely declined to allow me to speak at any meeting over which they had control. It made no difference as far as the State Committee is concerned because my work here is so engrossing that I could not go to any place whence I could not return by the night train; for I cannot afford to be absent a single entire day; and all the State Senators within a striking distance of New York are Platt men pure and simple; but you can gain an idea from this of the absolute hopelessness of my trying to do anything with the machine as it now is. Nevertheless, I speak for the State and City Republican ticket every night and two and three times a night. The meetings I address are more largely attended and more fully reported than those of the regular party organizations.

Last evening, I spoke at an immense Republican mass meeting in Baltimore, where I was the guest of the evening. We have a good chance of carrying Maryland. I went to Baltimore on the 3:20 P.M. train, and took the mid-night train back. I have so far, with no little self command, refrained from hitting at any of the Republican people; but after election is over, I am far from certain that I shall keep my hands off them. However, if possible, I shall wait until I see you before taking action. Their conduct toward me has been base to a degree; and they have greatly injured themselves by flinching from the issue. Thanks to the way I have rallied the church-going people and the City Vigilance people, we stand a fair chance of winning (in spite of the idiocy of the "goo-goos"); but had they made the fight boldly along the lines I had marked out, there would not have been a shadow of doubt as to the result in either State or City.

Last Saturday night I spoke at an immense meeting over which Joe Murray presided; the other speakers included the Paulist Father Doyle, and a Methodist preacher Dr. Iglehardt, both of whom attacked Tammany Hall ferociously. If the Republicans had followed my lead this would have been a regular Republican meeting under the auspices of the City Committee; while as it was I had to hold it under the auspices of one of my own assembly district Republican Clubs.

In great haste, I am, Always yours,

THEODORE ROOSEVELT.

P. S.—Tom Reed appeared here on Thursday and called on me at once. I went around to see him on Friday morning. I had a very pleasant talk with him. I was amused at his humorous and thorough understanding of my own relations with the machine here. He asked me with great interest about you; and laughed himself purple over my account of the persistency with which you look at my position here through spectacles which are not merely rosy but crimson. He is in excellent health and temper, and thinks the drift is his way. He tells me I may have to go on to Boston next week to speak at a dinner for him.

POLICE DEPARTMENT
OF THE CITY OF NEW YORK

300 Mulberry Street,
Dear Cabot: NEW YORK, October 20th, 1895.

On Monday last in pursuance of a long standing promise I had to deliver an address in Boston. I found the audience much more in sympathy with me than, I regret to say, a corresponding New York audience would be. I was more touched than I can say to see in the very front row your dear mother and John. I only had time to shake hands with them afterwards. Sturgis Bigelow was present too, so that all your immediate belongings showed their usual loyalty to me. Sturgis took me around to the Club for a small hot supper before I caught the midnight train to come home.

I am sorry to say Quigg will no longer have anything to do with me. He insisted upon being given the Police advertising which, as you may recollect, was taken away from the *Tribune* last year and given to the *Press* by Platt. The *Tribune* also applied for it, as did the other Republican papers. I followed what was obviously the proper course of giving it to the lowest bidder. Quigg, himself, then put in a bid of just one-sixth the amount that he charged the City last year; but the *Tribune* under-bidding got it. Quigg took the result in high dudgeon and went about explaining that I was his "creation," his personal appointee, and had been guilty of base ingratitude. He is a goose.

This morning I had a note from Edith (I have not seen my family for nearly a week) in which she says "I think you have been wonderfully judicious in your speeches. I think Cabot would approve of them. I only wish you had not said the Goo-Goos had gone silly."

Edith always keeps you in view as a mentor. I did completely lose my temper with the Goo-Goos, and gave them two or three slashing blows.

Our fusion ticket is on the whole very good. It is decidedly better than the fusion ticket last year. It is of the utmost importance to elect it over the Tammany ticket; and it is hard to control my indignation at the action of the Goo-Goos in running a ticket of their own on grounds that are so trivial that it is really difficult to state them; as for understanding them, why the Goo-Goos themselves don't do that.

Last night there was a big Republican meeting held by the County Committee in Carnegie Hall. Of course I was excluded, so I went up and addressed a meeting of the same size in support of the fusion ticket and against Tammany, this meeting being organized specially for me. So far the incident is common place; but to my immense amusement the audience at Carnegie Hall most loudly demanded me. They are all Republicans of course, and they gave Lauterbach and Quigg and the other speakers perfunctory applause; and then of their own accord they would cheer for me. The result was that Lauterbach in his speech had to incorporate some statements as to my worth and services.

I spoke at the Republican Club dinner in Massachusetts where we gave Tom Reed a send off. I sat on Greenhalge's right. He spoke to me most feelingly of you, and said he never could say how much he had missed you and longed for your advice and help this summer. He remarked that he had no idea how much he leaned on you until you went away, for that there was literally no one who could in anyway take your place.

It was like a fresh spring after a fetid pool to get among those Republicans; I mean Greenhalge, Wolcott, Lyman, Frank Appleton, Frank Lowell, George Meyer, and that very good young fellow Moody,* who is running in Cogswell's place. What a contrast they are to the men who manage our Republican campaign here. Of course they are literally unable to understand why any Republican could possibly question the propriety of what I have been doing here, or indeed the necessity for it; and they were most curious in their inquiries as to what Platt and his lieutenants could mean.

I enclose you a speech which Lauterbach has just made. He and his allies have been going all around attacking me in this manner. Of course they do the ticket an incalculable amount of harm. They have for months been sedulously inculcating

* W. H. Moody—afterward a member of Roosevelt's Cabinet and a Justice of the Supreme Court.

among the Germans and doubtful voters that we are wrong in our Excise policy. I really think they seem anxious to beat the fusion ticket, so that they may turn around and say it is my fault. As for the Goo-Goo people, who are running a straight ticket, their folly is literally incalculable. I enclose you a letter I wrote them about it.

I have revelled in your description of Southern France. I am taking the letter out to show Edith. Don't think because I am so absorbed in my work here that I don't appreciate to the full your letters; but it has been an awful struggle, and I have been very lonely. I have not had one political friend of any weight from whom I could get a particle of advice or of real support. Now it seems to me as though, through no fault of mine, we are to meet defeat in this City. The only thing that can save us is the campaign that I and three or four of my friends have waged. I doubt if this will be sufficient in view of the folly and stupidity of our own party managers and of these Goo-Goos. However, whether defeat comes or not, I am entirely prepared for every attack that will be made; and I shall not alter my course here one handsbreadth, even though Tammany carries the city by fifty thousand. I cannot but believe that in the end decent Republicans, not only here, but elsewhere, will support my course.

Always yours,
THEODORE ROOSEVELT.

PARIS,
Oct. 23rd, [1895.]

Dear Theodore:

I have had two letters from you that of Oct. 3d (undated) in Madrid and your note of the 11th here last night. The situation has been most trying—I can only say that I think you have behaved most wisely and exactly right and your position is impregnable and will bear fruit. The Germans behave very badly. They prefer beer to principle. What amazes me most about the machine is not their being wrong but their utter stupidity. The issue was their chance and they neither rejected you nor sustained you. Anything more idiotic I have never seen. The Goo-Goos have behaved as they always do. I am amazed at what you tell me of Strong. Meantime the substantial victory is with you. The convention stood by you, you have a good fusion ticket and even the city Republicans did not dare officially to throw you over. You are strong with the people, you have their ear, your party standing before the country is unimpeachable, you are right and you have made a very big national reputation. All this will bear fruit besides being worth while itself. I am glad you got that hit at Godkin. You are quite right in refusing to speak except at Republican meetings. Let it be known quietly that the committee will not let you speak—not as coming from you of course but let the fact get out. It will help. I have not much hope of the City but I think you will get the State and it is of the last importance to hold the Assembly for the Senator. The news I have seen the last day or two as to England and Venezuela has put me on pins and needles to get home. If we allow England to invade Venezuela nominally for reparation, as at Corinto, really for territory our supremacy in the Americas is over. I am worried and angry beyond words at what I see. England is simply playing the Administration for what she can get. I hope to hear something from home by tomorrow's papers. I have written Edith of our doings.

Ever yrs., H. C. L.

PARIS,
Oct. 23rd, 1895.

Dear Edith:

Your letter came to me just as we were leaving Madrid and so I delayed my answer until we reached Paris. You were so good to write to me and you cannot think how pleased I was to have you tell me of the book. I confess I thought very slightly of the tales written by me except the Lowell*

* Charles Russel Lowell:

"To him who, deadly hurt, agen
Flashed on afore the charge's thunder,
Tippin' with fire the bolt of men
Thet rived the Rebel line asunder."

and I am not only pleased but greatly relieved to know that you think well of them for I have as you know a great deal of confidence in your literary taste and judgment. The omitting of the table of contents with the names seems to me utterly inexcusable and as if it must have been wilful. I was also very glad to know from you about Theodore and how he is for I have worried a little as to the effects of the fatigue and anxiety upon him. I shall enclose in this a note to him on his affairs. I believe when I last wrote Theodore I had not been to the bull fight. Bay and I went with our Minister, Taylor, and saw the show a week ago Sunday. One bull and part of another round satisfied Bay and he cleared out. I remained and saw four. I wanted to satisfy myself in regard to it. I expected it to be bloody and brutal and it was. I had also expected to be excited and I was not. I found it stupid and tiresome. One round is exactly like another. The bull, a most splendid animal, is doomed. He has no chance. The only doubt is whether he will get the matador in whose fate I felt but a mild interest. The men are very skilful, strong, bold and marvellously active. But the goring of the horses, poor blind-folded beasts, is hideous. I saw 4 bulls tortured and killed and they gored and killed 9 horses in the ring and mortally wounded three others. The place was a shambles. It is the last remnant of Rome surviving in an age where it has no place. The Span-iards love it. It is about all they are fit for and if the world were suddenly put back 400 years the Spaniard is the only person who would find himself at home. He would not do in the Roman time for the Roman if bloody could also fight and govern and the Spaniard nowadays can do neither. I have a terrible suspicion that I wrote all this to Theodore before. If I did forgive me for I have so many letters to write that I get muddled as to dates.

Mr. Hannis Taylor was very polite to us. He is a man of ability but anecdotical. Mr. Taylor had us to dinner with the Chamberlains who happened to be in Madrid. Then Canovas the Prime Minister sent word that he would like to see Mr. Chamberlain and myself and so Taylor and an old Count Saldanha of the Privy Council escorted us there in state and we had a long and pleasant call on Canovas, who is a clever and interesting man, the ablest in Spain, Taylor says. We talked of many things and to me Canovas discoursed of Cuba and I replied guardedly. They are in a state of mind over it and dreadfully afraid we shall intervene. Altogether the call was an interesting incident. We lived in the gallery in Madrid and it is beyond words. We also went to Toledo, a wonderful old place with some beautiful bits of Moorish architecture as well as its cathedral which in its way is one of the examples of Gothic building best worth seeing. That was our ultima Thule and thence we sped here—sped is figurative applied to Spanish trains—as fast as we could. We expect Bamie here tonight which will be very delightful. Two weeks here and then we shall sail and altho' the outing has been a great success I shall be very glad to get home. I am so glad to hear of the children and that. the god-baby* loves Jessie— Best love from Nannie.

Ever yrs., H. C. LODGE.

POLICE DEPARTMENT
OF THE CITY OF NEW YORK

300 Mulberry Street,
Dear Cabot: NEW YORK, Oct. 29, 1895.

This will be the last letter you will have from me. I congratulate you much. I enclose you at Edith's request a clipping from the *Sun* which will rejoice your heart. The exhibition of snobbery in regard to the Duke of Marlborough this fall has been loathsome.

The Boston *Herald* and the *Evening Post* have made long and vicious attacks on me for my jingo speech the other night. Senator Vilas has also written me an exceedingly angry letter because of my article in *Scribner's* in which I touched on him and his Civil Service Record. Joe Quincy has also made a public attack upon me for having "violated the principle of

* Archie Roosevelt.

nonpartisanship," by going around the country speaking for
the Republican party. So you see I am having a good deal of
outside fun. I now speak two and three times every night. I
am inclined to think the tide has begun to set our way. For
one thing the Police have done excellent work—work such as
has never been done before—in preventing fraudulent registration. The registration has fallen off somewhat in the Republican wards; but it has fallen off far more in the Tammany
wards, thanks to the thoroughness with which we have gone
over the so-called lodging-house or mattress vote. In Diver's*
district it is one-third less than last year. As I said, the tide is
now our way; whether it is flowing strong enough to reach
flood before election day I don't know.

After election day I shall try to get a day or two in the
country every week, for the strain is beginning to tell on me a
little; but after all it is not enough to speak of, for I feel as
strong as a bull-moose.

When I see you I want to tell you all about my colleagues.
I have had two or three rough times with them recently, and
it has only been by a mixture of tact, good humor and occasional heavy hitting that I have kept each one in line.

Give my best love to Nannie. I suppose you will turn up
about the twenty-fourth.   Yours always,

THEODORE ROOSEVELT.

P. S.—Your cable has just come. Edith was in town to
spend the night with me, and was more moved than she often
is at your sending it. "Dear Cabot," she said, "I do believe
that next to myself he cares more for you than any one else in
the world does." All right! I won't attack any one.

Kerwin, my predecessor, who has been so praised for his
"stalwart Republicanism," and compared to whom the Platt
people said I was a mugwump, has just declared his adherence
to the Tammany ticket!

* Paddy (?) Diver a well known Tammany leader of that time.

PARIS,
Oct. 30th, 1895.

Dear Theodore:

You may have been surprised to get a cable from me today, but one sentence in your letter of the 18th troubled me and that was where you said that you might attack the Machine after election. That I would not have you do for the world. I know how trying it all is, I know how stupidly and outrageously they have behaved but to come out and denounce Platt is simply to play Platt's game. He cares nothing for attack and it would enable him to say that you were attacking the party. Their reading you out of the party shows that you are in it and that they want to get you out. They can't get you out. You can only do that yourself. Mr. Lauterbach looks important in N. Y. City—he is pretty small in the State and absolutely unknown outside of it. You are known all over the country and known as a Republican. What Mr. Lauterbach says is of no consequence. What you say and do is of vast consequence. If the time has come for you to fight Platt as I think quite probable—say nothing—be *very* regular but go to work and organize the anti-Platt forces,—Warner Miller, Brookfield, Fassett, Pavey, etc., he has enemies everywhere— and fight for those delegates who are anti-Platt. Robertson did it against Conkling, a far stronger man in 1880 and got 24— You may get 5—10—20— The moment you hit him then you reach him. Attack by words helps him. There is material for such a fight as there was in 1880. It only needs courageous leadership and organization. They let Platt do all the organizing and so he wins. At all events say nothing and make no attack until I see you. Your present attitude is admirable and impregnable. Hold it. I may be over sanguine about you and that fat man from Maine and you may laugh at me but I am a better politician than the pair of you rolled into one and "just" you follow my advice. Love to Edith.

Yrs.,
H. C. L.

POLICE DEPARTMENT
OF THE CITY OF NEW YORK

300 Mulberry Street,

Dear Cabot: NEW YORK, Dec. 2nd, 1895.

I enclose a clipping from the *Evening Post* which really pleases me. I wish you would show it to Reed, and then send it back again. The *Post*, in view of my attitude on Reed and our foreign policy, has been obliged to give up all attempt to support me in my police work.

This is comic rather than serious; but the attitude of the Platt people here in New York *is* serious. Nothing ever done by Tammany or by the Southern Democrats in the way of fraudulent management of primaries and of stuffing and padding the district associations, has surpassed what Platt has been doing recently. The decent Republicans are getting savage, and there is very ugly talk of establishing a separate county organization and of sending a rival set of delegates to the National Convention. These delegates will represent the best element in the party here, the element without which the party will be in a hopeless minority, and will in point of character stand not much above Tammany; but the evil feature of it is that many of them will not be Reed men. I am getting seriously alarmed . lest Platt's utter unscrupulousness and cynical indifference to the wellfare of the party, unless it redounds to his own personal benefit, should make the decent people here indifferent on the Presidential question and muddle everything in a desire to beat Platt. I wish Quigg could have gotten me a chance to see Platt, talk with him, and sound him on the Reed matter.

I now see two rocks ahead; first that Platt may decide to throw over Reed; and second, that the anti-Platt people, many of whom are for McKinley or Harrison, may be thrown by Platt into a combination against him and whomever he supports. The minute I find out anything of importance I shall communicate at once with either you or Reed. Don't think that I am gloomy as to the outlook, it is only that I wish to keep the dangers in mind.

Always yours,

THEODORE ROOSEVELT.

POLICE DEPARTMENT
OF THE CITY OF NEW YORK

300 Mulberry Street,
NEW YORK, Dec. 6th, 1895.

Dear Cabot:

I was delighted to see that you put in your Venezuela resolution. If I ever see Smalley I am going to talk with him about
the Venezuela matter now. The seriousness with which you
spoke of *The Evening Post* editorial made me think I might
have sent you the wrong one, so I accordingly enclose what I
thought was a duplicate; glance over it, and send it back. My
soul was delighted over the wounded bird's flutterings, and it
made me think that I wrote a pretty good article in *The Forum.*
Yours always,
THEODORE ROOSEVELT.

P. S.—A little later most certainly Edith and I will come on
to visit you. I should very much like a holiday; but I know
you appreciate as well as I that now and then you get hold of
a thing you can't drop. If you see Quigg give him the hint
that Platt and I ought to meet. It is barely possible I may be
on for the afternoon of the 12th; and to dine that evening; it
may be impossible for me to get out of a speech to the National
Civil Service Reform Ass:

POLICE DEPARTMENT
OF THE CITY OF NEW YORK

300 Mulberry Street,
NEW YORK, Dec. 13th, 1895.

Dear Cabot:

Pray treat this letter as strictly confidential, except as
regards Tom Reed whom it concerns, and to whom I wish you
to show it. I find that Gov. Morton is angry over my support
of Reed, and is in consequence relied upon to support some of
the bills aimed at the Police Department and especially at me.
There will evidently be a resolute effort to legislate me out of
office, in some manner this year. I consulted with Reed last
summer, and he then advised me that I should support Morton

if the delegation did, and if he was in the field. Of course as a matter of fact I would have to anyway, or otherwise I could not do anything whatever in this State; but I may find it necessary to tell Morton that I have told Reed this and that I will as a matter of course support him, (Morton) if he is put in nomination. Now will you show this to Reed at once, and let him write me absolutely frankly, or rather let him speak to you frankly, and you write to me, so that I can get it by Tuesday morning. I have a sufficiently difficult road anyhow, and if I can legitimately avoid trouble I want to. Of course you and Tom understand that if you think it wise to go for him at the outset I shall do so; but I think this would merely hurt all chance of my being useful to him in the end and it seems to me the best thing on every account that I should be for Morton if Morton is the State's candidate.

Pray write me at once.   Always yours,
THEODORE ROOSEVELT.

POLICE DEPARTMENT
OF THE CITY OF NEW YORK

300 Mulberry Street,
NEW YORK, Dec. 20th, 1895.

Hon. Henry Cabot Lodge, Senate Chamber, Washington, D. C.

Dear Cabot: I am very much pleased with the President's or rather with Olney's message*; I think the immense majority of our people will back him. I earnestly hope he will receive full support from both houses of Congress. This is a most remarkable vindication of your attitude last Spring; I think that feature of it has given *The Nation* peculiar anguish. I am angry with General Grosvenor's speech, here in New York; he is most willing to show the white feather, and has no sense of honor, official or personal. I do hope there will not be any back down among our people. Let the fight come if it must; I don't care whether our sea coast cities are bombarded or not; we would take Canada.

* The Venezuela Message.

The fool of a Mayor could not resist making a sinuous attack on me, but he got the worst of it, I think.

Always yours,

THEODORE ROOSEVELT.

P. S.—Last evening I dined at Cruger's to meet the various heads of the City Departments, Brookfield, Collins, McCook, LaGrange, Murray, Wright, etc. We had a very animated talk; the overmastering feeling among all was bitter indignation with Platt; not mere factional indignation, but anger at the scoundrelly dishonesty with which the primary associations have been padded, as even Tammany has never dared to pad. They were most anxious to form a new county committee; but we Reed men succeeded in stopping this. The danger is over at least for the present. The decent Republicans who are not for Reed are getting perfectly willing to throw the whole apple cart over; and if Platt continues in his present frame of mind we shall undoubtedly have some ugly talk to meet if Reed is nominated through him. For this very reason I was of course most anxious to prevent any split in our local party organizations. A year hence, after the Presidential election, I am perfectly willing it should come; and indeed it is evident it has got to come unless the Platt people see a great light; but I finally carried my plans, and there will be at present no break. If we can secure a few decent Reed Republicans as delegates from this city through the regular organizations it will prevent much of the criticism which would certainly arise if Platt delegates of the stamp of the Abe Gruber, Lauterbach and Company are the only ones that go for Reed from this city. As I said the danger is temporarily over, but the Lauterbach people seem literally crazy in their desire to run any risk to the party if they can benefit themselves; and I don't know how much more the decent Republicans will stand. The Primaries next Tuesday will of course go overwhelmingly for Platt, and it is a very bitter thing for the decent Republicans to have to submit to a victory of people at least half of whose vote will be fraudulent; there never has been anything like the frauds of the late registration.

I write you so much at length because I think it most important that you should try to shape the Reed canvass so that it won't look as if he was being nominated by Platt and Quay. I get nervous for fear of popular clamor being aroused by this. If Morton is a candidate all will have to go as Morton men from here.

T. R.

SAGAMORE HILL,
OYSTER BAY, LONG ISLAND, N. Y.,
Dec. 23d, '95.

Dear Cabot,

Just a line to wish a merry Xmas to you and Nannie; Edith and I have been rather gloomily commenting on the fact that our last five Xmas dinners were eaten at your house; and now we shan't see you at all. Early in January I must get on to see you if only for a couple of days, for I must unburden myself.

Here I am living in a welter of small political intrigue, of the meanest kind. Quigg has been telling me he wished me to go with him as a delegate; and I find he has also promised Abe Gruber, and is merely waiting to see which way he can best turn over his own forces. I find that Whitelaw Reid was given orders that in the *Tribune* I am not to be mentioned save to attack me, unless it is unavoidable; this came to me in a curious fashion, first hand. Mayor Strong has been guilty of flagrant double dealing, and intends to attack us in his message to the Board of Aldermen. The Platt people are planning to legislate me out of office under cover of a necessary amendment to the Greater New York bill; and are getting Morton's help by insisting that I am for Tom Reed, whereas *they* are for Morton—and are trying to impress Reed to the contrary meanwhile. Many of the Brookfield wing, headed by the Mayor, are really hostile to me because they wish either McKinley or Harrison.

Every now and then I feel a momentary discouragement; for it really seems that there *must* be some fearful shortcoming on my side to account for the fact that I have not one N. Y.

city newspaper or one N. Y. city politician of note on my side. Don't think that I even for a moment dream of abandoning my fight; I shall continue absolutely unmoved on my present course and shall accept philosophically whatever violent end may be put to my political career.

There! I've made my wail to the only person to whom I *can* make it, and feel better.

The 4th volume of my "Winning of the West" is done.

By the way, the *Century* people have been asked to bring out in form for the blind, or rather allow to be brought out, our "Hero Tales" and Kipling's "Jungle Book." Kipling consented; and I told them of course we consented too. You have done admirably in your speeches about Venezuela; I do hope we shall not back down. Reed seems to have done excellently with his committees; of course I regret the choice of Brosius for the C. S. R. Committee; he joined with Raines to attack me on behalf of Wanamaker.

Yours, T. R.

POLICE DEPARTMENT
OF THE CITY OF NEW YORK

300 Mulberry Street,
NEW YORK, Dec. 27th, 1895.

Dear Cabot:

Your two letters were a great comfort and pleasure. Don't imagine that I really get very blue. Every now and then I feel sullen for an hour or two when everybody seems to join against me here; but I would not for anything give up my experience of the last eight months; I prize them more than any other eight months in all my official career. You were more than wise in advising me to come here.

I am deeply interested in what you say about Harrison. It looks now as if Platt was going to make a serious effort on behalf of Morton, and if that proves useless to go in for Reed. I must say it irks me a little to have to be for Morton. I like the old gentleman well enough; but my whole heart is in the

Reed canvass and I feel all the time that very uncomfortable sensation of sailing under false colors. However, I suppose that by what I have written and spoken about him I have really given him more help—slight though this help was—than I could give him by an attempt to get a Reed delegate in some one New York district. I doubt if I can get to St. Louis myself, and may have to limit my exertions to get in two delegates from our district who will be straight out Reed men for second choice.

It seems to me that our action on the tariff under Reed's leadership was admirable; we have countered on Cleveland most effectively.

I most earnestly hope that our people won't weaken in any way on the Venezuela matter. The antics of the bankers, brokers and anglomaniacs generally are humiliating to a degree; but the bulk of the American people will I think surely stand behind the man who boldly and without flinching takes the American view.

As you say, thank God I am not a free-trader. In this country pernicious indulgence in the doctrine of free trade seems inevitably to produce fatty degeneration of the moral fibre. Did you read the *Sun's* admirable editorial upon the damage done to England by American correspondents of the British Press, who utterly misrepresented the whole tone of American thought?

Smalley's whole attitude is contemptible beyond words. As for the Editors of the *Evening Post* and *World* it would give me great pleasure to have them put in prison the minute hostilities began. I felt I must give utterance to my feelings. I am more indignant than I can say at the action of the Harvard people. Do you think there would be any harm in my writing to the *Crimson* a smashing letter as per enclosed giving my views and saying a word for Patriotism and Americanism; unless I hear from you to the contrary I think I shall send this on. I wish to at least do what I can to save Harvard from degredation. Our peace at any price men, if they only knew it, are rendering war likely, because they will encourage England to persist; in the long run this means a fight. Personally I

rather hope the fight will come soon. The clamor of the peace
faction has convinced me that this country needs a war.

Give my best love to Nannie.

Always yours,

THEODORE ROOSEVELT.

If you like what I say to the *Crimson*, return it, and I will
send it.

1896

SAGAMORE HILL,
OYSTER BAY, LONG ISLAND, N. Y.,
Jan. 2d, '96.

Dear Cabot,

I entirely agree with you and Nannie as to your action on
the Cuban resolution; vote against it in Committee, and if
it comes up in the Senate explain your vote just as in your
interview, making it clear that you will support any such
resolution the moment there is hope of making it effective,
but that until then you will not take part in worse than waste
of time, and in blocking needed legislation. I am going to
write to Wolcott.

Here matters are worse than ever. The machine is really
infamous. Not only do they back Parker, but they have
induced Grant by the promise of their aid with McKinley,
and he has openly gone in with Parker. I have said the latter
is a liar a dozen times; I cannot shoot him, or engage in a
rough-and-tumble with him—I couldn't even as a private
citizen, still less as the chief peace officer of the city; and I
hardly know what course to follow as he is utterly unabashed
by exposure and repeats lie after lie with brazen effrontery.

Best love to Nannie.

Yours,   T. R.

POLICE DEPARTMENT
OF THE CITY OF NEW YORK

300 Mulberry Street,

Dear Cabot:—   NEW YORK, Jan. 2nd, 1896.

I thought your speech admirable. You had a great historic question and you handled it in a way that I seriously think entitles you to feel that your speech will rank as a public document with the speeches of the great men in time past when they discussed great questions; that is, with some of the best speeches of Webster and some of the State papers of Adams. It was a great opportunity and you took advantage of it.

Edith will soon write Nannie asking if we can come on toward the end of this month, I think she says on the 24th, Friday, to stay over Sunday and return Tuesday. Whether I can spend more than three days I rather doubt. I want to see Reed and Cushman Davis; and any one else you wish— Adams, Phillips, the Hays, the Wolcotts, the Hagues. We are in a very ugly fight here and I am nearly as bitterly opposed by the Strong-Brookfield crowd as by the Platt people. I finally broke with the *Tribune* last week, and they have come out as our open foes because I would not give in to the Milholland and Cornelius Bliss effort to make a separate county committee. Here the people who most earnestly demand this committee are secret foes of Reed; and this has been part of the trouble with the *Tribune*, though of course it began when I refused to give them the advertising, and let it out by open bidding.

I shall send on the letter to the *Crimson*.

Moorfield Storey's course is just what I should expect from him; but I regret that some of the Harvard Professors could be led into doing what they have done. They are rapidly confirming me in the feeling that there ought to be a war.

All right! I will find out about the "Hero Tales" from the Century people as you suggest.

We all came in town today. As for my own endless troubles in this office I shall not try to tell you about them until I see you. At present I literally have not got a friend in this city of any note, whether a newspaper man or a politician; and I am rather inclined to think that they will succeed in legislating me out of office; but they will not succeed in making me alter my position one handsbreadth.

I feel that Morton's candidacy will have a very serious side.

Always yours,

THEODORE ROOSEVELT.

P. S.—   Jan. 3rd, 1896.

I find that the first edition of two thousand copies of the "Hero Tales" is sold and over half of the second edition of the same number.

POLICE DEPARTMENT
OF THE CITY OF NEW YORK

300 Mulberry Street,
NEW YORK,
Jan. 6, 1896.

Dear Cabot:—

I quite agree with you on every point. Just as far as I possibly can I am now striving to avoid all possible rows with Parker, and to confine them to as courteous a basis as possible. The trouble is that in this issue, the *Sun*, which, in any emergency of the kind referring to municipal affairs, always rises above consideration of truth and honesty, backs Parker because that is part of the agreement with the machine.

At the Greater New York hearing the other day the alliance between him and Lauterbach and Lexow was entirely open. The *Tribune* dislikes me, and will take no stand either way; they have never forgiven my refusing to supply them with the printing business as a job; the *World, Journal* and *Herald*, of course wish to attack the Police Department for being decent, and so they side with any one who will attack me.

I was at the dinner to Cornelius Bliss at the Republican Club last evening, and he called on me to speak, which I did. I think I could go to him frankly myself for my relations are entirely cordial. What do you think about my calling on him?

I have received an extremely kind letter from Harry Davis, which I shall answer at once.

Always yours,

THEODORE ROOSEVELT.

POLICE DEPARTMENT
OF THE CITY OF NEW YORK

300 Mulberry Street,
NEW YORK, Jan. 10th, 1896.

Dear Cabot :—

I wish we could stay longer, but I am afraid it is impossible; you see we will occupy four days any how; I shall take the night train home on Monday, so as to get here in time on Tuesday and let Edith follow next day. Until we get the Albany matters settled one way or the other I would not feel comfortable if I was too long away.

There has been a certain stern satisfaction in fighting against such heavy odds; I have not the slightest doubt as to the propriety and wisdom of our own course. The Police Force is better than it ever has been; the aggregate of crime smaller than ever before in New York. I do earnestly hope that my own party will not legislate me out of office; but it is less for my own sake than for the force and the party itself. The full details I shall have to tell you when we meet.

My letter to *The Crimson* about Harvard's attitude toward England drew blood. There was a delightful attack on me in the Boston *Herald*. I have had twenty or thirty letters from Harvard men thanking me for having written it.

I greatly enjoyed yesterday in Boston at the Overseers meeting.* I went on there one night and came back the next, so I am feeling rather sleepy just at this moment. I stopped with Sturgis Bigelow, and had a dear call on your mother. She is so sweet and cunning and so absorbed in your speech and your triumph; and so wrought up over the attacks on me.

Give my warm love to Nannie.

Yours always,

THEODORE ROOSEVELT.

* He had been elected an Overseer of Harvard in 1895.

POLICE DEPARTMENT
OF THE CITY OF NEW YORK

300 Mulberry Street,
NEW YORK, Jan. 15th, 1896.

Dear Cabot:—

I am sorry to say that Platt and his people, headed by Lauterbach, are resolutely bent upon legislating us out of office. It merely depends upon whether they think the religious vote is sufficiently worked up on the matter. The eager demand of the Brooklyn clergymen and priests to have the law enforced as it is here in New York will make them hesitate a little.

I am going to speak before the conference of Methodist ministers next Monday, and I am going to give the Republican majority some pretty plain talk. I hear from inside that Platt is trying to see what candidate for the Presidency will promise him most!

Yes! I think my interview was a success. It produced a raving letter from Hart*; the kind of anger which showed shame underneath.

I lunched with Norman† today. It certainly looks as if we were getting out all right in the Venezuela matter; and no man is entitled to more credit to it than you.

I need hardly say how I am looking forward to seeing you. I have very, very much to tell you. I have staunch friends among the Republican Senators and Assemblymen, no less than among the Republican masses, but I am ashamed to say that the *Evening Post*, which is of course ferociously attacking me as a "jingo" has nevertheless on the whole stood up better for my work during the last eight months than any single Republican paper in New York.

Love to Nannie!

Always yours,
THEODORE ROOSEVELT.

---

* Professor Albert Bushnell Hart; later a very warm supporter of Roosevelt. They were classmates.
† Henry Norman of London.

689 MADISON AVENUE

Dear Cabot,   Jan. 19th, '96.

I have written to the Century people for the accounts.

Nothing can be done with Wolcott*; he is an impossible person to work with. Indeed I think it would be well if all the ultra silver men left our party. They are on the whole a weakness.

The Harvard Graduates Magazine is now assailing me with the ineffective bitterness proper to beings whose cult is non-virility.

I had a very interesting conference with Platt, and shall tell not only you but Reed all about it. We got along very well, in an entirely pleasant and cold-blooded manner. They intend to legislate me out in about 60 days; and are confident they can do it—sure of it in fact; but I think there may be delays and obstacles which they don't take into account which may keep me in until some time in April. I shall not break with the party; the Presidential contest is too important; and I never sulk when I don't go to extremes. I can't go as a delegate; Quigg and Gruber are slated from my district; and I will not join the Brookfield people in a bolt which would be sure to turn out anti-Reed as well as anti-Platt.

Can't we breakfast with Henry Adams (making him ask Willie Phillips) some time? But what I chiefly wish is to see as much of Nannie and you as you can stand. I must have a good talk with Tom Reed; if possible you must be present.

Yours, T. R.

689 MADISON AVENUE

Dear Cabot,   Feb. 16th, '96.

The three days with you made an oasis. I have been working like a beaver ever since. One of my most difficult tasks is to keep my colleagues together. We *must* not have a split now; and I have to put up with all sorts of compromises in order to avoid it. But gradually I am getting an immense amount of work done. The factional bitterness here is intense. Only

* Senator E. O. Wolcott of Colorado.

the deep distrust felt for the Democracy can save us from a defeat even this year. On the fight for Presidential delegates I fear greatly I shall have to assist the Platt people. In my own district I can do nothing; Quigg and Gruber represent the majority very well. But in the district above, which the anti-Platt people hold, I fear Joe Murray will have to turn against them, and join with a Platt man, in order to prevent two anti-Reed delegates being sent by the Strong forces. This is a disagreeable thing to do; and I shall take as little open a part as may be; but of course I wish to strengthen Reed in every way possible. Is Morton looked upon as a real candidate outside New York?

Your speeches on civil service reform were excellent; and the whole debate was so characteristic and natural! Allen's speech especially, made me feel quite homesick.

The chances still favor my being legislated out of office; but I hardly see how they can put me out until about May; and most of my work will be done then.

Give my love to Nannie.

Yours, T. R.

POLICE DEPARTMENT
OF THE CITY OF NEW YORK

300 Mulberry Street,
NEW YORK, Feby. 25th, 1896.

Dear Cabot:—

This letter is to be shown to Reed as well as being for your own use. I hope your friend will give me warning before he comes. I am eagerly looking forward to your visit on March twenty-fifth.

During the past month I have had my hands full in the political business here aside from the fact of the work I have done in the Police Department. It has been exceedingly difficult to prevent the Brookfield men from bolting; all the more so as there was ample justification for it; and I should have been inclined to head the bolt myself if the Presidency, and especially Reed's chance for the Presidency, had not been at stake.

The absolutely cynical disregard of decency of Platt and his followers can hardly be imagined. I will give you two little instances, in the district in which Tom Sturgis is one of the leaders on the anti-Platt side. The Platt people carried the primary by fraud so unblushing as to be comic. On examining the rolls of their voters there were found over six hundred from vacant lots, from houses where no such men lived, from houses of ill fame, and the like; of course all of these men were merely repeaters. Moreover there were actually one hundred and three delegates to the Tammany Hall General Committee; whose names were published in the list of that General Committee, who nevertheless voted and were recorded on the Platt side at the primary. In certain streets the Platt people simply took the names on the signs in all the shops along the streets and voted under them right in order. The leader of the Platt forces was Stewart. Platt promised him a Gas Inspectorship if he could carry this district and Morton actually carried out the bargain; although the fraudulent character of the vote was laid before him, and though even the Platt County Committee struck nearly a thousand men off the rolls of this district—when once they had served their purpose and the district had been safely carried. A very large number of the decent men of the party are naturally growing to feel that no democratic success could be worse for them than to be put under Platt's heel, and they will not do anything to rivet Platt's power upon them.

It is thus pretty difficult for me to keep them from bolting; and Platt makes my task no easier by quite openly announcing his intention of using my forbearance as a weapon against me. I am hampered by the fact that I wish the Party to win, and wish Reed to win. He wishes nothing of the kind, unless it is to redound to his benefit; and he regards us as fools who play into his hands because we do not destroy the party if he is to benefit by the party's success. There is a certain small bill pending in the legislature to help the Police Department; it doesn't affect us personally at all; it is simply a small measure for the good of the Department. Grant (who is not overwise and whose blunders cause me more trouble than Parker's cold blooded treacheries and intrigues) went to Platt and said he wished him to support the bill; Platt refused, remarking "I would like to please you Col. Grant, but I don't care nearly as much to please you as I do to worry Roosevelt." This gives just about a fair estimate of the man's size and of his public feeling; he is quite incapable of considering the good of the community, or anything but his own advantage.

Moreover, I have no question that he honestly (so far as you can use such an adverb about him) desires Morton's nomination, because he would have complete control over him. So that in preventing a split, which I have hitherto succeeded in doing, I can't be certain I am working in Reed's interest directly; indirectly I am, however, because the anti-Platt people are steadily verging toward McKinley. As I wrote you I shall have to in my own district turn against the Strong or Brookfield men and probably join with the Platt men in running Joe Murray and one of their own number; not even their hostility for Brookfield can make them support me personally.

I have never had a much more severe trial put on my steadfastness than through this winter. I quite sincerely believe Platt to be as bad a man as Hill, Murphy or Croker, and just so long as the party is under his domination it is no better than the old ring of Democracy that we overthrew. Yet I have prevented a revolt against it because of the damage that revolt would work to other interests.

As for my own police work, I am steadily, and in spite of infinite obstacles, re-building this Police Force. I suppose we shall be legislated out, but it can't be for a couple of months I think, and by that time most of my work will have been finished.

Always yours,

THEODORE ROOSEVELT.

P. S.—I have just seen a quotation purporting to give an interview with me in which I boom with delight Morton's candidacy. This is an absolute fake. I have been in doubt whether to deny it or not, but it seemed to me best to take no further notice of it. Will you ask Tom Reed whether he would like to have it denied? If so, I will deny it at once; but it seems to me to be one of the things that is best left alone. It is a pure Chicago invention. Congressman Aldrich will tell Reed what I said out there the only time I spoke of him; Aldrich was present.

I thought your speech on Cuba excellent; one of the best things you have done. I talked very straight doctrine to the "peace at any price people" both in my address at the Chicago Auditorium and to the Chicago Harvard Club. I wish I had been at the New York Harvard Club to give them a little straight talk too.

T. R.

POLICE DEPARTMENT
OF THE CITY OF NEW YORK

300 Mulberry Street,
NEW YORK, Feb. 25th, 1896.

Dear Cabot :—

Just a line more. The only thing outside of my present work in which I take a real interest is the question of our attitude toward foreign powers and therefore of our defence. What has been done in the Navy? Surely Tom Reed cannot be going to try to throw us down on a question of an addition to the naval forces and proper preparation for coast defense.

Yours always,

THEODORE ROOSEVELT.

To Hon. Henry Cabot Lodge,
  Washington, D. C.

UNITED STATES SENATE
WASHINGTON, D. C.

Feb. 27, 1896.

My dear Theodore :—

I have your letter of the 25th and will show it to Reed. It is a very miserable state of things which you depict in New York and yet I do not see that any course can be pursued at present except the one you are following out.

I saw your Chicago interview and thought very likely you might have said you were for Morton and that it had been exaggerated. Certainly I do not see how you can take any other ground at present and if I were you, I would pay no attention to it and let it go. If Reed thinks differently, I will let you know. (He does not think differently—says deny nothing.)

We are going to get a good appropriation for the Navy. The sub-committee has voted Boutelle down, who wanted to reduce the number of battleships from 6 to 4, and whatever comes over we shall probably add to it in the Senate. Even 4 would be the biggest authorization we have ever made, so you see there is no danger of the Navy being crippled. We are working hard on coast defenses in the Senate and the committee has reported a very good bill. I am in hopes we shall get it through. You do not tell me the writer of the letter in *The Author*, but it is extremely good. Sincerely yours, H. C. L.

POLICE DEPARTMENT
OF THE CITY OF NEW YORK

300 Mulberry Street,

Dear Cabot:— NEW YORK, March 13th, 1896.

I am delighted that you like the article. It made the *Evening Post* announce its decision that on the whole on foreign matters I was rather worse than you or Chandler.* It is difficult for me to restrain my indignation at the cowardice of so many of the men to whom we ought to look for aid in any movement on behalf of Americanism. I must say I am getting disgusted with both Hoar and Hale, and I am getting pretty impatient with Reed. More important than any other question is, it seems to me, the matter of providing an adequate coast defense and an adequate Navy. I can't say how earnestly I hope that Congress will come up to the mark in these two particulars. Surely Reed will help us on these two points.

* Senator William E. Chandler of New Hampshire.

The Strong men here have pretty well thrown off the mask and are out for McKinley. I have naturally had a most disagreeable ·time. In the only district which they controlled I was obliged, in the interest of Reed, to go in with the Platt men and run Joe Murray on a ticket with one of Lauterbach's friends against two of Mayor Strong's Commissioners. It was of course the only thing to do; but it was very disagreeable having to do it. Upon my word I do think that Reed ought to pay some heed to the wishes of you and myself. You have been his most effective supporter; and while my support does not amount to much, it has yet been given at a very serious cost to myself.

I have just received an attack from the Boston *Herald* enclosed in a letter from an anonymous Bostonian who thinks me a very bad man indeed.

You are emphatically right about the Spanish Minister.*

Always yours,

THEODORE ROOSEVELT.

POLICE DEPARTMENT
OF THE CITY OF NEW YORK

300 Mulberry Street,
NEW YORK, March 23rd, 1896.

Dear Cabot:

That was an A 1 speech of yours on Immigration. I have only just had time to read it all through. I have sent to France for those pamphlets by Le Bon. I am ashamed to say I cannot recollect whom your closing quotation is from.

Bigelow dined with us last night. I think that poem of Bay's "The Wave," is the best thing he has done yet. Upon my word it has a fairly Elizabethan touch. I shall go on with you Thursday on Deland's request to speak for Foot Ball, but I must come back by the night train. We expect you Wednesday.

Always yours,

THEODORE ROOSEVELT.

* Dupuy de Lome

POLICE DEPARTMENT
OF THE CITY OF NEW YORK

300 Mulberry Street,
NEW YORK, Apr. 11th, 1896.

Dear Cabot :—

I thought your speech admirable in every way. I was disappointed at the result, but you made a splendid fight.

Lauterbach queered us before the Senate Committee, showing the Senate a typewritten statement by Parker to the effect that he was responsible for every Republican promoted by the Board, and that I had recommended for promotion only Democrats. Andrews,* Grant and I sent a letter to Lauterbach, taking his statements up one by one and denouncing them as falsehoods. Grant is a broken reed to lean upon, for Parker is continually playing on him and using him for his own purposes. I fear now that the bill will not pass; but I am very glad to have got Parker in the open, where I could nail him. He is a thoroughly tricky and despicable fellow; but he is able and unscrupulous and it is not easy to catch him.

The other day I was asked to dinner to meet "Mr. Astor." At first I thought it was Jack Astor and accepted, for Jack Astor, with all his faults, is an American, but when I found it was William Waldorf Astor, I wrote again refusing, pleading inability to attend. I am not going to join in any way in greeting Willie Astor.

Best love to Nannie. All our children are reasonably well.

Always yours,

THEODORE ROOSEVELT.

POLICE DEPARTMENT
OF THE CITY OF NEW YORK

300 Mulberry Street,
NEW YORK, Apr. 29th, 1896.

Dear Cabot :—

It was very good of you to send that letter to Laura,† and she was deeply touched.

* Avery D. Andrews, one of Roosevelt's colleagues on the Police Commission.
† Mrs. West Roosevelt, whose husband had just died.

Did you see in *Scribner's* of this month the opening sentences in reference to yourself by the man who was writing about the Consulates? such a purely incidental tribute speaks more than all the resolutions of the Civil Service Reform Association for the good work you have done.

I was deeply interested in both the volumes by Gustave LeBon. He is really a thinker—not the kind of "thinker" whom the Mugwumps designate by that title—and his books are most suggestive. At the same time I think he falls into fundamental errors quite as vicious in their way as Brooks Adams', especially when he states positively and without qualification a general law which he afterwards himself qualifies in a way that shows that his first general statement was incorrect. I was rather amused at seeing that while his last summing up contained a sweeping prophecy of evil quite as gloomy as Brooks', it was based on exactly the opposite view. One believes that the mass, the proletariat, will swallow up everything and grind capital and learning alike into powder beneath the wheels of socialism. The other believes that the few men on top, the capitalists, will swallow up everything, and will reduce all below them to practical vassalage. But what LeBon says of race is very fine and true.

I see that President Eliot attacked you and myself as "degenerated sons of Harvard." It is a fine alliance, that between the anglo-maniac mugwumps, the socialist working men, and corrupt politicians like Gorman, to prevent the increase of our Navy and coast defenses. The moneyed and semi-cultivated classes, especially of the Northeast, are doing their best to bring this country down to the Chinese level. If we ever come to nothing as a nation it will be because the teaching of Carl Schurz, President Eliot, the *Evening Post* and the futile sentimentalists of the international arbitration type, bears its legitimate fruit in producing a flabby, timid type of character, which eats away the great fighting features of our race. Hand in hand with the Chinese timidity and inefficiency of such a character would go the Chinese corruption; for men of such a stamp are utterly unable to war against the Tammany stripe of politicians. There is nothing that provokes me more than the unintelligent, cowardly chatter for "peace at any price" in which all of those gentlemen indulge.

Give my best love to Nannie.

Always yours,

THEODORE ROOSEVELT.

POLICE DEPARTMENT
OF THE CITY OF NEW YORK

300 Mulberry Street,

NEW YORK, May 2nd, 1896.

Dear Cabot:—

I confess I feel a little downcast over the result in Vermont and Illinois. Oh! if only Reed would have made an aggressive and striking fight for sound finance, beginning at least six months ago. However, there is no use crying over spilt milk.

I was also very much depressed by the action of the Senate in reducing the battleships from four to two. I earnestly hope that the Conferees of the House will insist. I have absolutely no patience with men who are willing to vote to recognize Cuba and to approve of protecting Venezuela, but who are not willing to provide the means to make our action effective. I think I hate nothing more than a bluff where the bluffer does not intend to make it good. What a fearful muss England is in about the Transvaal. It is a very disagreeable business.

Faithfully yours,

THEODORE ROOSEVELT.

Dear Theodore: [WASHINGTON, D. C.,] May 3rd, 1896.

Yours of the 2nd has just come. I should think you would feel downcast over Vermont and Illinois. We are beaten although of course I do not say so outside and I have been practicing philosophy which is a poor business.

It was too bad losing the two ships but we should gain at

least one in conference. Boutelle whose mental processes are not always easy to follow is furious and is going to stand out for four at all hazards. He says he has opposed the Jingoes but believes in defense and when a Jingo like Sherman votes against ships the position is preposterous and he is going to beat him if he can. I send you the two *Records*, I want you to see not only my second speech but that of Wolcott which drew it out. We get 15 torpedo boats as it is. Chandler and I on general principles made a fight for 20. We get 500 extra marines and 1000 more sailors. Gorman tried to knock both out and we licked him. We shall do fairly well in the end. I grinned at Parker's moving your reelection, having failed, I suppose, in an intrigue to get Grant to stand. The supplementary legislation failed for which I am glad and you are in for another year for which I am not very glad—a complicated state of mind which Edith will appreciate. What a mess England is in and how old Kruger has whipped them. It was all a sordid speculation* of the money class, reckless, dishonest and feeble. This is a case which backs up Brooks' conception of the economic type.

My best love to Edith.

Yours, H. C. L.

POLICE DEPARTMENT
OF THE CITY OF NEW YORK

300 Mulberry Street,
NEW YORK, May 6th, 1896.

Dear Cabot :—

I read the two copies of the *Record* with great interest. That your speech was admirable goes without saying. I was also very much pleased with the lesson that Hawley drew from the burning of Washington. I must say I felt disheartened at reading what Wolcott said. How a man of his ancestry and training can be so indifferent to the national honor, I find it hard to conceive. Gorman is as cheap a scoundrel as exists. Hill is a scoundrel too, although of much higher grade. I

* The Jameson Raid.

thought he might act decently on the Navy. I was immensely amused at Peffer's idea that torpedo boats were to be used chiefly for preying on the enemy's commerce. Boutelle certainly follows an oddly tortuous path mentally, but I am glad of the stand he has taken now, at all events. Well, we shall get something out of it anyhow, and we are gradually building a navy which will, at least, prevent any but a first class power from insulting us with impunity.

I have continued a somewhat stormy career here. Yesterday I lost my temper with Fitch, which I should not have done; but he is so contemptible, and does so much mischief that I found it difficult to pardon him. As for Parker, I have made no progress; the Mayor ought to remove him, but I don't think he is prepared for such vigorous action. At any rate I have more than held my own during these last few weeks, but it is very hard work indeed to go on with such a scoundrel. With proper power I could make this Department of the first rank from top to bottom. We have done a good deal anyhow, but the way we are hampered is almost inconceivable, and I shall not be sorry when I leave it, though I would not be willing to go now under fire.

Best love to Nannie. Austin Wadsworth dined with us last night.

Always yours,
THEODORE ROOSEVELT.

POLICE DEPARTMENT
OF THE CITY OF NEW YORK

300 Mulberry Street,
NEW YORK, June 10th, 1896.

Dear Cabot :—

I was awfully sorry not to see you. I don't suppose there is any chance of your stopping on your way back from St. Louis, but telegraph me "on spec" any way.

I am now engaged in my usual fight with the amiable Parker. He is the worst kind of a hindrance to decent work that you can imagine. But the thing that I am most interested in is of course the Presidential nomination. It is evident that McKinley has it hands down; but I do hope that we shall have the most vigorous kind of gold plank, and that we shall be against free silver at any ratio. I am delighted to see that the free silver men seem not to be championing McKinley. We ought to disregard them utterly, and I hope our people will see that a straddle will gain absolutely nothing; we shall lose a great deal if the Democrats go for free silver; it will give us a hard fight in the west; but it is a fight which will be victorious only if we are just as positive on the right side as they are on the wrong. If we assume a timid, halting, negative position I fear we shall get whipped, and if so, disaster awaits the country.

I am glad you liked the fourth volume of my "Winning of the West." I don't know why I used "folk," I fear it must have been due to the unconscious memories of Green and Freeman; and as for "mutterless," I am very sorry it is a coined word; it seemed to come handy and I used it! Edith had not seen it, or at any rate when I read your note she promptly and with severity joined with you in denunciation and loudly insisted that I had not read to her that part of the proof.

Give my best love to Nannie. I think Harry enjoyed his night with us because he has volunteered to try to come out for another.

Yours always,

THEODORE ROOSEVELT.

WESTERN UNION TELEGRAPH COMPANY

NEW YORK 6/17 1896.

Senator H. Cabot Lodge, Massachusetts Delegation, St. Louis Mo.

Immensely proud of you* hope Civil Service will be heeded.

THEODORE ROOSEVELT.

* This referred to my fight for the word "gold" in the platform of the Republican National Convention.

SAGAMORE HILL,
June 20th, '96.

Well, you've scored again! and heavily. Every one here is talking of your splendid leadership, and is attributing much of the victory for sound money to you. Not only Massachusetts, but Boston, will be behind you now, stronger than ever.

I am dreadfully sorry and sore about Reed; but we must do all we can for McKinley, of course. He is an honorable man; and the platform is admirable; the only plank I don't like is the pension plank.

Give our best love to Nannie.

Yours, T. R.

POLICE DEPARTMENT
OF THE CITY OF NEW YORK

300 Mulberry Street,
NEW YORK, July 14th, 1896.

Dear Cabot:—

I am exceedingly disappointed not to be able to get to Tuckanuck,* but it is simply impossible for me to leave just now unless I shirk my work. I had hoped that by the first of July, at the latest, everything would be all clear; but it now looks as if it would be the middle of August or later before we dispose of the promotions one way or the other. Parker is still in, and, whatever the Mayor does, an appeal will be taken on his behalf to the Courts, and pending the settlement of this appeal I suppose he will continue to exercise his functions. This means that the promotions will have to be fought out step by step, and as the examinations have been delayed so that they are only now taking place I simply cannot get away. I got to Austin Wadsworth's because I only had to be absent one working day, taking the night train on and another night train back—for Sunday, and Saturday, which was the fourth, don't count—but for some little time to come I evidently cannot expect to get off for more than a Saturday and Sunday, or Sunday and Monday. It is a great deal more likely that I

---

* An island near Nantucket where Dr. W. S. Bigelow had a large place.

can visit Nahant than Tuckanuck, and even Nahant will be doubtful.

I had great fun up at Geneseo but as I was frightfully out of condition, as well as stiff and flabby, I came back sore all over. Dacre Bush distinguished himself, and I took a great fancy to him. As I was up there I went in for all the sports, and still bear traces of conflict with divers of the Carey brothers in the cavalry fight. I got rather a bad strain in a fall over a fence in the course of one of the canonical Sunday afternoon horse-back strolls. Austin was in at Oyster Bay the other day on a yacht.

Edith and the children are very well. Edith enjoyed Geneseo as much as I did. I shall have to be in town almost every night this week; but Grant LaFarge and Bob Ferguson will probably be with her at Oyster Bay.

What a Witches Sabbath they did hold at Chicago! Bryan admirably suits the platform. I can't help hoping that before November he will have talked himself out, and his utter shallowness be evident, but just at this moment I believe him to be very formidable, even in the Middle West and of course in the far West and South. As you know, and have long said, the hardest fight the democracy could give us this year was on the free silver issue. They have done wisely, (if one disregards considerations of morality) in making the issue so thorough going there is not a crook or criminal in the entire country who ought not to support them; and we have never had, save only during the Civil War, a party whose success at the national election would have argued so ill for national welfare. I am very glad that McKinley has come out so straight on the finance issue; we have got to meet them as boldly as they meet us. The bolt among the democrats here is fairly astounding; I have never seen anything like it, and I believe that most of the Germans everywhere will be on our side. The A. P. A. is, I think, eager to support Bryan; on this account as well as others, Bland would have been an easier candidate to beat. Still, Bryan has no real substance to him; I think the people will size him up by November, and that we shall beat him hands down; but we must not be deluded into the belief that there is not to be a struggle in the States along the Mississippi Valley.

Let me know your movements as soon as you can, so that if I can get a chance to see you I may avail myself of it.

Give my best love to Nannie.

Yours always,

THEODORE ROOSEVELT.

POLICE DEPARTMENT
OF THE CITY OF NEW YORK

300 Mulberry Street,
NEW YORK, July 29th, 1896.

Dear Cabot:—

First, a word as to literature. I do hope Bay will publish "The Wave." Every time I read it over I am more and more impressed by it. I won't repeat to you what I said about sonnets—if for no other reason than that you justifiably distrust my judgment upon them—but it seems to me that, while so many thousands of men write pretty good sonnets, or even more than pretty good sonnets, and while Shakespeare, Milton and Wordsworth still remain rather lonely in this line, there is a better chance in other directions to do work that will really stand in the first rank. I think "The Wave" stands quite alone, and with all due respect to you, it *does* combine a touch both of Whitman, and of Marlowe in his grand style. The combination seems queer, but the result is good. I do wish it could be published.

Now for politics, I saw George Lyman* just as I was about to call on Hanna. With Hanna I had a very pleasant talk, and I dwelt especially upon the fact that in Massachusetts if he wished to get money help, which he so urgently needs, he must tie to you and Lyman; and he assured me that he quite understood Osborne's† position, and indeed the attitude

---

* At that time chairman of the Republican State Committee of Massachusetts.

† William McKinley Osborne, at that time a police and license commissioner in Boston—cousin of President McKinley.

of the other original McKinley men in Massachusetts, and that he intended to work through the regular organization, and recognize Lyman and yourself as its exponents, and the people to be considered; and that you were those whom he regarded as the people to be considered, both now and after election. Of course I can only tell you what he *said* he would do, and not what he *will* do.

As for matters here, he evidently feels rather sore with Platt, and not inclined to call on Platt first; while Platt foolishly stands on a point of punctilio in refusing to make the first advance. I am going to send an urgent request to him today through Quigg to see Hanna by all means. Fortunately Hanna is entirely against any split in the Party here.

Always yours,
THEODORE ROOSEVELT.

POLICE DEPARTMENT
OF THE CITY OF NEW YORK

300 Mulberry Street,
NEW YORK, July 30th, 1896.

Dear Cabot :—

This is an explanatory appendix to my note of yesterday. Like yourself I am a man of one idea, and yesterday as an under-current of thought running through my battles with the ungodly in the shape of Fitch, Parker and the like, there was present a sense of irritation that my favorite "The Wave" should not be published. All that I meant to do was to make an ardent plea for "The Wave"; but after I sent the letter it suddenly occurred to me that it might read like an attack on Bay's sonnets. To accentuate my feelings, on my way to a meeting of the Greater New York Commission to testify about the Police Department, I read in *Scribner's* the only one of Bay's other poems which I think ranks with "The Wave"; that wonderfully beautiful sonnet "After." I know that my own judgment about sonnets is not of the best, and that one's sense of perspective is not good when too close, but really I feel that this equals any of Wordsworth's. I recollect that when Sturgis Bigelow read this and "The Wave" to me, I had very strongly the feeling that I was listening to a couple of master-pieces, by a man who ranked as a poet; and there are not many poets in this century. This is all by the way of explana-tion, though I don't suppose you could really think I did not appreciate Bay's sonnets; but it is not given to any man in one lifetime to write many such sonnets as "After" and I don't want him to desert the other forms of poetry entirely.

I had a second talk with Hanna, the conversation coming around to Massachusetts. I again dwelt on the fact that the only people who could help him were the men represented by you and Lyman, and that if there was the slightest suspicion that there was an effort to build up a machine against you by the use of patronage, it would be impossible to get any real solid help from the only Bostonians who could give Hanna the help he needs, that is money. I think you ought to make every effort to see a good deal of him, and to have him meet you at a dinner with but two or three other men, at the most, present. He is the type of man that despises big dinners, and any appearance of fuss; and he realizes that there is a very big fight on in the Middle West, and that he needs all the finan-cial aid possible from the East. He is a goodnatured, well meaning, rough man, shrewd and hard-headed, but neither very farsighted nor very broad-minded, and as he has a reso-lute, imperious mind, he will have to be handled with some care; and yet he must be shown that the financial issue must in many quarters be made the foremost issue, and must every-where be made one of the two foremost. I don't mean to ad-vise dropping the tariff; on the contrary, we must force the tariff issue well to the front; but we must not subordinate to it the issue of sound money.

Give my best love to Nannie.

Always yours,
THEODORE ROOSEVELT.

POLICE DEPARTMENT
OF THE CITY OF NEW YORK

300 Mulberry Street,
NEW YORK, July 31st, 1896.

Dear Cabot:—

I do not often write three letters in three days even to you, but your note of yesterday, which crossed my two made me feel that I had the authority to go around on my own hook to see Burlingame; so round I went, and Burlingame jumped at the chance of seeing "The Wave," and told me that he was sincerely obliged to me for giving him the opportunity. He meant this, for he repeated it three or four times, saying that he considered himself under a personal obligation, because he felt that "young Lodge" was doing noteworthy work, and he told me to write and have it sent on at once, being evidently afraid that some other Magazine would get the first choice; so please send it on at once.

The first part of our conversation, by the way, was hampered a little by his inability to understand that "George Cabot" was pronounced "Bay,"* but after this phonetic trouble was once over, we got on capitally. Incidentally, he volunteered the remark that I must not think that he did not appreciate "Richard the Third,"† that it was simple lack of space that weighed with him, and that he quite understood and acquiesced in any criticism I might make as to that growth of the "popular" element in Magazines which took away from what ought to be a tolerably serious periodical the chance to put in such an article. As he seemed contrite, and as at any rate he had a proper appreciation of Bay's poems, I magnanimously forebore to say anything.

I know just how you feel about my work here. It is irritating to the last degree to have to spend my strength in an obscure fight with a scoundrelly intriguer like Parker, who derives his power solely from the ridiculous features of the law foisted upon us by these preposterous machine leaders. I should never go into such a struggle on such conditions, which are utterly unfair to any honorable and self-respecting man; the

* Nickname of my eldest son.
† An article of mine published in *Scribner's*.

law being framed to give power to the trickster and to prevent the exercise of the qualities which can alone permanently reform this force. But I am in, and I shall see it through; six or eight months will enable me to do all that I have to do; meanwhile, it is possible that I can break the neck of either Conlin or Parker, and most glad I shall be to do it. At any rate, I have done something; and on the whole I have enjoyed my work, albeit grimly.

Always yours,

THEODORE ROOSEVELT.

POLICE DEPARTMENT
OF THE CITY OF NEW YORK

300 Mulberry Street,

Dear Cabot:—   NEW YORK, Aug. 8th, 1896.

I don't see any chance of my being able to get on; you will understand that I am working fairly hard when I tell you that during this week of sweltering heat, I have been obliged to stay in town without going out for even a night at Oyster Bay. A fortnight hence I shall go out for a short visit to my ranch. I have told the Republican Committee that I am at their disposal as a speaker if they wish me, and that I will make one or two speeches for them, if they so desire, while going to or returning from Dakota.

The silver feeling among our farmers, and to some extent among our laboring men, is undoubtedly serious, and it will receive a great temporary boom next week from Bryan's speech here in New York. I cannot but think, however, that after that the tide will begin to set steadily our way. At National Headquarters they tell me that there is no demand whatever for literature on the tariff, but that they have to send out tons of mail matter on finance, and that they only wish they had more documents. I am glad you are speedily to begin at Vermont and Maine, much though I know you dread it.

Give Nannie my best love. We are all well, though Edith writes me that the heat has told a good deal on Archie. While

I am out West, she is going to take the children up to Lake Champlain, and I think it will do both her and them good.

Let me know what Burlingame says about "The Wave." What he says, I may mention, will affect merely my opinion of him, not of the poem.   Always yours,

THEODORE ROOSEVELT.

POLICE DEPARTMENT
OF THE CITY OF NEW YORK

300 Mulberry Street,
NEW YORK, Aug. 13, 1896
Dear Cabot :—

If I can get out I shall for I have begun to feel a little knocked up; I have had splendid health up to this time.

As I know you will see the *Sun*, I wish to say that every other paper in New York, no matter of what politics, spoke in the highest terms of the way the Police handled the crowd at the Bryan notification meeting. The trouble with the *Sun* was that its reporter got there after the house was full, the notification people having issued just twice the number of tickets that there were seats, and after the house was filled the Police of course had no other alternative than to turn every one back.

By the way, Bryan, himself, fell perfectly flat here in New York, his big notification meeting has simply hurt him.

Oh! how I do long for a chance to see you and to talk with you.   Always yours,

THEODORE ROOSEVELT.

POLICE DEPARTMENT
OF THE CITY OF NEW YORK

300 Mulberry Street,
NEW YORK, Aug. 19, 1896.
Dear Cabot :—

I am off on Friday for three weeks, and I am very glad to go for I think the endless strain and worry had told on me a little.

The meeting to hear Bourke Cockran was a phenomenon. It is extraordinary that a mere private citizen should be able to gather such an enormous crowd; a crowd quite as large inside the Madison Square Garden and almost as large outside, as that which came to hear Bryan, the candidate for the Presidency. Cockran made a first class speech. I cannot but believe that the tide is beginning to flow against the free silver-ites; but of course it all depends upon the big States of the Middle West. Down at the bottom the cry for free silver is nothing whatever but a variant of the cry for fiat money or a debased and inflated currency. Brooks Adams' theories are beautiful, but in practice they mean a simple dishonesty, and a dishonest nation does not stand much higher than a dis-honest man. The hatred of the East among many Westerners, and the crude ignorance of even elementary finance among such a multitude of well meaning, but puzzled-headed, voters, give cause for serious alarm throughout this campaign. I shall be able to speak more intelligently when I come back from the West. Cushman K. Davis has made a splendid speech in St. Paul.

This time I supervised the police arrangements myself, Conlin having run off to the country. Everything went off without a hitch; there was very little legitimate ground for complaint even at the first meeting; it was chiefly reporters' grievances, as a number of their passes were not honored. This time I saw that they were all honored, and the police kept complete control of the crowd, having them thoroughly in hand; and yet they behaved with the utmost good nature. I determined that I would be able to testify as an eye witness to all that happened.

I have written to Burlingame, but it seems to me simply impossible that he can fail to take "The Wave." Give my best love to Nannie and John, Bay and Constance, and to Sturgis Bigelow if he is anywhere around.

Always yours,

THEODORE ROOSEVELT.

I wish I could have joined you at the Whites.

P. S.—I have again had to make a break with some of the anti-Platt people; the Platt men locally are quite impossible,

but our anti-Platt men are such fools! They want to nominate
Saxton for Governor. Well! I should like to nominate him,
but it is simply out of the question; but the most important
think is to beat Aldridge, and he can only be beaten (if Morton
won't run) provided the anti-Platt men help those Platt men
who are in favor of Fish or Wadsworth. I don't think anyone
of these is at all an ideal candidate, but we don't get ideal
candidates for Governor in New York. Either will make a good
Governor, much above the average, and for either we can poll
the full party strength without leaving a break in the party
ranks, and without disgracing ourselves by putting up an unfit
man. The anti-Platt people behave with such folly that they
are apt to oppose quite as strenuously a decent fellow whom
Platt supports as the worst scoundrel.

POLICE DEPARTMENT
OF THE CITY OF NEW YORK

300 Mulberry Street,
Dear Cabot:—   NEW YORK, Sept. 14, 1896.

I thought your speech, which Edith showed me, admirable;
but then you have gotten into the habit of making admirable
speeches now. I haven't seen your Commencement speeches.
I suppose Maine will give a rousing majority today. I earnestly
hope so. I spoke in New York last Friday and was rapturously
received. The Organization had frowned on my being asked,
but after my reception I was rather amused to find that they
at once wrote me to know if I would not speak for them during
the campaign, and I of course answered that I would. We
have made a pretty good nomination for Governor. Black is
a Platt man, but a man of ability and integrity.

I looked into the situation very carefully in the West. I
spent two days at the Republican Headquarters at Chicago.
We have a very severe fight there, but we are going to win.
Illinois is now looking all right; Indiana will be venal as usual;
Ohio we shall carry of course, and the Germans make Wis-
consin as safe as New York; affairs are very much demoralized

in Michigan, but we shall win. In Iowa the defection has been *very* great and the result is still in doubt, but the drift is our way. The same is true of Minnesota, and there is an even chance in the Dakotas, and as I am informed by the Pacific slope men, in Oregon and possibly Washington and California; even in Montana McKinley has proved so strong that Tom Carter* has hastily gotten off the fence on our side. Nebraska, I believe, we shall carry. I don't know enough about Kansas to speak with any certainty.

What confounded fools the political G. A. R. men are. Just at present they are trying to have me imprisoned, under the peculiar provision of the New York law rendering public officials liable if they do not give veterans their rights. During the last fifteen years Tammany while in complete control of the Board, or dividing it with the machine Republicans, made twenty-six promotions to the rank of Captain, six of the men promoted being veterans. During the past sixteen months we have made twenty promotions, eleven of the men promoted being veterans; in other words, we have promoted relatively more than twice as many; yet the very men who never made a kick about Tammany are now threatening deadly measures aimed especially at me, because I will not promote certain entirely incompetent Grand Army men to positions in which they would have the responsibility for preserving order in this entire vast City, and because I have reduced an utterly incompetent and unworthy man, Patrick Buckley. They have taken the action partly of their own accord, but mainly at the instigation of Parker. They don't care in the least for the fact that of the eleven veterans promoted (eight of whom incidentally are Republicans) Parker voted against five. They care still less that Parker does not really want their men promoted, but desires to interfere with the promotions of the only men who are just at this moment fit to be made Inspectors. All they wish to do is to try to put forward two or three incompetent professional G. A. R. policemen, and having failed to do this by threats, they now are proceeding to law, and the Platt people are egging them on. However, though a little irritating,

* A Senator from Montana.

I have been much amused at this. They went before the Grand Jury to get me indicted; the Grand Jury positively refused. What they will do next, I don't know.

I have had a rather amusing experience with the English reviews of my fourth volume of the "Winning of the West," which offer a commentary on the supposed indifference of the British to American criticism. In the first three volumes I had no occasion to say anything bad about the British. In the fourth volume I had to tell the truth about their conduct in the Northwestern frontier. Every English paper, from the *Athenæum* to the *Times*, has confined its review to a perfect yell of rage over this part of my volume. The *Athenæum* put it that "he (I) panders to vulgar passion and prejudice; he either cannot or dare not make the attempt to write with candor and historical truth when a question concerning Great Britain and America is discussed."

Scribner's having accepted "The Wave" I now most earnestly hope it will be produced very soon.

I have just had a long and really very interesting letter, from, of all persons in the world, Tom Watson,* in reference to an article of mine in *The Review of Reviews*. I shall show it to you when we meet.

Give my best love to Nannie and to Bay and John, and Constance if you see her. Gussie† has been distinguishing himself on the polo field, I see.	Always yours,

THEODORE ROOSEVELT.

P. S.—I have just received your letter which was very welcome. That was an exceedingly stupid slip of mine about Jefferson, due to my having to dictate the article late at night just as I was leaving for the West. I have written you above my forecast of the West. The wage-earners are drifting our way and the revolt among the farmers is shrinking rather than spreading. In my own county of Billings and the extreme West of North Dakota the sentiment was for gold among the

* Subsequently Senator from Georgia.
† My son-in-law, Augustus Peabody Gardner—afterward member of Congress, major in the war with Germany and died of pneumonia in camp.

small ranchmen and they will give McKinley two to one majority there. But the situation in the West generally has been one of great danger. The drift our way was very perceptible, however, and the change was distinctly visible even during the three weeks I was out there. Of all the States Iowa made relatively the worst showing. I went over a careful canvass of the State with their National Committeeman; even the names of the voters were down, and it showed a net loss of thirty thousand republicans, for the ten thousand gold democrats could not be depended upon to vote against Bryan. However, matters are improving, even the improvement in Minnesota was very marked. When I was going to my ranch the people there were all nervous, and the men with whom I talked were very doubtful; coming back it was evident that the tide had begun to set our way. At present the Dakotas are a little against us, but with proper care I believe there is at least an even chance of carrying them. There is a great need of money to spend in an entirely legitimate way for educational purposes. Maine like Vermont has done even better than we had hoped.

POLICE DEPARTMENT
OF THE CITY OF NEW YORK

300 Mulberry Street,

Dear Cabot:—   NEW YORK, Sept. 18, 1896.

I was overjoyed to receive your letter. I at once went up to see Hackett where I met a large number of the gentlemen who have been endeavoring to get my scalp for the last year or two, and we grinned at one another like an assembly of Roman Augurs, and greeted one another with hilarious politeness. The lovely Lauterbach was prominent among them. I never can help being amused with that graceless person. Hackett was very pleasant and both he and Lauterbach were evidently a good deal struck by my speech the other day. He at once said that he would only be too glad to have me go with you through the State and speak at Utica, Buffalo and Jamestown on the 29th, 30th and the 1st.* Your first speech on the 28th here in New York Hackett told me might possibly be the big opening of the campaign, with only yourself and Black as the speakers, and, if so, they would not want me. But the great point is that I shall be able to go with you through the State. Now about Canton. I may possibly have to come right back after our tour. If by any chance I can I shall go with you; but Bellamy Storer made me promise sometime ago that I would not go to Canton without him, he was here this morning; I told him our plans, and he said all right, that if I would let him know in advance he would come up to Canton to meet us. This seemed to me the best way out of it, as of course if I go at all, I shall go with you. Yet I don't want to hurt Bellamy's feelings, and I know you would not object to meeting him there, as he is a stanch friend of yours.

It was just like you, old man, to think of me; and of course of all things I should most like to go on the stump with you. General Clayton has just written me that they may have to put me on in Maryland and West Virginia as for some inscrutable reason there is a demand for me there.

I am immensely interested in what you tell me about Gussie. I don't think he has fallen off in his polo; the polo men here think he has not. But it delights my soul to have him go into serious work. From the very beginning I took a great fancy to him; he is a *man* in every way, and I hated not to see him doing a man's work. I am more than delighted at what you tell me about him.

I think you will be amused at Watson's letter. I was really very much pleased at Nannie's appreciation of my article. I have had letters about it from all over, but I care a good deal more for Nannie's liking it than for anything.

I have a howling mob, metaphorically speaking, waiting for me in the ante-chamber and must close this letter.

Always yours,
THEODORE ROOSEVELT.

* We made this trip and spoke at various meetings—from Jamestown we went to Akron, arriving there in the very small hours. After sleeping briefly in a garret room in an alleged hotel, went to Canton, where we saw and had a full talk with McKinley—turned back to New York and to Boston.

POLICE DEPARTMENT
OF THE CITY OF NEW YORK

300 Mulberry Street,

Dear Cabot :— NEW YORK, Oct. 6, 1896.

I regarded our trip as a real holiday; it was simply delightful to be with you for the five days. A piece of good luck has befallen me. They want me to speak at a big meeting at Chicago, and so they have put me into Illinois and Michigan instead of West Virginia and Maryland. This will be far more comfortable.

Now, I was a little disturbed at what you said to me about Hart Merriam. On most matters I accept your judgment as much better than mine. On this will you for the time being follow me? The only two scientific men in the country who rank with Merriam are Agassiz and Jordan. Those monographs of which the *Sun* made such fun were, I find, *not* published among the documents to benefit farmers; but as part of the work of the Biological Survey which he has been conducting; and which ranks among European men of science as perhaps the very best piece of work of the kind that has been done anywhere of recent years. Always yours,

THEODORE ROOSEVELT.

POLICE DEPARTMENT
OF THE CITY OF NEW YORK

300 Mulberry Street,

Dear Cabot :— NEW YORK, Oct. 21, 1896.

Just a line to tell you about my Western trip. First, and least important, as to myself. I made a success of it, and got in good form and spoke to immense audiences, who always listened attentively, and sometimes, as in Chicago and Detroit, went mad with enthusiasm. The only serious interruption I had, funnily enough, was by Moreton Frewen* in Chicago. After a little sparring I used him up so that he left the hall.

Now as to the result. We shall sweep the West very much as we shall the East, although, of course, not to the same extent. Altgeld will run way ahead of Bryan in Illinois, but the land-slide will be so great that we shall probably down him too. In Minnesota there has been a check as there has been in Michigan, Indiana and Ohio, so that our people are not quite as confident of overwhelming majorities as they were a month ago; nevertheless the majorities will be large. I went through Minnesota the same time Bryan did, and in three different towns spoke on the same day. At the moment he frightened our leaders; but I really believe his visit did us good rather than harm. The conduct of Pingree† in Michigan is however most unfortunate. He has hardly supported McKinley at all, and his men are trying to trade so as to carry him (Pingree) through at all costs; while on the other hand I did not meet a decent Republican in the State who intended to vote for him. The scoundrel actually asked the Bryan people to let him introduce Bryan at his great meeting in Detroit. They refused. He has great influences with the labor people, and a large number of the leaders of the latter will be against us. Moreover, Michigan is the one place where I did actually come across serious defections among the Republican farmers on the silver question. On the other hand, the sound money Democrats have been a tower of strength to us there. In one small town I visited, out of 450 votes one hundred and three were actually enrolled in the McKinley sound money league; there were 50 others who had not enrolled but who will nevertheless vote our way. Indiana is a bad State, as always, and our men are not wholly free from anxiety. Hanna told me that he thought it quite as doubtful as Kentucky. Personally, I think this an exaggeration. Iowa is coming our way with a sweep, and we have more than an even chance of carrying Nebraska, and two out of three of the Pacific coast States.

* An English friend of ours.   He was an ardent bi-metalist.
† Governor Pingree.

Will you tell Curtis Guild* that wherever I went I heard his speeches spoken of with general admiration. Also tell me if that was Gussie's article in the last *Bachelor of Arts*.

Give my best love to Nannie and tell her how much I enjoyed her note.

Always yours,

THEODORE ROOSEVELT.

SAGAMORE HILL,
OYSTER BAY, LONG ISLAND, N. Y.,
Nov. 5th, '96.

Dear Cabot,

We shall spend Sunday the 14th with the White's chiefly because Nannie and you are to be there; so you mustn't go back on us.

We were so sorry not to see Brooks and his wife. He has asked me to review his book in *The Forum*, which I shall do; I may send the article to you or Nannie first, so as to be sure there is nothing in it to which he could object; for it will not be too easy to write. I have just come across the paper you and I drew up on our stumping tour as to the States which would go for McKinley; it was a rather curiously exact prophecy.

Well, this was a fight of such vital and tremendous importance that I am very glad you and I were able to do our full share of the fighting.

Love to Nannie.

Always yours,

THEODORE ROOSEVELT.

SAGAMORE HILL,
OYSTER BAY, LONG ISLAND, N. Y.,
Nov. 28th, '96.

Dear Cabot,

All right; I'll sound Brander† as soon as I can make time to see him. I don't believe the *Century* people know how to push a book; but it may now be too late for the other company to take it.

---

* Subsequently Governor of Massachusetts. He accompanied Roosevelt through the West in the campaign of 1900.

† Brander Matthews.

I liked your interview; but I am glad you are to send me the complete text. Still, what was quoted was excellent.

I am very glad McKinley seems inclined to be so friendly; I'm really a good deal worried by Reed's seeming purpose to refuse to be on good terms with him. Bryanism, with all that it implies, is too real and ugly a danger, and our hold on the forces that won the victory for us by no means too well assured, to make me feel we can afford needless quarrels among ourselves.

Love to Nannie.

Yours, T. R.

P. S.—I can't get the review of Brooks'* book to you in time; they demand it now. It has been a rather difficult thing to do. I have written with the warmest admiration for the book, but have emphatically dissented from parts of his thesis.

UNITED STATES SENATE
WASHINGTON, D. C.

Private.

Dec. 2, 1896.

My dear Theodore :—

I went to Canton Sunday night, as I wrote you, got there Monday morning, passed two hours with Major McKinley, and lunched with him. I first talked with him about Hawaii. I did not go into our policy in that respect, but simply obtained his permission to have Cooper, their Secretary of State, who is here, stop and see him on his way to Chicago. He then asked me about Cuba, and we went over the whole of that very perplexing question. It is very much on his mind and I found he had given it a great deal of thought. He very naturally does not want to be obliged to go to war as soon as he comes in, for of course his great ambition is to restore business and bring back good times and he dislikes the idea of such interruption. He would like the crisis to come this winter and be settled one way or the other before he takes up the reins, but I was greatly pleased to see how thoroughly he appreciates the momentous character of the question.

* "The Law of Civilization and Decay," by Brooks Adams.

This led him to say that he regarded it as of the utmost
importance to have the strongest possible man for the Secretaryship of State and he voluntarily proceeded to talk over a
number of people with me. He of course did not tell me what
he was going to do, although he asked my opinion very freely.
I am satisfied that he has no idea of taking Depew. On that
point he was very explicit. The fact is the whole cabinet is
hinging on Hanna. If Hanna takes the Treasury, it will be
made up one way; if he does not, it will be made up another.
With Hanna out of the cabinet, I should think that Hay's
chances are extremely good. With Hanna in the cabinet I
should say that it was very likely to go West—and probably
to Allison.* I do not think it will come East, but these are
nothing but my own inferences. I do not think that a cabinet
portfolio has been offered to anyone. I think it is all waiting.
Probably I am all wrong in my guesses, but I think I have
some foundation for them and I give them to you for what they
are worth.

We then talked about tariff legislation and extra session and
on that his position is as wise and firm as possible. He is entirely prepared to face the responsibilities at the earliest possible moment and deal with them. Indeed his whole attitude of
mind struck me as serious, broad in view, and just what we
all ought to desire. I brought from it many good hopes.

After the tariff he spoke about you. He spoke of you with
great regard for your character and your services and he would
like to have you in Washington. The only question he asked
me was this, which I give you: "I hope he has no preconceived
plans which he would wish to drive through the moment he
got in." I replied that he need not give himself the slightest
uneasiness on that score, that I knew your views about the
Navy, and they were only to push on the policies which had
been in operation for the last two or three administrations.

We then had some general talk during which he asked me
about the range of the recent civil service extension and, while
he commented on the fact that they had managed to shut in
a good many Democrats with them, he said there should be no

* Senator William B. Allison of Iowa.

going back from what had been done. Nothing could be more satisfactory on this point, which was entirely incidental.

Later when we were sitting in an outer room and had been chatting about a good many indifferent things, I said to him: "I have no right to ask a personal favor of you, but I do ask for Roosevelt as the one personal favor." He said very warmly: "You must not say that. I have no feeling about what went before the nomination. You have a perfect right to ask a personal favor and I understand what you want." When I was leaving him after lunch I said just as we were starting that I was very much obliged to him and had enjoyed our talk and that he knew the one thing which was near my heart and that I should say no more about it. He said very cordially that he did. In a word he gave me every encouragement. But after all I am not one of his old supporters and the person to whom I look now, having shot my own bolt, is Storer. I have just written him, told him that I have been at Canton, and therefore should not go to Ohio later, and urging him as strongly as I know how to press your case. I have told him that he must look after it, because he is the one who is in constant communication and who can without intruding keep the matter steadily at the front. If he looks after it, all will be well. One thing is certain. The matter is thoroughly in McKinley's mind. He is not going to forget it and, although I am not over sanguine about such things, I believe we shall succeed. You will be kind enough to remember that in all I have done, I have been doing for myself and what I particularly want and that your interests are wholly secondary!

I need hardly say that all this is in the most absolute confidence. No one outside my own family knows or will know anything about my conversation out there. No one is likely to guess, for they imagine I went about office, whereas I went about questions of policy and you. I was glad I went and I feel very much encouraged. If he holds to the attitude which he has expressed to me, all will go well. Not only do his views seem sound, but his desire to have a very strong cabinet seemed uppermost in his mind.   Always sincerely yours,

H. C. L.

POLICE DEPARTMENT
OF THE CITY OF NEW YORK

300 Mulberry Street,

Dear Cabot:— NEW YORK, Dec. 4, 1896.

I need hardly say with what intense interest I read your letter. I am delighted at what you say about McKinley. I do hope he will take a strong stand both about Hawaii and Cuba. I do not think a war with Spain would be serious enough to cause much strain on the country, or much interruption to the revival of prosperity; but I certainly wish the matter could be settled this winter. Nothing could be better than the attitude you describe him as having on the tariff, and on civil service reform.

Now, old man, as to what you say about myself, I shall not try to express any gratitude, for I don't suppose that between you and me it is necessary for me to say what I feel. Of course I have no preconceived policy of any kind which I wish to push through, and I think he would find that I would not be in any way a marplot or agitator; but I really look upon the matter with philosophical equanimity. The main reason why I would care to go to Washington is to be near you. If you were not in Washington, I should certainly prefer to stay here, even under the present unsatisfactory law, and I am so absorbed in this work that I would not leave it if I had the proper power, or if I did not feel that I had about come to the end of what I could accomplish that was worth accomplishing. Rather to my amusement today General Wilson—"Cavalry" Wilson, of Delaware—turned up, and I lunched with him and Charles A. Dana.* Wilson had been writing to me hoping to have me made Secretary of the Navy. I told him that was all nonsense, and he then earnestly begged me *not* to take the Assistant Secretaryship. I did not say anything to him, because I thought it better not. Dana evidently did not share his views, but wanted me to call on Platt, and see if I could not get him to give us proper police legislation. Of course I did not give either of them a hint that you or anyone else had approached

* Editor of the New York *Sun.*

McKinley (Storer has just written me that he went to see him, and evidently Mrs. Storer spoke to him about me at that time).

I wish I could call on Platt and see Governor Black. I have nothing to ask for myself, but I would like them not to do anything, or permit the legislature to do anything, which will damage the Republican Party. I wonder if Platt would misinterpret my calling on him? What do you think?

Now old fellow! you must not mind in the least if McKinley does not offer it to me. I think Storer will write him, but I don't suppose there is anyone else that would, and I hate to ask anyone to, for I don't like to appear in the position of a supplicant—for I am not a supplicant. I think I could do honorable work as Assistant Secretary. If I am not offered it, then I shall try to do honorable work here as long as I can, and then I shall turn to any work that comes up.

Give my best love to Nannie and Bay.

Always yours,

THEODORE ROOSEVELT.

UNITED STATES SENATE
WASHINGTON, D. C.

Dec. 7, 1896.

Dear Theodore :—

I have just come from talking over the telephone with Platt. He said he was not going to Canton, as he had not been asked. I told him that I wanted to talk with him about a matter personal to myself and that I was going to ask a favor of him. I then stated what I wanted for you. He said that he was most anxious to oblige me in any way he could, but he did not feel ready to say he would support you, if you intended to go into the Navy Department and make war on him—or, as he put it, on the organization. I replied with some surprise that I did not see how you came in contact with the organization in the Department at all. He said, "Oh, yes, there is the

Brooklyn Navy Yard." I said I did not think that that would be likely to stand in the way. He then said that he should like very much to see you, that he had nothing but the kindest feelings personally toward you and that your personal relations had always been extremely pleasant, that in fact he liked you very much, that his only objection was on the single point he named and that he wished very much you would call and see him. I said that you had been thinking of calling to see him about some state matters and that you had hesitated because, I knew, you thought your doing so might possibly be misunderstood by him. He said there was no danger of that, that he wished very much you would come, and he would be much obliged if I would say so to you, and that he should hope to see you soon. There is nothing in that Brooklyn Navy Yard business. It is practically all under the Tracy rules, which have been maintained by Herbert and which McKinley will not abrogate. The patronage there is perfectly trivial in any event and whatever there is, be it much or little, is handled by the Secretary and not by the Assistant Secretary. It is really to my mind not a matter of any consequence. The questions in the Navy Department with which you will be called to deal will be the big questions of naval policy. The matter of Navy Yard patronage died out of the Navy Department some years ago—a fact which I do not think Platt appreciates. Platt also said that he was absolutely sure that Bliss was to be Secretary of the Navy, but that the fact of your both coming from New York would not make the slightest difference. I do not think that any cabinet place is sure. Everything is in the air in my opinion in regard to it, but Bliss would be a very pleasant man to get on with and he and Platt could settle patronage between them, although there is really, as I have said, no serious patronage there. If I were you, I would see him. I do not want him to ask anything for you, nor do I want to put you under the slightest obligation to him, but I do not want his opposition. I want him to be friendly and not fight.

I saw Wolcott last night. He has had a terrible summer in Colorado, but he is tremendously interested in you and is going to tackle Hanna with all his might and main. He is an old and intimate friend of Hanna's. Today Senator Davis was asking me about you and I told him what I was trying to bring about. He said you ought to have it if you wanted it—in fact that you ought to have anything in reason that you want and that he would especially like to get you back to Washington. He then said voluntarily, "I will write to McKinley tonight and give my personal estimate of Roosevelt and say all I can for his appointment." You would have been gratified by his warm expression of admiration and real affection for you. I would not have you make a single effort yourself for this place, but I think as Platt has expressed to me the desire to see you and as he is likely to be the Senator from your own State, it is perfectly right and proper and certainly advisable that you should see him. I would let him do the talking and I have no doubt that it will all come right. He wants really, I think, more than anything else to feel that you are not to be shoved in over his head and that your idea in going there is not to make war on him. That is of course a perfectly absurd notion, for as a matter of fact you would not come in contact with him or the Brooklyn yard at all and I can see no objection to disabusing his mind of that idea, if he has got it. At all events a talk with him can do no possible harm and you will have the chance to discuss the other matters of greater importance than the Brooklyn Navy Yard, about which you said you wanted to see him. I am to meet Hanna at dinner tonight and shall open up on you then. I saw him Saturday evening, but did not at that time get an opportunity. From all I can learn Hanna likes you extremely, but I propose to get his energetic and active support, if I can.*

Always sincerely yours, H. C. L.

* The reason for Senator Platt's kindly feeling toward me at that time was that we had been closely associated in the great fight in the National Convention to put the word "Gold" into the currency resolution. To this cause Mr. Platt had rendered great service.

POLICE DEPARTMENT
OF THE CITY OF NEW YORK

300 Mulberry Street,
NEW YORK, Dec. 9, 1896.

Hon. H. C. Lodge, Senate Chamber, Washington, D. C.

Dear Cabot:—I feel really ashamed, when I think of all you are doing; and yet I ought not to, for I have become quite hardened to all manifestations of your interest in anything that concerns me. I shall write Platt at once to get an appointment to see him. Of course I should not go into the Department to make war upon Platt, and so far as I had any influence, I would not allow the patronage to be used for any such purpose. As a matter of fact, the Civil Service Law would prevent any such use anyhow.

Now, ought I to write Senator Davis and thank him for his kindness? I am very much touched by it.

Indeed, I do not think the Assistant Secretaryship in the least below what I ought to have. Except you and one or two other equally mis-guided people who persist in getting my personality out of focus, and except the other people who do not realize that there is work to do for the Navy, no one would think so. All I meant was that I had become so interested in the fight here, and was so reluctant to leave it half done, that if I had full power I should hesitate about leaving—though even in that case, I think I should resolve my doubts in favor of going back to where I could be near you and Nannie, the only people for whom I really care outside of my own family.

The Century people made just the same request of me, and curiously enough, I like yourself, took the opportunity to make a plea for the "Hero Tales." I shall go in and see them at once. I return the letter. Tell Nannie to look in the next *Forum* for my Review of Brooks' book.

Ever yours,
THEODORE ROOSEVELT.

POLICE DEPARTMENT
OF THE CITY OF NEW YORK

300 Mulberry Street,
NEW YORK, Dec. 17, 1896.

Dear Cabot :—

We had an exceedingly pleasant dinner at Witherbee's. I must say I was most favorably impressed with Black, and I can't help feeling he is sound at heart, though his machine training is most unfortunate. Unless he is a skillful dissimulator he also liked me. I am going to have a good deal of correspondence with him not only on the liquor law, but about civil service matters. Platt was exceedingly polite.

I don't like the election of the Populist Mayor in Lynn. It shows that the workingmen are inclined to demand the impossible in the way of immediate prosperity; and I fear some of our own people made a great error in not following on the lines you laid down, and in making all kinds of promises of immediate prosperity as a result of Republican rule, instead of merely saying that we would give conditions which would allow the chance of prosperity.

Best love to Nannie. It was delightful to see Bay and yourself.

Always yours,
THEODORE ROOSEVELT.

SAGAMORE HILL,
OYSTER BAY, LONG ISLAND, N. Y.,
Dec. 26th, '96.

Dear Cabot,

A very merry Xmas to Nannie and yourself. Edith and I have felt it a serious loss to be away from you these two years at Xmas, although we of course take peculiar pleasure in passing Xmas out here in the country at our own home. The weather this time has been ideal; cold, and with lots of snow, so we have been able to ride and sleigh, and Bob and I in addition have had much fun on the skis, and chopping.

Grant has suddenly gone in with Parker, to carry out (which of course he can't do) the dictates of the Republican county managers, Lauterbach and Gruber; he is hoping to get something good from McKinley, and relies upon the backing of the local machine. I refused to speak at the Choate meeting; of course if I have to declare, I shall be for Choate against Platt, for the feeling about Platt is ugly; but it is a futile and useless fight, and as I have my hands full of fights which are neither futile nor useless, I do not care to be dragged into this.

I wish the Cuban question could be forced to an issue before Cleveland went out. What is the matter with Olney? Edith sends her love. Look at the *Forum* article; I had an irritating experience with the *Review of Reviews* and the Watson article is scarcely worth looking at.

Yours,   T. R.

POLICE DEPARTMENT
OF THE CITY OF NEW YORK

300 Mulberry Street,
NEW YORK, Dec. 29, 1896.

Dear Cabot :—

I am in a great quandary how to answer you. I have read and re-read your interview a dozen times. All I am afraid is that it may be misconstrued; there is not a sentence in it which is not entirely proper, but I am nervous lest it's general purport may be misunderstood. Would it not be well to add, even if it may be surplusage a tag in which you state that you wish it definitely understood that you favor immediate steps for the independence of Cuba, even at the risk of war with Spain, and that you wish it understood also that conditions may at any time change so as to render it absolutely imperative at any cost to try to secure prompt action; but that as things are now it is evident that nothing can be done, and when this is the case it is your plain duty not to allow the wheels of legislation to be blocked by a resolution which at the moment means nothing. Of course your judgment is better than mine, and don't add this if you think it unwise. I am inclined to think, however, that some such addition would make it all right, and that then it would be a good thing to put out the interview; but I do not want to allow any chance of your being misunderstood, or being hampered in any future action.

How I wish I could see you on the new horse, and accompany you on the long rides, and watch your management of the Cary pet with respectful admiration.

Grant's folly has made things almost intolerable here. He is a heaven-sent tool for Parker. I have written to Cushman K. Davis.

Best love to Nannie. By the way, don't you think that "Father Archangel of Scotland" was an amusing little book in some ways?

Yours,   T. R.

1897

POLICE DEPARTMENT
OF THE CITY OF NEW YORK

300 Mulberry Street,
NEW YORK, Jan. 20, 1897.

Dear Cabot:—

I am rapidly growing hopelessly impatient to see you and talk over everything from the Arbitration Treaty to myself. I do not suppose there is any chance of your having to go to Boston, or your coming to New York within a month or so, is there? I rather hate to go to Washington as things are now.

Cornelius Bliss wishes me to write to McKinley on behalf of Horace Porter for a place in the Cabinet. I do not like to refuse Bliss, and I have always been very friendly to Porter. What is your judgment as to my writing McKinley? Quigg is laying his plans to be Mayor. He has many good points; but I wish he was less conceited and carried more guns, both intellectually and morally.

Rather to my amusement I am being attacked for having dealt too gently with Brooks; old Charles A. Dana and Austin Wadsworth forming part of the incongruous group of critics.

The enclosed letter from Mrs. Jones explains itself. I do not know whether Macmillans would be the best firm to put out these text books, even if we had time to write them. What do you say?

My work has begun to let up a good deal, and I have been able to do a little for that English Naval work.

Always yours,

THEODORE ROOSEVELT.

POLICE DEPARTMENT
OF THE CITY OF NEW YORK

300 Mulberry Street,
NEW YORK, Jan. 27, 1897.

Dear Cabot:—

Good! I was delighted to see that at last *Scribner's* had your article, and I think it even better than I thought it when I first read it.

I was immensely amused the other day at Mr. and Mrs. William E. Dodge coming back from Washington highly enthusiastic about you, and seriously shaken in their faith in the *Evening Post*, which had led them to expect in you an understudy of Scannel and Croker.

Always yours,

THEODORE ROOSEVELT.

POLICE DEPARTMENT
OF THE CITY OF NEW YORK

300 Mulberry Street,
NEW YORK, Jan. 30, 1897.

Dear Cabot:—

To my horror the *Sun* yesterday put me down as opposed to the restriction of immigration; this being the way they had construed an ardent appeal of mine to the labor union men to restrict it. I corrected it in the *Sun* of this morning. I had an extremely interesting conference with the union men, though I was much irritated at certain jacks immediately trying to undo the good, by saying that I ought to get their support as candidate for Mayor.

I wrote to Platt telling him how much I approved his speech at Albany, except on the Cuba question.

I really don't know that there is any one I care much to see at Washington unless it is Cushman K. Davis; and if I get a chance I shall stop in for five minutes to see Olney. You and Nannie are my objective points!

Always yours,

THEODORE ROOSEVELT.

POLICE DEPARTMENT
OF THE CITY OF NEW YORK

300 Mulberry Street,
NEW YORK, March 1st, 1897.

Dear Cabot:—

I was much amused at the German publication. It seems to me my utterances are mild when compared to yours. Your speech about Cuba made me feel proud. I got the Southern Society literally standing on the table on Washington's Birthday when I talked about Crete and Cuba.

Yours,   T. R.

SENATE CHAMBER
WASHINGTON

March 8th, 1897.

Dear Theodore:

You have been in my thoughts day and night and your name has been on my lips daily and yet I have not written you. The simple reason has been that in this town of crowds and rush, with a dying Congress and an incoming President, with struggling ambitions and an air filled with contradictory rumors it has seemed to me that it would be a useless annoyance to tell you all the phases and fluctuations and all I was doing in the campaign I am making for you—the only thing I care about winning out. I knew you would know that I was not lying idle but doing all that could be done. Now I have

something to report. I have seen Long.* He says he is entirely
open-minded, has not yet taken the question up—will not for
some little time—that McKinley will appoint but he supposes
he will be consulted. He spoke unfavorably of the other candidates—in the highest terms of you. The only thing resembling
criticism was then given out. "Roosevelt has the character,
standing, ability and reputation to entitle him to be a Cabinet
Minister. Is not this too small for him!" The hitch, if there
be one, is not with Long but at the White House and in this
Wolcott agrees with me. Whether there is any real resistance
I cannot tell and the only, absolutely the only thing, I can
hear adverse is that there is a fear that you will want to fight
somebody at once. I have not seen McKinley because I want
to strike in a little later. Meantime I have been massing the
forces, most of them, let me say, volunteers. You have enough
friends earnest for you to make a Secretary of State.

Wolcott, who will ask—as I have done—for it as his one personal favor. I am more grateful to Wolcott and for his stand in
this than I can say. Reed who has written to Long and will
speak to McKinley as Wolcott and I have spoken, perhaps has
done so already. I have not asked him to speak for I would
not until I was sure it would be granted. I would not have him
refused. Reed and George Lyman are less particular, George
Lyman made it his one request to Reed to ask your appointment of McKinley.

John Hay has written and spoken and urged in the most
earnest way at all opportunities. Davis, as you know, has
written and will do anything more I ask.

Hanna is entirely friendly and wants you here—has so many
things that I do not suppose he presses it, but he is all right.

Judge Taft, one of the best fellows going, plunged in last week
—got Herrick, a close friend of the President, to take hold which
he did most cordially. John Addison Porter—volunteered
doing all he can—wants you very much and talks to the
President. Platt not lifting a finger against you. I shall have
further talk tomorrow and see if I cannot carry him still further.

I saw Bliss this morning. He spoke of you in the warmest

* John D. Long, Secretary of the Navy.

and most affectionate way. Said you were just the man, and that he had meant to have you altho' he did not commit himself when you talked together. He will talk to the President and Long. McAdoo* who is acting as assistant wants you to succeed him and will talk to Long at first opening.

After adjournment today Hobart came up and said, "You are I know interested in Roosevelt. He is a splendid fellow. I think everything of him—just the sort of man we ought to get. What can I do?" This was an unexpected recruit. I took him in at once. He had an appointment with the President this afternoon and said that he would urge you then upon him. I believe I am going to win. I say "I" with egotism. I mean all these men who are friends of yours. Whence the resistance comes I do not know; nor do I know that there is any; but some one I am sure has been trying to influence the President and possibly Long against you. I cannot think they would pay heed to Grant and yet I can hear of no one else. I believe we are coming out all right. In any event you have, I think, a right to be proud of such support as that I have described and you have not raised a finger and it has all come voluntarily. All I have done is to mass and direct a little. Poor Storer (this in deepest confidence)is thrown over for the State Dept. I will tell you about it when we meet. What he will get I cannot say. Some small thing abroad I suppose. I have had some dark hours in this business but I feel so cheerful and hopeful now that I thought I could report to you fairly as it looks at this moment.

Best love to Edith.

Ever yrs, H. C. L.

689 Madison Ave.,
New York,
March 10th, '97.

Dear Cabot,

Your two letters made Edith and me feel very much as you and Nannie felt when your own Nahant people came up to serenade you—a little like bawling. I do think you are the staunchest and most loyal friend in the world. I feel ashamed

* William McAdoo of New Jersey.

to feel you have had me so on your mind, just at this time, with the defeat of the immigration bill and everything else to weigh on you. I have never felt much hope about the Assistant Secretaryship; for the pressure on McKinley is very great, he has no reason to care for me personally; and of course if he has some one else in mind, that makes the chance very small.

Parker and Grant between them have deliberately brought the whole machine to a standstill, and have created a situation so bad that in my heart I hail this bill to legislate us out as a relief. It is bitter to have that knave and that dolt able to undo what it has cost me much intense effort to do. Nothing possible that I would get, not the Senatorship or a place in the Cabinet, could be to me what you have done—and the way it was done—have been. And I am more touched than I can say at what you tell me the others have done—men whom I never dreamed cared a rap about me. As for you, old man, I don't mind in the least being under the greatest obligations to you; and I have written notes of thanks to Hobart, Addison Porter and Secretary Bliss.

I am awfully sorry about poor Storer.

Best love to Nannie.

Yours ever,

T. R.

POLICE DEPARTMENT
OF THE CITY OF NEW YORK

300 Mulberry Street,

Dear Cabot :— NEW YORK, March 17, 1897.

I am very much obliged to you for that pamphlet. It has a rather extraordinary collection of books of travel; there are one or two I think I must get. By the way, I have about finished my piece on The War of 1812, for the Laird Clowes outfit. It contains a pretty strong plea for a powerful navy, and the ability of handling that navy effectively when necessary.

At present there seems to be a hitch in the project to legislate us out of office. I think the project so bad from the civic and political standpoint that I am glad, but as regards myself I am really disappointed; I should like very much to see the bill go through as far as I am concerned. I can say conscientiously, and as a matter of honest, and, as I think, well justified belief, that no man could have done more than I have done in this position, and that no man who strove honestly to do his duty could have avoided the difficulties I have encountered. It simply was not possible to keep in any longer with either Parker or Grant. The rascality of the one, and the weakness of the other, simply rendered it out of the question. One of the utterly harassing features of it is that they care nothing for the good of the Force, whereas, I do, and so I continually have to accept compromises and make a vigorous fight for measures of which I only half approve, while they positively desire to see the Police Force stand badly. In consequence, the entire brunt of keeping the Force straight and of defending it from unjust attack comes upon me, and they by their actions merely give weight and point to the attack on it. During the two years I have been here, I have in every way avoided any kind of attack upon the organization Republicans, and all I could legitimately do that they have asked me, I have done. In the greatest struggle in which they engaged, that about the Presidential nomination, I backed them in every way, and the only feeling they have in return is a desire to cut my throat, not for any mistake I have made, but because I have administered the office honestly; and in the same breath in which they denounce me as not being a good Republican because I will not do dirty work for them, they turn round and insist upon making a deal with Parker and Conlin, both of whom are Democrats, and who are probably corrupt. As for the Anti-Platt Republicans, upon my word, I believe them to be almost a shade worse. The *Tribune* has added insincerity to the catalogue of the machine vices, and has in every way opposed me ever since I declined to give them the police advertising; and to work under Mayor Strong, is soul-harrowing, for he never follows out a consistent course, and never resolutely backs any man up. The so-called Independent

Republicans of the Seth Low stamp are but little better. The only comfort is that I resolutely strive to give as good as I get.

There! I feel easier, having burdened you, as usual, with my parochial woes.

Are you going to try to do anything about your Immigration Bill again? You have never written me very much about that. I suppose no action whatever will be taken in reference to Cuba for some time to come. The tariff bill is all right, is it not? At any rate, if we can once begin to raise enough revenue the most serious part of our troubles will disappear, and the definite knowledge of our tariff policy for the next four years will enable business to become stable and revive.

Best love to Nannie.

Always yours,

THEODORE ROOSEVELT.

POLICE DEPARTMENT
OF THE CITY OF NEW YORK

300 Mulberry Street,

Dear Cabot:—   NEW YORK, March 19, 1897.

I have received both your letters. Edith got hold of the first immediately on her return from Philadelphia, where she had been spending three days, and insisted on reading it aloud to me, and endorsing all the views it set forth with fairly rabid emphasis. I have no more speeches in view excepting one a fortnight hence at the Young Men's Republican Club of Brooklyn, which is a rather representative body, and where I cannot conceive of anything unpleasant happening.

As for talking about "forgiving" you for writing me advice which was most sound, and which merely added a needless proof of the depth of your interest in my welfare—why, I shall simply decline to discuss *that* proposition.

I had abandoned all idea of the Assistant Secretaryship, and was not thinking about it until those two last letters of yours came. Now, a word of justification as to the Social Reform Club incident. I have had nobody back of me for the last two years here and every ounce of strength I have got is due to my own personal exertions. I have found that especially among workingmen, and Germans, and political organizations on the East and West sides, there was a good deal of distrust of me and misunderstanding of my position, which I could often remove if I came before them in person. If I had not been able to get some sentiment in my favor I should have been out of this office long ago. The other day the clergy all declared in my favor, primarily because I have spoken so often at their meetings, and have made them partners, so to speak, in my work. I have, at least, prevented many of the East side organizations from taking any hostile steps against me by what I have done, and have won a few of them over. Nine times out of ten by going to speak before them I do good; the tenth it works badly. Of course this does not excuse me for failing to take every possible measure to prevent such an occurrence as that of the other night, for I appreciate fully the discredit attaching to what looked like a joint debate with an abusive socialist blackguard. The Social Reform Club has at its top a lot of thoroughly well-meaning philanthropists like Mrs. Josephine Shaw Lowell, Dr. Rainsford, Ernest Howard Crosby, etc., and it also has a large number of Labor Union Leaders. It ought to be influential and responsible, but I doubt if it is either. For over a year they have been begging me to come, and this winter I finally consented. Waring addressed them the other day, and so have two or three of the heads of City Departments without anything disagreeable happening; but they are a lot of utter cranks, and they showed this when they came to deal with me. Their body contains many socialists and anarchists, both of the parlor and practical kinds, and these men, I am happy to say, regard me with a peculiar hatred. Without giving me a word of warning they asked this Oppenheimer, who is a European refugee, and who has been in prison abroad, and who is a violent socialist and agitator, to answer me. I knew nothing of it until Oppenheimer got up with his typewritten manuscript in his hand, copies of which he had already sent to the papers, and the room was filled to overflowing with the people who had come round to cheer the attack. In short, it was a put-up-job, for which the well-meaning fools who had invited me were really responsible. The *Sun* has recently had rather a relapse about me, and anyhow is always willing to chronicle with delightful indifference a hard blow struck, whether it happens to be a foul or not. The reporters on most of these City papers are, as I have found out during the last Presidential Campaign, predominantly of the free silver, socialist stripe, and they had all been informed in advance by the Oppenheimer people of what he was to do. As soon as he began to speak I saw what I was in for, and the only way to make the best of a bad business was to fight it out. Now, I am going to say something in which I fear even you will believe my judgment is entirely wrong. The impression conveyed by the morning papers, with the possible exception of the utterly unimportant *Times*, was wholly erroneous. I never won a more complete triumph, of a small character, than in my answer to Oppenheimer. I was addressing hostile socialists who began by hissing me. When I had finished my speech I had driven Oppenheimer out of the room, and I had the audience perfectly crazily on my side. They cheered me and cheered me again and again, and thronged around me so to shake hands, and to tell me that they had changed their opinion, that I was not able to get away for half an hour. But of course this did not count for anything, as they were an unimportant aggregation of warring microbes, and the papers made it look the other way.

I was very glad that the Mayor acted. I do not suppose that the Governor will sustain him, but the Mayor's action itself strengthens me; and it furnished an additional reason for refusing to pass the bill. At present it seems probable that the bill will not go through, but no one can tell.

I myself doubted whether it would be wise for you to go abroad this summer, but I did not like to say so. I am glad you have begun the fight on your Immigration Bill again. I took a kind of grim satisfaction in Cleveland's* winding up his

---

* It is only fair to say that I heard some years later, that Mr. Cleveland spoke of the veto of the Immigration Bill which contained the first illiteracy test as one which he had since greatly regretted. It was said at the time that he had been

career by this action, so that his last stroke was given to injure the country as much as he possibly could.

I am immensely surprised and pleased about Senator Chandler. I shall do just as you advise. I quite understand the embarrassment of the matter so far as Platt is concerned, both from his standpoint and from ours. It is of course very hard for him to have the big places go to his political opponents; but on the other hand his trusted lieutenants are a dreadful lot. I was much amused at Chandler's telling you this, for, of course, that is the fundamental trouble I have had with the machine. When they have put up a man like Health Officer Doty, or District Attorney Olcott, I have jumped at the chance of supporting them with all enthusiasm; but the men they have asked me to promote and appoint in my Department have usually been men of such low character that it was a simple impossibility to do anything with them. I do not mean that they were politicians, or merely negative persons, I mean that they were guilty of blackmail, personal corruption, ballot-box stuffing and the like. I think it extremely kind of Hobart and Hanna to have done what they did.

No human being except Edith shall know anything about Chandler.   Always yours,
                                                        THEODORE ROOSEVELT.

P. S.—Harry White wrote me a very nice letter. Naturally enough he seemed fairly awed by the energy and resolution with which you had been working for me. I think it is the kind of disinterestedness to which he has not been accustomed in politics. Best love to Nannie.

689 MADISON AVENUE

Dear Cabot,   March 20th, '97.

Immediately upon receipt of your telegram I called upon Olcott, and then talked with Doty, who is stationed on Staten Island, over the telephone. They both responded in the nicest way possible; it really made me feel that I did not mind being

much influenced by the representations or misrepresentations of the German Steamship people in New York. But however this may be, I am now very certain that he was not only a strong but an honest man and thoroughly American as was shown by his action in the Venezuela case.

under the obligation to them. I have had very intimate official relations with both; and I was genuinely pleased at the heartiness with which they at once responded. Olcott saw Platt last night and again this morning; and Doty came all the way in from Staten Island to see him early this morning. Olcott has just been up to see me and told me the result of the interview. It was not favorable. Platt said substantially just what you have reported. He said he should not oppose me, if I was nominated as a man whose nomination was not to be charged to him or New York; but that Bliss and Porter were anti-organization men and the remaining places should be given to the organization; and that my appointment would mean one place less for the organization people, to which he could not well consent. He said he thought I was honest (which was kind of him), and that from what they said I was evidently a good executive officer, with whom it was not so difficult as was popularly supposed to get along; and that in one way my appointment would please the machine, as it would take me out of my present office, as there now seemed little chance of accomplishing this by legislation; but that he felt both they, and I, ought to understand that he could not assent to my receiving a place which ought to be credited to the organization. Do you know, I hate to write you this, for I believe you will mind it a good deal more than I do.

When you think proper, I wish to write to Long and thank him very heartily, and to explain to him that I should have been entirely loyal and subordinate.

Best love to Nannie.   Always yours,

                                                T. R.

POLICE DEPARTMENT
OF THE CITY OF NEW YORK

                                300 Mulberry Street,
Dear Cabot:—   NEW YORK, March 22, 1897.

I was delighted to get your letter this morning. I felt a little down-cast over the prospect after what Olcott and Doty told me, for they are the only Platt men I know who could go to Platt about me, and they took the greatest trouble to go, and I have no doubt they backed me in every way. It may be that Platt will consent to my nomination if some of his friends go in at the same time; but I don't feel very hopeful in the matter. I hate like poison to have you pull such a laboring oar on my behalf, when I can do nothing. Olcott and Doty were so pleasant and so delighted to speak for me, even at some inconvenience to themselves, that I did not mind a bit having asked them the favor. I was a good deal touched too at the heartiness with which they responded, for they have been thrown into close contact with me, and if I were an unpleasant person to get along with, they would certainly know it. There does not seem much chance of the bill to turn us out passing, and still less chance of Parker being put out.

Just at this moment Lauterbach has called me up over the telephone, and volunteered the information that he and Quigg at the regular Sunday conference yesterday, advised Platt to favor me for Assistant Secretary. Now, I have not the slightest idea whether this is true or not, but it evidently does mean that good resulted from the visits of Olcott and Doty, and that the matter was brought under discussion. I daresay if Platt got other things at the same time, or some other one thing which he wants very much, he might consent to me; but at bottom I fear their objection to me is radical.

Whenever you say, I shall write Long. I want him to understand that I know enough to go into this position, if I am offered it, with my eyes open, and shall work hard, and shall stay at Washington, hot weather or any other weather, whenever he wants me to stay there, and go wherever he sends me, and my aim should be solely to make his administration a success.

From what Lauterbach says I think it evident that Platt is really making the machine's hostility to me merely an excuse. I think the machine would be quite willing to see me appointed so as to get me out of the city; at least Lauterbach's words were what if Platt would consent the rest would be entirely willing; but he told me to keep what he said entirely confidential, so that you must not let Platt know that Lauterbach has talked to me.   Always yours,

THEODORE ROOSEVELT.

POLICE DEPARTMENT
OF THE CITY OF NEW YORK

300 Mulberry Street,
NEW YORK, March 23, 1897.

Dear Cabot :—

Just a line to tell you that the machine people here evidently
have it in their heads that I am to be made Assistant Secretary
of the Navy, and evidently approve of it as a means of getting
me out of New York. I rather wonder whether some of what
Platt told Doty and Olcott was not merely said with the hope
of making me give him something in connection with this
office, or else to establish a ground for holding off, so as to get
something from the Administration.

Always yours,
THEODORE ROOSEVELT.

P. S.—Harry White has just turned up: and he was really
touching in describing how you have worked for me. There
is nothing I can say except that I am well aware of it, old man.

March 29th, '97.
Dear Cabot,

Immediately on receiving your second telegram I started;
I picked up a good deal of negative information; but unless I
am greatly mistaken I excited, and had to excite, some suspicion. But of that I shall write you tomorrow.

Of this much I am certain. The Mayor has now no idea
whom he would appoint, were there a vacancy on the Board.
The only man of whom he has ever so much as spoken a word
is Edward Mitchell, and this was a mere casual expression.
He would be well inclined to a machine man like Olcott or
Doty, but would on no account appoint any of the ordinary
gang of machine heelers. He would doubtless listen to anything from a man like Cornelius Bliss. But he would not
agree (and I should not advise him to agree) to anything in
the nature of a bargain, by which he would take some organization man, not fitted for the place; and I very much fear that

this is what Platt means. Strong would wish in my place only some man of the very highest type.

You are awfully good not to have sent those letters I wrote; I only felt that when you did so much I ought to do *something*, and not be a mere dead weight! I didn't like to write them.

Now, show this letter to Tom Reed, and if you think it wise show the next sheet to Platt; for it contains something I would like to say to *him*, but which it is useless to say to the corrupt gang behind him; and they are simply awful!

I do wish I could lay before Senator Platt what seems to me to be *the* important feature of the situation in the Police Board now. Commissioners come and go, but the Chief stays, and the Chief is far more important than any Commissioner. The Senator would find it far more to the benefit of the organization to get the right man for Chief than to get anything else; and he could get that man now in the shape of Acting Inspector McCullagh, if he could be made Chief.

Conlin is utterly weak and treacherous; he is a Democrat; he is even now dealing with Tammany; and he will turn on the Platt people the minute he or Parker think it advantageous to do it. McCullagh is an organization Republican; he is a strong, brave and discreet and able man; he is far and away the best man for Chief; he is already a follower of Senator Platt; and he is a man who never forgets a friend, and never loses heart or abandons the side which he has championed. He would "stay put!"

To Lauterbach or Hackett I would not dare to praise McCullagh, because they would think I had some personal end in view; but I believe Senator Platt would know I had none, save to help the Force, and also the party. McCullagh would make the best Chief the Force could have; and he is the only man in the Force who when Chief would surely remain a Republican in foul as well as fair weather; and he is an organization Republican at that. At last I now have Andrews for him; should Grant favor him, and let Conlin get out, the whole difficulty in the police board would be solved and I think solved in just the way Senator Platt would wish.

Yours,

T. R.

New York,
March 30th, '97.

Dear Cabot,

As I expected, my inquiries resulted in my being called before the Mayor, with whom, however, I am bound to say, I had the pleasantest interview I have yet had. He told me that Bliss had recently spoken to him about my going, and that he hated to have me, but that "he knew I was in hell" and he would take the utmost pleasure in writing to McKinley on my behalf. As to my successor, he said about what I told you yesterday. He has no idea himself who it would be, or who would take it; but it must be some one who will work as I have worked, and who will be steadfast against Parker, Grant and Conlin.

In this he is quite right. A decent man like Olcott the Mayor would gladly appoint; but Olcott hates and distrusts Parker and Conlin as much as I do; being an honest District Attorney he speedily found them out; and he told me he had nearly quarreled with Platt on the subject, telling him that it was incomprehensible to him how the machine could support that pair of scoundrels in their effort to ruin the police department. You see the whole trouble comes from this attitude of the machine leaders. For the last year Parker's whole strength has been due to his deal with the machine; and Platt acquiesces in it; this is all that gives Parker his power for evil; and the machine, with a shamelessness rather worse than Tammany's, seeks its profit out of the mischief he makes. Lauterbach, Lexow, and the other machine leaders are now moving heaven and earth to prevent the Governor from removing Parker. Every decent man in the machine wishes him removed; but the fundamental difficulty with the New York machine at this moment is that the great majority of its leaders are not decent, and their quarrel with me is because I am. I wish you would show this to Tom Reed.

I feel this is rather a gloomy note to have to write you; but of course I simply cannot try to have chosen as my successor the kind of man who, I fear, would alone be acceptable to Platt; and if I did try it would do worse than no good.

McCook was most pleasant. I feel like a heavy lump of dough to be so unable to help you while you are making such an extraordinary fight for me.

Yours,

T. R.

WESTERN UNION TELEGRAPH COMPANY

Apr. 6–97.

Hon. H. C. Lodge, 1765 Mass. Ave., Washington, D. C.

Sinbad has evidently landed the old man of the sea.*

T. R.

POLICE DEPARTMENT
OF THE CITY OF NEW YORK

300 Mulberry Street,

Dear Cabot:—

NEW YORK, Apr. 8, 1897.

That was not only a lie, but an exceptionally mean lie. One of the editors of the *Journal* travelled with me to Chicago, having been introduced to me as the cousin of Dr. Lyman Abbott; I was cordial to him, but of course, said nothing whatever that he could quote against me. Two weeks later he gave out an alleged statement by me in the first person, but carefully refrained from giving himself as authority, until I publicly taxed him. The statement was of course an absolute lie. Any one who has ever heard me speak knows that I am quite incapable of using such expressions as "meeting Altgeld sword in hand at the head of my regiment" and, "standing up the silver leaders against a wall to be shot."

I wish you would drop me a line to tell me what effect that lie has. As soon as it was published I denied it in the most explicit terms; among other places, in the *Sun* of October 31st.

I am just on my way up to see Nannie.

Always yours,

THEODORE ROOSEVELT.

* He had been nominated for the place of Assistant Secretary of the Navy by President McKinley.

NAVY DEPARTMENT
WASHINGTON

Dear Cabot,   June 17th, '97.

I am very much pleased you are better; don't come back
Sunday unless you are all right; things are very quiet here
(though I personally hope you *will* get back; for Long is off
until July 2d and wishes me then to take ten days at O. B. so
as to get in trim for the hot months alone!)

I am very much pleased over the Hawaiian business. Last
evening I spent very pleasantly at the White House. The
President was as cordial as ever; was much pleased with what
I told of your support of and adhesion to him; and expressed himself very strongly as in favor of going on with the
upbuilding of the Navy—Hanna backing up this like a man. I
have dined three times at the Harry Davises; I struggle hard
to keep Hobday from over-feeding me; Bella has nine puppies;
and I have two or three stories for Nannie—to whom give my
warmest love.

                                    Yours ever,
                                                      T. R.

NAVY DEPARTMENT
OFFICE ASSISTANT SECRETARY
WASHINGTON

Dear Cabot: August 3, 1897.

Yes indeed, the President has come out finely on the civil
service; and you will be pleased to hear that in a recent interview he told Proctor* that he should keep him when he reorganized the Commission. Proctor, by the way, is very grateful
to you, and fully appreciates all you have done for him.

I entirely agree with you. We have every reason to be
proud of what the President and Congress have done during
the five months of office; and unquestionably times are improving. Of course to prophesy about our politics is a little
like prophesying about a kaleidoscope, and no human being
can foretell anything with any accuracy; but it certainly

* John R. Proctor of Kentucky, Civil Service Commissioner. An admirable
man and official.

seems to me as though this administration was opening, unlike every other administration of the last twenty years, with the prospects steadily brightening for its continuance during a second term.

I had a most interesting trip in the West among the Naval Militia, and also at Newport and Sandy Hook. My speech to the Naval Reserve of Ohio was entirely straight, and it was reported with substantial accuracy; but the headlines and comments, for which I was in no way responsible, nearly threw the Secretary into a fit, and he gave me as heavy a wigging as his invariable courtesy and kindness would permit. I told him of course that I was extremely sorry to have said anything of which he disapproved, and that I would not do so under any consideration, but that at the same time I thought what I said was, or ought to be, true, for most certainly the United States ought to decide whether or not it will annex Hawaii wholly without regard to the attitude of Japan or any other Power. I send you a clipping of a kind of which I get many. By the way, in Ohio they were very anxious that some action should be taken about Cuba. The President has done so much that I don't feel like being discontented, but of course I do feel that it would be everything for us to take firm action on behalf of the wretched Cubans. It would be a splendid thing for the Navy, too. I am feeling rather blue over the armor business. I am afraid it will be difficult for us to get them to go on with the building up of the Navy, and if they stop I fear they will never begin again.

I was immensely amused to see that Congressman Walker has announced his intention of beating you for Senator. I think he has quite a job on hand, and that your attitude can afford to be that of the Texan who examined the tenderfoot's 32 calibre revolver—"Stranger, if you ever shot me with that, *and I know'd it*, I would kick you all over Texas." I saw it stated that he intended to use the Secretary against you as a candidate, but I don't believe that the Secretary has the vaguest idea of running. However, it doesn't make any matter who tries to run; it will amount to the same thing.

Edith is on here with me; and fortunately the weather is

cool. She is grappling with desperate energy with the new house and the old furniture. The house will have a certain incongruous look next year, being furnished scantily in some directions, and over-abundantly in others, but we are very much pleased with it nevertheless. It seems very comfortable indeed, much more so than our old one. When Edith goes I shall probably spend some of the hot weather with Harry* at the observatory.

It is a great relief to think of you as at last having a little rest and being either at Nahant or at the Island. Give my warmest love to Nannie. Except in general terms I never heard exactly how John† passed, and as soon as you find out what Bay intends to do, be sure to let us know. I wish very much I could see Bay.

Always yours,

THEODORE ROOSEVELT.

NAHANT, MASS.
Aug. 5, 1897.

My dear Theodore:

I am very glad to hear what you say about Proctor. I not only spoke to the President about him, but I wrote a long letter putting the case as strongly as I could. You were all right in what you said about Japan. The headlines, I suppose, were what disturbed the Secretary. The Haverhill *Gazette* is a very influential paper in my county, and the editor, I am happy to say, a cordial friend of mine.

The Secretary said to me the last time I saw him, that I would be elected without opposition and ought to be.

What I hope for is that there will be no fight, and everything points in that direction.

I am very glad to hear what you say about the Observatory, and also that Edith managed to get through what she had to do so comfortably.

John, considering his illness, passed very well, getting

---

* Captain Davis was then in command at the Naval Observatory.
† My younger son.

nothing lower than C. Bay is getting together some verses for a little volume and wants to strike out and see what he can do for himself with literary work. I am going to let him try the experiment.

It seems inconceivable that the President should send Grant to China, and I hope there is no truth in the rumor. After the way he behaved to the President I should think the appointment was to say the least unlikely.

It is very disturbing about the armour, but the whole trouble has arisen from the greed of the companies. Hale told me that he could not get ten votes in the Senate for the higher price, and it is just as bad in the House. We may have some trouble about getting more ships, but if the President stands firm, we shall come out all right.   Always sincerely yours,

H. C. L.

NAVY DEPARTMENT
WASHINGTON

Aug. 8th, '97.

Dear Cabot,

Edith has very nearly finished with the house, and will go back to Oyster Bay in two or three days; most fortunately we have had really cool weather, and she has actually enjoyed herself. (Nannie will smile incredulously and say: "poor dear!") Rockhill dines with us tonight; last evening we dined at Overlook Inn, saw a lovely sunset, and had a beautiful moonlight drive home; one night the Davises dined with us and went to see an amusing farce; and another night we dined with them. They have a very comfortable and indeed handsome house. Harry is in fine form. He said of his predecessor: ". . . is a Kentuckian; he had not a single book, and he kept his chickens on the porch. He had for furniture in the dining room an oak table, nine mahogany chairs, a black walnut bookcase, and a washstand!" Harry made an excellent investigation at the Brooklyn navy yard; but I had to do much cutting of his report, which contained a violent assault on the

G. A. R. and on all the Brooklyn Congressmen by name; together with such sentences as "The military spirit is now totally extinct in the American people." You probably recognize the style.

Our house will be furnished largely from the wreck of Edith's forefather's houses sixty years back, with an occasional relic of my own family thrown in—all of the mesozoic or horse-hair furniture stage. We have come across some lovely mementos of a bygone civilization; including especially a number of stereopticon plates—"The Wedding Breakfast," "Dressing the Bride," "Evening near Windsor Castle," or, varied with views of the family tombs in Greenwood cemetery; which our ancestors always deemed highly edifying.

I am, as usual very much interested and occupied with my work. I have the armor board at work, and the cruising squadron of battleships and torpedo boats under my eye. With the docks I have nothing to do; I believe we need a radical revision of our whole dock system.

Edith and I were very glad to hear about Bay and John. Give our love to Nannie.

Yours,   T. R.

NAVY DEPARTMENT
OFFICE ASSISTANT SECRETARY
WASHINGTON.

Hon. H. C. Lodge, Nahant, Mass.   August 17, 1897.

Dear Cabot:—I have had a delightful few days with Harry. Day after tomorrow he goes off, and I shall be alone. The evenings are not particularly exhilarating, but the days I like, as I really am accomplishing a certain amount. Having done away with the needless paper work on the torpedo boats, I have now put Harry on a board to do the same things for the battleships and cruisers. I have also started a board on the question of dry docks. I don't know whether the Secretary will wish any information about these or not, but when he comes back I am going to have a definite plan to propose to him; and, what's more, a plan that will work. I acted on my own responsibility with the diagonal armour, for I found that the Secretary had feared to allow them to complete the armour unless they completed all, but he has been most kind, and acquiesced in what I did. I haven't a doubt on the subject myself, for it means the saving of nearly a year's work, and will be of very great importance. My torpedo boat flotilla is in fine shape. Of the six torpedo boats they have got only two with the proper commanders, which is a real misfortune, but still, though I can't get the best work out of the flotilla, I shall get pretty good work. I have spent my spare hours in getting together a most interesting series of quotations from the messages of the Presidents to Congress on behalf of the Navy. In some form or other I am going to try and have them made public. The first week in September I hope to spend three days with the squadron of battleships off Hampton Roads. From all of which you can readily gather that I am really enjoying my work.

I am very much pleased that you are loafing, and I am sure that you will very soon be yourself again. Any man who throws himself with such intense energy into his work as you do, and who therefore accomplishes so much, must pay the penalty in one way or another, especially if he not only *does* things, but *feels* them. I am also glad that you are working a little at your revolutionary piece.* I think that's going to be one of the most successful things you have ever done. By the way, I had a long and very pleasant letter from Senator Chandler the other day, in which he spoke with delight of your Webster and Hamilton, but especially your Webster. I am correcting the proof of my essays.

That good times are coming is now beyond a doubt. Wheat and gold together, and the fact that the tariff is out of the way, and the uneasiness abroad, all help. I am particularly glad for the sake of the contest in Ohio.

Faithfully yours,
THEODORE ROOSEVELT.

* "Story of the Revolution."

Private.   NAHANT, MASS.,
                                                 Aug. 19, 1897.
Dear Theodore :

The work you are doing is admirable and you really seem
to be accomplishing a good deal. It is a good idea to get together quotations from the Messages in regard to the Navy,
but do not on any account put them out with your name on
them or as coming from you in any way, for it would look as
if you were trying to force somebody's hand. It will be easy
enough to let that get out at the proper time, but before doing
anything about it in the way of publishing I think you ought
to submit them to the President and Secretary. Excuse my
volunteering this advice, which is probably unnecessary.

I am particularly glad in regard to what you did about the
armor. I did not know that we owed it to you, but I might have
guessed it.

Our friend Moorfield Storey has been making a speech in
which he has denounced the annexation of Hawaii; the reason
being that because we cannot govern New York and Boston
with perfect success we ought not to undertake anything else.
I simply mention this to show you the direction which our best
thought here is taking.
                           Always sincerely yours, H. C. L.

                        NAVY DEPARTMENT
                          WASHINGTON
                                                 Aug. 26th, '97.
Dear Cabot,

Before receiving your letter I had sent Long the proof of my
proposed article (I don't think it would quite do for me to send
it to the President, after the Secretary has passed on it) and
I enclose you the last two pages of his answer; on the first
page he had merely told me about striking out the parts where
I urged an increase in size of the Navy. His letter, as you will
see, is most kind in tone towards me; it shows that he is against
any increase whatever of the Navy; and I especially wish you
to look at the paragraph I have marked. It is precisely what
Carl Schurz and Godkin have written, to me or about me; and
if it were true I should of course have stayed in the Police De-

partment. Well, we must do what we can with the tools available. Please return me the letter; also the other, from the Commander of the new torpedo flotilla, which I send simply because it is so appreciative that it quite touched me.

Will you write me Bigelow's address abroad? I would like it moderately soon.

Did you notice that Conlin had retired, and that Parker was bowled over? Events in the Police Department have more than justified every action I took.

Give my love to Nannie; I sent her letter to Edith. It is very cool and pleasant here—for Washington; and, though I get rather homesick in the evenings, I thoroughly enjoy my work in the day time.

Mahan has a really noble article in *Harper's Monthly*.

Yours ever,   T. R.

NAVY DEPARTMENT
WASHINGTON

Hon. H. C. Lodge, Nahant, Mass.   September 11, 1897.

Dear Cabot: Many thanks for sending me the editorial from the *Journal*. By the way, after thinking it over I came to the conclusion you were right, and, before making my piece public, I sent a copy to the President. I didn't ask his approval, because I thought that might look as if I wanted something more than the Secretary's, so I merely sent it to him with a statement that I wished him to see it in advance; and that the words "in my own opinion" had been put in by direction of the Secretary. Apparently it has done good.

I have never enjoyed three days more than my three days with the fleet, and I think I have profited by it. In fact I know I have, for there are a lot of things I am doing now because of what I saw there. I was very fortunate in the weather, which was wonderfully calm. Think of it, on the Atlantic Ocean, out of sight of land, going out to dinner to a battleship in evening dress without an overcoat! I saw for myself the working of the different gear for turning turrets—electric, hydraulic, steam,- and pneumatic. I was aboard the *Iowa* and the *Puritan* throughout their practice under service conditions at the targets, and was able to satisfy myself definitely of the great superiority of the battleship as a gun platform. I was on the *New York* during the practice at night with searchlights and rapid fire guns at a drifting target, the location of which was unknown. I saw the maneuvers of the squadron as a whole, and met every captain and went over with him, on the ground, what was needed.

Harry has come back; I shall see him today. We are having a spell of hot weather now, but I don't mind it. When the Secretary will return I haven't the slightest idea. I hope the President gets back next week, as there are a number of things I should like to talk to him about.

With warm love to Nannie.

Yours ever,

THEODORE ROOSEVELT.

The London *Morning Post* has an article on me as "a Jingo of the Lodge and Morgan* school"; and the *Evening Post* of N. Y. is filled with wrath and contempt at my visiting the squadron because I am a "civilian."

Personal.   NAHANT, MASS.,
                                             Sept. 13, 1897.
Dear Theodore:—

Many thanks for your note of the 11th. You spoke of receiving the editorial from the *Journal*. I hope you also received my letter from Tuckanuck, with which I returned the Secretary's letter and the note from Capt. Kimball. You say nothing about it and I have a fear that it may have miscarried.

Your three days with the fleet must have been delightful. I read the account of it in the newspapers with a great deal of interest. The London *Post* seems to have hit you about right, but the remark of the *Evening Post* that you should not visit

* Senator John T. Morgan of Alabama—a very able man. Ex-Confederate general, in politics a Democrat.

the fleet because you were a civilian is one of the funniest things I have heard for a long time.

I have come back from the island much improved and quite ready for our little campaign here, which will not amount to much.

My book of essays* is out and I think it looks pretty well.

Always sincerely yours,

H. C. L.

NAVY DEPARTMENT
OFFICE ASSISTANT SECRETARY
WASHINGTON

Hon. H. C. Lodge, Nahant, Mass.   September 15, 1897.

My dear Cabot: Murray Crane was in yesterday with a couple of Massachusetts men, whose business I was able to attend to. I then got him to tell me about you and the Senatorship. He says there is absolutely no danger whatever. All he wants is that you and your friends should do nothing, and stay quiet; that there mustn't be the slightest acknowledgment that there is so much as a contest. It must all be taken for granted that your renomination is a matter of course.

The President has returned, and yesterday I went out driving with him. He was very much pleased with your letter to him some little time ago in reference to his civil service order and the course of the administration generally; and laughed heartily when I told him how you had written me at once to send my pamphlet to him before publishing it. He had previously told me that he hadn't had time to read the pamphlet when it came, but seeing how much attention it attracted in the newspapers he had afterwards read every word of it, and was exceedingly glad that I had put it out. Somewhat to my astonishment he also said that I was quite right in my speech to the Naval Militia, in which I mentioned Japan; that it was only the headlines that were wrong; and, in fact, generally expressed great satisfaction with what I had done, especially

* "Certain Accepted Heroes."

during the last seven weeks that I have been in charge of the Department. Of course the President is a bit of a jollier, but I think his words did represent a substratum of satisfaction.

He is evidently by no means sure that we shall not have trouble with either Spain or Japan; and, though he wants to avoid both, yet I think he could be depended upon to deal thoroughly and well with any difficulty that arises. I told him that I thought we ought to have some warning in the Navy Department, and that we ought not to be kept ready all the time. We can get ready for any time set us, just as you can get horses ready for any particular time; but you can't keep horses ready minute after minute for 24 hours and have them worth much at the end of the period. I also told him that I would guarantee that the Department would be in the best possible shape that our means would permit when war began; and that, as he knew, I myself would go to the war. He asked me what Mrs. Roosevelt would think of it, and I said that both you and she would regret it, but that this was one case where I would consult neither. He laughed, and said that he would do all he could, and thought he could guarantee that I should have the opportunity I sought if war by any chance arose.

To my great pleasure he also told me that he intended we should go on building up the Navy, with battleships and torpedo boats, and that he did not think the Secretary would recommend anything he (the President) did not approve. Altogether I had a very satisfactory talk.

We have had a very hot spell this month.

As I wrote you, I had three delightful days with the squadron. It was a wonderful and beautiful sight, and did me a lot of good, and the squadron some good.

I lunched with Harry on Sunday, and we then took a long bicycle ride. With best love to Nannie, and all,

Faithfully yours,

THEODORE ROOSEVELT.

NAVY DEPARTMENT
OFFICE ASSISTANT SECRETARY
WASHINGTON

Dear Cabot: September 21, 1897.

I shall not reply again to the *Journal*. Curiously enough, I did it this time on a hint from the President, who I found to my astonishment had taken the statements about the *Indiana* with entire seriousness and felt much worried, and was correspondingly relieved when I told him that the story was an absolute fake; that the damage done was a dent, at its deepest point an inch and a half in depth, which in a battleship 350 feet long no one but a trained expert would be able even to discover, and which, during the month the vessel had been at sea, had not caused even the tiniest leak. However, I sha'n't have another interview.

The President has been most kind. I dined with him Friday evening, and yesterday he sent over and took me out to drive again. I gave him a paper showing exactly where all our ships are, and I also sketched in outline what I thought ought to be done if things looked menacing about Spain, urging the necessity of taking an immediate and prompt initiative if we wished to avoid the chance of some serious trouble, and of the Japs chipping in. If we get Walker with our main fleet on the Cuban coast within forty-eight hours after war is declared— which we can readily do if just before the declaration we gather the entire fleet at Key West; and if we put four big, fast, heavily armed cruisers under, say Evans, as a flying squadron to harass the coast of Spain until some of the battleships are able to leave Cuba and go there; and if at the same time we throw, as quickly as possible, an expeditionary force into Cuba, I doubt if the war would last six weeks so far as the acute phase of it was concerned. Meanwhile, our Asiatic squadron should blockade, and if possible take, Manila. But if we hesitate and let the Spaniards take the initiative, they could give us great temporary annoyance by sending a squadron off our coast, not to speak of the fact that if they were given time, when once it was evident that war had to come, there would be plenty of German and English, and possible French, officers instructing them how to lay mines and use torpedoes for the defence of the Cuban ports. Besides, we would have the Japs on our backs. However, I haven't the slightest idea that there will be a war.

I am very much obliged to you for sending me Long's speech, and I shall write to him at once about it. His allusions to me were most kind and generous.

Yesterday I saw for the first time your new volume of essays, and I read it all through again from beginning to end. I think they make as good work of the kind as was ever done on this side of the water, and so far as I know, the only work of the kind that has been done here by a man who was a doer as well as a writer. I am particularly pleased that you put in your article about our foreign policy. It was timely, and it all goes to build up the body of public sentiment on the subject. I don't think it comes up to the seriousness and weight of the essays.

Give my best love to Nannie.

Faithfully yours,

THEODORE ROOSEVELT.

NAVY DEPARTMENT
OFFICE ASSISTANT SECRETARY
WASHINGTON

September 24, 1897.

Dear Cabot:

Now don't be absurd and speak of yourself as carping or critical in comments on me. All I perpetually fear is that your very great over-appreciation of me may lead you to minimize, or rather to overlook entirely, my very obvious faults. I entirely agree with you about not answering the papers. I sha'n't do it again. I should never answer an attack on myself, but when an attack on the Navy comes along it is sometimes hard not to respond.

Long is just a dear. The *Herald* piece did render me a little uneasy because I was so afraid it might represent some feeling on his part that I was usurping a position to which I was not entitled. He has wanted me to act entirely independently while he was away, and to decide all these things myself, even where I have written him that I was going to decide them in a way that I doubted whether he would altogether like; and I have at times been a little nervous in the effort to steer the exact course between bothering him on the one hand, and going ahead with something too widely divergent from his views, on the other. However, on the whole I think he has been satisfied with these two months during which I have had charge of the Department. He is a man of whom one really becomes fond, and I am looking forward to his return.

Really I cannot take very much interest in the solitary man against you being beaten. I don't care whether you come in by a vote of four hundred and odd to one, or of four hundred and odd to nothing. You are just as certain of your next term in the Senate as you are of finishing out your present term! Seriously, I am of course delighted to know that even this little pebble has been kicked out of the way.

Next week I hope to get back to Oyster Bay for a fortnight.

Faithfully yours,

THEODORE ROOSEVELT.

Personal.   NAHANT, MASS.,
                                                  Sept. 24, 1897.
Dear Theodore :

I was at Hamilton last night when I added a few lines to my letter to you about the watchmen, and did not thank you for what you said about my little volume of essays, which pleased me very much. It is needless to say that I value your opinion more than anyone else's, and when you are satisfied I have an encouraging sense that I have not done ill, because I know you would be the first to detect failure and have enough regard for me to point out the errors which might exist.

Always sincerely yours, H. C. L.

NAVY DEPARTMENT
WASHINGTON

Dear Cabot: Sept. 27th, 1897.

Captain Crowninshield tells me that the Secretary has already promised the command of the *Enterprise,* and even gave what might be called the promise of an alternate to that vessel.

Brander* has written me most enthusiastically about your essays saying that he had already read all but the one on our foreign policy and that he re-read them with real pleasure because "they were sturdy, wholesome, keen and scholarly."

The Secretary comes back tomorrow or day after and I shall be off for a fortnight. I shall get Arlo Bates' little volume at once.

Love to Nannie.

                                         Yours,
                                                    T. R.

Personal.   NAHANT, MASS.,
                                         Sept. 27, 1897.
Dear Theodore:

I have your letter of the 24th. The Secretary told me that he was entirely satisfied with all you had done and praised in the highest the work and service you were doing for the Navy and the spirit with which you are inspiring the Department. He was really delighted at your success and you need have no apprehension on that score. He talked of all you had been doing and approved of everything. The only thing I recall on which he said he was inclined to disagree with you was in your opinion in regard to floating docks. He seems to doubt very much whether they are good for much, and I confess my own prejudice runs that way; but this was a mere matter of policy and simply showed to me that he had been carefully following all you had been doing, and was really entirely satisfied.

What a mess they have gotten into in New York. I had supposed that Low was a man of too much practical sense to allow the Citizens Union to nominate him, and still more to accept the nomination before he had made all his arrangements

* Brander Matthews.

with the other forces. Without doubt he has dished himself completely, I should think, unless he can come to some agreement with the Republicans. I do hope they will and by uniting on some candidate against Tammany.

What news do you get from Ohio? I had supposed that under the reviving prospects everything was all right there, but what I have heard lately, from private sources, brings rather disquieting rumors.

Always sincerely yours, H. C. L.

NAVY DEPARTMENT
OFFICE ASSISTANT SECRETARY
WASHINGTON

September 29, 1897.

Dear Cabot:

The Secretary came last night. He is just as kind and cordial as possible. I really think he is pleased with what I have done.

I don't disagree with either of you about floating docks. I think that we ought to have one because it can be used for certain contingencies that others cannot be, and because it is so much cheaper and quicker to build. But concrete docks are what we really need, and especially one concrete dock at Boston.

Barrett* has been clamoring for places so much that I had a little brush with him about the shipkeepers. When the Secretary left it seemed there would be two vacancies as shipkeeper, and he told Barrett he could have them. However, later it turned out there were three. I gave Barrett the two which the Secretary had said he should have, but I did not hold myself bound to give him the third, about which I telegraphed to you and ultimately put in MacCabe's man. This, and my putting in Wilson instead of one of the veterans whom Barrett recommended, evidently angered him not a little, and he wrote me, in effect asserting his claims to all the places in the navy yard. I wrote him very politely but very firmly in return, and have not heard from him since.

* William E. Barrett, Congressman from Massachusetts.

I have had one or two horrid times with the patronage. I got on all right with the Grand Army men in New York, and indeed I think with the Congressmen there and Senator Platt —at any rate so far as I know; but in Norfolk a G. A. R. man got drunk and was absent for a week (which he himself stated in his telegram now on file) and before he could be removed he resigned. Twelve days afterward the commander of the local post demanded his reinstatement. I refused, stating the facts, and he then wrote me a grossly impertinent and abusive letter, to which I simply responded that when he learned how to write a proper letter I should answer it and not before. I have kept the correspondence complete.

What creatures those Pennsylvanians are! Even so good a fellow as Bingham is almost impossible to deal with, and Boies Penrose is worse. They have almost had epilepsy over a promotion from a $1200 to a $1400 clerkship, made under the rules in accordance with the recommendation of the commandant, just as we have made promotion after promotion in Brooklyn and Boston. It never occurred to me to consult them about it any more than I would have consulted you or Platt about similar affairs, for of course I knew nothing of the man's record and simply acted on the recommendation of the commandant. But this procedure very nearly gave them a fit. I have just had Bingham to lunch to smooth him down.

By the way, Penrose asked for an increase of salary for the League Island shipkeepers. I spoke to the Secretary in reference to your request, but he seemed rather disinclined to make any increases, fearing it would involve increases all along the line.

Indeed New York politics are in a muss! Low was exceedingly foolish to let the ultra-wing of the Citizens' Union force him into such a position; and this same wing has dominated the policy of the Citizens' Union with most disastrous results. On the other hand, the antics of the New York machine have passed belief. The fraud in conducting the primaries is now so open that it does not attract the least attention and is hardly even alluded to in the papers. But this year it has been carried fairly to the last point in the determination not to allow Low a delegate from New York. It was silly because it was entirely unnecessary. He would not have had, at the outside, more than 25, who could not have created even a fight; but in order to prevent so much as one being chosen, tactics were employed which no morality could have allowed and for which there was no excuse on the ground of self-preservation. In my own district they voted Tammany men openly, laughing and boasting about it; and for fear this might not win they changed the place of meeting at the last moment, notifying their own people by word of mouth, and the others by postal cards which were received the following day. Moreover, having taken their stand upon the "responsible Republican party government," they proceeded to nominate Ashbel P. Fitch as controller—one of the worst I ever met in Political life—and declined to give any approval whatever to Strong's administration, which with all its faults has been the best the city has had for half a century. Still, all this does not excuse in the least the worse than idiotic conduct of the Citizens' Union, and I am heartily glad I am out of it all. You may imagine, by the way, the wild appeals I am receiving from Mrs. Josephine Shaw Lowell, and others of that stamp.

I was delighted with Arlo Bates' book. It seemed to me as good as anything of the kind I have recently read and I am going to bring it on to Edith.

For the next fortnight I shall be at Oyster Bay. Edith forwarded me Nannie's letter which I greatly enjoyed reading.

Faithfully yours,
THEODORE ROOSEVELT.

P. S.—I asked the Secretary's permission today to talk to him very seriously about the need for an increase in the Navy, and the damage which the opposite course might do to America and the Republican party and the administration and himself, telling him that I wanted to speak plainly because I so esteemed and admired him, and I wanted his administration to be a success. He listened to me with the greatest fairness and with the utmost attention, and I half believe that I made some impression on him.

SAGAMORE HILL,
OYSTER BAY, LONG ISLAND, N. Y.,
Oct. 5th, '97.

Dear Cabot,

I'll have you sent the data about the *Constitution*. The Secretary has just written me that he wishes me to go on to Boston to the celebration on the 21st; the President had just previously informed me that he wished me to speak at the Cleveland Chamber of Commerce on the 19th; if I can get away that night I suppose I shall be able to get on to Boston in time to run down to Nahant for the night, if you can put me up. I don't know where the celebration is to be, or at what hour.

Corinne and Douglas have just gone away after spending a night here; both in excellent health. All here are well. You will be pleased to hear that at Washington I finally developed a playmate who fairly walked me off my legs; a Massachusetts man moreover, an army surgeon named Wood.*

As long as I can't take active part in shaping the fight here in N. Y. I am glad I am out of it. The result is utterly uncertain. No one can tell how much George will pull from Tammany; it is impossible to measure the strength of one or the weakness of the other. As to Tracy and Low, there is genuine public irritation that there should be a divided front; and, aside from the rabid minority in the following of each, there is a strong tendency to flock to whichever of the two seems strongest. At present any incident might turn the scale towards either.

Always yours,
T. R.

I am very much pleased with Gussie's success.

SAGAMORE HILL,
OYSTER BAY, LONG ISLAND, N. Y.,
Oct. 9th, '97.

Dear Cabot,

Send me back John Hay's letter after you have shown it to Nannie; she may like to see it.

I haven't Sir Howard Douglas' book anywhere round. Prac-

* Afterwards General Leonard Wood.

tically all the lessons he draws from British victories are from duels in 1812–15. In that book which you have so wisely purchased you will find that I quote from him several times. But the greatest tribute is paid by the greatest of the French authorities, Admiral Jurien de la Gravière. The only single ship actions which he even mentions are ours, and he gives the same attention to these that he does to the great fleet actions of the preceding twenty years; this, too, in a book written merely for the French naval public. Shall I send it to you? I quote it quite fully. We fired on the falling wave.

I shall be only too glad if I *don't* have to speak!

Yours,   T. R.

SAGAMORE HILL,
OYSTER BAY, LONG ISLAND, N. Y.,
Oct. 13th, '97.

Dear Cabot,

The Governor will address *me;* and *I* shall deliver an impassioned reply in which I shall anticipate or refute all your statements.

The Secretary has sent me word that he wishes me to go to a dinner of the Norfolk Club, in his stead, on Saturday the 23rd, so I shall have to go; if convenient I'll spend most of the time from the evening of the 20th until the 23rd at Nahant; one "Surbridge" has asked me to speak at Worcester at a Republican rally on Friday evening. I referred him to you; I'll accept unless you think otherwise.

I saw Burlingame the other day. He is really delighted with your series; he says your account of the Jersey campaign fairly thrilled him. Tell Nannie that he also told me that Kipling had sent him a remarkable out-of-doors poem for the December number, dedicated to the memory of Willie Phillips. I am very glad. Poor Willie Phillips! * What a gap he did leave.

---

* William Phillips, of Washington—a most delightful man. Great friend of us all. He was drowned while yachting on the Potomac.

I shall be very glad to be on the stump for the Republican party, away from a contest in which my party loyalty conflicts with my loyalty to the principles of decent government.

Always yours,

T. R.

SAGAMORE HILL,
OYSTER BAY, LONG ISLAND, N. Y.,

Dear Cabot,   Oct. 16th, '97.

I think you did very wisely in refusing to mix yourself in this ugly contest. There is too much intricate folly on both sides. Imagine making a deal with the George men after refusing even to confer with the Republicans, on the ground that deals were abhorrent! And the "Cits" Union have as a leader Reynolds who sizes up below the level of an ordinary election district captain.

On the other hand, the Republicans are running on a "straight party" issue, with Fitch, a free trader, a double traitor, in the second place; and denounce Low for voting twice for Cleveland when the Judge who is our only nominee on the State ticket did so three times. Moreover the really ugly feature in the Republican canvass is that it *does* represent exactly what the populists say, that is corrupt wealth. The Pierpont Morgan type of men forced Fitch on the ticket; and both Platt and Tracy represent the powerful, unscrupulous politicians who charge heavily for doing the work—sometimes good, sometimes bad—of the bankers, railroad men, insurance men and the like. I am glad I am out of it. I would have no heart in a campaign against my own organization; and yet I could not with self respect support men who have done everything they could to nullify the work I did for two years, whose triumph would mean the undoing of much of that work, who have declined to endorse Strong's administration, and whose rule would be but one degree better than that of Tammany—while nineteen out of twenty of my staunch supporters are on the other side.

I'll wire you from Cleveland whether I'll be at Nahant the evening of the 20th, or meet you at the Old South the following day.

Yours,

T. R.

P. S.—As for the election, no man can now foretell which candidate will come out ahead. Van Wyck has the call.

SAGAMORE HILL,
OYSTER BAY, LONG ISLAND, N. Y.,
Oct. 18th, '97.

Dear Cabot,

Can't I get out of going to Worcester? Tell Surbridge that as I must speak at the Norfolk Club Saturday, by request of the Secretary, and must make that my real speech, I am going to ask him to excuse me from Worcester. I shall reach Boston 10:30 A.M. Thursday, and will go to the Parker House, as that is near the Old South. I'll not take five minutes with my remarks. The Ohio people have been wanting me to spend this week there, for Hanna, and I should much have liked to do so; but my Massachusetts engagements forbid. The enclosed letter from "Drydollar" Sullivan may amuse you; I had asked him to give me his confidential views as to the canvass. Of course it is merely the Tammany view (the worthy statesman is not a goo-goo) and I think he underestimates the strength of George and even of Low. Nevertheless his forecast is *probably* right; for there are two bodies of regulars against two bodies of militia. But the unrest and disintegration are great; and as yet it is anybody's race with Van Wyck ahead, and Tracy and Low neck and neck for second place.

Yours,

T. R.

NAVY DEPARTMENT
WASHINGTON

Dear Cabot,   Oct. 28th, '97.

At first I had written out a dedication to you, stating that more than any other man you embodied what in the book I tried to set forth, that you realized the ideals of American life; but I never could get it in satisfactory shape, though Edith and I both worked over it again and again. If I said all I thought it made the thing look a little fulsome; and to say less than I thought I was not willing. So we decided simply to put in your name; and after all we thought that, taken in connection with the title, this showed well enough why the book was dedicated to you. Yes, it preaches the gospel of honesty, efficiency and patriotism which we have both striven to put into effect; you of course on an infinitely more important and larger scale. It represents why we have thought a certain kind of life well worth living.

Edith and the family have arrived tonight, very tired of course. Tomorrow I start for a hideous forty-eight hours in order to speak for Hanna, at the President's request. The old jollier assured me that he was strictly neutral in the New York contest!—which, by the way, may turn out on any line. Both Low and George seem to have gained, instead of losing, strength.

That venerable impostor, old Garland, was never on the *Constitution* until about 1830. Love to Nannie.

Yours ever,   T. R.

NAVY DEPARTMENT
OFFICE ASSISTANT SECRETARY
WASHINGTON

Hon. H. C. Lodge, Nahant, Mass.   October 29, 1897.

Dear Cabot: Most certainly I shall keep that gem from Charles Eliot Norton. If we are threatened with a domination of his kind I am not only for Platt and Lauterbach, but I am for Croker and Sheehan. Anything is preferable to that stuff.

Word has just come over the telegraph that Henry George died this morning of apoplexy. This greatly complicates the New York fight. I believe the bulk of his vote will go to Van Wyck and Low. As you say, the conduct of the Low people

and of Low in not insisting upon some kind of union with the
Republicans was not merely stupid, but from the civic standpoint almost criminal. The explanation they all give me is that
their have been betrayed so often and lied to so often when they
have tried to go in with Platt, Quigg, Lauterbach & Co., that
they were afraid to have any dealings with them. There is a
great deal of truth in this, but the fact remains that they
unquestionably ought to have taken the risk. It was the only
thing to do. Some of the machine men might have knifed them,
but they would have gotten the great bulk of the vote that
will now go for Tracy; and though they would have alienated
some tens of thousands of men they would have more than
made up the difference. What a grim comedy the whole canvass
is! The Low men hand in glove with Henry George, and making
deals with him alone, refuse even to confer with the Republicans on the ground that deals are immoral. The Republicans
are running a straight ticket because only straight tickets are
proper, and putting upon it in the second highest place a
democrat who is a renegade republican and a man of exceedingly bad character; and Henry George has with him on the
ticket for comptroller a gold democrat, Dayton, who last year
refused to support his party on the silver issue, and now runs
on the ticket which is largely gotten up as a rebuke to Tammany
because it didn't come out flatfooted for silver. Did I tell you
that Amos Cummings the other day told me he thought Low
had an even chance of election, as Van Wyck was weak, and
Tracy had no show whatever? On the other hand the regular
republicans I think are sincere in their belief that though
Tracy may be beaten by Van Wyck, he will beat Low.

I start today to make my speech at Columbus for Hanna.
They are evidently suffering from apathy out in Ohio. They
have made a foolish campaign. Instead of trying to get
speakers of national importance in New York, where their
presence arouses animosity, they should have put them into
Ohio where they would have aroused enthusiasm.

Well, I guess you can understand more than ever now why
I feel a bit lonely in the politics of New York, and why I wel-
comed such a glimpse as I got of you at Nahant. Tell Nannie

I had a long and very nice letter from Mrs. Chanler. Of course she has heard from her too.

Always yours,

THEODORE ROOSEVELT.

P. S.—There is one phase of this New York matter that has not attracted general attention. Platt's attitude has done more than anything else to jeopardize republican success in Maryland. This I was told by various Maryland republicans. Our chance of carrying Maryland depends upon having the sound money democrats vote with us. Platt's position in New York (in spite of his alliance with Fitch!) is that we must have a mere straight ticket, and must absolutely decline joining with the independent element. In consequence, I am informed on every side that the people in Maryland and in Kentucky who would have been with us are feeling reluctant to come with us. I very firmly believe that if Platt had endorsed Low and gone in for him from the beginning, there wouldn't have been a question of our ousting Gorman and gaining a United States Senator.

NAVY DEPARTMENT
OFFICE ASSISTANT SECRETARY
WASHINGTON

Hon. H. C. Lodge, Nahant, Mass.   November 4, 1897.

Dear Cabot: If, as seems certain, Hanna is elected, and if, as seems probable, Gorman is defeated, it seems to me that we have won what it was most essential from the national standpoint to win this Fall. That there should be some reaction was to be expected. Ohio and Maryland on the popular vote went as they did last Fall, although of course by greatly reduced pluralities; but in proportion not much more reduced than in New Jersey and Massachusetts. In New York the conditions were singular. We should have seen a reduced majority anyhow; but the majority would have been still very large in our favor, say over 100,000 without doubt, if it had not been for the criminal folly with which Platt and the machine have been behaving for the last two years, and I am almost tempted to say for the last three years. The first year of victory stunned them so that they permitted the mass of decent republican voters to have their say in a good many things. We got a first-class constitutional convention, a good man for Governor, and another good man for Mayor, and in the first and second Legislatures there were many representatives of decency; but after the first shock was over Platt followed his invariable principle of seeing that republican success meant the success only of men who were venal or weak enough to be his tools, and every possible step was taken to alienate the decent elements. New York will be all right again in 1898, even if Platt keeps in power, provided we have to fight Bryanism (although the hatred of the Platt machine inspired among decent people is so intense that the State will offer some pretty hard fighting under any conditions if it retains power). If Bryanism is thrown over by the Democracy, New York will be more than doubtful, but in that case we should get the West; so that from the national standpoint I see nothing discouraging in what has happened. From the standpoint of civic decency there is of course very much to be regretted. The figures make it clear that no possible alliance in which Platt was allowed any particular hand could have won. If a compromise ticket in any way agreeable to Platt had been put up it would have been beaten overwhelmingly, for Platt's machine people would have probably been disloyal to it, as they were in '95, while tens of thousands of gold democrats and independents, and even of Republicans, would not have touched anything with which Platt was connected; for, as always happens in a fight like this, the hostility aroused finally passes the bounds of common sense. Platt could have saved his State ticket and gained twenty Assemblymen in Greater New York by heartily, and without reservation, and without exacting stipulations of any kind, approving the Citizens' Union ticket. It was of course impossible to expect him to do this; but if he had done it he would have undoubtedly received full recognition from Low in the improbable event of Low's being elected; and, as I said, he would without doubt have carried the republican judge on the State ticket, and have gained from fifteen to twenty Assemblymen. Half of the republicans in Greater New York voted for Low, and the Tracy republican vote came from democratic districts. The native American republicans were almost exclusively for Low. Tracy did not carry a single assembly district. Low carried 13. In my own district Low polled three times as many votes as Tracy, who did not poll in the district much more than half as many as Van Wyck; yet, by absolute shameless fraud, this is one of the districts where the organization does not allow a single delegate to the anti-machine people. I don't see much hope in the situation in New York. The Citizens' Union people are very foolish, and the unspeakable scoundrelism as well as folly of the machine has alienated decent republicans more deeply than you could imagine. As soon as I got back from my visit to Nahant I found that the tide among all decent republicans was setting very strongly in favor of Low against Tracy; and one of the most potent causes was the attitude of the *Sun*, which has been not merely mischievous, but, what is unusual with the *Sun*, wholly ineffective with regard to gaining its ends. Platt will doubtless keep the machine in his control, and unless he chooses to exercise some self-restraint we shall run serious risks of being beaten outright in New York until we again come to a national campaign where the national issues swamp the local. As it has turned out, the Citizens' Union were quite right in nominating Assemblymen; and in the three best republican districts in New York they carried their men through; while had they been out of the field the Republican machine men would have unquestionably been beaten by the Tammany men, who were not one whit worse. The two Republicans elected were candidates who had been endorsed by the Citizens' Union.

There! All this you either will not care for or will know as well as I do; but I have to blow off steam. My two speeches in Ohio were very successful.

Give my best love to Nannie.

Yours ever,

THEODORE ROOSEVELT.

NAVY DEPARTMENT
WASHINGTON

Dear Cabot,   November 5th, '97.

As a personal addition to my political wail of yesterday, I may mention that Edith and I have been selfishly exultant, in the midst of our political depression, that you got us here, so that I am part of the Administration, with the prospect of honorable work, instead of being part of the wreck in New York.

Now, in strict confidence, we have won as regards the *principle* of extension of the Navy with the Secretary; he will recommend one additional battleship, and additional torpedo boats. It is too little, but it is a recognition of the principle that we are not to stop.

He carefully explained to me that he had always intended this! and that I must be careful not to give the impression that he was converted. So I'll be careful about this. Aside from this little warning, and the brush over the canteen, he has been as kind and friendly as ever.

Love to Nannie.

Yours always, T. R.

NAVY DEPARTMENT
OFFICE ASSISTANT SECRETARY
WASHINGTON

Hon. H. C. Lodge, Nahant, Mass.   November 8, 1897.

Dear Cabot: I was awfully glad to get your letter. I enclose you a letter from an extremely good fellow in New York —one of the only two aldermen we elected. He is a regular republican, and was elected over the Citizens' Union as well as over the Tammany candidates. It was one of the cases where I, and other decent men, felt the Citizens' Union had no business not to endorse, and we helped him all we could. He had advocated the nomination of Low by the republicans, but stood by the organization when the split came. I send you his letter just so that you may see how the decent men in the organization feel over the matter.

Did I tell you that Joe Murray finally came out for Low, as indeed did every other machine man in my district with whom I have ever acted in the past. It is a horrid muddle and I am very glad you kept out of it. Of course our hindsight is better than our foresight; but as things have turned out it is a real misfortune that Bliss should have got so mixed up in it, and that I should have so ostentatiously kept aloof. Of course, as always happens, the wrath that was visited on Platt, and therefore on the Republican Party, represented the stored up revolt against innumerable injuries and insults, and not merely anger at the misdeeds of this year. The Presidential election drowned everything last year; but in 1897 the men felt that there was really no one overmastering issue, and the vengeful memories of a hundred insolent injuries were uppermost. One feature which I very sincerely lament is that the anger at the machine, which the machine has so richly deserved, is so great that there will be, even among rational and practical men, a strong tendency to pardon even the worst vagaries of the so-called independents; and this in turn means trouble of another kind in the future. I am very anxious to see you and to talk over the thing at length. Outside of New York, as you say, I regard the result as on the whole encouraging, and if Van Wyck puts into office the same old gang, it will in its turn produce a reaction which cannot but help us. But oh, how I wish I thought Platt would be willing to learn even a little. It is worse than useless to try to regain power by driving out of the party, or keeping out of the party, that half of the party, including the great bulk of its intelligence and morality, which is against Platt, and which in New York supported Low.

Ever yours,

THEODORE ROOSEVELT.

Your volume of essays drew blood and tears from the *Evening Post* to the extent of a column and a half.

NAVY DEPARTMENT
OFFICE ASSISTANT SECRETARY
WASHINGTON

Dear Cabot: November 16, 1897.

Leutze is a first-class man. I have already suggested him to the Secretary as the best appointment. Another man, Commander Swift, is about as good; that is, as a member of the Secretary's cabinet he would be better—merely as head of the Yards and Docks perhaps not quite up to Leutze.

I thought your speech excellent. O, Lord, how I wish we had some man in New York like you! Platt's last letter will of course merely serve to intensify the bitterness of the anti-machine republican leaders. He could not have done anything that would more have aggravated the situation; but then I am not at all sure that the situation can be bettered. Both sides have gotten to the point when their mutual hostilities surpass that which either feels for his ordinary opponents. I only hope the Administration can keep out of the muss sufficiently to give us a fair chance to carry the State on national issues.

I suppose you will be on here in ten days or so. We are looking forward to your coming.

Always yours,

THEODORE ROOSEVELT.

1898

NAVY DEPARTMENT
WASHINGTON

Dear Cabot: April 14, 1898.

General Lee* is going to Richmond on Saturday, so he accepts with pleasure for Friday evening, at eight. He will write you himself, but the good old "Southron" has an immense mass of unopened mail on his desk, and I am not certain when his acceptance will reach you. I told him that you

* General Fitzhugh Lee.

wanted Morgan and Davis and one or two others, including Baron von Sternberg.

I have just had word that the Administration is very anxious for the House resolution, because under it they will not have to take immediate action. They regard that resolution as requiring immediate intervention, by which they understand diplomacy to be included, but as not requiring them to use the Army and Navy at once. I earnestly hope that it will not be passed by the Senate, and that you will stick to your own resolution; otherwise we shall have more delay and more shilly-shallying. The House resolution means delay; it is nearly as inconclusive as the message; it may mean a humiliating fiasco; and you must have no part in it.

Faithfully yours,
THEODORE ROOSEVELT.

NAVY DEPARTMENT
WASHINGTON

Dear Cabot: April 19, 1898.

This letter seems to be meant for you, though it was sent to me. I congratulate you, old man, upon the way events have justified all that you did.

Faithfully yours,
THEODORE ROOSEVELT.

Enclosure.

THE WESTERN UNION TELEGRAPH COMPANY

SAN ANTONIO, TEX.,
May 15, [1898.]

Senator H. C. Lodge, 1765 Mass. Ave., Washn., D. C.

All officers of this regiment nervous because their commissions were not confirmed by Senate. Will you see Attorney General confidentially and find out about this, it is under special act for three regiments.

THEODORE ROOSEVELT.

First Regt. U. S. Vol. Cavalry,
In Camp, near San Antonio, Texas,
May 19th, 1898.

Hon. H. C. Lodge, Senate Chamber, Washington, D. C.

Dear Cabot: Will you tell Gussie* that I know he will pardon me for not writing. I am told that he is with Wilson's† staff, and much appreciate his sending me the note. Here we are working like beavers and we are getting the regiment into shape. It has all the faults incident to an organization whose members have elected their own officers—some good and more very bad—and who have been recruited largely from among classes who putting it mildly, do not look at life in the spirit of decorum and conventionality that obtains in the East. Nevertheless many of our officers have in them the making of first rate men, and the troopers, I believe, are on the average finer than are to be found in any other regiment in the whole country. It would do your heart good to see some of the riding. The Eastern men are getting along very well. You would be amused to see three Knickerbocker club men cooking and washing dishes for one of the New Mexico companies. We have a number of Indians, who are excellent riders and seem to be pretty good fellows. The bulk of the men are quiet and self-respecting, often men of very considerable education and I think generally men of some property. The order has been excellent; we have had but one fight and one case of drunkenness. —— is turning out only fairly well as a major. I have been drilling his squadron and one of the others this afternoon. The dust, heat and mosquitoes prevent existence being at all sybaritic. I am heartily enjoying it nevertheless, and as the Spanish squadron has so far eluded our people, I think this regiment will be in trim to move whenever the advance on Cuba is to be made; but you can have no conception of the interminable delays of the Ordnance and Quartermaster's Departments.

I have a couple of scrawny horses, which they say are tough.

* Captain A. P. Gardner—my son-in-law.
† Major General James H. Wilson. He commanded the troops sent to Porto Rico.

I hope so, as otherwise I shall probably have to eat them and continue my career on foot.

I feel pretty homesick, of course. If it were not for that, I should really be enjoying myself thoroughly.

Wood is doing splendidly and the amount of work he has accomplished is incredible.

Give my best love to Nannie, and do not make peace until we get Porto Rico, while Cuba is made independent and the Philippines at any rate taken from the Spaniards.

I have given a note of introduction to you to a big stockman from Texas, Simpson, formerly of Forrest's cavalry, who went with us last trip on the gold issue.   Yours ever, T. R.

UNITED STATES SENATE
WASHINGTON, D. C.

Personal.

Dear Theodore :—   May 24, 1898.

It is a great delight to get your letter. Gus went off today, and these partings begin to come pretty hard. I was very much interested in all you tell me about your regiment, and I do not doubt you will make it a first rate one. The one point where haste is needed is the Philippines, and I think I can say to you, in confidence but in absolute certainty, that the administration is grasping the whole policy at last. The *Charleston* has gone and the *City of Pekin* goes today with a thousand men. The *Monterey*, which I have been breaking my heart to send, is now coaling for the trip, and will be off inside of a week. We are not going to lug that monitor across the Pacific for the fun of lugging her back again. They mean to send not less than twenty thousand men to the Philippines. As to Cuba I am in no sort of hurry. Our troops are fresh and raw. They ought to be hardened up. They also stand sadly in need of equipment and all this takes time. As I understand it they intend to put one hundred thousand men into Cuba when they do move so as to sweep the whole thing up at one quick stroke, and this is right. Porto Rico is not forgotten and we mean to have it. Unless I am utterly and profoundly mistaken the Administration is now fully committed to the large policy that we both desire. We have had some dark days since you left, and my very humdrum and unexciting part in the struggle has been one of constant work and anxiety. I think now however, from the information I get, that the cloud has lifted.

Give my best regards to Wood.

Always sincerely, H. C. L.

First Regt. U. S. Vol. Cavalry,
In Camp, near San Antonio, Texas,
May 25th, 1898.

Hon. H. C. Lodge, Senate Chamber, Washington, D. C.

Dear Cabot: Just a line to tell you how we are getting on. I really doubt if there ever has been a regiment quite like this. I know you will believe that more than ever I fail to get the relations of this regiment and the universe straight, but I cannot help being a little enthusiastic about it. It is as typical an American regiment as ever marched or fought. I suppose about 95 per cent of the men are of native birth, but we have a few from everywhere, including a score of Indians, and about as many men of Mexican origin from New Mexico; then there are some fifty Easterners—almost all graduates of Harvard, Yale, Princeton, etc.,—and almost as many Southerners; the rest are men of the plains and the Rocky Mountains. Three fourths of our men have at one time or another been cowboys or else are small stockmen; certainly two thirds have fathers who fought on one side or the other in the civil war. Of course, a regiment cannot be made in a week, but these men are in it because they want to be in it. They are intelligent as well as game, and they study the tactics, talking all the movements over among themselves; in consequence we have made really remarkable progress. You would enjoy seeing the mounted drill, for the way these men have got their wild half-broken horses into order is something marvellous. I am surprised at the orderly manner in which they have behaved; now and then a small squad goes to town and proceeds to paint things red, and then we get hold of them and put them into the guard-house, but the great bulk of the men are as quiet and straight as possible. I am very confident there has been much less disturbance than there would have been with the ordinary National Guard or the ordinary regular regiment. I have been both astonished and pleased at my own ability in the line of tactics. I thoroughly enjoy handling these men, and I get them on the jump so that they execute their movements at a gallop.

Wood is the ideal man for Colonel. Woody Kane has risen to be first lieutenant, and Goodrich, the captain of the Harvard crew, a second lieutenant. The First Major is a dandy—Major Brodie, of Arizona—a grizzled old frontier soldier, who was in the regular army. —— is a pitiful failure, between ourselves; and some of the other officers are very poor.

We most earnestly hope we can be sent to Cuba, and if for any reason Cuba should fail, then to the Philippines—any-where so that we can see active service. Of course, if we do not see active service, I am left, but if we do, I shall feel amply repaid for the loss of what I liked to make myself believe was a career in the Navy Department.

Give my best love to Nannie. I wonder how Bay* is enjoying himself? I do not suppose either he or I will see much fighting.

If they begin to send troops to Cuba, I shall wire you to see that we go. We are all ready now to move, and will render a good account of ourselves. I earnestly hope that no truce will be granted and that peace will only be made on considera-tion of Cuba being independent, Porto Rico ours and the Philippines taken away from Spain.

Give my respects to the members of the Senate Committee on Foreign Relations and tell them I pin my faith to them; and will you give my love to Secretary Long when you see him?

Faithfully yours,
THEODORE ROOSEVELT.

* My older son was in the Navy--volunteer officer U. S. S. *Dixie* commanded by his uncle, Captain C. H. Davis, U. S. N.

UNITED STATES SENATE
WASHINGTON, D. C.

Personal.

May 31, 1898.

Dear Theodore :

My best thanks for your letter of the 25th which I have read with great interest. I have no doubt your regiment will turn out first class when you get them drilled into shape. The Secretary of War told me on Saturday that he had ordered your regiment to Tampa so that I suppose you will be in a position to go with the first expedition. I do not think they mean to send any men to Cuba until they can get a large army together and sweep up the whole at once. I think this is wise. For various reasons I am in no hurry to see the war jammed through. We shall come out better if we take our time. Moreover, the Administration are continuing very earnestly and I believe will soon undertake an expedition to Porto Rico, which I believe is useful. We ought to take Porto Rico as we have taken the Philippines and then close in on Cuba. Let us get the outlying things first. The Administration I believe to be doing very well and to be following out a large policy. The opposition now comes exclusively from Reed,* who is straining every nerve to beat Hawaii,† which the Administration is very eager to get on military grounds. I am in strong hopes that the President will act without Congress, but the attitude of the minority in not giving the Administration this important military measure is in the highest degree discreditable.

I hear but little from Bay but that little is good. There is no news here but what you see in the papers. It looks this morning as if we had really got their fleet at Santiago.

Always sincerely yours,   H. C. L.

* Thomas B. Reed.   † Annexation of Hawaii.

TAMPA BAY HOTEL
TAMPA, FLA.

Senator H. C. Lodge, Washington, D. C.   June 6th, 1898.

Dear Cabot: Edith has been down here for the last three days and it has been a perfect treat having her. I think she really enjoyed it. She saw the camp and the mounted drill this morning—at which by the way, all the representatives of the foreign armies were present and expressed great wonder at the way we had gotten this regiment into shape.

We expect to start for Cuba on the transports tomorrow. Those of us who come back will feel mighty glad to get home no matter what fate they encounter in Cuba, I guess.

I had an awful morning for the orders first came out that only 4 troops out of our 12 were to go, in which case I should have had to stay here with the remaining 8; but they have now sent 8 and so I go. The 4 that are left behind feel fearfully.

They send us dismounted but we should be glad to go on all fours rather than not to go at all. It will be an outrage though if they do not send the horses after or together with the remainder of our men very soon. If not too much trouble I wish you would see the Secretary and have him keep us in mind, and have the horses sent to us very early. It is a little bit rough to make us fight on foot with only two-thirds of our strength. If I had been left behind I should have had to telegraph you to use your endeavors to have me put into the front.

Give my warm love to Nannie. Edith and I have spoken about you both all the time and about Bay, John, Harry and Gussie.

Ever faithfully yours,
THEODORE ROOSEVELT.

First U. S. Volunteer Cavalry, Troop A,
PORT TAMPA, FLA.,
June 10th, 1898.

Senator H. C. Lodge, Senate Chamber, Washington, D. C.

Dear Cabot: No words could describe to you the confusion and lack of system and the general mismanagement of affairs here; a good deal of it is the inevitable accompaniment of a sudden war where people have resolutely refused to make the needed preparations, but a very great deal could be avoided. For a month the troops have been gathering here in a country where lines of temporary railroad could be laid down for miles in 24 hours, yet to this day, while the troops are at Tampa there is but a single line connecting them with the point of debarkation 9 miles off and there are no switches to speak of and no facilities whatever for unloading freight or troops. There are hundreds of freight cars containing stores of all kinds which nobody knows anything about, and the single line is so jammed that it is impossible to move over it as fast as the muletrains go alongside. When we unloaded our regiment at Tampa we had to go 24 hours without food and not a human being met us to show us our camp or tell us anything about what we were to do. When we were ordered to embark here it took us twelve hours to make the nine miles of railroad, and on the wharf not one shadow of preparation had been made to receive any regiment; no transports had been assigned in advance, and there was actually no office for either the commissary or Quartermaster. We had to hunt all over the dock among ten thousand people before, by chance we ran across first one and then the other, and each regiment had to seize its transport and hold it against all comers; nothing but the most vigorous, and rather lawless, work got us our transport. Under these circumstances it, of course, took over three days to embark the troops. No sooner were they embarked than we received word from Washington not to start. We have been here two days now; the troops jammed together under the tropical sun on these crowded troop ships. We are in a sewer; a canal which is festering as if it were Havana harbor. The steamer on which we are contains nearly one thousand men, there being room for about five hundred comfortably. We have given up the entire deck to the men, so that the officers have to sit in the cabin, and even so several companies are down in the lower hold, which is unpleasantly suggestive of the Black Hole of Calcutta. We are apparently to be kept here three or four days more, for they say we are to start on Monday. The officers' horses were embarked last Sunday with the artillery horses; they have had to disembark them for the simple

reason that they began to die. Of course there was no shadow
of a reason for putting them aboard until the last moment.

If the people at Washington understood the fearful danger
to health that lies in keeping these troops on the transports,
and understood further that they cannot be disembarked and
reembarked under five days' time, they would surely make
up their minds in advance whether they intended to start or
not, and when they once did put us on would let us go. Four
or five days of this will reduce the efficiency of the landing
force just about ten per cent, and must inevitably shake the
morale of the men. Our men are behaving peculiarly well, as
they have behaved all along; we have a remarkably fine set;
they never complain; but surely they should be put into
action as soon as possible before letting some malignant disease
break out in the crowds here on shipboard. They won't even
let us put out into the bay, where we should all swim in spite
of the sharks, and we stay crowded in this fetid ditch, the men
not allowed to swim or go ashore, where indeed there is nothing
to do in the thick sand. Last night Gen. Young, who is our
brigade commander, together with Gen. Sumner and Gen.
Wheeler, spoke to me and said they wished that the people at
Washington could know how hard it is upon the cavalry to
leave behind their horses. We do not complain of this, for we
would go on all fours rather than not get there at all, and if we
are to rush Santiago of course we must do it on foot; but I do
most earnestly hope (and they wish me to write you this) that,
without bringing my name in, you will try to see that our horses
are forwarded to us as soon as possible. With two brigades of
cavalry we can do a tremendous amount of work in Cuba;
we can drive the Spanish foragers from the fields and take the
small towns and close the larger ones—and it is a shame to
dismount all our men.

Do, old man, try to see that the expedition is not longer
deferred, because the bad effects of so deferring it are evident
to everyone, and do see that our horses are sent after us at
the earliest moment. But above all, let us get over now, to
Cuba or Porto Rico; and have neither peace nor armistice
until the job is thoroughly done.

Count von Goetzen and Captain Lee* told Wood and myself the other day that the two things that astonished them most were, first: the rapidity with which this regiment had been raised, armed and put into so fairly efficient a state, and, second, the utter lack of system and organization in the way matters as a whole are managed. They got quite confidential and I think said more than they intended. Still I am having genuine soldiering even if we have not seen the enemy, and oh how I hope we shall soon see him.

Let me know about Bay and John and Gus, and give my warm love to Nannie and Constance.

Ever yours,   T. R.

P. S.—One man should be in absolute control here, with autocratic authority, especially over the railroad people who have behaved very badly.

On Board U. S. Transport Yucatan,
Port Tampa, Fla.,
June 12th, 1898.

Hon. H. C. Lodge, Senate Chamber, Washington, D. C.

Dear Cabot: I wonder if it would be possible for you to tell the Administration, that is, the President, and if necessary the Secretary of War, just what is going on here and the damage that is being done. Of course, I cannot speak publicly in any way; I should be courtmartialed if I did, but this letter I shall show to Wood, my Colonel, and it is written after consultation with Gen. Young, my brigade commander. I shall not show this first paragraph to Wood or to Young, for I want to say that it would be impossible to get a better man for Colonel than Wood has shown himself to be, and so far as I am concerned I am entirely content with Young as a Brigade General, but otherwise the mismanagement here is frightful. Wood thinks that if Miles could be given absolute control he would straighten things out and I most earnestly wish the experiment could be tried, though personally I cannot help feeling that Miles might have remedied a great deal that has

* Captain Arthur Lee, British Military Attaché. Now Lord Lee of Fareham.

gone wrong if only he had chosen or had known how. Think of embarking troops by sending their regiments higgledly-piggledly from their camp to the port ten miles away on a one-line railroad without ever assigning to each regiment its transport and without having a single officer detailed to meet the regiment and show them where to go or what they were to do. Our experience was that of every other regiment. We were up the entire night standing by the railway track at Tampa, hoping for trains that did not come. At dawn we were shifted to another railway track, and then owing to some energetic work of Wood and myself succeeded in getting the troops on empty coal cars, in which we came down to the wharf. At the wharf we could find no human being who could tell us what our transport was. Gen. Miles and Gen. Shafter both told us that if we did not find out soon we would not be able to go, and said they knew nothing more about it. The Quartermaster General and the Commissary General were allotting the boats. Neither had an office nor any place where he was to be found. The wharf was over a mile long, jammed with trains, with boats everywhere alongside, ten thousand troops embarking. Through this crowd Wood and I had to hunt until almost at the same time we both found the Quarter-master General. He allotted us a transport and advised us to seize her instantly if we hoped to keep her. The advice was good, for it proved she had been allotted to another regiment—the 71st N. Y. While Wood went out into the stream in a boat which he had seized for the purpose and got aboard the transport and brought her in, I brought up my four hundred men at a double and took possession in the very nick of time to head off the 71st regiment, which was also advancing for the purpose. Meanwhile they unloaded our stores about a mile off and we had to bring them up by hand. However, all this we could stand, but just as soon as we were all loaded and ready word came that there had been a complete change of plans and that the expedition was indefinitely postponed. As it had taken three days to load all the troops and would take six to unload them and load them again, it was obviously unwise to do anything but keep them on board until there was definite information from Washington. So, thanks to this vacillation of purpose at Washington this is the fifth day we have spent (and the eighth day some of the troops have spent) packed and sweltering on these troop ships in Tampa Bay under the semi-tropical June sun. In spite of the sharks, we let the men bathe morning and evening, as it is too hot during the rest of the day. The shore is mere sand, but fortunately we have been moved out of the fetid ditch beside the wharf where we first lay, so that the men can be very rarely sent ashore. We have given them the entire deck and they are packed so close that they can get no exercise and no drill, while the officers, except when inspecting the ship or attending a disembarkation, have to keep to their own cabins.

Now, if this were necessary no one would complain for a moment, and the men are perfectly cheerful as it is; but it is absolutely unnecessary; the five days' great heat and crowded confinement are telling visibly upon the spirits and health of the troops. It seems incredible that a place like Tampa should have been chosen without previous inspection, that no improvements should have been made in the railroad facilities at the place during the last month and that the Ordnance and Quartermaster Departments should have fallen into such inextricable confusion; a confusion partly due to their own dilatory inefficiency and partly due to the utter incompetence of the railway managers here and the inadequacy of their system. Finally, it was inexcusable to get the troops to Tampa unless it was intended to embark them, while it seems literally incredible that they could have been embarked before it was intended to use them.

All this is in the past now, but at least it may be possible to prevent such blunders in the future. It should be well determined in advance, before sending troops, that they are to sail, and when they are once sent aboard they should sail forthwith. Agents of the Government, men of push and intelligence, and above all men of youth, should be sent to every point of debarkation to tell exactly the difficulties and the needs and how they can be met. It, of course, goes without saying, that men should be appointed as Generals of Divisions and Brigades who are physically fit, as well as morally and mentally. The Ordnance Dept. in particular needs a thorough shaking up; and there should in every port like this be. one responsible head who would be held to a rigid accountability. Some of the regular army officers were saying today that every day we had remained on these transports had reduced the efficiency of the force just about five percent, while to disembark the men now would mean a serious harm to the morale. They will get over it, of course, just as they would get over the effects of a repulse by the Spaniards, but it would be about as serious as a repulse.

I did not feel that I was fit to be Colonel of this regiment and I was certainly much less fit than Wood, who has done better with it than I possibly could have done, but I am more fit to command a Brigade or a Division or attend to this whole matter of embarking and sending the army than many of those whose business it is to do the work. I do not know whether the circumstances at Tampa were exceptional; if not, there is need of an immediate and radical change or the inefficiency of our Government in 1812 will be more than paralleled.

Naturally this is not a letter that can be shown to anyone, but I am going to keep you informed as to the facts, and for the credit of the country and administration I wish you would try to straighten things out. I know what a fight you have on strictly the line of your own duties, old man, and of course you must not neglect that, no matter what happens to the Administration. You must get Manila and Hawaii; you must prevent any talk of peace until we get Porto Rico and the Philippines as well as secure the independence of Cuba. These jobs are big enough, but if besides doing them you can make the Administration realize that we have to go into this thing with a good heart and have to put the best men into the important positions and insist upon efficiency as the one vital requisite, you will add enormously to the debt the country already owes you.

I see Bronson and my old aid Sharp both got into the fight at Santiago. Lucky fellows! Harry and I are left, so far, but I do most sincerely hope we shall yet be able to get in. We are already in the yellow fever zone and at the beginning of the yellow fever season, and I only hope that no weakness or vacillation will prevent our being put where we can do some service inasmuch as we are already running the risk. I doubt if Cuba is much more unhealthy than the low coast of Florida now.

Give my love to Nannie.   Faithfully yours,

THEODORE ROOSEVELT.

UNITED STATES SENATE
WASHINGTON, D. C.

Personal.

June 15, 1898.

Dear Theodore :—

I got your letter last week and supposing that you would be immediately on your way to Santiago did not reply. Yesterday came your second letter and I now reply to both, although where I shall send this letter and when you will get it seems rather vague. I knew pretty well what a state of things existed at Tampa, but your description brought it home with a vividness which no other account did. We were entirely unprepared and the disorganization is something frightful. The greatest trouble is in the bureaus of the War Department and in the fact that the Secretary of War does not have the nerve to clean out his bureaus and put in competent men. The underlying fact of all is that we never have a sufficient army and are always caught unprepared when we go to war. In some respects it is quite wonderful to me that we get along even as well as we do. The suffering on the transports must have been something awful, and I sympathize with you and your men I assure you.

You are likely, I think, to have some sharp fighting at Santiago, but I cannot but believe that the town will soon be in your hands.

I will do everything in my power about your horses, but my power is very little and I feel very helpless when I come up against the immobility of the War Department. Still there is nothing like trying.

The Navy has done splendidly all along. Allen,* you will be glad to hear, is doing extremely well. He is methodical and firm and has got hold of the business with great rapidity, but it would have amused you to see at first his pathetic surprise at his inability to get some action on this or that which seemed to him of the most pressing importance. He had a telegram about a matter which ought to have been acted on at once. He said to me, sadly, "I have been carrying this about for three days and cannot get any one to look at it"; but he is really doing most admirably and shows great capacity, and sympathizes, so far as I can see, entirely in all your policies. The Secretary has been quite ill, but is now better again.

As for myself I am going along in a humdrum way which would seem very tame to you who are in the midst of such exciting scenes. I have, I think, done something to force Hawaii to the front, and the House votes on it tomorrow. It will carry there by a large majority, and I do not believe the Senate can hold out very long, for the President has been very firm about it and means to annex the Islands any way. I consider the Hawaiian business as practically settled. The whole policy of annexation is growing rapidly under the irresistible pressure of events. You may judge a little of the change when I tell you that Judge Day† said to me two or three days ago, "there is of course no question about Porto Rico, everyone is agreed on that, the only question for us to consider is how much we should do in the Philippines."

I was in New York for two days last week and found Anna‡ and Cowles both very well. He very impatient at the delays over the *Topeka*. I heard that Edith had arrived safely at Oyster Bay but did not see her.

Some very comic incidents happen which I should like to enjoy with you. William Lloyd Garrison has denounced Charles Eliot Norton as a "jingo" because he said the administration should be furnished with funds to bring the war to a

* Charles Allen of Massachusetts, who succeeded Roosevelt as Assistant Secretary of the Navy.
† At that time Secretary of State.
‡ His elder sister, Mrs. W. S. Cowles. The *Topeka* was Captain Cowles's ship.

speedy close, although it was an infamous war. Then Gamaliel Bradford and Moorfield Storey are to hold a meeting at Faneuil Hall tomorrow to denounce the adoption of an imperial policy by the United States. The drift of public opinion in favor of an imperial policy seems to be absolutely overwhelming, and the Democrats here seem to be going to pieces on it.

I trust this may reach you and find you well, unwounded and victorious. If it ever does reach you do write me and be sure to let me know if there is anything I can do.

Always sincerely yours, H. C. L.

UNITED STATES SENATE
WASHINGTON, D. C.

Personal.

June 24, 1898.

Dear Theodore :—

I have written you two letters which I sent to Tampa, but I have such faint hopes of their ever getting to you through the confusions which reign in post offices as well as elsewhere in that place that I am going to send you a third by another channel. If you ever get my other two letters you will know how much I sympathize with you in all the disorganization from which you suffered at Tampa. It is pretty well known here, but people are very shy in making public criticisms for fear of hampering the government in any way. I think matters are slowly improving, but the trouble is, as it has been from the beginning, in the War Department. I noticed with great interest that when it came to landing the troops under naval management at Santiago it was most rapidly and perfectly performed. You can imagine the intense interest with which we are waiting for news from Shafter's expedition, and our particular anxiety is greatly sharpened by the knowledge that our best friend, who is conspicuous for recklessness, is there with his regiment. I anticipate some very sharp fighting before you get the town, but the quickness of the landing and the apparent rapidity of movement since are encouraging.

I have been to the Department about your horses, and as I wrote you, they told me they would try and send them as soon as possible and hoped you might be able to get some there after you were established, which seems a difficult and wholly vague provision. I will do the best I can, but I feel very hopeless and helpless at the War Department.

The *Dixie* reached Santiago last Saturday. What has become of her since I do not yet know, but she is there and I hope will have a part in the fighting and that Bay and Harry may get out creditably and safe.

As I wrote you before—for I want you to know what was in my other letters—I was in New York a week ago for two days and found Anna and Cowles very well—but he was chafing very much over the delays about his ship. I see by the papers that she has not sailed and I am very sorry for him, for I know how trying this waiting is.

The first troop ship ought to be at Manila today with the *Charleston.* The *Monterey* must have reached Honolulu by this time. The second expedition must be between Honolulu and Manila, and the *Monadnock* sailed yesterday, and the third expedition will start early next week. Day tells me there is no longer any question in any one's mind that we must have Porto Rico; that he said to me sometime ago was a matter of course. He dined with me the other night and Mahan and I talked the Philippines with him for two hours. He said at the end that he thought we could not escape our destiny there. The feeling of the country is overwhelming against giving the Philippines back to Spain. That is clear to the most casual observer. Bryan has announced that he is against colonization, and Cleveland, in a ponderous speech, has come out against war as much as he dares and utterly against annexation. We shall sweep the country on that issue in my judgment. The Republican Conventions are all declaring that where the flag once goes up it must never come down.

To you, in the midst of war, the things we are doing here must appear very tame, and it seems hardly worth while to tell you that I am devoting all my strength to securing the annexation of Hawaii. It is humdrum work compared to that in which you are engaged, but not, I think, useless. The resolutions passed the House by a magnificent majority, and we now have them up in the Senate and are face to face with a dogged filibuster, led by White* and Pettigrew.† How long they will hold us here I cannot say, but we do not mean to adjourn without action, and I hope they will give way before very long.

We had a letter from Edith this morning who tells us all is well at Oyster Bay.

I hear little or nothing from Gus, but Wilson wrote me that he was a most admirable officer. He is hard at work at Chickamauga, and I suppose will get his share of the fighting later, for I do not think this war is going to be very brief.

If this, or any of my letters reach you, drop me a line if you can and let me know. I will write from time to time and tell you about things here. The best of fortune go with you always.

Always sincerely yours,

H. C. LODGE.

Camp 5 miles from Santiago,
June 27th, '98.

Dear Cabot,

Well, whatever comes I shall feel contented with having left the Navy Department to go into the army for the war; for our regiment has been in the first fight on land, and has done well. It was nothing more than a brisk skirmish, for Young's brigade, the advance guard of the army, had but 900 men on the ground, of whom over ninety were killed or wounded. Our regiment furnished over half the men, and over half the loss. Young did well. So did Wood; and in fact the entire regiment. I had command of the right squadron, until, in the advance we got touch of the regulars, who had come up separately. Then Major Brodie was shot, and I took command of his squadron, the right, and led it in the final charge. It was very thick country, and the Spaniards were in a very strong position. I thought they shot well. Our Cuban scouts and guides ran like sheep at the first fire. The smokeless pow-

* Stephen White, a Senator from California.
† Richard F. Pettigrew, a Senator from South Dakota.

der made it very hard to place the men who were shooting at us; and our men at, times dropped thickly when we could not tell where to fire back. Shafter was not even ashore! The mismanagement has been maddening. We have had very little to eat. But we care nothing for that, as long as we got into the fight.

Yours ever, T. R.

UNITED STATES SENATE
WASHINGTON, D. C.

Personal.

Dear Theodore: June 29, 1898.

Perhaps among the alarms and excursions of your active war you may like to turn your thoughts to something frivolous. I have two little stories which I think will amuse you. The second one is confidential. The first is this: A Madrid paper has given the following description of you. "He was born at Harlaam and immigrated to America at an early age. He was educated at the town of Harvard where there is a commercial school, as there are no colleges or universities in the United States. He then became a policeman in New York and is now the commander of the American Navy." This is perfectly genuine and is a translation from a Spanish paper. The second story is this: Whenever I go in to see the Governor [Long] he is very apt to close the doors and call upon me for sympathy in regard to his worthy colleague in the War Department. Day before yesterday he had a story which was not serious like most of his plaints but which had tickled his sense of humor immensely. The Secretary of War had come over and said that he wanted a convoy at once to take a tug and lighter to Shafter. The Governor asked him why he did not send his lighter with the expedition. He said that he did but that the lighter had been lost. I may say, in parenthesis, nobody knows where that lighter was lost, but it seems to have disappeared somewhere. Alger then said that Shafter was telegraphing for a lighter and that he must send him òne at once. Very well, Long said, I will furnish you with a convoy, you can have the *Fern*, which will answer your purpose. The Secretary said he was very much obliged and then he hesitated and said, now that you have given me a convoy don't you think you could furnish me with a tug and a lighter, which I am bound to say was what ultimately happened. It forcibly reminded me of your pet story about the Irishman, the only difference being that the Secretary did not even have a stopper for his pipe.

It would gratify you very much I am sure to hear the expressions of delight and pride from your friends, especially your friends in the Senate, at the victory won by the Rough Riders. There was some disposition to say, as I wrote you, that it was magnificent but too expensive, and so I took pains to let the President's opinion, which I wrote you, get out. From all the accounts which I have read it seems to me that you were caught suddenly in a very difficult place by a superior force, and nothing saved us from a serious check but the extreme steadiness and gallantry with which your men went forward in the face of a deadly fire.

The newspapers are nominating you for Governor of New York and I have not the least doubt that you can go to Congress if you want to, which I think you would like by and by, and if you keep on as you have been doing and succeed in living through the war you can hope for much better things than a seat in Congress. All of which is very satisfactory to me.

I do not remember whether I wrote you that the *Dixie* is included in the Squadron which is to go to Spain, and the Governor assures me that they mean business and are going to raid Spanish commerce, attack Spanish towns and find Camara's fleet if they can. Harry and Bay will be perfectly delighted, and really I do not suppose the war would have brought them a better chance than this if they really go as I believe they will. I saw by the despatches yesterday that the *Dixie*, of which we have heard nothing for ten days, has been feeling around Cienfuegos and had incidentally smashed a Spanish battery there, so I suppose the gallant captain and his crew feel better.

I dare say by the time my letters reach you they contain

old news which you have read in the newspapers, on the other hand they may contain some little items which you would not get otherwise, so I will keep on sending them with a childlike trust that they may reach you.

The filibuster on Hawaii is about broken down. Everything is looking promising and we expect to vote and annex the Islands next week and then adjourn.

If you can find time to send me just a line and let me know whether any of these letters get to you and how you are I shall be greatly delighted. Remember me always to Wood, whose conduct seems to have been most magnificent in that hot fight, and whose praises are on everyone's lips.

Always sincerely yours, H. C. L.

Trenches outside Santiago,
July 3d, 1898.

Dear Cabot:

Tell the President for Heaven's sake to send us every regiment and above all every battery possible. We have won so far at a heavy cost; but the Spaniards fight very hard and charging these intrenchments against modern rifles is terrible. We are within measureable distance of a terrible military disaster; we *must* have help—thousands of men, batteries, and *food* and ammunition. The other volunteers are at a hideous disadvantage owing to their not having smokeless powder. Our General is poor; he is too unwieldy to get to the front. I commanded my regiment, I think I may say, with honor. We lost a quarter of our men. For three days I have been at the extreme front of the firing line; how I have escaped I know not; I have not blanket or coat; I have not taken off my shoes even; I sleep in the drenching rain, and drink putrid water. Best love to Nannie.

Yours ever, T. R.

UNITED STATES SENATE
WASHINGTON, D. C.

Dear Theodore: July 4th, 1898.

Great news this morning and I cannot resist sending a line
to tell you how rejoiced we all are. You again brilliantly distinguished yourself at San Juan on Friday. You are one of
the popular persons of the war and deserve to be. Pray God
you come out all right. We have been living with our hearts
in our mouths.

Still fighting over Hawaii but we are determined and are
going to put it through. Glass* took the Ladrone Islands,
left soldiers, ran up the flag and brought the Governor prisoner
to Manila.

A letter from Edith this morning says all well at Oyster Bay.

I congratulate you and admire you more than you can
conceive.

Best love from Nannie.

Yrs.,   H. C. L.

Trenches outside Santiago,
Dear Cabot: July 5th, '98.

Not since the campaign of Crassus against the Parthians
has there been so criminally incompetent a General as Shafter;
and not since the expedition against Walcheren has there been
grosser mismanagement than in this. The battle simply fought
itself; three of the Brigade Commanders, most of the Colonels,
and all the regiments individually did well; and the heroism
of some of the regiments could not be surpassed; but Shafter
never came within three miles of the line, and never has come;
the confusion is incredible. The siege guns have not yet been
landed! The mortars have not been started from the landing
place. Our artillery has been poorly handled. There is no
head; the orders follow one another in rapid succession, and
are confused and contradictory to a degree. I have held the
extreme front of the fighting line; I shall do all that can be
done, whatever comes; but it is bitter to see the misery and

* Captain Glass, U. S. N., in command of the *Charleston*, also took Guam.

suffering, and think that nothing but incompetency in administering the nation's enormous resources caused it. The fighting has been very hard. I don't know whether people at home know how well this regiment did. I am as proud of it as I can be; and these men would follow me anywhere now. It was great luck for me to get the command of it before this battle.

Best love to Nannie.

Yours ever, T. R.

UNITED STATES SENATE
WASHINGTON, D. C.

Personal.

Dear Theodore :—

July 6, 1898.

How much I miss you at such a time as this just after our great naval victory. The brilliant fighting of our Army doing, with insufficient numbers and very insufficient artillery, work which I do not believe any other army in the world could do, so alarmed the Spanish that Cervera thought his time had come and left the harbor. Do you believe that there has ever been such perfection of workmanship as that which destroyed four great cruisers of the highest type and two torpedo boats with the loss of only one man killed and two wounded? You, in the midst of your own triumphs and dangers I know will have many thoughts for the glory won by the American Navy, which you did so much to prepare.

You have won for yourself a high place already as one of the popular heroes of the war, and I wish I could see you and tell you how we all feel about you. I enclose an article from the Washington *Times*, which is a little Bryanite, Democratic paper, but which gives you some conception of the way people talk about you, which is also a curiously just article to the other two persons mentioned as well as to yourself.

I was in the War Department on Sunday when Shafter's disheartening despatch came, and was alone there with the Secretary and his assistants. I was perfectly appalled by the utter lack of efficiency, organization or plan there displayed by the head of the Department. I was a rank outsider and have no military education or experience, but I could have taken those questions up which they were muddling over and settled them in an hour. There is no plan in the War Department that I can see, and a great deal of time is spent asking why the Navy does not do this, that and the other. As it is, the Navy has taken its own warships to carry the troops, but Alger seemed to think that to blow up the *Iowa* in an attempt to enter Santiago would be a trivial incident, for, as he wisely said, "what's the loss of one ship after all." How we get on as well as we do I cannot imagine, and I have been filled with an anxiety about the Army in the last two or three days (owing to the state of things at the Department) which it is difficult to describe. However I hope and believe all will come out well.

General Wilson and his Division, with Gus of course, left Chickamauga yesterday, and are on their way to Santiago as fast as rail and boat can take them. Possibly you may meet there.

We heard from Bay yesterday for the first time. The *Dixie* has been coasting and cruising on the South Coast of Cuba. They destroyed two blockhouses at the South end of the Trocha, and they went in near Trinidad and engaged the battery there twice and apparently used up a couple of gun boats. Thence she is to return to Santiago and go to Europe. Bay has two gun crews under him and was complimented by the First Lieutenant on the way he handled his guns in the engagements the ship was in. To you, in the midst of such fighting as you have had, this will of course seem pretty tame, but I know that you are almost as fond of Bay as I am, and on that account will be glad to know that he is doing his duty in a commendable fashion.

I hear talk all the time about your being run for Governor and Congressman, and at this moment you could have pretty much anything you wanted. Although I do not take a great deal of stock in the Governor part of it I think it by no means impossible that a seat in Congress could be brought about, and I think if you could be elected in your absence by the time you were to take your seat the war would be over and you would come back into public life in a great popular body with an immense enthusiasm behind you. Perhaps something still better than this will offer, but I know that you think as I do about the House and I think you would find it without much difficulty the road to the Senate.

Always sincerely yours,
H. C. LODGE.

Our 2nd regiment shows many losses but I am glad the old State was at the front tho' it was hard on the poor boys with Springfields, so smoky that they could not be kept on the firing line. I enclose a little absurd advertisement which shows how the man on the street has you in mind. Your regiment has suffered terribly and is covered with glory. It looks as if we were pretty near a vote on Hawaii but anyway it is bound to come.

Trenches outside Santiago,
July 7th, '98.

Dear Cabot,

As I only write you and Edith you must pardon my persistent jeremiads. First, the unimportant, which is personal. Wood has commanded his brigade, and I my regiment, in the hardest battle of the war; they lost a heavier percentage than any other regiment or brigade; and we feel we are entitled to the promotions rather than outsiders. If it is judged that other men in the field have shown greater efficiency, why we have nothing to say; but we ought to receive the promotions rather than men who have not been in the fight. Gen. Wheeler says he intends to recommend me for the medal of honor; naturally I should like to have it. And, when we take Santiago, do try to see that we are sent to the front again, and not kept as garrison. I think we have shown we can fight.

Next, as to the important. It is criminal to keep Shafter in command. He is utterly inefficient; and now he is panic struck. Wheeler is an old dear; but he is very little more fit than Shafter to command. Our part of the battle fought itself under the brigade and regimental commanders. Sumner deserves more credit than Wheeler for it—but as I say the regiments themselves really fought it. The mismanagement has been beyond belief. We have a prize fool—who handled a balloon so as to cause us very great loss. We are half starved; and our men are sickening daily. The lack of transportation, food and artillery has brought us to the very verge of disaster; but above all the lack of any leadership, of any system or any executive capacity.

Best love to Nannie. Do go and see Edith. I wish I could hear about Harry and Bay.

Yours ever, T. R.

Outside Santiago,
July 10th, '98.

Dear Cabot:

We on the firing line are crazy just at present because Gen. Shafter is tacking and veering as to whether or not he will close with the Spaniards' request to allow them to walk out unmolested. It will be a great misfortune to accept less than unconditional surrender. Thanks to Gen. Shafter's incompetency and timidity we were, on the night of July 1st, in grave danger. By hard fighting and hard work, without any aid from him, we have steadily bettered our position, until we have the upper hand completely; the reinforcements of artillery which we so sorely needed have come (in spite of outrageous delay here, at headquarters, in hurrying it after it reached the landing); we can surely get the whole Spanish army now, at the cost of probably not more than a couple of days' fighting, chiefly bombardment.

I am delighted that Wood got the Brigadier Generalship; he earned it. I think I earned my Colonelcy and medal of honor, and hope I get them; but it doesn't make much difference, for nothing can take away the fact that for the ten great days of its life I commanded the regiment, and led it victoriously in a hard fought battle. I never expected to come through! I am as strong as a bull moose, although I sleep out on the firing line, on the ground, often wet through. My last horse is going and I am practically afoot. The sun prostrates many of our men; the rain and the drinking water more. But our chief loss has been by bullets—a quarter of our strength. I have just received your first two letters. Hurrah for Hawaii!

Yours ever, T. R.

NEW YORK,
July 12th [?], '98.

My dear Theodore:

Before I go to Tuckanuck I write you a line to give you the last news from Washington. As I wrote you before I left, we succeeded in passing the Hawaiian annexation very handsomely —it is a very great victory and very important. I also had a long talk with the President on Thursday, as I believe I also wrote you, and you know long before this he promoted you, as he told me he would. I don't know whether I also told you that he said that you would have your star before very long—he means to make you Brigadier General I am sure at the first reasonable opportunity. I believe that he is all right in his conception of our policy and that his intentions are equally all right as to what should be done,—but at the same time I cannot help feeling very anxious—I am very much afraid of an armistice because if we once accept an armistice rather than go to war again I am afraid that he might settle on terms which we should all regret. He is entirely clear as to Cuba,— and I think also as to Porto Rico. He is also very firm against European interference, but he is worrying over the Philippines—he wants to hold them evidently but is a little timid about it. There is one thing that has given me great encouragement and that is the taking of the Ladrone Islands—he must have ordered this far back in May when the *Charleston* left San Francisco. I do not know whether you have seen enough of the papers to know what a delightful incident in war that has been—it will amuse you more than anything that has happened. Capt. Glass in the *Charleston* stopped at the Island of Guam and proceeded to shell the forts, whereupon the Spanish Governor in full uniform came off and said that he regretted that he had no powder with which to return the salute. Glass thereupon replied that he did not understand the situation—that this was war—the Spanish Governor expressed surprise and disgust, whereupon Glass took him prisoner with the entire government and the entire Spanish army consisting of fifty-four men and carried them off to Manila—but the most amusing feature of the whole thing was that Glass found on this remote island an American resident whom he appointed Governor—I believe that in every spot of the world there is an American resident ready to become Governor—so this American was made Governor and we left a company of soldiers with him and those islands are ours today—now why the President should have taken those islands unless he expects to hold on to the Philippines I cannot conceive. He intends to hold something in the Philippines and the single point that I have made with him and have made with everybody is whatever happens we cannot return to Spain the people whom we have set free. To hand Aguinaldo and his men back to Spain would be an act of infamy. Day is very weak about the Philippines but I am hoping for the best. Since I have been here I have seen the *Sun* people and they are going to use all their influence which is very considerable with the President in the right direction. I also had a long talk with Laffan* and Paul Dana about you. I must say that you have no two better friends anywhere. Laffan agrees with me that what we want for you is the Senate but it looks as if the drift was very strong to make you Governor and that may lead to the Senate next winter. At least we are looking after your interest as well as we can, and you must not think that I am dreaming about these things because you can have no idea of your popularity here. We are waiting with intense interest for news from Santiago. I hope that the town will soon surrender for now that the fleet is destroyed Santiago is of little value to us except for moral effect and we want to move on Porto Rico as rapidly as possible. Douglas and I have cordially agreed that we were all wrong about your going into war and that you were all right. We have also agreed that ordinary rules do not apply to you, and Douglas said in this connection

* William M. Laffan of the New York *Sun*.

that there were no rules that could apply to drunkards and
madmen—I don't know exactly what he means by this, as
you are neither, but perhaps you can get the connection. We
know that you will take every possible opportunity to get
killed if you can, but now that you are Colonel of the Regiment we venture to suggest that your first business is to look
after it and not run ahead of it in every charge that is
made. I wish you were here to take hand in keeping the policy
of the country straight but you are doing far better work where
you are and we can only hope that you will come through all
right. You can't win more distinction than you have already
won so far as mere personal heroism is concerned! Harry and
Bay, I suppose, sail tomorrow with the Eastern Squadron,
they are likely to see some sharp fighting in any event and if
they meet Camara's fleet there will be action. You can imagine
the intense anxiety in which we live but I cannot help being
glad that they are going. Gus I suppose has sailed from
Charleston before this and if the expedition goes on to Porto
Rico you will probably fall in with him. Wilson speaks of him
in the highest terms and he is evidently making a very fine
officer.

All are well here and with best love, I am as always,

H. C. L.

In Camp near Santiago de Cuba,
July 19th, 1898.

Hon. H. C. Lodge, Senate Chamber, Washington, D. C.

Dear Cabot: It was the greatest pleasure to receive your
two letters of the 24th and 25th, which came in inverse order,
a couple of days ago. Wood was immensely flattered at your
sending him your regards in so kind a way, and I was, naturally, deeply touched, old man, by the whole tone of your note
and especially by your thinking now that I was justified in
coming. Somehow or other I always knew that if I did not go I
never would forgive myself; and I really have been of use. I
do not want to be vain, but I do not think that anyone else
could have handled this regiment quite as I have handled it

during the last three weeks and during these weeks it has done
as well as any of the regular regiments and infinitely better
than any of the volunteer regiments, and indeed, frankly, I
think it has done better than the regulars with the exception
of one or two of the best regular regiments. We have moved
up to the foothills, but fever is making perfect ravages among
us. I now have left less than half of the six hundred men with
whom I landed; but the gallant fellows struggle back to me
from the hospital just as soon as their wounds are healed or
the fever or dysentery lets up a little.

Well, the fight is over now and we have won a big triumph,
so there is no use in washing dirty linen, except that surely we
ought to profit by our bitter experiences in the next expedi-
tions. Even now with Santiago taken and our ships in the bay
and with a month in which to have gotten ample transportation, food and medical supplies, our condition is horrible in
every respect. I have over one hundred men down with fever
in my own camp out of my regiment of four hundred, 200 having previously died or having been sent to the rear hospitals.
The mismanagement of the hospital service in the rear has
been such that my men will not leave the regiment if they can
possibly help it; yet here we have nothing for them but hard-
tack, bacon and generally coffee without sugar. I cannot get
even oatmeal and rice except occasionally by paying for it
myself, which seems a little needless in as rich a government as
ours. I have to buy the men canned tomatoes and tobacco.
The regiment was moved yesterday and I was given one wagon
in which to transport everything, which simply meant a night
of exposure for the men and a couple of very scanty meals,
while as Gen. Shafter made us move at midday we had fifty
cases of heat prostration, the tropical sun working its will
upon men weakened by poor food, constant exposure and the
grinding hardship of labor in the trenches. Curiously enough
the part in which we have broken down has been the administrative and business part, and to a less extent in the mechanical
part, while we have been saved by the dogged fighting of the
individual regiments. The engineers and artillery have done
poorly and the hospital division worse. But the prime diffi-

culty has been lack of transportation, including lack of means to land from the ships. We should have had a great number of barges, lighters and small steam craft as a matter of course. During the month that has passed, Gen. Shafter should have insisted upon having a sufficiency of wagons, mule trains and small craft of the kind mentioned above. Even now we keep the wagons idle while the ships are in the bay, and our men half starved and in tatters. If only I could get decent food for my men!—rice, cornmeal, canned fruit, dried meat. I hope you will not think I grumble too much or am too much worried; it is not in the least for myself; I am more than satisfied even though I die of yellow fever tomorrow, for at least I feel that I have done something which enables me to leave a name to the children of which they can rightly be proud and which will serve in some sense as a substitute for not leaving them more money. But, as any honorable man must, I feel very keenly my share of the responsibility for this army and especially my responsibility for this regiment. I am deeply touched by the way the men of the regiment trust me and follow me. I think they know I would do anything for them, and when we got into the darkest days I fared precisely as they did. Certainly in battle or in the march or in the trenches I never went anywhere but I found them eager to follow me. I was not reckless; but with a regiment like this, and indeed I think with most regiments, the man in command must take all the risks which he asks his men to take if he is going to get the best work out of them. On the day of the big fight I had to ask my men to do a deed that European military writers consider utterly impossible of performance, that is, to attack over open ground unshaken infantry armed with the best modern repeating rifles behind a formidable system of entrenchments. The only way to get them to do it in the way it had to be done was to lead them myself. Now, naturally, I feel terribly to see them suffering for lack of plain food, to see my sick men in high fever lying in the mud on their soggy blankets without even so cheap a comfort as a little rice or even sugar for their tea or coffee.

Lt. Day was promoted for conspicuous gallantry. He was

sent to the rear wounded with some of our men. They were kept in the hospital 48 hours before they were given a mouthful of food, and as for water they had to depend upon those of their number who could walk. My men's shoes are worn through; two of them went into the last battle barefooted. Their clothes are in tatters. They have not changed their underclothes since they landed a month ago; yet do what I can I cannot get them spare clothing.

However, enough of grumbling. Did I tell you that I killed a Spaniard with my own hand when I led the storm of the first redoubt? Probably I did. For some time, for your sins, you will hear from me a great many "grouse in the gunroom" anecdotes of this war. I am just wild to see you and spend an evening telling you various things. For the first hour of the last battle we had a very uncomfortable time. We were lying in reserve under orders, where the bullets of the enemy reached us, and man after man was killed or wounded. I lay on the bank by Lieut. Haskell, talking with him. Finally he did not answer some question of mine; I turned to find that he had been shot through the stomach. I gave an order to one of my men, who stood up and saluted and then fell over my knees with a bullet through his brain. But then came the order to advance, and with it my "crowded hour"; for there followed the day of my active life. I got my men moving forward, and when the 9th regiment of regulars halted too long firing, I took my men clean through it, and their men and younger officers joined me. At the head of the two commands I rode forward (being much helped because I was the only man on horseback) and we carried the first hill (this was the first entrenchment carried by any of our troops; the first break in the Spanish line; and I was the first man in) in gallant shape and then the next and then the third. On the last I was halted and for 24 hours I was in command, on the extreme front of the line, of the fragments of the six cavalry regiments, I being the highest officer left there.

Two of my men have died of yellow fever, but we hope to keep it out of the camp, and if we succeed we also hope we shall soon be ordered to Porto Rico.

Remember that I do not hear any news and do write me about anything, especially about Bay, Harry and Gus. You have done everything where you are. You have been more useful than any General, for you occupy the larger field; it would have been criminal for you to leave your task.

Warm love to Nannie.

Ever yours,
THEODORE ROOSEVELT.

Private. NAHANT, MASS.,
July 23, 1898.

Dear Theodore :—

Your three letters from the trenches in front of Santiago have just reached me, and before I go off for a few days of rest on Bigelow's island I am glad to have an opportunity to answer them. On the 3rd of July when you were writing me in a strain which was naturally pretty gloomy I was at the War Department, as it happened, urging the sending of reenforcements and advising strongly against the full publication of Shafter's despatch, which had just come in. My advice was in a measure successful, but I think that day was one of the worst that I have ever passed. The news of the great victory over Cervera, which came that night, relieved the tension, but your later letters make no mention of it, and I suppose its enormous effect was not as visible to you in the trenches as it was to the world at large. Between the time when you wrote and that at which I received your letters a great deal has happened and Santiago has fallen. I think we came out of it astonishingly well, and I do not in the least wonder at your distress of mind. On one point however you were strangely mistaken. I do not think any two men have received as much credit as you and Wood. If you have received my letters— which went in a pretty steady stream from Washington—you will know how warmly the President appreciated your work from the beginning, and of course you are aware that Wood and you were in the first list of promotions. You are both popular not only at the White House but at the War Department, and I see this morning that Wood has been made

Governor of Santiago. You can form no idea of the impression which your brilliant charge and splendid leadership have made on the country. You are one of the heroes of the fight and one of the most conspicuous and everybody thinks so.

I do not see how it is going to be possible for your regiment to go to Porto Rico, for it is stated here that no men are to be taken from the infected district and placed with fresh troops in a non-infected district like Porto Rico. I am very sorry that this should be so, but you have covered yourself with glory already and will have plenty to do in Cuba in my opinion before the work there is finished.

I had a long talk with the President before leaving Washington and he was very clear and strong about both Cuba and Porto Rico. He is not giving much consideration to the Philippines but the question in his mind is how much he will take there. I think his imagination is touched by the situation, and I think he grasps it fully. We ordered the taking of the Ladrones way back in May, and they are of value only as a stepping stone. He did everything to secure the annexation of Hawaii, and speaks of it as a step in a policy. I enclose a copy of a letter from Laffan, who went on to see him at my suggestion after the adjournment of Congress, which will give you an idea better than I have been able to do myself as to his present frame of mind.

The *Dixie* had a very active time harrying the South coast of Cuba, and is going as a convoy to Porto Rico and will go thence to Europe with the Eastern Squadron. They leave soon and are likely to see plenty of service.

Gus sailed day before yesterday for Porto Rico. General Wilson writes to everyone about him in the highest terms, and in a letter to Henry Higginson said he was one of the very best men he had and a first class Adjutant General. He is only an Assistant Adjutant General but has been doing the duty of the higher place.

Winty* was wounded when the expedition made their landing, which apparently was very badly managed. He is

* Winthrop Chanler of New York. He went with an insurgent expedition to Cuba.

not much hurt however and is back in this country and writing the most cheerful letters.

From everything I hear I get a very poor impression of the insurgents, and if you get time I wish you would write me about them.

Cowles is blockading off Nipe Bay.

I tell you all these things which you may hear from a dozen sources, but on the other hand, you may not and so I take the chances.

We are all well, but, as you may imagine, are very anxious about you and the others near to us who are in the fighting.

Let me know if you receive any of my letters. I have kept sending them to you steadily but do not know yet if a single one has reached you. Everything I get from you of course I send to Edith. You know that I have been laboring to cure the defects and troubles which have borne so hardly on the Army, but there is very little I can do. One cannot make any public attack, because that would be at once sent abroad and to Madrid, and private expostulation does not go very far.

Give my best regards to Wood.

Always sincerely yours,   H. C. L.

First Regt. U. S. Volunteer Cavalry,
In Camp near Santiago de Cuba,
July 31, 1898.

Senator H. C. Lodge, Nahant, Mass.

Dear Cabot: I was delighted to get your letter from New York; and with it came my commission as Colonel, which resulted in my now being in command of the Brigade, for bullets and disease have worked havoc among the higher officers.

I suppose Gussie is now in Porto Rico. I wish him all possible luck.

It is part of the grotesque mismanagement of our campaign that half of this army has not been sent there.

During the past fortnight the yellow fever cases have been

very few and have been confined to Siboney, a port 15 miles away. If we had been shipped a week ago there would have been absolutely no danger; if we were shipped now there would be practically no danger; but it is simply infamous to keep us here during the sickly months that are now on and which will last until October, to serve no possible object, but merely because the authorities to whom the United States has entrusted the lives of the men as well as the honor of the flag are helplessly unable to do their duty. We have had at Siboney a few cases of yellow fever; two of my men who were sent to the hospital there caught this yellow fever and died, as did a few others from different regiments. Here at the front we have had no yellow fever whatever but any amount of malarial fever, probably 1500 cases in the Cavalry Division alone; not a death has resulted, and the men all go back to their work after a few days, but very much shattered and weakened and in fine shape to catch yellow fever or anything. The malarial fever is no more contagious or infectious than a cut finger; yet Alger in his message to us absolutely seems to treat the yellow fever and the malarial fever as if they were alike; he says that he will take the troops back when the fever shows signs of lessening. Of course, the malarial fever won't lessen; it will increase, and if he does as he says he will simply keep us here, growing weaker and weaker, until Yellow Jack does come in and we die like rotten sheep, and this for absolutely no end whatever and with absolutely no excuse. Among the doctors here the name of this fever is the Five-day Fever; and because the Secretary cannot distinguish between this Five-day Fever and the Yellow Jack, he actually proposes to keep us here until we catch the latter. I am determined that my skirts shall be clear of this particular form of murder, and so I have written the enclosed letter.

I am not in the least alarmed about myself; in the first place I don't think I should die if I caught it, and in the next place should the worse come to the worst I am quite content to go now and to leave my children at least an honorable name (and, old man, if I do go, I do wish you would get that medal of honor for me anyhow, as I should awfully like the children to have it, and I think I earned it). But these men under me, who have fought and worked and marched and endured hardship and exposure and semi-starvation without complaint, and whose fellows have met death bravely and quietly, are entitled at least to just treatment. I have spent their blood like water myself when there seemed an object and have flung them straight against entrenchments and kept them hour after hour, dropping under rifle and shrapnel fire, and now if there was need of our holding a town against any foe, I would care not one jot more for yellow fever than for Spanish bullets and would not mind sacrificing the lives of my entire command; but to sacrifice them pointlessly from mere stupidity and inefficiency is cruel.

I do not suppose you can do anything, and when you receive this it may be too late anyhow, but if the army is not brought away from here with all possible expedition and if an epidemic does really break out, the President and the Secretary of War will have incurred a debt as heavy as Walpole incurred when he wasted the lives of Admiral Hozier's 3000 men in these same West Indian waters against this same Spanish foe. Perhaps you think I write too bitterly. I can only say, old man, that what I have seen during the last five weeks has been enough to make one bitter.

But, Oh, how well the Navy has done. The courage and fighting capacity of our soldiers on shore cannot be surpassed by their brethren on the sea, but Oh, the difference in the Departments and in the men in the higher ranks.

I know just how you feel about Harry and Bay. You cannot help being nervous and yet you would not for anything in the world have them elsewhere than where they are. Mark my words, however, that they will not suffer any more than the Navy has hitherto suffered. The remaining war vessels of the Spaniards will fight less effectively than those which we have captured or have sunk have fought, and Bay and Harry, and any other officer, will off Spain do as they have done off Cuba and the Philippines, that is, win undying honor and glory at a cost that we may disregard.

Oh, how I wish I were in Porto Rico with Gussie and under

General Wilson. He'd be proud of this command. Frankly, I think anyone would be.

Do write me again, old man, and don't think I am not having a good time, for I am; this has been, aside from Edith, *the* time of my life; but there have been a good many grim features to it, and you're the only man to whom I can write of them.

As for politics, I am not really able to take any steps about them now, because while this war lasts the only thing I want to do is to command this regiment and get it into all the fighting I can. As I told you, I am at present in command of the Brigade, and I enjoy handling that, too, for I feel perfectly competent to handle a Brigade in the field now. Of course, if I can possibly get out of it I do not intend to stay in the army merely for police work; I only want to be in while there is actual fighting on a fairly big scale. If I could get down to National politics instead of dealing with sewers and police boards in New York, I should greatly prefer it, but I haven't any real knack of getting on in politics, and the favor of the multitude (especially when extended about equally to our regiment, which has an almost unequalled record, and the —— New York, which did very badly) is a matter of about ten days. The good people in New York at present seem to be crazy over me; it is not very long since on the whole they felt I compared unfavorably with Caligula. By the time election day comes round they may have reverted to their former feeling; and in any event I don't know how to get on with the New York politicians. If I had money enough to keep in National politics it would not be difficult, because the average New York boss is quite willing to allow you to do what you wish in such trivial matters as war and the acquisition of Porto Rico and Hawaii, provided you don't interfere with the really vital questions, such as giving out contracts for cartage in the Custom House and interfering with the appointment of street sweepers.

Warmest love to Nannie, John and Sturgis Bigelow.

Faithfully yours,

THEODORE ROOSEVELT.

Our regiment ranks with the regulars; aside from us, it was purely the regulars who did the real fighting. The National Guard regiments, with their black powder muskets, were nearly worthless.

Copy.   Headquarters, Second Brigade Cavalry Division,
In Camp near Santiago de Cuba,
July 31, 1898.

Major-General Joseph Wheeler, Commanding Cavalry Division.

Sir: I feel it my duty as commander of this Brigade to lay before you with all possible earnestness a request that measures be immediately taken to ship it to the North. I should feel most derelict in my duty to the Brigade if I failed not only to make this request but to make it in as urgent a manner as possible, for I feel that the welfare of this Brigade, its efficiency as a fighting machine, and the lives of the individual members in it, depend in all probability upon its being taken away immediately from where it now is. As you know, I have long wanted to go to Porto Rico, and I feel now that we could get from this Brigade the nucleus of a good fighting force if the squadrons and troops left behind in the United States could be added to it, although of course, the force would be nothing like so efficient as it would have been had we been put aboard transports for shipment to Porto Rico ten or twelve days ago, for every day's delay here has meant the weakening by so much of the Brigade and the impairment of its fighting qualities.

But I understand there is no talk of sending us to Porto Rico. This means that the question is not one of using up the Brigade in service for of course we should be only too glad to be used up in any manner in the service but of preserving it in shape for when it can do service in the future, and there is only one way in which it can be preserved and that is by having it shipped immediately as far north as possible.

I respectfully call your attention to the letter sent by Surgeon Major Church of the First Volunteer Cavalry to Surgeon Major Harris, the Division Surgeon. This letter, I understand, expresses practically Harris' own views and it sets forth the conditions which apply not only to the First Volunteer Cavalry but to the First and Tenth Regulars, that is, to the entire Brigade.

Up to the present time there has not been, so far as I have been able to find out, a single case of yellow fever in this Brigade here at the front, but there have been several hundred cases of the malarial fever peculiar to this country and climate. In not one of these several hundred cases has the patient died and in almost every case he has gotten back to work after a few days, but he is always a shattered and weakened man, far less fit for work than he formerly was and liable to a recurrence of the fever, being more apt to have it than he was before his first attack.

This malarial fever is neither infectious nor contagious; to quarantine against it is just about like quarantining against the toothache. Just as long as the command is kept here these fever cases will keep up; they would keep coming up if we were kept here for three years. While the malaria does not kill it weakens the men so that they are in exactly the condition to die like sheep if the yellow fever really gets among them. To keep this Brigade here for August and September is, in my judgment, to invite an epidemic of yellow fever among the troopers, and surely such an epidemic should not be courted unless for some real and good reason. The Brigade should be moved North, not next month or next week but now, today if possible, tomorrow if possible; it should be put on transports at once and shipped to Long Island or to Maine or elsewhere. It has not got yellow fever now and there is nothing whatever in its condition to warrant the slightest anxiety among any people where it would be sent, especially if sent to a northern climate, in which the yellow fever germ never has thriven and never will thrive and where no yellow fever epidemic has occurred or can occur. Every day the Brigade is kept here means running just so much avoidable risk; every day means that the Brigade is so much less fit to withstand the yellow fever if it should come; every day means that it will take so much longer to get into good trim if it gets up North; every day renders it more likely that some epidemic will arise that would justify the quarantining of the Brigade, whereas now there is not the slightest reason of any kind, so far as the fever which has been prevalent in the regiment is concerned, why we should not be sent anywhere at once, for the fever is in no way contagious or infectious.

The situation seems to me so serious, and the responsibility for the lives of the men under me and the efficiency of the Brigade, which is now under my command, so heavy, that I would feel derelict in my duty if I did not in the strongest possible manner urge that arrangements be immediately made, without the loss of a day more than is necessary, to have this Brigade put on roomy transports and shipped North. If this is done the Brigade will speedily be restored to all its old-time efficiency; if it is not done, every day that we remain in Cuba during the sickly months upon which we are now entering means risking the outbreak of an epidemic of yellow fever, which would result in literally appalling disaster.

Very respectfully,
THEODORE ROOSEVELT.

Personal.   NAHANT, MASS.,
                                                 Aug. 15, 1898.
Dear Theodore :

Your very interesting letter of the 19th [July] has just come. I shall not undertake to answer it at any length, for I see by the papers that you have arrived at Montauk, and as soon as you are out of quarantine and can arrange to get away for a day I will run down to Oyster Bay and see you. I have so many things to say to you that can be better said than written. It is a great relief to know that you are safe at home with your men. The war is over and so far as the West Indies is concerned all is right. The administration seems to be hesitating about the Philippines, but I hope they will at least keep Manila, which is the great prize, and the thing which will give us the Eastern trade. Everything will depend upon the character of the Peace Commission. A great many names are suggested

which would not be fortunate selections, but if Davis* goes, as
reported this morning, all will be well.

Always sincerely yours,   H. C. L.

Personal.   NAHANT, MASS.,
                                             Sept. 1, 1898.
My dear Theodore:

Let me call your attention to this judicious paragraph from
our good friend John Wright of the Haverhill *Gazette*. I like
his way of putting things, and if some time you could send
him a photograph of yourself with your autograph it would
greatly please a very good fellow. How I wish you could be
Secretary of War. You could do an immense work for the
country at this moment, and your appointment would be the
most popular thing the President could do. It would put an
end to the attacks now being made and would save us from all
the scandals which are now being raked up and which I dread,
because they will cloud and tarnish the great glories of the
war. If the President would make any good change and take
Wilson, for example, it would have the same effect. As it is the
Democrats are going to make an issue of the War Department,
and we have no defense to make. It is too bad to make the
party responsible for Alger. I do not know how it is in your
State, but it is going to cost us, I fear, a great many votes
here if Alger is kept in, and we shall lose Congressmen. The
feeling is intense—to a certain extent extreme, no doubt—
but none the less bitter, especially in the Western part of the
State where the Second Regiment comes from. If the President
does not move before election the results may be extremely
serious politically.

It is a great trial to me not to be able to do something for
you at this juncture in New York. I know of course that there
is nothing that I can do and your own course is absolutely
perfect, but at the same time I hate to sit by helpless when you
are concerned in a matter of so much importance. I have not
even the opportunity to criticise or find fault, your own con-

---

* Cushman K. Davis, a Senator from Minnesota.

duct is so entirely discreet and judicious. It seems to me pretty clear that the nomination is coming to you because it must, which is the best possible way, and which will leave you independent. You will be handsomely elected, but with this muss in the War Department anybody else would, in my judgment, be beaten.

After I got home I had a letter from Gus written after the protocol was signed. A day or two after Coamo he was sent out with thirty men under him to make a reconnoissance toward Aibonito, which was the next point. He was in the saddle thirty hours. After the first two hours the Spaniards opened on him and he was exposed and under fire all the rest of the time. He said that he had apparently been selected for this duty of making reconnoissances, and that if it had continued he felt sure he would have been bagged, so that the news of peace came to him without an unpleasant shock. Old army men tell me here that making reconnoissances of that character is the most dangerous kind of work, and that it is an immense compliment to the officer to be selected for it. I confess that I feel very proud of Gus and very thankful that he has come through safely.

After all my good resolutions about not taking additional work the publisher has tempted me and I have fallen. The Harpers offered me $4500 for six articles on the Spanish war, to begin in February, and I have accepted. The political and diplomatic part I know personally. The other part must be written from the accounts of on-lookers, and will necessarily be very imperfect because it is of course about fifty years too early to write a dispassionate history. It will not, I think, be much of a book, little more than an account of how it strikes a contemporary, but I have the consolation of knowing that the operations of the war were so widely scattered that no one man could have seen it all and therefore no one man could write the history from personal observation, as Kinglake wrote the history of the Crimea.

I thought that Davis' account of Las Guasimas in *Scribner's* was extremely good, and as I had your vivid account of the fight fresh in my mind it seemed to me very accurate as well.

It is a story which will bear telling a good many times, but I rather wished that you could have been the first to tell it, because it is so peculiarly your own.

Poor Tiffany's death after actually getting home seemed to me extremely sad. He was a very gallant fellow, like all your men.

The accounts in the papers of Camp Wyckoff are appalling.

I see in the account of the arrival of our Ninth Regiment this morning that those who were on the *Panther* in charge of the Navy were perfectly well fed and taken care of, while those on the Army transport suffered terribly. It is inconceivable after all that has happened that they cannot even now make an improvement.

I hope you will soon be mustered out, and if you are do come on here and get out of the way of politicians in New York and give us the delight of seeing you.

Always sincerely yours, H. C. L.

Camp Wyckoff,
Montauk, L. I.,
Sept. 4, 1898.

Hon. H. C. Lodge, Nahant, Mass.

Dear Cabot:—I am in horrible disfavor with Edith, because I have been so busy here I haven't been able to write more than fragmentary letters to her; but tonight there is a good deal of a let-up, so I am able to sit down and dictate a letter to you. In the first place, I have just written to John Wright and will send him a photograph as soon as I get one, as I want to have him know how I appreciate what he has done.

Today the President came to visit Camp, and was more than cordial, for when he saw me, just after he got into his carriage, he promptly got out again and stepped toward me so that I had to get off my horse and shake hands with him. Hobart and Griggs did the same thing.

I am very much afraid that with Alger the trouble is congenital. He simply *can't* do better; he *can not* learn by experience. Now I don't want to grumble, and I am doing my best to keep the "Rough Riders" from grumbling, but we did not have good food on our transport coming back here; we did not have good water; and we were so crowded that if an epidemic had broken out, we should have had literally no place in which to isolate a single patient. On our ship we managed to keep the standard fairly healthy and just got through with only one death; but a very trivial change in the health of the men the day we came aboard, or in the rigor of policing the ship, would have meant just such an experience as befell the 9th Mass. I do most earnestly wish that the President would change Alger before election, and change him for some man who would himself begin to uproot the evils in the Department. It is absolutely necessary that it should be done, if we are going to get the Army to the point of efficiency which the Navy has reached, and make it compare favorably with other modern armies. Furthermore, it is absolutely necessary in my judgment if we wish to avoid serious political losses. The anger and dissatisfaction here are quite as great as you describe in Mass.,—indeed I think greater; and as always happens at such a time, the feeling produced by what is really blameworthy is augmented by sensational accounts that give a wrong color to what is not blameworthy, or else deliberately invent misdeeds.

As for myself, old man, I do not think that even you could do anything for me here. If the popular feeling is strong enough, and steady enough, I shall be nominated and elected. If it is merely temporary, then I shall be neither; and I don't believe that any effort of mine would alter the result one way or the other. I have been very busy with my Regiment, and have let the other matter attend to itself. If I am nominated, well and good; I shall try to be elected, and if elected, I shall try to rise to the extremely difficult position in which I shall find myself. If I am not nominated, I shall take the result with extreme philosophy and with a certain sense of relief, and shall turn my attention to the literary work which is awaiting me. I am delighted that you are going to do that for Harpers. The most valuable part will be the political and diplomatic chapters, all of which you have seen and very much of which you have been; and the other part will be valuable too, for you were ever a fighter, and ever will be, and those who were closest and dearest to you have borne arms in this conflict.

Gus could have had no higher, (although no more dangerous) compliment paid him than that of entrusting to him reconnoissance duty in a hostile country. It is the greatest test for a young officer, and is never given, save to an exceptionally cool, daring and able man, who is ambitious enough to be willing to take heavy risks. If we ever fight again, I only wish it may be my good fortune to have Gus high under me. Indeed you may well feel proud of him.

Yes, Davis wrote that account very well; I was extremely pleased with it. Poor Tiffany's death was very sad.

I don't believe you can realize old man, what a keen, keen pleasure it was to see you at Sagamore. Next to Edith and the children there was no one whom I so desired to see (and never is anyone). If I can go down to see you, I most certainly shall when we are mustered out, but of course I don't know in the least what my plans will be.

Give my warmest love to Nannie.

Faithfully yours,

THEODORE ROOSEVELT.

Personal.   NAHANT, MASS.,
                                         Sept. 8, 1898.
Dear Theodore :—

I was delighted to get your letter of the 4th. I had seen in the papers what a pleasant meeting you had had with the President. You are entirely right about Alger. The trouble is congenital. He has striven to do his best and the difficulty is that he can't do any better than he has done. The Rough Riders do not grumble any more than the regulars. When you were first at Santiago there were a few letters published by injudicious relatives and the interview with Thomas came which had a good deal of complaint, but since then I have not seen or heard a word from any of your men, and I think their patience is very remarkable, for the other volunteers are talking and writing all the time, and the papers exaggerate the actual evils—

which are bad enough as we all know. The feeling about Alger is very strong. I think it has subsided a little, and perhaps it may subside a good deal before election. There is some reaction apparent on the ground that the complaints and attacks have been overdone by certain newspapers.

I send you an article from the Boston *Journal* which contains some interesting statistics and which illustrates the talk, which is beginning to be heard. I send also another article from the *Journal* in reference to you which I thought very nice. None the less after all allowances there is a deep feeling about the War Department, and it will continue, I fear, with great strength if the President does not do something.

Everything seems to be going right with you in New York and I should say from this point of view that your nomination and election were assured. When it becomes certain that you are to be nominated I hope you will insist that the platform on which you are to stand takes good ground on our foreign policy. I do not mean that it will necessarily incorporate a demand that we take all the Philippines, but I think it ought to leave the door open for that if necessary, and certainly take ground against returning to Spain any people whom we have freed, or Manila which was the prize of Dewey's great victory. This would be very important in its effect on national opinion and on the action of the Peace Commission, and you as the candidate will have the right to insist that the platform should conform to your general views and to the position you intend to assume in the campaign. I shall try for a similar declaration in our platform here.

I enjoyed my day at Sagamore more than I can say. I wish after your regiment is mustered out that you could come on here for a week out of the way.

Bay has been at home for a few days leave. The flag of Spain which he hauled down at Ponce and the banner of the city are both hung in my entry at Nahant and make two very handsome trophies, which I think the boy fairly earned.

Gus has left Porto Rico and ought to be in New York next week. I wish by some chance you could see him.

Always sincerely yours, H. C. L.

Camp Wyckoff,
Montauk Point, L. I.,
Sept. 11, 1898.

Hon. H. C. Lodge, Nahant, Mass.

Dear Cabot: Just a line as I am nearly driven to death by the work of mustering out the regiment. The outcry about the suffering of the troops is fast becoming mere hysteric nonsense.

Those figures in the *Journal* were most interesting: I shall keep the clipping; it told the exact truth.

Give my hearty congratulations to Bay; I envy him his two trophies; I haven't any. As for politics I haven't had a moment even to think of them.

Ever yours,
Theodore Roosevelt.

Personal.   Nahant, Mass.,
Sept. 12, 1898.
My dear Theodore:—

The Middlesex Club is one of our oldest and strongest Republican organizations; a very active and vigorous set of men, and always strong friends of mine. They have been to see me about getting you to speak for them on Grant's birthday, the 27th of next April. I told them that you would probably be Governor with your Legislature in session and that it would be impossible for you to make an absolute engagement so far ahead, but that I would write you in regard to it. They are very earnest and anxious for you, as you can see from their coming to see me so early. Write me a genial and as encouraging a letter as you can which I can give to them, for they are good fellows, and I want to oblige them as much as possible. It might be possible that you could run on for just a night and make a speech. Their meeting is always a great occasion in our politics, and they have had our very best men to speak.

Everything seems to be moving right for your nomination. A mugwump correspondent of a mugwump newspaper here stated the other day that there was a dark conspiracy to have you elected Governor and then when the time came elected to the Senate, leaving Mr. Woodruff to be the acting Governor.

I can only say that if a Senatorship comes in your way take it, for it is better than many Governorships. Of course our mugwump friend denounced this as an infamous dicker and I do not suppose there is any truth in it but to an unscrupulous fellow like myself the thought of getting you into the Senate over-rode all other considerations.

Always sincerely yours, H. C. L.

Personal.   NAHANT, MASS.,
                                             Sept. 14, 1898.
My dear Theodore :—

I am afraid you will think me a great bore about my own particular belongings in the war, but you have always taken such an interest in Gus that I cannot resist sending you a copy of a letter I have just received from General Wilson, which I am sure you will be glad to read. It seems to me that it is rather an unusual thing for a commanding officer to write about one of his staff, and I cannot help feeling that Gus must have done exceptionally well.

Always sincerely yours, H. C. L.

                                             OYSTER BAY, L. I.,
Hon. H. C. Lodge, Nahant, Mass.   Sept. 19, 1898.

*Dear Cabot :—*Will you tell the men of the Middlesex Club that, while I cannot promise, yet if I possibly can come to their dinner, I most certainly shall. You know the peculiar feeling I have for Massachusetts and for the Republican Party in Massachusetts.

If I can get away at the time they give their dinner, I certainly will. As to the Republican Club, tell them that there is nothing I should like more than to speak for them, but that if I am nominated, I *cannot* leave the State. My managers would not permit it.

Will you also tell Hayes that I telegraphed right and left to try to get Turner, but never heard from him or saw him.

That letter of Wilson's, I think, is something that should be kept as an invaluable heirloom for Gussie's descendants. It is as different as possible from the ordinary letter of commendation; in fact, I have never known any letter precisely like it, except one which Gen. Lawton wrote about Wood. I wish I could see Gus and Bay.

Apparently, I am going to be nominated. I saw Platt the other day, and had an entirely satisfactory talk. Of course, I shall have great trouble in the governorship, but there is no use in shirking responsibilities. The first installment of trouble is already on hand, for I cannot accept the so-called independent nomination and keep good faith with the other men on the Republican ticket, against whom the independent ticket is really put up. I would give a great deal were you where I could talk over things with you now and then, but I am being as circumspect as possible and am trying to commit as few mistakes as possible.

Give my best love to Nannie.

Faithfully yours,
THEODORE ROOSEVELT.

P. S.—I wish, if you are willing, that you would write a line to the President for Wood for one of the vacant Brigadier Generalships in the Regular Army. It would be rather revolutionary to put him in over the heads of the elder men, but it would be one of the best things that could happen to the Army. We want young Generals of Wood's capacity, sound good sense and extraordinary energy.

Personal.   NAHANT, MASS.,
                                                 Sept. 21, 1898.
Dear Theodore :—

Gus came home last Friday and has returned to join Wilson in New York. He was very thin and looked rather wan as if he had been carrying a great many anxieties. He has a decided touch of fever which occurs each afternoon, but is I think getting over it. He has brought home a report on schools, churches and taxation in Porto Rico which is quite masterly, and which Wilson means to submit to the President. He would not talk about himself at all, and it was with the utmost difficulty, and only incidentally, that I extracted anything from him. I found however that he had had his first chill when sleeping out on the side of a mountain in the pouring rain on a sweaty horse blanket, down which he slid at intervals as the ground got wetter.

I have seen a very nice fellow who joined the Rough Riders too late to get to Tampa, as he had been in Nicaragua on the canal. He stayed at Tampa through the war. He is a son of Rear Admiral Belknap and wants to get into the Regular Army. Like all the rest of your men, with the few exceptions of the early days, he had no complaint of any sort to make, and impressed me as an extremely good sort. You certainly had an exceptionally fine lot with you, to judge from the specimens I have seen.

I gather from the papers that some of your simple followers from the West had a troublous time in New York after they were mustered out.   Always sincerely yours, H. C. L.

Personal.   NAHANT, MASS.,
                                             Sept. 23, 1898.
Dear Theodore :—

Many thanks for your letter of the 19th. I will convey your message to the Middlesex and Republican clubs with pleasure.

Bay has gotten home finally. He was promoted to the rank of Ensign and obtained his honorable discharge, so that I think he ends his service very creditably.

There is of course no doubt about your nomination. I saw by the papers that you had had a talk with Platt, and I was much amused to see in a Washington despatch that Platt had told the President with great frankness that what you wanted was to be Secretary of War. It is curious that the President cannot see how much he is sacrificing, both in regard to himself and to the party, in keeping Alger.

The Governorship is a great place and full of opportunities

as well as responsibility. I cannot but believe that it will lead you to the Senate at least, where I have always especially wanted you to be.

You are absolutely right in refusing that independent nomination. That whole business, under present existing circumstances, is simply cut throat, and would have but one result, which is the defeat of sound money men and supporters of the administration and the bringing in of Democrats who will vote for free silver and who will oppose the administration and the results of the war. I think your refusal will probably break the movement down, so that it will not be powerful. You not only are circumspect but I honestly think that nothing could have been wiser or more judicious than your entire course. If I thought you were making any errors I should tell you so with the utmost frankness, for your election is quite as near my heart as my own, but I do not see where you have made a single mistake of any kind so far. Your speech at Oyster Bay was very good and just right.

I will write to the President with the greatest pleasure in regard to Wood, or do anything I can to help him. Is it best for me to write now or wait until I go on in November, when I can make a personal appeal? My letters to the White House seem to disappear in the void without any effect, but I would just as lief write if you think it should be begun early. I do not know what the powers of the President are in appointing volunteer officers to positions in the Regular Army. Perhaps you can tell me. He has no authority to appoint volunteer officers into the Regular Navy.

I enclose a letter from a man whom I used to know quite well when I first started in politics here. He was then a clever young Irishman, just beginning the practice of the law in Lynn. He afterwards moved to New York where I understand he has done well. He is intelligent and fervent. As to his standing in New York politically or otherwise I know nothing whatever, but I think his party attachments have always remained very loose, as they were when he was here. He always seemed to me to be loyal to the man whom he liked. I have written him that I would refer his letter to you, but that all such matters of the campaign would, I supposed, be referred by you to the party managers. I think it could do no harm if you were to see him and tell him the same thing, then if he is genuine it is an easy matter to put him into communication with Odell. Of course you do not want to have anything to do with it yourself.

You say nothing in your letter about the platform. I hope you have the plank on foreign relations in mind and will keep it as straight as you can.

Always sincerely yours,

H. C. L.

Dictated.

OYSTER BAY, L. I.,
Sept. 26, '98.

Hon. H. C. Lodge, Nahant, Mass.

Dear Cabot:—I have felt ashamed not to write you more at length, but I have, literally, hardly been able to eat or sleep during the last week, because of the pressure upon me. Probably when you see this the whole residence business will have been made clear in the papers, so I shall not go over it now. I will write you in full about it' in case it is used to stop my nomination, merely so that you may know the exact facts.

The Citizens' Union or Independent Movement has been worse than silly, and some day I will tell you of their exceedingly tricky conduct to me. I hope you like my letter to them. I will write to Ronayne as you suggest.

I am very glad to hear about Bay. As I have said, I cannot express how anxious I am for a real talk with him and Gus.

About those orders to Dewey, when you were present, I merely remember the general tenor. Will you give me, as exactly as you can, your memory? I am exceedingly amused at the Secretary's caution in the matter. It is not necessary to say that I should naturally be delighted to shoulder the responsibility for them myself.

With warm regards, I am,

Faithfully yours,

THEODORE ROOSEVELT.

Personal.   NAHANT, MASS.,
                                             Sept. 28, 1898.
My dear Theodore :—

Thanks for your letter. It is too bad that I should have given you the trouble to read letters even at such times as this. We are all delighted this morning with the news of your nomination and all the household send you their best love and congratulations. Crowninshield has managed to send me all the information I want about Dewey's orders, so do not give that matter another thought. The conduct of the Independents toward you, is the most emphatic exhibition of their dishonesty that I have ever seen. The residence business never gave me the slightest uneasiness; it was absurd on its face. Your platform seems to me excellent.

Always sincerely yours, H. C. L.

                                        OYSTER BAY, L. I.,
                                        Sept. 28, 1898.
Hon. H. C. Lodge, Nahant, Mass.

*Dear Cabot :—*You have probably seen in the *Sun,* Root's statement of the residence question.

I was to blame, for having left the whole matter, as I have left all my business affairs, to Douglas, Uncle Jim and John.* But, most fortunately, they had preserved my letter, in which I not only explicitly stated that my residence was to be kept, but also explicitly directed that my taxes were to be paid, either at Oyster Bay or in New York. Uncle Jim's death was the only reason they were not paid at Oyster Bay.

Of course, it was a peculiarly ugly business, for I hated to have any combination of incidents make me look for a moment as if I were doing something shifty.

Of course, the Democrats will ring the changes on the original charge from now until election, and while I want to win, still I am more anxious that no colorably just accusation can be brought against me. I think that my published letters remove all fear of this.

As for the election, I can form no idea how it will go. There is a great enthusiasm for me, but it may prove to be mere

* His cousin, John Roosevelt.

froth, and the drift of events is against the Party in New York this year, while the Germans are very likely to oppose me; and if Earle is nominated by the Democrats they will have a very strong man.

Faithfully yours,
THEODORE ROOSEVELT.

Warm love to Nannie and both boys; also to Constance and Gus. How busy will you be in your canvass? You are right about waiting and *speaking* to the President concerning Wood.

NAHANT, MASS.,
Sept. 30, 1898.

My dear Theodore :—

I have your letter of the 28th. There was more legal quibbling in the matter of residence than I expected. I see just how it arose—largely through accident; but I never knew of a legal quibble of that kind which had no foundation in truth or fact, having any effect. They seem to have nominated a pretty weak man to run against you, and I do not feel the slightest doubt, myself, about the result. I think that the money issue ought to be pressed very hard in New York, as well as that of sustaining the President's policy.

Gus is in New York with Gen. Wilson and I have asked him to see you. I do not know how busy a campaign I am going to have. Our State Convention comes off next week, so the campaign will be short in any event.

Very truly yours, H. C. L.

SAGAMORE HILL,
OYSTER BAY, LONG ISLAND, N. Y.,
Tuesday, P. M.
[October 5th, 1898.]

Dear Cabot:

I believe a speech from you in the city would be of very great use to me; and of course the Committee would be overjoyed to have you.

I had a great time with the President and Platt on foreign policy; and to get anything like a good plank in the platform I had to agree to be moderate myself in return.

On the surface things seem to be going my way. Whether this is all mere froth I can't tell. Of course it is too early for a forecast that amounts to anything.

I had a really delightful time with shrewd, able Gus; what a man he is! as well as a soldier.

That goose Parkhurst is giving me some trouble. Warm love to Nannie. Edith is fairly well; Ted not well; the other children in bounding health.

Yours, T. R.

Personal.

NAHANT, MASS.,
Oct. 6, 1898.

Dear Theodore :—

Your speech of acceptance was admirable; just what it ought to be, and all that it ought to have been. I can say the same of the report of your speech at Carnegie Hall which I have just read. It is curiously like what I am going to say to the Convention today, and of which I will send you a report, although you will hardly have time to look at other people's speeches. Some of our Congressmen here are uneasy about taking any part in the Philippines and we have had a troublesome time with the resolution, but thanks to Mr. Hoar we have come out all right. It has required however a good deal of steering.

Your class-mate, Charles G. Washburn, has been nominated for the Senate in Worcester. He stands deservedly high as a representative and I have no doubt will make a good Senator. I understand that like everybody else he is for me, but if instead of writing three hundred letters a day you could write three hundred and one and congratulate him and say incidentally how much interest you feel in me, he would appreciate it. Don't do it if it is the least bother of course, for I do not hear as yet of a ripple of opposition to me anywhere.

Gus is down with typhoid fever at Hamilton, and I am more anxious than I can say, although the doctors give us hope that it is not a very severe case.

Always sincerely yours, H. C. L.

Personal.   NAHANT, MASS.,
                                              Oct. 7, 1898.
My dear Theodore :—

   I enclose a letter which comes to you in my care, which from
the handwriting, I guess it to be from Moreton Frewen. It
amuses me to think that he should address you in my care,
but perhaps as he is a Silver man, and Tammany doubts about
your citizenship have reached him, he may think you are a
citizen of Massachusetts.

   Your speech at Carnegie Hall, which I have now read fully,
was an immense success. Nannie was delighted with it and
thinks it the best speech you ever made.

   I got your note of Tuesday last night. Do not in the least
have me on your mind for a speech in New York. I only said
what I did because I wanted you to know that if I could be of
the slightest service by making a speech of course call on me.

   I think your plank on the foreign relations was excellent, and
just what it ought to be. You will see that ours is substantially
the same by the copy of the Boston *Journal* which I send
you. The report of my speech, which was not written out, is
rather ragged, but it will give you an idea of what I said,
and the speech appeared to be ·a success and there was no
doubt of the splendid reception that the Convention gave me.
There has been no appearance of any opposition to me anywhere, but the tone of the Convention yesterday settled the
thing if any settlement was needed.

   We, of course, are very anxious about Gus, but at least he
seems to be no worse.

   Bob* is here and he is in very poor condition. I do not
mean that he is in the least dangerously ill, but he is worn
out, very sick, and requires rest and care, which, I think, he
is getting here.

   I am very glad you saw Gus, and I know how much it pleased
him.

   Unless my judgment is completely at fault you are going
to be elected by a very large majority. Every indication seems
to me to point that way. I thought Low's speech at the meet-

_____
   * R. M. Ferguson, a young Scotchman, a friend of us all. He was one of the
"Rough Riders."

ing very good, but I was disappointed in Choate's. It seemed
to me rather labored and not to reach the real point.

Always sincerely yours, H. C. L.

REPUBLICAN STATE COMMITTEE
FIFTH AVENUE HOTEL

NEW YORK,
Oct. 11th, 1898.

Dear Cabot:—

Just a line to say how distressed I am about Gus. I have
written poor Mrs. Hoar. Sherman* was· a fine fellow and he
gave his life for his country.

I am very glad you like my speech. It was not received
with any particular favor here; neither by the mugwumps on
one side nor the practical politicians on the other. However,
I would not have been willing to refrain from making it. The
surface indications are in my favor but I am not over sanguine
for I simply do not know in this state what the undercurrents
really amount to and Croker is certainly confident and has
any amount of money. Your speech was splendid. Infinitely
better than mine. I like your allusion to the Germans. But
indeed, your speech was the speech of a Statesman and should
be kept in your works. It was just like you to mention me.

How I wish I could see you.

Always yours,
THEODORE ROOSEVELT.

Personal.

NAHANT, MASS.,
Oct. 14, 1898.

Dear Theodore :—

I have your note of the 11th. Gus seems to be doing quite
well, and we are beginning to feel very hopeful.

There is no doubt that your speech was a good one—unusually good. It would not have pleased the mugwumps
here, but every Republican in this State would have delighted
in it. I see that Croker has a great deal of money, but I cannot conceive that you should be in any danger.

* Sherman Hoar, son of Judge Hoar; rendered fine service during the war.

I am glad you liked my speech. I had an extremely difficult situation here to handle, which I will explain to you more at length when we meet.

I do ·not know what day I shall come to New York. Mr. Barnes said he would let me know, but I do hope that I shall not have the ill luck to be in New York when you are speaking at Buffalo or some other distant place, for I should like a little talk with you very much.

I heard yesterday in a round about way that your letter to Washburn had been received, and apparently made much impression in Worcester, although my informant said that Washburn was for me any way, but was none the less pleased to have a line from you. Many thanks for it.

Always sincerely yours,
H. C. L.

Dictated.   OYSTER BAY, L. I.,
                                Oct. 14, 1898.
Hon. H. C. Lodge, Nahant, Mass.

Dear Cabot:—Lord! How I would like to live in a civilized community where I could make speeches like yours. Here, I press them just as far as I possibly can, but it is astonishing how little they will stand.

I enclose you a letter of Wood's, which gives an idea of what he is doing, which it seems to me, shows him in a pretty good light. If I am elected Governor, I shall do my best to use all my influence to try to have Wood made a Brigadier General in the Regular Army, for I think it would be a splendid thing for the service.

If Alger should get out, what would you say to Frank Greene* as Secretary of War? I lunched with him yesterday, and it did me good to meet a man so solid on expansion and foreign policy, as well as upon his views of the War Department.

Will you send the enclosed to Gus, if he is well enough to read it; if not, then to Constance. I don't know whether he now is in shape where anything can be told him or read to him or not.

* General Francis V. Greene, a distinguished officer in the Philippine campaign.

I am deeply concerned that Constance and Nannie and you should have this grief and worry now, and I grieve on my own account too, for Gus is a man for whom I have grown to feel a steadily increasing regard and affection. He is every inch a man; a good citizen and a good American.

Always yours,

THEODORE ROOSEVELT.

REPUBLICAN STATE COMMITTEE
FIFTH AVENUE HOTEL

Private and Confidential.

NEW YORK,
Oct. 16th, 1898.

Dear Cabot :—

This may be the last letter I shall write you for the canvass is not looking well and I shall evidently have to work like a beaver for the next three weeks. At first all the managers were anxious that I should do nothing, should take as little personal control of the canvass as possible and should make very few speeches but the result has shown that they were wrong and they have changed their minds. On the very point where they ought to have done the best work, that is, in the matter of registration, they have failed signally. The truth is that the Republican machine, especially in New York City has devoted itself for two or three years to getting delegates for Conventions and not to getting votes at elections and now it works a little rustily in the new direction. Senator Platt and Congressman Odell are doing all they can for me and I could not wish the canvass to be in better hands; but in the city all of the vote-getters, and all of the men who can influence the doubtful vote which is not corrupt, have partly by their own fault and partly through the fault of the machine, left the party and it is exceedingly hard to get into touch with them. The Gold Democrats have returned to Tammany, being perfectly satisfied if only their party will dodge the issue of honest money. The Germans are inclined to be against me and the Independents care very much less for honest government than they care to register themselves against my views of expansion and of an efficient Army and Navy. In addition to this, Algerism is a heavy load to carry and Lou Payne and Aldridge and the canal business and Tillinghast and the militia make up another burden with which it is difficult to deal. In fact, taking it as a whole, New York cares very little for the war now that it is over, except that it would like to punish somebody because the Republican administration did not handle the War Department well. It is not interested in free silver for it never looks more than six months ahead or behind and it thinks free silver dead; and the things against which it cries are things for which the Republican Party has been responsible. The result is that I am not having an entirely pleasant campaign. I may win yet, and I am going in to do everything that can be done. As I said, Senator Platt and Congressman Odell are doing everything and I am more than satisfied with the way the State canvass is being run, but there is great apathy among the Republicans; and, as for the Independents and Democrats, their feeling is precisely Croker's, viz.: that they wish me well as a good soldier, but that they intend to vote against me as Governor. In New York county we are exceedingly weak.

Yours,   T. R.

Private.   NAHANT, MASS.,
                                                  Oct. 19, 1898.

Dear Theodore :—

I have your letter of the 16th. I had begun to get very anxious about the campaign in New York. Sometimes an outsider at a distance sees the general trend of a campaign more clearly than those in it, just as a traveller will remark leading characteristics in a new country which would slip out of sight if he stayed there a year. You give me the reasons for what I saw, which was that the campaign was lagging. At the time you were writing to me I felt very blue and worried, but since then the situation seems to me to have greatly changed. Croker's assault on the judges has had an immense effect. It has frightened the conservative class, and a great many people who took no interest will now go to the polls, and a great many others who started in simply to elect Judge Daly will end by voting for you. That is the way those things always work. An attack on one part of the ticket, no matter how they try to confine it, always ends by putting the leader ahead. Then again your tour through the State is having an immense success. It is rousing things up. This letter will reach you only after you return, and so the suggestions I make will perhaps not be of much value, but still you will have a few more speeches to make and then I want you to consider them.

Argue more than you do. The people of New York know perfectly well that you will carry out your promises, and that you do not say one thing on the stump and do another at Albany, so that there seems no need of saying that too often, whereas you have got lots of subjects on which you can make most effective arguments and with great variety. I think that one of the most effective speeches you made was your first talk about the judiciary.

Another good point was in regard to the National Guard. If I were you I would argue this question, and also the money question, as often and as strongly as possible.

I would press home too the necessity of standing by the President against Spain. You made one admirable statement under this last head at some point on your journey, and I noticed that it was received with tremendous applause. That is a very telling argument.

We are in danger of losing two or three Districts here, none of which ought to be lost, and we have an immaculate State Government and as little as is adverse to carry as any party could possibly desire, but the failures of the War Department have damped enthusiasm, and the astonishing indifference of business men to the election of a free silver House is something inconceivable. If we lose Congressmen it will be due to these two causes alone.

The President's trip out West and his speeches have done good. I think I see an improvement in the Republican campaign all along the line, and if things continue to move as they are now moving the party will go to the polls and carry the House all right.

A week ago I took a bad cold from speaking. I went on

speaking last week and that made it worse, and now the doctor has shut me up in the house and forbidden any speeches for this week. I am very anxious to get in perfect trim so that I can go on next week to New York and make a speech for you. I saw it was announced that I was to go through the State, but that is really impossible. I can make one speech in New York City, but in view of my work here that is all I can undertake.

Wood's letter came yesterday and I have read it with a great deal of interest. Since then I see that Lawton has been recalled. Does not this put Wood in nominal as well as actual command? If you think best I will of course write the strongest kind of a letter to the President, which I shall get an answer to from Porter that it has been received and referred to the Secretary of War. I fear I cannot do anything effectually until I get back to Washington, but if you think I ought to write say the word and I will do so. Anything I can do for Wood I am more than anxious to do at any time.

Of course I should like the Mauser which he is kind enough to suggest sending me to add to my collection of war relics.

Always sincerely yours, H. C. L.

Personal.　　　　　　　　　　　　　　NAHANT, MASS.,
　　　　　　　　　　　　　　　　　　Oct. 25, 1898.
Dear Theodore :—

I telephoned to the White House about the medal as soon as I got down to the *Sun* office and gave the message to Mr. Montgomery, one of the clerks whom I know, and put it in the strongest possible terms. After I had gone Laffan received word from the White House as follows: "President says he is appointing Board to award those medals and will be glad to comply with your wishes by seeing to it that there is no delay in T. R.'s case." I do not feel myself that this is very satisfactory, because I do not believe a board can be appointed in time to do it. Laffan expected to go to Washington today, and if he does will urge the thing personally. I am going to write to the President now and reiterate what I said over the telephone. I trust it may not be all in vain.

We had a fine meeting last night and I do not see how it could have possibly gone off better. I came away from New York feeling very confident as to the result. I passed the afternoon at the Republican State Committee and had a long talk with Odell, who seems to me a very conservative and reserved man, but who impressed me with confidence. I saw a lot of other people and the result of all my enquiries and investigations was great confidence in the outcome of the election.

Always sincerely yours, H. C. L.

Personal.

To the President:

NAHANT, MASS.,
Oct. 25, 1898.

I took the liberty of telephoning yesterday from New York in regard to giving to Colonel Roosevelt at this time the medal for distinguished gallantry for which he was recommended by General Wheeler. I assume that there is no doubt that that medal will be conferred upon him sooner or later. Just now it would have a very important meaning and value and would put at rest many stories which are being circulated by the Democrats. In view of the immense importance of the New York election I felt justified in bringing the matter to your attention, and desire to express my most earnest hope that this medal may be awarded to Colonel Roosevelt in the course of the next few days. I would not be so urgent were I not thoroughly assured of the importance of the action at this time.

I have the honor to be, with the highest respect,

Sincerely yours, H. C. LODGE.

WESTERN UNION TELEGRAPH COMPANY

LOCKPORT DEPOT, N. Y.,
Oct. 26th, 1898.

To Hon. H. C. Lodge, Nahant, Mass.

Your speech was the best delivered in my entire campaign.

THEODORE ROOSEVELT.

Personal. NAHANT, MASS.,
Nov. 3, 1898.
Dear Theodore :—

I noticed in the papers last night that you were to begin your course of Lowell lectures about which I had entirely forgotten on November 16th. As ill luck will have it I shall have left Nahant by that time and be at my mother's for a day or two on my way to Washington, so that I shall not have the shelter of my roof-tree to offer you, which is very trying. Moreover on that night I have got to speak before a business association, but we must in some way arrange to meet. I suppose of course that you will stay over for George Lee's wedding on the 17th, and in that case I do hope that you will remain through the day and dine with George Lyman, as he is having a dinner for me that evening. It seems too bad that I should be houseless just at the moment when you come here, and my mother's house will be filled up with the boys who are on their way to Washington.

I firmly believe that you are going to be elected, but I am so anxious about the result, more anxious than I have ever been about any election contest in my life, that my anxiety confuses my judgment. You have made a most wonderful and splendid fight, and your speeches have been most telling and wholly admirable. The enormous enthusiasm which greets you everywhere will certainly be translated into votes. It is too genuine for anything else. I believe too that the tide throughout the country is setting in our favor, and this will help us.
Always sincerely yours, H. C. L.

REPUBLICAN STATE COMMITTEE
FIFTH AVENUE HOTEL
NEW YORK,
Nov. 4, 1898.
Hon. H. C. Lodge, Nahant, Mass.

Dear Cabot: All right; I will dine with you at George Lyman's on the night of the 17th.

I have no idea how this fight is going. It is evident that the National Guard will give a majority against me, partly on account of my letter to Alger, but more on account of the fact that they were really not very good soldiers and are sore and angry and mortified about the hardships they have encountered. I have had a very hard campaign; but at any rate I have made the best fight I could, and if Blifil and Black George win, why, win they must.   Always yours,

THEODORE ROOSEVELT.

Personal.   NAHANT, MASS.,
                                              Nov. 7, 1898.
My dear Theodore :—

I have your letter of the 4th and am delighted to know you are going to dine with Lyman.

I am devoured with anxiety about your election in New York. The news I get from there this morning seems very good, and I. cannot believe that we are to meet with such a calamity as your defeat would be. I think you will show a much greater strength at the polls than any one imagines, but although this is my opinion it does not diminish my anxiety. You have made a magnificent campaign, especially since you took up the issues both State and National and argued them on every stump as you have done with the greatest force. But there is no use in my speculating. You will not get this letter until all is over, and you know whether it is victory or defeat I share with you in all your feelings. I got a letter from Chandler this morning, and here is the last paragraph, which, although it gives me more credit than I deserve, I think will gratify you even after the battle is over.

Always sincerely yours,   H. C. L.

NIGHT MESSAGE
WESTERN UNION TELEGRAPH COMPANY

                                        OYSTER BAY, N. Y.,
                                        Nov. 7th, 1898.
To Hon. H. C. Lodge.

Hearty thanks old fellow best love to Nannie.

ROOSEVELT.

UNITED STATES SENATE
WASHINGTON, D. C.

Private.

Dear Theodore: Nov. 30, 1898.

I enclose a passage from Allen's report. He spoke to me yesterday about it and said that Miller and Weeks* and some of the Naval Militia people were going to hold a convention in Philadelphia in opposition to his recommendations and in behalf of the present organization of militia; that he had no objection to the Naval Militia, and appreciated what they had done, but he thought it was of the highest importance to have a true Naval Reserve. He said that he had learned that the opposition were going to try to enlist your aid and sympathy in their attempt, and that he hoped you would feel that the Department was taking the right ground in the matter and that you would not do anything about it, certainly not without first talking with him. I told him that I agreed with him as to what the Naval Reserve should be, and that I was certain that you did also, but that I would call the matter to your attention, so that you might be forewarned. There is no question that the Naval Reserve ought to be such as he describes in the paragraph I enclose, and I remember that you and I had some talk on the same lines when you were in Boston.

You would be pleased to hear the expressions of delight from every one here over your victory and the universal agreement that without you and the fight you made we could not possibly have carried New York. The President spoke of you to me on Monday, when I had a long talk with him, not only in terms of the highest commendation and personal regard, but with the utmost gratification in your election. Bliss, next to whom I sat last night at dinner, was most emphatic in the same direction.

It looks to me as if they were going to send Choate to England—this of course in confidence—and I think it would be a very happy solution.

I have your letter in regard to Andrews. In the note I wrote you after seeing Platt I said that I understood from him that

* John W. Weeks.

you had decided to take Andrews and that he thought it very wise. After thinking it all over I reverted to my first opinion, that it was the best solution, and after reading the letters you enclose, I feel that way more than ever. Personally, I like Andrews very much and think his appointment would be an excellent one. The objections that I suggested only arose from my extreme anxiety in regard to anything which concerns you, and I am clearly of the opinion now that his appointment is best, not only from the point of view of the National Guard but politically. As to Hendricks, you know of course that I would not for one moment suggest that you appoint any man against whom there was any real reason whatever, but on the contrary, if there was any substantial reason I should be the first to say to you to stand out at all hazards. It seemed to me, however, from all I could learn in New York, that if Hendricks was an honest man of good character and fair ability there was not enough difference between him and Clinton to make a sufficient ground for a serious contest. I know how imperfect my knowledge is, and therefore advance this opinion with great diffidence, but from the little I know I still think that, assuming that Hendricks is a man of fair ability and good character his appointment would be on the whole the best solution.

I wish you and Edith could get down here for a few days. I really think it would do you good to get the change.

Always sincerely yours,
H. C. L.

SAGAMORE HILL,
Dec. 1st, '98.

Dear Cabot,

Many thinks for your letter. I sent you General Wilson's letter to Andrews, did I not?

Hendricks would be a good appointment in ordinary times. He is a machine politician of a good kind. But he is ultra-machine, and has been engaged in desperate fighting with the Belden faction, in the course of which a good many things have been done, in the way of fighting fire with fire, that have an ugly look. I think Hendricks is clean and honest; but I do not think the State at large would believe that he intended to punish corruption in the Canal Department in any aggressive manner. It may be that I can do no better than take him; but as yet I am not convinced of this. Clinton, who says he would under no circumstances take the place, has written a very strong protest against him.

Now, one of my usual worrying requests! On Sept. 17th Meiklejohn wrote me that there was in the War Department the recommendation for me for the medal of honor, by Wood, Wheeler and Shafter. Can you get me a copy of it? Can you get any idea as to when they are likely to take action?

Give my love to Nannie and the boys. I only hope we can get on, if only for a day or two, to see you before Xmas.

Yours ever, T. R.

UNITED STATES SENATE
WASHINGTON, D. C,

Personal.

Dear Theodore :—

Dec. 5, 1898.

I went to the War Department this morning and saw Meiklejohn,* who was most obliging. He said he would have copies of all the letters made at once and sent to you directly and he gave the order while I was there. If they do not turn up very soon let me know. He said that the statement of the Secretary in regard to medals was a complete mistake, and sent for Col. Ainsworth to confirm him, which he did most fully. The only requirement is that the service should have been rendered in action and should have been most conspicuous. Both Meiklejohn and Ainsworth said you would receive your medal as a matter of course, and that the Board would act upon all these cases now in a very few days. I enclose a copy of the law in regard to medals, and of the regulations of the War Department in regard to it.

Sincerely yours,
H. C. LODGE.

* George de Rue Meiklejohn, Assistant Secretary of War.

REPUBLICAN STATE COMMITTEE
FIFTH AVENUE HOTEL

NEW YORK,
Dec. 6th, 1898.

Dear Cabot:—

Hearty thanks! The attitude of the Secretary of course simply means that the War Department does not intend that I shall have the Medal of Honor.* If I didn't earn it, then no commissioned officer ever can earn it. I was not acting in accordance with orders. I had been told to *support* the attack of the Regulars with my regiment. I moved through the 9th Regiment, of my own accord, and gave the order to charge, and led in person that portion of the line on horseback, being the first man on the Hill, and killing a Spaniard with my own hand. I led in person the next charge on the second line of block-houses; I led in person the third charge; and then at the extreme front commanded the fragments of the six cavalry regiments and brigade until the next morning. I don't ask this as a favor—I ask it as a right. Wood, Wheeler, and Shafter joined in making the request for me; Miles has told me it certainly should be granted as a matter of course; and General Sumner, and Captain Stevens of the 9th, Captain Steele and Captain Howze, of General Sumner's staff, and Captains Mc-Blaine and McAnee, of the Ninth, and Captain Ayres of the Tenth, could all be summoned as eye-witnesses—not to speak of my own men. I have stood, without making a counter attack, the Secretary's publication of my private letter, and the President's failure to interfere with it. I do not feel much like standing the refusal to give me the only reward they possibly can give me. Remember that though I had commanded a brigade, and though I had been singled out in reports for special commendation, I was given no brevet rank. For this I don't care, but I am entitled to the Medal of Honor, and I want it.

The Daly matter has rather complicated matters, and may result in my appointing Hendricks. I will tell you about it when we meet.

Faithfully yours,

THEODORE ROOSEVELT.

* For some unknown reason it seemed finally to appear that the War Department did not intend he should have the medal. It was an outrage. No man ever had earned the medal more completely than he.

P. S.—I have seen that Spanish report. Do get me a copy of the Wood-Wheeler-Shafter recommendation. I feel rather ugly on this medal of honor business; and the President and War Dept. may as well understand it. If they want fighting, they shall have it.

UNITED STATES SENATE
WASHINGTON, D. C.

Personal.

My dear Theodore:—

Dec. 7, 1898.

It was stupid of me to write to you about that conversation with Alger, for it simply upset you when you have enough on your mind without an irritation like that. It was especially useless as I felt sure at the time that there could be nothing in what Alger said, and this has been proved by my conversation with Meiklejohn and Ainsworth, which I reported to you yesterday. You are unjust, I think, to the President, for when I saw him the day after I got here and he spoke of you in the highest terms as I wrote you he referred to the matter of the medal and said that the Board would award it to you as a matter of course. I do not think you need have any apprehension about it at all. All that Alger said was his own stupidity, but I will watch the matter carefully and if there should be the slightest hitch, which I do not regard as in any way possible, I will bring the matter up in Congress.

I may be as mistaken in my advice about Daly as in anything else, but I do not think I am, because it seems to me that there is a question of principle involved, which I did not think was at stake in the case of Hendricks. I agreed entirely with your view that after the attitude the party took in the campaign you ought to appoint Daly at the first opportunity, and I adhere to that opinion. The selection of Hendricks seems to me entirely secondary to the question involved in Daly's appointment, and if you can soothe feelings by taking them both, as you say is possible, it appears to me it would be a very wise solution.

We are going to have trouble over the Treaty. How serious I do not know, but I confess I cannot think calmly of the rejection of that Treaty by a little more than one-third of the Senate. It would be a repudiation of the President and humiliation of the whole country in the eyes of the world, and would show we are unfit as a nation to enter into great questions of foreign policy. I cannot believe that the opposition which is of course composed of Southern Democrats can succeed.

Always sincerely yours, H. C. L.

REPUBLICAN STATE COMMITTEE
FIFTH AVENUE HOTEL
NEW YORK,
Dec. 7th, 1898.

Dear Cabot :—

Hearty thanks. I am very much pleased. If they want a detailed statement of what I did, I know Wood will gladly submit it.

Faithfully yours,
THEODORE ROOSEVELT.

OYSTER BAY, L. I.,
Dictated.   Dec. 12, 1898.

Hon. H. C. Lodge, U. S. Senate, Washington, D. C.

Dear Cabot :—I have just got back from Boston. I inquired about you, and found, of course, that there was not a ripple of opposition to you.

You seriously alarm me about the treaty matter. It seems impossible that men of ordinary patriotism can contemplate such an outrage upon the country. As for my own affairs, you probably saw the outcome of the Daly matter. As soon as I announced definitely, that I would appoint Daly, Croker made O'Brien keep on the bench.

I have offered Gen. Frank V. Greene the commissionership of Public Works, but I very much fear he cannot accept. I shall very possibly have to take Hendricks; but I shall try Roberts who is sufficiently better to justify a fight.

Always yours,

THEODORE ROOSEVELT.

Corbin writes me that Wood's recommendation is not sufficiently specific to justify awarding me the medal. I have written Wood.

UNITED STATES SENATE
WASHINGTON, D. C.

Personal.

Dec. 15, 1898.

Dear Theodore :—

I have your note of the 12th. Glad to hear what you say about Boston. I do not hear that there is the slightest opposition to me, but I wish it were out of the way, simply because no one cares to have that sort of thing to look forward to.

I was amused by the Croker performances on the Daly matter, but it seems to me as if you had gotten all the glory of the action without making the appointment.

Frank Greene would be an ideal Commissioner, but I suppose he can hardly take it. About the others I do not know enough to judge.

I cannot believe there will be any doubt about the medal, but keep me posted and if it doesn't come there will be a row if nothing else.

Always sincerely yours, H. C. LODGE.

UNITED STATES SENATE
WASHINGTON, D. C.

Personal.

Dec. 20, 1898.

Dear Theodore :—

I saw the President yesterday and handed him the letter from Howze, which he read with a great deal of interest and asked me to leave with him. He said of course you ought to have the medal and would have it, but that he had been very reluctant to pick out any one man ahead of all the others and give him the medal, because he did not think it quite fair, and he also felt that it would lead to a great rush and clamor for them from all quarters, which could be best stopped by the report of the Board. For this reason he has taken no action for any of those specially recommended for gallantry and did not mean to until the Board sent in their report. I told him that you ought also to have the brevet, to which he agreed, and I think I shall be able to bring that about also. He said that no one had reaped more from the war than you or more deservedly, and that there was no one in whose success he was more interested than he was in yours.

I have had some very interesting talks with him about our international policy. He has risen up during the summer to the level of the great events in a very striking way, and I think you will be much impressed with it when you see him and talk with him. I think, as I wrote you, that we are going to ratify the treaty without trouble. Reed is terribly bitter, saying all sorts of ugly things about the administration and its policy in private talks, so I keep out of his way, for I am fond of him, and I confess that his attitude is painful and disappointing to me beyond words. What a singular collection the so-called anti-imperialists are getting together—Bryan and Carnegie, Pingree and Cleveland.

Always sincerely yours,   H. C. LODGE.

OYSTER BAY, L. I.,
Dictated.   Dec. 21, 1898.

Hon. H. C. Lodge, Senate Chamber, Washington, D. C.

Dear Cabot:—I enclose a copy of a certificate, which has been sent to the Adjutant General in my case. I will get one or two more like it, and then, if they do not grant the medal, I shall feel, at least, that they have been deprived of all excuse.

In a letter to me, Howze adds that in his judgment, I was the one man of the entire cavalry brigade who did earn a medal that day. Howze is, himself, a medal-of-honor man and, perhaps, the most reckless dare-devil, as regards his own person, whom I met at Santiago.

Would you mind keeping the copy? It might be worth

while to show to the President, and I should like to have it anyhow, later.

As I look more and more into the canal matter, I become very reluctant to appoint Hendricks. The worst trouble has come from using the canals for political purposes. Among the men singled out for especial criticism by the investigating committee, were a number put on by Hendricks, who has been given, by Aldridge, the entire patronage of his district, to use against Belden. For this, and for other reasons connected with Hendricks' extreme subserviency to the Machine, in for instance, coming to Albany to do everything he could for Lou Payne's appointment, etc., etc., I feel that if I can get some better man, I should try. Frank Greene is wavering. I think, if you wrote him what a big place it was and how important, not the highest merely in New York but of the country, that he would be very much impressed.

Give my love to Nannie and the boys. Little Speck is to pass Christmas with us. I shall strive to get on for two or three days to Washington, as soon after the Inauguration as possible.

I want to see you and talk over the big questions of National politics.

Always yours,
THEODORE ROOSEVELT.

UNITED STATES SENATE
WASHINGTON, D. C.

Personal.

My dear Theodore :—	Dec. 22, 1898.

It seems too bad to ask you a question when you are so bothered, but I cannot help it, for I am in trouble myself about one of my articles. I cannot get any statistics as to the number of Spanish troops at San Juan, or as to the number of the killed and wounded on the Spanish side. The little that I can gather from the Spanish account is so grotesquely false as to be beyond use. Could you tell me where to look, or give me any idea of how many men they had there, and how many they lost in the action with your division and Kent's?

Always sincerely yours,   H. C. L.

UNITED STATES SENATE
WASHINGTON, D. C.

Personal.

My dear Theodore :—   Dec. 23, 1898.

I have your letter of the 21st and the copies of the letters you enclose. I intended to have a talk with the President about it tomorrow, and am glad to have these letters with me. No promotions or medals have been awarded as yet to anyone, and I do not think any will be until the Board reports.

I hope you can get Frank Greene. If I could only see him I would say anything to him that you wanted said, but I do not know whether I know him well enough to write him in regard to it. If you think he would not regard it as unwarranted interference for me to do so, just let me know and I will write him a letter at once. He is by all odds the man to get if you can possibly get him.

It looks now as if the treaty would be ratified without serious opposition.

Always sincerely, H. C. LODGE.

SAGAMORE HILL,
Dear Cabot,   Dec. 26th, '98.

First, do tell Nannie how lovely it was of her to remember all the children, who reveled in her books.

Now, as to the Spanish numbers. I think that the best figures are those of Frederic Ramsden, the British Consul, who puts the Spanish force on July 1st as 6,000; 4,000 regulars, 1,000 guerillas, 1,000 marines and sailors. On July 2nd 5,000 more regulars marched in.

On July 1st Lawton at Caney fought only about 800 Spaniards, or even less. Wheeler fought about 4,000; or rather over. But these 4,000 could and did retreat; while those at Caney really could not, save in a last desperate, disorganized rush. We had over 12,000 men. But only four brigades, those of Chaffee, Sumner, Wood, and Hawkins, were really fought. With any kind of generalship, our practically untouched brigades could have gone on into the city in the afternoon.

As for the Spanish losses I do not believe they were as heavy as ours. We advanced, exposed largely in the open, and shot at their heads in the trenches, and at the apertures in the block houses. When we took the city we found nearly as many sick and wounded in their hospitals as we had in ours. I think a thousand would cover their losses, as against our 1,500.

I have Miller's book in the Spanish. By the way, tell Allen I took a fall out of our friend Captain Miller on the Naval Militia business. In my inaugural I came out on expansion and the Army and Navy pretty well; Platt and Odell didn't want me to touch it, but I thought an allusion was all right.

Yours, T. R.

UNITED STATES SENATE
WASHINGTON, D. C.

Personal.

Dec. 27, 1898.

My dear Theodore :—

It was very good of you, in the midst of all your cares, to write me your note of the 26th, which I have just received. I have seen Ramsden's figures but did not know how trustworthy they were, so that your note tells me exactly what I wanted to find out. I had made out from the reports and the table of losses that the brunt of the fighting was borne by the brigade you mention. It is of course very obvious from the report of Chaffee's brigade at El Caney that the whole army was practically engaged, more or less, and I confess that it does seem to me after studying the situation that it was an extraordinary movement which moved the whole army forward without any reserves.

After I have completed my articles, if I still live, I think I shall escape to Europe, for I do not think that it would be safe for me to be here at the time of their publication, .as I have written, of course from the standpoint of the historian, and as I have tried to do justice to every one no one will be satisfied, and those I have criticised will fall upon me heavily.

I think it is all right your making the allusion in your message to the events of the year, which have been of such a great character that I do not think they could possibly be passed over in silence. I am glad the children like the books.

Always sincerely yours,
H. C. Lodge.

Oyster Bay, L. I.,
Dec. 27, 1898.

Dear Cabot :—

Now, please don't, in the midst of all your worry over big matters, do another thing in connection with the medal. I shall try to get one or two letters like that of Captain Howze, not getting them from men in my regiment, unless absolutely necessary, as I prefer to rely upon the testimony of regular officers. Then I shall simply let the matter go.

I do not think that the War Department has treated me well in the matter. It must be remembered that there is no occasion "to invite a rush of applicants" by giving me the medal. So far as I know, I was the only man in the entire army at Santiago, and certainly the only man in the Cavalry Division who, on the spot, (or indeed since) was recommended by his brigade, his division, and his corps, commanders, all three, for the medal; and granting it to me at once, would only be a precedent for granting it to others who were *similarly* recommended. In other words, I was singled out by the Generals in command on the ground, as having, on that particular day in the big fight of the war, earned the medal above any other man in the Cavalry Division, and I am inclined to think, above any other man, except Hawkins, in the Army.

At Montauk, about four months ago, I wrote to the War Department to find out if the application had been received and was in proper form. Not a hint was given me that any additional testimony would be required. On the contrary I was told, up to within a month, as you were told by General Corbin, that it was all right. Then I was suddenly told to get new testimony; but I was no longer with the army and the witnesses of the act were scattered everywhere. I could have gotten scores of men while I was at Montauk, because I should have asked the regular officers, who were in the Cavalry Division, whether or not they had seen me. I don't know who saw me throughout the fight, because I was almost always in the front and could not tell who was close behind me, and was paying no attention to it. It was by a mere accident that I happened to find out that Howze had been an eye witness of what occurred. I have written to two or three other regular officers whom I think saw me; but I cannot be certain whether they did or not. Wood and Wheeler told me of their own volition that they had recommended me for the medal, and it never occurred to me to ask the men of less rank as to my conduct.

Don't bother about the brevet. It is the medal for which I care. I commanded a brigade as acting Brigadier General for over a month, being paid as such, and exercising command not only on the field, but on the transport coming home. I was the only officer who thus commanded a brigade who was not made a Brigadier General by the President in our Santiago army. If he had seen fit then to promote me, as he promoted the others, who certainly did no more, I should have been very much pleased; but I do not care for the brevet. From the people at large, including the people of my own State, I received a more than ample recognition for my services, and so I did from the regulars with whom I served, from Generals Shafter, Wheeler, Young and Sumner, down to the Captains and Lieutenants of the 1st and 10th Regular Cavalry, who were really overjoyed at my being given the brigade. From Washington, I have received no recognition whatever, except that when the vacancy of Colonel had to be filled, I was put into it, in the regular order of events, as is done in every regiment with every Lieutenant Colonel, whether he has been in battle or not.

This will seem, even to you, very egotistical. I wish you would look at a book of Lieut. Parker's, of the Regular Army, called "The Gatlings at Santiago." He saw more of our regiment than any other outside officer, and I would like you to see what he says of us, and indeed, of me.

There! Pardon this. I shall not allude to it again; but I did want you to understand just why I feel that the War Department people have not behaved with justice toward me. You see, that if the Board is now sitting, it cannot have my documents before it, for my documents have not been brought in; thanks to the conduct of the War Department in never letting me know that there was any need of extra recommendations, until within the last two or three weeks, and then, only owing to vigorous prodding of yourself and myself. I could hardly regard such conduct as due to other than design. The Board, if now sitting, does not have before it the full case of the only officer who was recommended in the field by all of his superior officers.

I am terribly disappointed that Greene won't take the Commissionership of Public Works. It would have been the ideal solution, especially as the appointment would have been particularly acceptable to Platt. I am now at my wits ends who to get. The more I look into the place, the more I realize that at this crisis, good work cannot be done by the ordinary party "hack," even of the best type; and the really high-class men will not take it. The candidates of the "Mugwumps" it is not necessary to say, are wholly unfit. Platt is working hard for Choate for Ambassador, which is an excellent appointment.

By the way, Choate told me, (to his own and my intense amusement) that one of the English papers has gotten hold of the story about the St. Patrick's Day dinner, and solemnly takes his speech as being meant seriously, stating that Choate is a "Jingo" who has publicly advised the Irish to leave the United States and return to Ireland, for the purpose of conquering it and freeing it from English rule.

Tell Nannie that I am enjoying the "American Revolution" as much as Edith. Corinne gave *me* a copy; which has been returned! I think it even better in book form than when it came out in the magazine.

Always yours,
THEODORE ROOSEVELT.

UNITED STATES SENATE
WASHINGTON, D. C.

Personal.

My dear Theodore :—   Dec. 31, 1898.

I have your letter of Dec. 27th. I share your feelings entirely, but I am not going into detail about the matter. I
only want to say that I have the medal at heart almost as much
as you, and without bothering you as to what I am doing I
propose to get it for you if I can. I have accomplished more
difficult things than this, which is the merest act of justice.
You ought also to have your promotion, and that is why I
wanted the brevet given to you. I know that you care nothing
about it, but it is only decent that you should have that recognition. Do not worry about it, but rest assured that however
slow I may be I have got this constantly in mind and am at
work on it in my own deliberate fashion. I had a little talk
with the Vice President about it this morning. He sympathizes entirely and says the medal ought to have been given
to you long ago, and is going to speak to the President. He
thinks the delay is merely stupidity on the part of the War
Department. I hope he is right, but I am not quite so charitable. He was all that is friendly and right-minded in regard
to it, and will give the thing a push. I am going to speak to
one or two other judicious persons and keep it going until
they tire of me. I do not want, if I can avoid it, to make a
public fight, but if they push me I will.

I am very much interested in what you say about New York
appointments. You seem to get on capitally. I cannot see
how you can do better. Do not get worried over the Superintendent of Public Works, and do not be hurried. Reports
say that the second man there is a competent man, and if he
is you can let the thing run along until you are able to secure
a Superintendent who is exactly to your mind.

What you say about Choate's speech on St. Patrick's Day
and the European view of it is perfectly delicious.

Let me disabuse your mind about the copy of the "American
Revolution," which I sent to Edith. You and she naturally
inferred that you owed it to Nannie. In this case you were

at fault. It was wholly my own idea and thought, and Nannie had nothing to do with it. I want to get all the credit I can. If you find a moment to look at it I wish you would read the last chapter, of which I am rather proud, not only for what is said but for the way I have said it. I hope also, in some spare moment, you may get a chance to look at Bay's poems. I think there is a note of decided promise in some of them which indicates a prospect of good work in his maturity. I wish particularly you would read a poem entitled "They." He is working very hard just now on a story, and seems to have gotten thoroughly into the harness, so far as laboring diligently is concerned. I hope that he will stick to literature, for it is a fine career, and it is also a great pleasure to me to think— although it cost me some very anxious hours last summer —that when war came he entered the Navy, was under fire several times, and showed himself an active, efficient and creditable officer, coming out with a promotion and the praise of his superiors. I find his name is in the official reports of what was done at Ponce. It is a small niche, but it will be a fine memory to him, and he has taken part in great events and lived the life of his time.

My best wishes go with you and Edith at the opening of this new year, which is so important to you both.

Always sincerely,   H. C. Lodge.

1899

STATE OF NEW YORK
EXECUTIVE CHAMBER
ALBANY
Jany. 9th, 1899.

Hon. H. C. Lodge, Senate Chamber, Washington, D. C.

Dear Cabot: I think that on the whole your last chapter* is the best thing you have done. Edith thinks as highly of it as I do. I am especially delighted with the way in which you show that so far from our reversing our attitude towards England, we have kept the same attitude and England herself

* My "Story of the Revolution" is the book referred to.

has accepted it, so that we can appear as in hearty friendship to her instead of in opposition to her.

Let me again repeat how greatly I appreciate, not merely the matter, but the manner of your book. As I re-read it, I am more and more struck by the style. It seems to me to be higher, purer, more vivid and stronger English than we have yet had from any American historian, and the thought matches the diction.

As for Bay's poems, as you know, I think he has the "touch of the purple" in him. My favorites in his book are: "The Song of the Wave," "The Song of the Sword," "The Mothers of Men," "The Norsemen," and the First and Fifth Sonnets— especially the Fifth, although I am not absolutely clear what it is about!

I enclose you four letters which I do not want you to do anything about, but I simply want you to know of their existence. One of them is Alger's letter to me apologizing for publishing my private letter. You may notice its opening sentence. The other three make, with Captain Howze's, the four certificates from eye-witnesses, which I submitted as soon as I was informed (five months after the event) by the War Department, that these certificates were needed. The rules call for only two. These certificates include one from the Major General who was at the time the Acting Division Commander; one from a Captain on his staff, a regular officer and himself a medal of honor man; one from a Captain of the 9th Cavalry through whose regiment I moved my men to the charge; and one from the Major of my own regiment, the senior officer next to myself. With General Sumner's letter, I now have recommendations for the medal from both Brigade Commanders and the Division Commander of the Cavalry: that is, from every officer of superior rank to mine in the field, who could speak or had a right to speak of the matter.

Will you send me back the letter of Captain Howze? I find I have not got a copy of it. If the President has lost it, a copy can be obtained from the War Department. Will you also hand the enclosed letter to Bay? It is nothing that he need bother about, but I am utterly unable to get anything from the War Department myself. They have even refused me the detail of a young officer who was down at Santiago with us, whom I wanted to have look after the militia here, although this is something that is always granted and there is one here now about to be relieved, and though I had seen the young officer's immediate chief at West Point who said he could be spared.

I have your telegram but not your letter about Webber. I do not intend to appoint him. I shall probably appoint Partridge, upon whom the machine and anti-machine people of Brooklyn have agreed, and who seems to be a very good man. So far I have gotten along beautifully. You may possibly have noticed that in the matter of the Naval Militia I took exactly the ground you indicated. I hope Allen was pleased. I continue to be on excellent terms with the Senator * so far as I can find out. He is treating me perfectly squarely and I think he is satisfied that I am treating him the same way; at the same time, I think every one realizes that the Governorship is not in commission.

Give my love to Nannie. I must soon get down to spend a couple of days with you.

Always yours,
THEODORE ROOSEVELT.

UNITED STATES SENATE
WASHINGTON, D. C.

Personal.

My dear Theodore :—   Jan. 9, 1899.

I saw General Wheeler Saturday morning, and asked him if he had recommended you for a medal. He said he had most strongly, and that his letter was in the War Department. I asked him to look the matter up and see if his letter had been sent before the Board, and he promised he would do all he could to assure your having it. He assured me very cordially that he would go to the Department at once in regard to the matter. I had a long talk with Chandler yesterday. He has been away but is going to take the matter up now. This morn-

* Senator Platt.

ing I went to the Department and saw Meiklejohn. He said that the letters recommending you for the medal were all in the Department, and that he had sent you copies. I asked him if those letters were before the Board. He said they were. I asked him if he was perfectly sure. He said he had himself handed them to the Adjutant General to go before the Board, and that if they were not there now they would be as soon as the Board took up the question of medals, which it has not yet done. I told him with considerable frankness that they must go before the Board, to which he entirely agreed. I then went to see Colonel Carter, who is on the Board, and missed him, but as luck would have it I found Frank Greene there, who had come to talk to Carter about the medal. I told him what I wanted first to make sure of was that the letters were before the Board, and he said he would find that out also and let me know this afternoon. I do not want to give way to suspicion but I do strongly suspect that there has been an effort somewhere to withhold those papers from the Board. I think my inquiries and the people I have set going have forced the sending of those letters to the Board, if it had not been done before, but at any rate I am on the right track at last, and before the Board those papers shall go or I will know the reason why by a Senate inquiry. They will hardly let it come to that in my judgment, and if the letters of Wheeler and the rest go before the Board the medal will be awarded to you I feel sure without the slightest difficulty and in the pleasantest way. You know how difficult it is to get at things in the Departments, and how skillful they are in putting one off and covering up tracks, but I have finally proved the existence of the papers in the Department, and now there is nothing to do but to follow up their transmission to the Board. I am looking after the matter every day and will keep you informed in regard to it.

I telegraphed you about Webber on Saturday, because Chandler and Schulteis had some very serious information in regard to him which I knew you ought to see, although I had no reason to suppose you were going to appoint him. I suppose you received their letters today.

My mind has been so occupied with this question of the medal that I have not said anything to you in my letters about your message, which seemed to me most admirable, and I like all you said about national affairs, and thought it entirely appropriate and just right. From this commendation I exclude your declaration in favor of woman suffrage, a sad weakness you have always had.

Always yours, H. C. LODGE.

WESTERN UNION TELEGRAPH COMPANY

ALBANY, N. Y., Jan. 10, 1899.

To Hon. H. C. Lodge, 1765 Mass. Ave., Washn., D. C.

It was a matter of course but still I am delighted.*

THEODORE ROOSEVELT.

UNITED STATES SENATE
WASHINGTON, D. C.

Private.

Jan. 11, 1899.

Dear Theodore : —

I have received your letter of the 9th, and am extremely glad you sent me the copies of your letters. I will try to get the Howze letter again. I did not realize it was your only copy when the President took it. These copies are just what I want in the way of ammunition, so that 'I may be prepared at all points. I heard yesterday through my second line of communication with the Board, that your papers were before them, so we have passed that point all right. I learned quite by accident that the President did not know that any recommendations for a medal had been made in your behalf, and that he had understood there were no such letters. You can see that he could not take in what I meant when I talked with him, barring of course the letter from Howze which I gave him. He shall now see the copies of the others.

Many thinks for your telegram, which came last night. It was pleasant to get a word from you, and to know that you

* About my renomination as Senator by the Party Caucus of the Legislature.

were thinking about me. There was of course no doubt as to the outcome, but it is good to have it settled. I confess I am greatly touched and pleased by the unanimity of action.

Bay will write you about the matter of getting reports. I have been unable to get Puerto Rican reports for my article, although I have been up to the Department every two or three days, the simple reason being that the War Department is behind hand and the reports are not in print.

It was a great pleasure to me to know that you liked my last chapter, and thanks also for what you say about Bay's poems.

Always sincerely, H. C. Lodge.

STATE OF NEW YORK
EXECUTIVE CHAMBER
ALBANY

Jany. 12th, 1899.

Hon. H. C. Lodge, Senate Chamber, Washington, D. C.

Dear Cabot:— Thank Bay for his efforts on my behalf. If I do not get the reports in time I will send in the article anyway.

I heard through a friend that the War Department is indignant at what it is pleased to call my "efforts to coerce the Board into giving me the medal," saying that I had gotten you to bring pressure to bear upon them through the President; at which they express much indignation. I told my friend that when the head of a department repeatedly states in public that I am not to have the medal, it certainly looks to me like coercion of the Board of subordinates who are supposed to decide whether I ought or ought not to have the medal. I am recovering my equanimity in the matter. After all, whatever the Board does, the fact remains that both Brigade Commanders, the Division Commander and the Corps Commander recommended me, and the letters of Howze, Stevens and Jenkins, besides the letter of Sumner, give the testimony of eye-witnesses. There is a subsequent letter of Wood as to what I actually accomplished; so that as far as my friends are concerned, my record in the matter is entirely clear. Indeed the offer of the brevet would stop the Department from saying that I had not acted well. All I am concerned in is to know whether these four letters have gotten before the Board. Do you think you could possibly find out? If they only have the bare recommendations of Wood, Wheeler and Shafter, they very possibly would not act.

Now, old man, after finding this out, if you can do so without any trouble, do not do anything further in the matter. You have great and serious interests to deal with and you ought not to worry over small matters.

My chief difficulties at present arise ·from the fact that really first class men will not accept small State positions where there is neither enough salary nor enough glory to tempt them. I have secured a good and upright Superintendent of Public Works who is acceptable to all Republicans, but I do not think he is a very strong man.

I send you an advance copy of a poem of Kipling which is rather poor poetry, but good sense from the expansion standpoint.

Last night, by the way, I met Whitelaw Reid at dinner. He was, as always, delightful. He was excellent about the Philippines. However, I am glad we have Choate as Ambassador. Think of the odd partnership between Bryan and Hoar!* Well, it is a great comfort to feel that you have six more years of good work in the Senate, come what may thereafter. It almost seemed nonsensical to telegraph you, but Edith and I were so pleased when Mr. Young, my Private Secretary, telephoned us the news, that I could not resist sending a line.

With best love to Nannie, believe me,

Always yours,
THEODORE ROOSEVELT.

Wood has sent me a captured Spanish Mauser rifle and machete for you. I'll send them on at once.

---

* In opposition to approval of the Treaty of Peace with Spain on account of the Philippines.

UNITED STATES SENATE
WASHINGTON, D. C.

Personal.

Dear Theodore :—

Jan. 14, 1899.

I have your note of the 12th. I have sent you today the reports.

I think the medal matter is all right. I took to the President yesterday copies of those letters you sent me. He was evidently greatly surprised to see them, and read them all with attention and kept them. Wood saw him later, and he told Wood that you should have the medal, and said a great many other pleasant things about you, all of which Wood will tell you when you see him. By the way, I always knew that Wood was a fine fellow, but he came home after all his experiences down there a great man. He has impressed me immensely, and every one here, and his work in Cuba is certainly most splendid. He has the entire confidence of the President, which is of vast importance, and I want him to keep it.

I saw you had finally decided on your Superintendent of Public Works, and it seems to me all right.

Thanks for the advance copy of Kipling's poem. I like it. I think it is better poetry than you say, apart from the sense of the verses.

They are trying to make trouble in Massachusetts by resolutions, etc., but we are masters of the situation, and they tell me that I shall have every Republican vote on Tuesday.*

The fight that is being made on the Treaty is disheartening, and every day that it is delayed increases our difficulties in the Philippines and the danger of bloodshed. The Spaniards are filling the papers with false reports in the hope that the rejection of the Treaty will throw back the Islands to Spain, and the attitude of American Senators is helping them. It is not very easy to bear.

Always sincerely yours,

H. C. LODGE.

* When the Legislature voted on the nominee of the Caucus.

STATE OF NEW YORK
EXECUTIVE CHAMBER
ALBANY

Jany. 19th, 1899.

Hon. H. C. Lodge, Senate Chamber, Washington, D. C.

Dear Cabot:—I trust that when the occasion comes, the Republicans of Massachusetts will see that the Republican representative who is alleged to have voted against you, is made to understand that the weak and silly variety of traitor is not particularly encouraged in the Bay State.

As for that infernal medal of honor, I really wish and ask that you do nothing more about it at all. Alger has succeeded in putting the matter in such a position that now if it is granted it will look as though I had to get political influence to have it granted. Of course, as a matter of fact I have done nothing at all except through your kindness in finding out what the Department refused to inform me personally, viz.: That there was not sufficient evidence; and then to furnish the evidence required. But the War Department, including the members of the Board who were to award the medal, have been stating that I have sought to bring pressure to bear through politicians to force the giving of the medal, the same members of the Board being particularly careful not to mention Alger's outrageous conduct in publicly stating again and again that I should not receive the medal, which was in itself the strongest kind of pressure upon the Board to refuse it, these statements being made when he knew absolutely not one thing about the matter. I felt very angry about it at first, but I do not feel angry now, in view of all that is going on. I mean quite seriously what I say when I tell you that I think myself fortunate in having escaped some reflection by the War Department upon my conduct. This they are stopped from making by their published reports; especially as it is rumored they recommend me for a similar brevet to that recommended for Jack Astor!

Is there any way at all I can help you about the treaty? I suppose there is not the slightest. It is very hard to have patience in this matter.

Here in my own parochial affairs I am so far getting along very well and am developing considerable tact in a way. But

I must see you sometime in the not far distant future to tell you all about it in person. When I see a chance for a day or two off I am going to run on to Washington and get Edith to accompany me if she can. We will give you fair warning so as to be sure that you have not too many other boarders.

Ever yours,
THEODORE ROOSEVELT.

Have you seen Trevelyan's book on the American Revolution? It is good. He sent me a copy.

UNITED STATES SENATE
WASHINGTON, D. C.

Personal.

My dear Theodore :—   Jan. 21, 1899.

One alleged Republican Representative, but a disciple of the *Springfield Republican,* voted against me, but as I received the votes of two gold Democrats in the Legislature the defection was not material. One Senator from the same town as the Representative refused to vote, his ground being that I was the author of the Immigration Bill and was now standing by the President, propositions which seem to me to receive but trifling acceptance from the Republican Legislature. I have been extremely careful in all I have done about the medal, in fact I have spoken to no one except the President, Frank Greene and Wood in regard to it. I think you are entirely mistaken about the Board, although I think you are right about the Secretary. The Board from the beginning has, I know, been anxious to give you the medal. I also know they have been extremely sensitive and resented any attempts on the part of the Secretary to guide their decision. The reports in the newspapers to the contrary are unfounded I am certain; but the thing is all right now and there is no use in giving it any further thought.

I think we shall come out all right on the treaty by the sheer force of events, but they have enough men, all Democrats but two, who say they are against the treaty, to defeat it if they could make them vote as they talk, which they cannot.

I wish you would come on to Washington for Sunday and

bring Edith if you possibly can. Let us know in time so that I can get some of the Senators you like to meet you at dinner.

Trevelyan sent me a copy of his book, and I have just read it. He has a great charm of style and of narration, and it is curious to see how completely he justifies our position.

Always sincerely yours,
H. C. LODGE.

STATE OF NEW YORK
EXECUTIVE CHAMBER
ALBANY

Jany. 23rd, 1899.

Hon. H. C. Lodge, Senate Chamber, Washington, D. C.

Dear Cabot:—I have just read the first chapter of "The War with Spain."* I think it admirable. You have the same style as in your History of the Revolution, and so far as a man who himself is still in the heat of the matter can judge, you are singularly impartial. I wonder if Reed will see the sentence in which you allude to the Speaker's position as to there not being any trouble in Cuba?

On thinking matters over, it seemed to me it might help if the New York legislature passed a resolution in favor of the treaty. I consulted with Paul Dana about it and then spoke to Senator Platt. The Senator really is against the Philippines, but he stands by the President and was exceedingly nice, saying that he would do what he could to have the legislature pass the resolution. I believe it will be arranged.

Always yours,
THEODORE ROOSEVELT.

UNITED STATES SENATE
WASHINGTON, D. C.

Personal.

Dear Theodore:—   Jan. 25, 1899.

Thanks for your letter of the 23rd. I am glad that you like my first number. There are one or two numbers that I shall not be able to do much with, notably that on the Puerto Rican campaign, but the main number which describes the land and

---

* Then appearing in *Harper's Magazine.*

sea fights at Santiago is, I believe, at the end the best thing I have ever written. I am afraid that you will feel that I have not done sufficient justice to the Rough Riders, but you must remember when you read it that I had to tell the whole story of the war in six papers and the consequent necessity of space and proportion cut down a great many things on which I should like to say more.

It will help very much to have a resolution from the New York Legislature demanding the ratification of the treaty. We have just agreed to vote on February 8th. The result is doubtful. On the surface they have more than a third, but they have some very weak supporters, and it is quite on the cards that we shall ratify all right. We need all the support from outside that we can get, and we have ten days to do it in.

I am thinking of coming on on Saturday to pass Sunday in New York.

Always sincerely yours,

H. C. LODGE.

STATE OF NEW YORK
EXECUTIVE CHAMBER
ALBANY

Dear Cabot :—   Jany. 26th, 1899.

Your speech was splendid. I confess I am utterly disheartened and cast down at the thought that the treaty is in such serious danger. It is difficult for me to speak with moderation of such men as Hoar. That our barbarian friends on the other side of the political fence should be against us is not to be wondered at or wholly to be regretted; although of course it must be *really* a matter of regret that any American should go wrong at a time like this. I would give anything if I could be of any help to you. Thank the Lord I have at least done what little I could to keep things right! This huge materialistic community is at bottom, either wrong or half-hearted on the Philippine question, and I can say that my influence has been one among the causes that have kept the Republican Party straight here.

I fear I shall have to wait until a little later, probably until the Spring, before getting on to Washington. Edith cannot come now and my own work is exhausting beyond anything I have had since the first months in the Police Department. Let me know as well in advance as you can when you will leave Washington.

As for my own small business here, it seems to be getting along well. Of course, I have any amount of trouble ahead of me, and serious trouble at that; but the first month (which is perhaps the most important), is over and in almost every big question I have taken the first and decided steps. I shall have great trouble and shall receive much criticism, and at times my relations with my own party leaders will be strained, but I think I have got things moving in the right direction and that there is a growing body of public opinion which is behind me, because it is convinced I am honestly striving to do well by the commonwealth, while Senator Platt and the organization people are, on the whole, satisfied, because they know I am a good Republican; that I am not trying to build up a machine for myself; and that I am sincerely desirous of doing what they wish, whenever I conscientiously can.

With best love to Nannie.

Always yours,

THEODORE ROOSEVELT.

STATE OF NEW YORK
EXECUTIVE CHAMBER
ALBANY

Feby. 7th, 1899.

Hon. H. C. Lodge, Senate Chamber, Washington, D. C.

Dear Cabot:—I am more grateful than I can say, partly to the Senate, partly to Providence and partly to the Philippinos. They just pulled the treaty through for us. This of course means that you will leave Washington sometime in March. Could you have me and if possible Edith on for Saturday and Sunday the 25th and 26th? I have written to Mrs. Senator Davis. Can you suggest my writing to anyone else.

The affairs of this parish continue to flourish fairly well;

but what do I care for the parish when such things are going on in the nation? However, I am having a very good time.

As always,

Yours,   THEODORE ROOSEVELT.

UNITED STATES SENATE
WASHINGTON, D. C.

Personal.

My dear Theodore :—   Feb. 9, 1899.

Many thanks for your letter of the 7th. Strange as it may appear we did not save the treaty by the fight at Manila. On Saturday we had 58 votes, four doubtful men to work upon. One of them, Heitfeld, went squarely over to the opposition on Sunday and was lost to us. The other three remained doubtful. We went into executive session on Monday at 2 o'clock with only 58 sure votes. At half past two McLaurin came over to us making 59. At five minutes before three McEnery agreed to vote with us and then Jones of Nevada dropped in giving us an extra vote after the first roll call had been completed, and we knew that we had the treaty ratified. In other words of the four doubtful men of Saturday we got three. The line of opposition stood absolutely firm, to my great astonishment. I thought the news from Manila would have shattered it, but it did not, marvelous as it may seem. It was the closest, hardest fight I have ever known, and probably we shall not see another in our time where there was so much at stake. Davis,* who is the best fellow in the world, cannot make a canvass and is no manager. He would ask me every morning how the vote stood, and I think that is about all he knew about it. Aldrich and I, but particularly Aldrich, made the hard fighting, which does not appear on the surface. Aldrich is a man of most astonishing vigor, courage and resource, and I cannot sufficiently describe the way in which he fought for this victory day and night. With him I worked, and also Chandler, Hanna, and the genial Elkins, and Hansbrough

* Cushman K. Davis of Minnesota, chairman of Foreign Relations.

and Carter. We were down in the engine room and do not get flowers, but we did make the ship move. George Gray came out in a splendid way on the floor and in every other direction, and of course Frye and Foraker, and all the men whom you would expect; but it was a desperate fight and there ought not to have been any fight at all. I saw the President nearly every day while it was going on. He was extremely anxious, but showed the greatest firmness and strength, and did everything he could do. If they had rejected the treaty he would have called an extra session in the next twenty-four hours. Until the fight was over I did not realize what a strain it had been, but for half an hour after the vote was announced I felt exactly as if I had been struggling up the side of a mountain and as if there was not an ounce more of exertion left in any muscle of my body. You feel such a deep interest in it that I know you do not mind these details. I think everything will now run pretty smoothly. There will be hitches and obstructions of course, but we have broken the jam and the whole drive is coming through.

We shall be perfectly delighted to see you and Edith here on the 25th and 26th. Let me know when to expect you as soon as you can, as I want to arrange to have some men to meet you at dinner whom you will be glad to see.

Always sincerely yours,
H. C. LODGE.

STATE OF NEW YORK
EXECUTIVE CHAMBER
ALBANY

Dear Cabot,   February 28th, 1899.

Need I say that the two days with you were the most delightful I have passed since returning from Santiago? Give my warm love to Nannie.

The enclosed explains itself. I do not know whether Dr. Doty can do anything for you or not.

Lieut. Col. Brodie has written me that he never can sufficiently express his appreciation of the way you behaved to him.

The idiots of the War Department Board of Inquiry, while I was literally with them on Saturday, solemnly wrote me to Albany asking when I could appear before them!

Yours, T. R.

STATE OF NEW YORK
EXECUTIVE CHAMBER
ALBANY

March 2nd, 1899.

Hon. H. C. Lodge, Senate Chamber, Washington, D. C.

Dear Cabot:—I am greatly concerned to see by the papers that the ridiculous price of $300 for armor* has been put on by the Senate. How can our dear friend Chandler take such an action? I love him; I respect his patriotism; but I mourn to see him take a position which may at some future time cause grave disaster to this country. When Hoar or Hale, Allen or Pettigrew, Butler or Jones† act on the army bill, on the treaty of peace, or on the declaration of war, as I think no patriotic American should act, I do not very much care; but it is a real grief to have Chandler on any account act in a way that may hinder very seriously the upbuilding of the navy with which he has been so prominently identified.

Always yours,
THEODORE ROOSEVELT.

STATE OF NEW YORK
EXECUTIVE CHAMBER
ALBANY

March 9th, 1899.

Hon. H. C. Lodge, Senate Chamber, Washington, D. C.

Dear Cabot:—I was very much disappointed with the outcome of the work in the Senate. It seems too bad that we should find such difficulty in learning our lessons. It was bad enough to have the session pass by without any effort to re-

* Armor for the ships.   † Senator Jones of Arkansas.

organize the Army on a proper basis and with only a miserable make-shift to enable the army to go on as it is, but I did not expect to see the Navy gone back on, and especially not by the Senate. Chandler and the others who voted for the absurd $300 price for armor will have a heavy load on their souls if in the course of the next four or five years we are forced into a war with a foreign power. To vote against war, to vote against peace, to vote against increasing the Army, or to vote to cripple the Navy—upon my word, it is hard to have patience with the man who is guilty of any of them! We may have serious work in Cuba and the Philippines, and I only hope that in doing it we shall not display the qualities displayed by the democratic opposition; by Hoar, Hale and the peace-at-any-price men; by the anti-armor plate men; and by Alger and the others who declined to break up the staff departments.

Lee, the British Military Attaché, told me a lovely story the other day. He met the Russian Military Attaché in London and gave him a dinner, at which the Russian waxed eloquent over his sufferings at Santiago, and as capping the climax described how when he went to present his respects and say good bye to General Shafter, the latter looked at him with his usual easy polish and grace, and remarked: "Well, good bye. Who are you, anyway, the Russian or the German?" I shouted. Think of the feelings of Yemiloff, the nice little military and diplomatic pedant, on the one hand, and on the other, of good, vulgar Shafter's magnificent indifference to ethnic and diplomatic niceties!

I am getting on here perfectly well, though the legislature is having rather a Kilkenny cat time.

When do you sail from New York?

Give my best love to Nannie.

Always yours,

THEODORE ROOSEVELT.

UNITED STATES SENATE
WASHINGTON, D. C.

Personal.

Dear Theodore :—   March 15, 1899.

Thanks for your note of the 9th. I do not think things are quite as bad as you regard them. The Army bill is, of course, a makeshift, but we get the main thing, which is the troops. The reorganization will take place next winter, and I think will then be well done—much better than we could have done now. The provisions of the present bill will of course bind the next Congress to nothing. The Democrats would not allow us to pass a proper bill, and with their votes in the Senate and the short time remaining of the session they were able to prevent action. If we had thrown the whole thing over and called an extra session we should not have gotten an Army bill through before May, even if we had done so then. Meantime the ratification of the peace would probably have been exchanged and all the Volunteers and all the Regulars—over twenty-seven thousand—would have had to be mustered out at once, with the result that we should have been left for two or three months with practically no troops. This seemed to me much the worse of the two evils, and I think we got out of it in the best way, for we have got men for the time being, we prevent a break in the Army, and we can reorganize next winter and do it much better than would have been possible now.

As to the Navy, we passed the Navy Personnel bill, which you regarded, as I do, as one of the greatest and most useful measures which could possibly have been passed. By it we have reorganized the Navy and put it on a permanent footing. At the same time we increased the Marine Corps to five thousand men. This was a very important piece of legislation.

In the appropriation bill we saved the authorization in full, but the armor fight will prevent our beginning work on any new armored ships, and is therefore deplorable. The House would not establish an armor plant, and the Senate would not agree to a proper price for armor plates. Between the two we have tied ourselves up until the next session of Congress, and all we can do under the new authorization is to build the cruisers.

It is disheartening and makes delays. You saw what I thought of it in the speech I made, but we shall come out of it all right.

The story of the Russian attaché is beyond words delightful.

We are just breaking up here, and intend to go to New York Monday, pass Tuesday there, and sail on Wednesday. I suppose we can hardly hope to see you on Tuesday, for I know how busy you are.

Everything seems to be going well with you, and I do not see that the fights in the legislature touch you at all.

Always sincerely yours,

H. C. LODGE.

STATE OF NEW YORK
EXECUTIVE CHAMBER
ALBANY

March 18, 1899.

Hon. H. C. Lodge, Holland House, New York. N. Y.

Dear Cabot:—I fear there isn't a chance of my getting down to say good bye to you and yours. These are the closing weeks of the legislature and the drive and push are tremendous. I am having my usual number of unpleasant experiences. At present my chief difficulty seems to come from some corporations engineered by our political friends, which have an entirely correct main purpose and which want to do something which will benefit the city, while at the same time escaping any taxation for what they get. This is all wrong. In one shape or another they should pay for the privileges they are to receive.

I agree absolutely with what you say in your letter as to what was done by Congress and the necessity of doing it. Your own position was exactly proper but the Democrats headed by Gorman and Company, and Hoar and Hale, (and on one point, Chandler) did show a lamentable indifference to the true interests of the nation. An indifference which it is difficult to understand in view of the war we have just passed through.

On the whole I am thoroughly enjoying this work, but I do get disheartened now and then. Of course it is only a temporary and slight discouragement, but it seems so difficult to accomplish even a very little and I have encountered so much unreasoning stupidity and sinister opposition from men on whose support I should be able to count. Well, my worse trials will be over in a month so far as this year is concerned and then the next year can take care of itself. Meanwhile, you will be having as righteously earned a holiday as any man in the United States could have. On the whole, there is no man of your age, or younger, in the United States who has quite as much right to be proud of what he has accomplished, quite as much right to feel that in his span of years he has done work which so redounds to the honor and advantage of his country. Now I do hope all of you will have a thoroughly happy six months. If you see Bryce, Trevelyan, Lord Spencer or Buxton, give each and all my regards. I know Nannie will enjoy herself thoroughly. Give my love to her and remembrances to the boys.

Faithfully yours,
THEODORE ROOSEVELT.

STATE OF NEW YORK
EXECUTIVE CHAMBER
ALBANY

4/27/99.

Hon. H. C. Lodge, c/o J. S. Morgan & Co., Bankers, London, England.

Dear *Cabot:*—I enclose you a Chicago speech of mine. It seems to have attracted attention of an adverse sort in Massachusetts as I have been continually receiving marked copies of the *Transcript, Herald* and *Springfield Republican* containing editorials and letters by thoughtful publicists which take a very black view of my character, antecedents and prospects. I made another speech in which I said that we had equally to dread the corrupt machine politician and the fool reformer. A large number of gentlemen, seemingly recognizing the fact that they came under the latter head, have written me in indignant denunciation, and the *Evening Post* is especially bitter about it.

I have just finished your chapter in the May *Harper's*, and I think it altogether admirable. The end really stirred my blood! You seem to have struck your "note" in style once for all. You did more than justice to the Rough Riders. Before publishing in book form I should like to submit one or two minor corrections to you, but nothing of the least importance.

Well, the legislature has just ended, and the heavy work, so far as I am concerned, is over for the year 1899. I think I may say that I have come out of it all right. I am on excellent terms with Senator Platt. He has treated me admirably in every way and is I believe equally satisfied with the way I have treated him, except that I have not been able to back up some of his views about corporations. Frank Platt* like Elihu Root has occasionally appeared before me on behalf of corporation measures. It has happened that I have decided against both of them in every case. I mentioned this to the Senator, saying that I was really sorry for it, but of course, I felt that they should appear before me exactly as they would appear before the Supreme Court, when any corporation measure for which they had a retainer was concerned. He told me he absolutely agreed with me.

I have had great success with my appointments. I do not believe there is a single one that I have made that was open to any serious criticism, and on the whole I believe they average better than those made by any Governor during as long a time as I can remember. I got an excellent Civil Service Law passed, a first class rapid transit bill, a first class measure for taxing franchises—or rather for laying the foundation in the matter of taxing franchises; together with a sweat-shop bill, the factory inspector's bills, a good banking law, etc., etc.

All together I am pretty well satisfied with what I have accomplished. I do not misunderstand in the least what it means—or rather, how little it may mean. New York politics are kaleidoscopic and 18 months hence I may be so much out of kilter with the machine that there will be no possibility of my renomination, and if renominated, my own conduct, or merely the general drift of events, may make it impossible to re-elect me; but at least I have a substantial sum of achieve-

* Senator Platt's son.

ment to my credit in the Governorship already, and I have kept every pledge, expressed or implied, that I made on the stump or anywhere else.

So much for my own parochial politics. As regards the nation at large, I do wish that President McKinley would get rid of Alger! Bryan is I believe a good deal stronger than he was three years ago, and it looks now as though it was going to be a serious struggle in 1900. Of course, McKinley must be renominated; so the success of the Republican party depends upon him. I believe that we shall carry him through, even with Alger, but when one has to make a hard fight there is no use of handicapping one's self. I told all this to Postmaster General Smith and to Judge Kohlsaat while in Chicago.

We have had a rather disagreeable experience with Captain Coghlan. He talked too much, but I confess that if I had been the President I should have told Germany that until they apologized for what Admiral von Diederich* *did,* they need not worry themselves about what Captain Coghlan *said.* The attitude of the *Staats-Zeitung* has been infamous; also that of some of the professional Irish leaders.

While Alger is in the Cabinet I always have a feeling of uneasiness about Cuba and the Philippines. We need to exercise much care in the former and to show unyielding resolution in the latter. There are symptoms apparently of a breakup among the Philippine insurgents, but if it does not come soon, I wish that McKinley would mobilize the 35,000 volunteers, and send a large force to the Islands.

Brooks and Mrs. Adams are passing a couple of days with us. Brooks is fairly revelling in his belief of our utter and absolute administrative breakdown and is firm in his conviction that the government is corrupt from top to bottom.

If you see Sir George Trevelyan give him my warm regards, and with best love to Nannie and the boys from both myself and Edith, I am,

Ever yours,

THEODORE ROOSEVELT.

* He commanded the German squadron at Manila during Dewey's capture and blockade of the harbor.

Private.   ROME,
Dear Theodore: May 11th, 1899.

It was a great delight to receive today your letter of April
27th—also your speech. Need I say how much I liked it and
how I agreed with every word. It is all the doctrine in which
I believe and I love to see it put with such splendid clearness
and force. It is pleasant to know that the "fool reformer"
recognizes himself when he is mentioned. I am so glad that
you liked the May number and thought what I said about the
Rough Riders adequate. Alas, I have corrected the proofs
for the book and so cannot avail myself of the corrections you
mention, of which I have made many and have a dreary consciousness that there are many more to be made. I like as much
as ever your *Scribner* articles and am looking forward to the
book. I cannot see how you could have done better in your
administration. The franchise bill seems to me an especially
sound measure. I know all the uncertainties of politics but
your success seems to me brilliant and I descry no cloud on
the horizon. When McKinley's foreign policy is so good it is
misery to see him keep Alger. It seems sheer madness for I
can see no reason whatever for retention. The general prosperity will pull him through if it holds but why load himself
and the party. And then the decision of the beef court! Alas!
Alas!—In the Philippines I think we shall have them under
before election and the army has done well. Funston seems a
very striking figure. Here it is curious to see everywhere the
fear and intent with which they regard us. We are shaking
them economically, they dread us politically and the Roman
Church is deeply disturbed by "Americanism" and by our
arresting Spain, and then with our great country striding forward, recognized as one of the great powers of the world one
reads the utterance of certain men and certain newspapers and
turns sick to think that there are such creatures crawling between Heaven and Earth in America.

We have made a most interesting trip through Sicily and
are now going, after two delightful weeks here with the
Chanlers, who are full of you and your doings, slowly through
northern Italy to London to see Constance and Gus off on

June 24. I am picking up a good deal of use in our foreign affairs, things well to know and to talk over when we meet. Barrett seems to have started a fight on my loyal and devoted friend Crane for governor which worries me, but I think Crane is all right. I hate to be away but I am realizing now how much I need the rest and shall stay out my six months, for there is much work ahead and I must husband my strength. Nannie was most glad to get Edith's letter and will write. Best love to Edith and the children. I hope the boys got the flag books.

Ever yours, H. C. L.

STATE OF NEW YORK
EXECUTIVE CHAMBER
ALBANY

May 27th, 1899.

Dear Cabot :—

I was delighted to get your letter, as was Edith. I greatly envy you your trip to Sicily. For some reason Sicily (which I have never seen) has always peculiarly attracted me. I suppose it is because the history of the Island gratifies to the full my taste for ethnic contests and the struggle of wholly alien civilizations.

You will be pleased to know that the Regular Army men seem to take to your history; I was with a group of them the other day and was interested to hear them mentioning that yours was the best account that had appeared of the general military operations of the war.

By the way, a perfectly preposterous incident of contemporary popular delusion is that Admiral Schley on his way through the West is being lionized with a mad enthusiasm.

Since I wrote you I called an extra session of the legislature, and after a very doubtful and anxious struggle, won a complete trumph. Platt, as was to be expected, bitterly and frantically opposed the Ford bill taxing franchises. As with every other political leader of his type where the boss system obtains, his power rests in great part upon the money contributed by the corporations. He was influenced to defend them partly by this consideration and partly by his honorable desire to acknowledge the benefits he had received from them; and partly because like most old men he is very conservative in such matters, and fails to see that to meet a just popular demand is often the best possible way of preventing a perfectly unjust popular demand, and that to do justice in the one case strengthens one in resisting injustice in the other. He and Depew and the rest were crazy to have me veto the bill. To this I would not consent. But the bill was crude in form and there were two or three extremely desirable amendments, notably one which would give the State the power of making the assessment, and I offered to call the legislature together for the purpose of making these amendments. At first they could not decide whether the corporations would be willing to have the amendments made; for not a few of them preferred to be black-mailed by Tammany rather than pay their just dues to an honest Board of State Assessors. Finally, however, the best made up their minds to try for honesty, and Platt then told me he wished the extra session called. Thereupon we began to prepare a new bill, and here the attorneys for the corporations. (including Frank Platt) tried to sell me a gold brick by putting in seemingly innocent provisos which would have made the taxation a nullity. I told them that unless they passed the bill exactly as I wished it, I should sign the Ford bill; for having the Ford bill in my hands gave me the complete mastery of the situation. They then all went in in good faith to pass my amendments. The demagogues and Tammany now became my opponents; but we held every Republican vote in the Senate, which was the close and doubtful body, and gained three democrats, and the net result is that we have on the statute books the most important law passed in recent times by any American State legislature; and we have to our credit a perfectly clean record in appointments and legislation for the session and a great deal of positive work of a good character accomplished. Moreover the break that was threatened between myself and the machine over the Ford bill has been healed by the passage of the amendments. I do not mean to say that they will entirely forgive me, or that they won't cut my throat when the time comes, but they will act with me, so far as I can now see, during my term, so that I shall have the chance of making a success rather than a failure.

I am very tired, for I have had four years of exceedingly hard work without a break, save for changing from one kind of work to another. This summer I shall hope to lie off as much as possible. Edith is very well and so are all the children. I hope Nannie received the copy of my book which I sent her.

Ever yours,
THEODORE ROOSEVELT.

OYSTER BAY, N. Y.,
July 1, 1899.

Hon. H. C. Lodge, c/o J. S. Morgan & Co., Bankers, London, Eng.

Dear Cabot:—On receiving your first letter about the Duffield incident, I looked up the official reports, and so was very glad to get your second. What you said was known by everybody to be the exact truth. I doubt if there was a man in the army who did not know that Duffield and his Michigan regiments let themselves be stopped by a resistance so trivial as to be contemptible. He had the greatest chance of the war, for if he had chosen to push home, I verily believe he could have taken the Morro, or at least could have put himself in shape to guarantee a detachment of the Army taking it. But he and Shafter arranged matters so that the official report holds Duffield blameless.

Incidentally, let me say that I think your last chapter on the war is almost the best. Every one has agreed that yours is the only good history of the war that has yet come out.

I have just come back from a week in the west where I went to attend my regimental reunion at Las Vegas. It would really be difficult to express my surprise at the way I was greeted. At every station at which the train stopped in Indiana, Illinois, Wisconsin, Iowa, Missouri, Kansas, Colorado and New Mexico, I was received by dense throngs exactly as if I had been a presidential candidate. My reception caused some talk, so I thought it better to come out in an interview stating, that of course I was for President McKinley's renomination, and that every one should be for it, and giving the reasons. Equally of course I am for Hobart's renomination, if he will take it.

Now as to what you say about the Vice Presidency. Curiously enough Edith is against your view and I am inclined to be for it. I am for it on the perfectly simple ground that I regard my position as utterly unstable and that I appreciate as well as anyone can how entirely ephemeral is the hold I have for a moment on the voters. I am not taken in by the crowds in the west or by anything else in the way of vociferous enthusiasm for the moment. It would be five years before it would materialize and I have never yet known a hurrah to endure five years; so I should be inclined to accept any honorable position; that the Vice Presidency is. As a matter of fact, I have not the slightest idea that I could get it, if I did decide to take it, and I should feel like taking any honorable position that offered itself. On the other hand, I confess I should like a position with more work in it. If I were a serious possibility for 1904, I should feel there was very much in what you say, but I do not think we need concern ourselves over the chances of the lightning striking me at that time rather than any other one of a thousand men. Meanwhile I could do more work in two years of the Governorship, although I might get myself in a tangle. What I should really most like would be to be re-elected Governor with a first class Lieutenant-Governor, and then be offered the Secretaryship of War for four years. Of course it would be even better if I could become United States Senator, but of that I do not see any chance. Of all the work that I would like to undertake, that of Secretary of War appeals to me most. There I think I really could do something, but of course I have no idea that McKinley will put me in the position.

Last night I dined with Wood and Greene and we went over at length the problems in Cuba and the Philippines. I have been growing seriously concerned about both, and this morning I deeided to send to John Hay a letter of which I enclose a copy. Having just come out in an interview for the President's renomination, I thought he might tolerate a little advice. I do not suppose it will do the least good, but I wrote on the off chance.

The President's civil service order was justifiable in part, and in part very unjustifiable. More than the matter, it was the manner of doing it that hurt, and especially the way in which it was trumpeted by Kerr, Grosvenor and similar cattle. By the way, I particularly liked what you said about the attitude of the Germans and French in the last war. It is just as well those gentry should have a reminder now and then as to the effect of their conduct. Did I tell you that Captain Coghlan came out and took lunch here the other day? He was most amusing. I told him that there were no reporters present and that like the old Chancellor with Mr. Pell, he might "damn himself in confidence."

My week's railroading in the west put the finishing touch and I am now feeling completely tired out. I hope to have six weeks of practically solid rest before me, for I have worked pretty hard during the last four years.

Give my best love to Nannie and the boys. Occasionally we see cables in the papers about you.

Ever yours,
THEODORE ROOSEVELT.

A Copy.   July 1, 1899.
Hon. John Hay, Secretary of State, Washington, D. C.

My dear Mr. Secretary:—Next to the man who is importuning for office ranks in the scale of nuisances and bores the man who gives advice. I am about to put myself in the latter category.

If you think it worth while after reading this letter, pray show it to the President. I have written on somewhat the same lines to Attorney General Griggs.

As a preliminary let me say, what I take for granted you know, viz.: that I am heartily in favor of President McKinley's renomination, as I have said publicly. Moreover, I am heartily in favor of Mr. Hobart's renomination for the Vice Presidency, and I have no earthly interest in what I am going to say except my interest as an American in the first place, and as a Republican in the second.

I am uneasy at the way things seem to be going both in the Philippines and in Cuba, and also at the mutterings of discontent with what we have done in those islands, which can be heard here and there throughout the country even now. A series of disasters at the very beginning of our colonial policy would shake this administration, and therefore our party, and might produce the most serious and far-reaching effects upon the nation as a whole, for if some political cataclysm was the result, it might mean the definite abandonment of the course upon which we have embarked—the only course I think fit for a really great nation. About Hawaii I know nothing. The men in whom I have the most confidence tell me that the condition of Porto Rico is very bad and that the people are really regretting the ending of Spanish rule. In Porto Rico there can be no revolt, but this does not render it less incumbent upon us to give it the best type of government. I earnestly wish that there should be no waiting for action by Congress. Let the Executive take the reins and establish any system of regulation about the tariff or anything else that is deemed wise, and Congress will simply have to stand by! A clear cut policy resolutely followed out is certain to be supported, if the Island does well under it, and this should be the prime purpose of any such policy.

In Cuba and the Philippines the conditions are different. In Cuba we may lay up for ourselves infinite trouble if we do not handle the people with a proper mixture of firmness, courtesy and tact. In the Philippines we are certain to invite disaster unless we send ample forces, and what is even more important, unless we put these forces under some first class man. Both in Cuba and in the Philippines what we obviously need, and need at once, is to have some man put in supreme command, in whom we can absolutely trust and to whom we give the widest liberty of action.

All this is of course sufficiently obvious as to seem almost trite. The great point is in choosing the men. I most earnestly urge the wisdom of the President putting Major General Leonard Wood in immediate command of all Cuba, with a complete liberty to do what he deems wisest in shaping our policy for the island, and with complete control over every other military and civil officer, and I also very earnestly urge that Major General Francis V. Greene be recalled to the service and put in complete command of the Philippines, being allowed the freest possible hand, with instructions not simply to defend Manila, but to assume aggressive operations and to harass and smash the insurgents in every way until they are literally beaten into peace; entertaining no proposition whatever from them save that of unconditional surrender.

This does not represent any sudden impulse on my part, but it is my very best judgment arrived at after months of thought—months during which I have gotten hundreds of side lights from soldiers, sailors, civilians, and in short, eye witnesses of every kind in the Philippine and Cuban matters. We need tact and judgment just as much as we need firmness in Cuba now. Wood is a born diplomat, just as he is a born soldier. I question if any nation in the world has now, or has had within recent time, anyone so nearly approaching the ideal of a military administrator of the kind now required in Cuba. Perhaps one or two of the Englishmen who have appeared in India during the last forty years come up to his level, but only one or two, and no one of their men who has yet made his mark in South Africa comes anywhere near it. He has a peculiar faculty for getting on with the Spaniards and Cubans. They like him, trust him, and down in their hearts are afraid of him. He always pays deference not only to their principles but to their prejudices. He is scrupulously courteous and polite. He understands their needs, material and moral, and he also understands their sensitiveness and their spirit of punctilio. Finally, he is able, while showing them entire courtesy and thoughtful consideration, to impress upon them the fact that there can be no opposition when once he has made up his mind.

General Greene is a man who has shown not only his ability

as a soldier by the extremely enviable record he made last year at Manila, but he is most successful as an organizer and chief executive officer in big business enterprises. He is a West Pointer, a man who has been trained in the regular army, a man who has commanded a division in the field victoriously. He is a born fighter; a born leader. I have watched him at close range as I have watched Wood, and in his case as in Wood's, I would be willing to stake my own reputation, the honor of the flag and the interests of the nation on my judgment that he is fit for the difficult and dangerous task for which I recommend him.

Wood and Greene are alike in possessing the by no means usual qualities of great capacity to earn money; with entire subordination of money-getting to what they feel to be nobler work. Wood, as you know, has just refused an offer of $30,000 a year from as big a combination of capitalists as there is in the country. Greene has risen to be one of the leading business men in New York. Each has shown to perfection those rare qualities which fit a man to succeed in business because they fit him to initiate, direct and supervise the most complicated and difficult bits of administration. Each has remarkable executive capacity. The objection will at once be raised that Wood is a young man who has already had very rapid promotion, and that he should not be put over the heads of his seniors; and that Greene should not be recalled to military life when he is now in civil life, and put over the heads of his seniors. Undoubtedly to take such action would invite a great deal of criticism of the wooden-headed sort. To this criticism absolutely not one particle of heed should be paid, and the objection counts for literally nothing. If we are going to try to administer Cuba and conquer the Philippines on the seniority plan, we had better abandon the two jobs at once, and it is not possible to carry either through successfully on such terms. We have got to push up our best men, wholly without regard to seniority, just as they were pushed up in the Civil War.

In last year's fighting, as the President knows, there was a good deal of hesitation in sending Dewey to the Asiatic squadron (before the war I mean—I include preparation as part of the fighting). It was urged very strongly by the Bureau of Navigation at the time, I remember, that Howell was entitled to go. Finally, and most wisely, the Secretary decided to disregard this argument and to send Dewey. If he had not done so, there would have been no Philippine problem at present, for our fleet would have done nothing more than to conduct a solemn blockade of Manila until our coal gave out, and then go away. The only trouble we have had in the Navy arose from appointing Schley because he was a commodore, to the position which Rodgers or Evans should have filled, just as Sampson filled his, or which Walker should have been recalled to fill. Again in this case the Bureau of Navigation fought for the appointment of Schley, as I very well recollect, because he was a commodore and a commodore should not be passed over for a captain.

In Cuba and the Philippines we now have and have had some excellent men and some entirely unfit men who are failures now and have been failures of the most striking kind in the past. But the best of them, however good, lack some of the qualities, if only the qualities of youth and bodily vigor which it is indispensable should be possessed by the man who is put in command of the entire business. Wood has administered Santiago with absolute success. Greene was one of the chief factors in the capture of Manila and knows exactly what ought to be done. Give to the first the complete control of Cuba and to the second the complete control of Luzon. In Wood's case there will not be so much as a jar, save from politicians. If any general does not like to serve under him, take that general home. If the friends of any general complain that they think that general ill-treated by being passed by or relieved, simply answer that we are not concerned with private feelings but with results for the nation as a whole, and that nothing whatever but results will be heeded. With Wood in command I venture the assertion that you would speedily have part of the regular force now in Cuba foot-loose for the Philippine campaign; that you would have necessary administrative reform inaugurated; and that the island would speedily be on the path to content and prosperity.

In the appointment of Greene there would be rather more serious dislocation, and I take it for granted that he would not be sent out to the Philippines until he had had a chance to do something toward organizing the forces to be sent there in the fall, but if he were sent out and were given complete control over the division commanders, and so far as possible the division commanders whom he thought best, and were allowed as free a hand as possible, I most emphatically believe that he would smash the whole Aguinaldo business in the campaign beginning when the rainy season closed, and meanwhile would organize a civil government which would work well. In short, he would put the Island upon an entirely satisfactory footing, for you have got to have a man able to start a civil government, no less than able to crush the insurgents, and he would leave of the hostiles only enough at the outside to justify such a subaltern's war, as for instance, the English carried on in Burmah for a couple of years after they took Mandalay.

There are one or two other points I should like to lay before the President. For instance, I earnestly hope that in appointing the officers of the new volunteer regiments, these regiments will be given to young regular officers who shall be their colonels, and that under them shall stand officers who did well in battle or in camp last summer. For instance, if a regiment should be given to Captain Robert L. Howze who was with the cavalry at Santiago on General Sumner's staff, and is now at West Point, I would guarantee that he would do the Government credit, especially if you would let him take among his volunteer officers, men such as I can recommend; that is, men from my old regiment like Dame, Fortescue and others, or men from the New York regiments like Andrews, and any number more whom I could enumerate.

But this is not the point about which I am writing you. What I am writing you is to urge as strongly as I know how that the President give Wood complete control in Cuba and Greene complete control in the Philippines, making them understand that if they fail, why their chance is gone and they shall be superseded by others, but that they shall be given every possible backing; and if this is done I am sure that they will succeed.

Unless you think it unwise, I wish you would show this letter to the President, and if he cares to talk to me about it, I should like to come on. Senator Platt I know would heartily back up Greene and Wood and so would Lodge, and these are the two Senators from their states.

Very faithfully yours,
THEODORE ROOSEVELT.

STATE OF NEW YORK
EXECUTIVE CHAMBER
ALBANY

At Oyster Bay, N. Y.,
July 21st, 1899.

Hon. H. C. Lodge, c/o J. S. Morgan & Co., Bankers, London, England.

Dear Cabot:—When Edith and I read over your last letter we began to feel various emotions which I am accustomed to consider as proper only to a member of the Latin race, and not to the "Dominant Peoples." Well, life certainly is not a failure when one has made such a friend as I have in you. I only wish there would occasionally come times when the manifestation of friendship would not be so one-sided; Edith can hardly speak of your letter even now.

Queer, nice, erratic, old Senator Chandler has been out here, taking your view of the Vice Presidency, a view which Senator Platt bitterly opposes. However, I think Hobart will accept the renomination, and that will end all our trouble.

I doubt if I send on your letter to the President, because Alger put in his resignation the day it arrived—*absit omen.* I had not written about Alger in *my* letter to the President because I had already spoken to the President about him, and he had shown scant inclination to hear me. After sending my letters to John Hay and Griggs, I received from the President a cordial invitation to go to Washington and spend a night at the White House. I accordingly went on and he received me with the utmost heartiness, being evidently very much pleased at my having come out for him. Meanwhile Alger's alliance with Pingree had resulted in Pingree's dragging Alger into some connection with his own assaults on the President, and the President, who had been quite insensible to Alger's shortcomings as a war administrator, and to the effect of his retention upon the country, was very much moved indeed by this new development. As soon as I saw him I told him I wanted first of all to say that nothing real could be done while Alger remained Secretary, and that whether Alger were right or wrong, the enormous majority of the American people regarded him as a curse, and that his retention was a source of the greatest danger to the administration. I felt it to be of the utmost importance that he should regard me as wholly disinterested, and so I told him that I wished it distinctly understood that I was not a candidate for the position of Secretary of War and could not leave the Governorship of New York now, and that I spoke as I did simply as an American and as a republican who felt that the welfare of our party, and, what was more important, of the country, was concerned in the President's re-election, and that Alger was the greatest bar to it and the greatest bar to our bringing the affairs of the islands into proper shape. He not only listened to me with the utmost attention, but, although he answered guardedly, gave me practically the assurance that Alger's days were numbered. If I had received your letter before my visit to the President I daresay I should not have spoken as I did about the Secretaryship, for I have implicit confidence in your judgment, and it is not necessary to say that I feel that the work of Secretary of War is more important than that of any other officer below the President just at this crisis; but, in the first place, it did not occur to me that I could very well leave the Governorship now when I had only been in it six or seven months; in the second place, it seemed to me of the utmost importance that the President should regard my action as entirely disinterested; and in the third place, I feel that if I went in as Secretary of War I ought to have a freer hand than the President would be inclined to give me. I am now backing Frank Greene very strongly for the position.

General Wilson would be a good man, but he is not nearly as young as Greene. The President has implicit faith in Otis. He assured me that Otis had things entirely in hand and that the insurrection would be speedily put down, certainly after the opening of the dry season, and said that he was thoroughly in touch with everything and that he knew Otis to be the best man he could put in, and that he had opportunities for judging of the matter which I could not have. He said this all in the pleasantest way possible, and I could only answer that of course the decision lay with him and he had more knowledge than anyone else of the situation, but that I begged him to consider nothing in dealing with even the least little part of the War Department's policy but the success of our arms and our principles; to make Otis understand, if he was to be kept, that he had to face facts as they were, and that he should be backed up and given everything which he needed in order to win.

As for Wood, I fear the President thought I was influenced mainly by my personal feelings. I assured him that this was not the case; that I advised as I did because I honestly thought Wood had developed qualities which fitted him for the peculiar work in Cuba making him stand a head above everyone else and waist high above General Brooke. He has given Wood another province, which is of course so much to the good, but he cannot make up his mind to take a decided stand in the matter. Wood and Wilson, who are, in that order the two best men in Cuba, advocate utterly different policies. Wood believes that we should not promise or give the Cubans independence; that we should govern them justly and equitably, giving them all possible opportunities for civic and military advancement, and that in two or three years they will insist upon being part of us. Wilson believes we should now leave the Island, establishing a Republican form of government and keeping a coaling station, etc., together with tariff arrangements which would include them with us as against outsiders, and he thinks that in a very few years they would drop into our hands of their own accord. I told the President (who is inclined to Wood's policy) that probably either policy would do, but that whichever is adopted must be followed out vigorously, intelligently and with tact. Wood writes me that things are in a bad way, I enclose a copy of his letter.

I send you a copy of an interesting letter I have just received from Funston. I answered that we must all stand by the President.

Frank Greene is coming up here tonight and I sail down with him to Coney Island to see Senator Platt tomorrow.

My parochial affairs seem to be getting along all right. I have devoted myself to them this year, and to good purpose. But of course it is really the larger interests of our country that give me concern and that interest me.

Give my warm love to Nannie and the boys; Edith sends hers to all of you. I am delighted that you had a chance to meet Balfour* and the rest and wish I could have been over with you, but I have had very little let up in my work. However, at present I have all my afternoons free and am rowing almost every day, with Edith, sometimes for several hours, taking our lunch with us and am in fine trim.

Ever yours,

THEODORE ROOSEVELT.

P. S.—I have just returned from a visit to Senator Platt at the Oriental, and you have by this time seen that Root has been made Secretary of War. I rather doubt if the President would have appointed me, even if I had not told him that I was not a candidate, for he has announced publicly and to Senator Platt that he wished to appoint a lawyer to the office and not a man who had any past connections with military affairs. He said this, my own belief is, chiefly because he did not wish to appoint either Greene or Wilson, for he fears trouble, and does not wish a sweeping reform of the office, or too thorough-going a policy. Personally, the desire to have a lawyer in the War Department seems to me simply foolish— so foolish indeed that I can only regard it as an excuse. But Root is an absolutely upright and very able man, and he will make a good Secretary. No dishonesty can exist under him,

---

* A. J. Balfour, now Lord Balfour.

and I believe that from sheer force of events, he will be obliged to work for radical reforms in the department. The President is absolutely confident that Otis will dispose of the Philippine matters before the New Year. If this is so, all will go well, for Root has a great regard for Wood and will, I think, pay much heed to his advice in Cuban matters. He will also be in close touch with you and men like you. Being a great corporation lawyer, he was violently opposed to the Franchise Tax measure, and in consequence, though still very friendly with me, is not nearly as close as he was last year. Personally, I am heartily glad to see him get the Secretaryship, and as all that is necessary in dealing with our problems is a mixture of resolution and common sense, I think he can handle the department all right, but it ought to have been given to a man with military experience, if the really best results are to be attained.

T. R.

STATE OF NEW YORK
EXECUTIVE CHAMBER
ALBANY

At Oyster Bay, N. Y.,
August 10th, 1899.

Hon. H. C. Lodge, c/o J. S. Morgan & Co., Bankers, London, England.

Dear Cabot:—I have just lunched with Root* and read him almost all of your last letter which was written evidently before you got my last. Root is taking hold of his work in just the right way. He went into it at all only because he felt the task was so serious, so difficult and of such vital importance to the nation. Otherwise as it is really out of his line, he would never have left his great practice for it. He has been a little disgruntled with me, or at least was last Spring, because of my action on the franchise tax matter, he being a great corporation lawyer and retained by Whitney and the street railway men. But he is such a good fellow that I was sure it would not last, and now I think every shade of it has vanished. I am confident he will do exceedingly well as Secretary of War.

* Mr. Root had just been made Secretary of War.

I very much fear that he will find difficulty in getting on with Miles. As you know, Miles unfortunately has the Presidential bee in his bonnet, even to the extent of wishing me to run as Vice President on the ticket with him. This occurred at your own house partly and on the train that night.* I don't know whether I told you about it, but I suppose I did. Above all, Root realizes that the first thing to do is to smash the Philippine insurrection, and he has got the President's authority to enlist additional regiments, but is keeping his intention absolutely secret, as he wants first to select the volunteer officers and escape as much political pressure in the matter as possible. Then I think he will undertake the reorganization of the army itself. Certainly it is now his present intention. So you see he is starting off first rate.

I am not easy over some of the developments of popular feeling here. Fortunately there is nothing much up this year; but we have an under swell against us. In the West I believe we are better off than in the last Presidential election. In the East we are very considerably worse off. The agitation against trusts is taking an always firmer hold. It is largely unreasonable and is fanned into activity by the Bryan type of demagogue, ably seconded by Gorman, Croker *et al* who want to change the issue from free silver. But when there is a good deal of misery and of injustice, even though it is mainly due to the faults of the individuals themselves, or to the mere operation of nature's laws, the quack who announces he has a cure-all for it is a dangerous person. Around the State of New York I am surprised to find how many of the working men who were with us three years ago, are now sullenly grumbling that McKinley is under Hanna's dictation; that Bryan is the only man who can control the trusts; and that the trusts are crushing the life out of the small men, etc., etc. I shall have much to tell you when I see you. In our local affairs, by industrious working I have got the republicans and the independents pretty thoroughly in line for a union on a legislative ticket. Quigg and the New York machine for once have acted with equal wisdom and virtue. The Brooklyn people are a very

* He had told me of Miles' proposal at my house just after the interview.

small lot and they have their own troubles, while in New York City the *Post* is so busy denouncing Platt and my imperialism that it can't see Tammany. Whitelaw Reid feels vindictively towards McKinley and Platt, and therefore towards the whole republican party, and he is deliberately striving to bring about our defeat. He has attacked Root most maliciously, saying that the President has added to his council merely a clever corporation lawyer, insinuating that he was appointed more to please great financial interests than to right the wrongs of the War Department. Recently he has even attacked me quite as bitterly as he has Root, seizing the occasion offered by the fact that Fox* and MacFarlane have reported that no indictments can lie against Aldridge and Adams in the canal matter. Fox and MacFarlane are two of the foremost democratic lawyers in the State, one of them being Cleveland's former district attorney, and there is not a reputable member of the bar of the State who does not know that though the canals were managed as they generally have been in New York—inefficiently and on a political basis—yet that nothing criminal was done and no prosecution could be had of the wrong doers, who of course went out of office when I came in, one of them by the expiration of his term, and the other because I refused to reappoint him. Whitelaw Reid knows all this perfectly, but it suits him to try to give the impression that somehow or other I have refused to prosecute criminals; and at the other pole, Mr. Rowland Blennerhasset Mahany and his little crowd of demagogues are attacking me because I won't give Aldridge a clean bill of health.

I am soon to start off on a tour of the county fairs. I have a special car and Edith had most unexpectedly volunteered to go with me. I rather think she has before her some experiences she wots not of. There is a Pioneer Picnic at Silver Lake, for instance, where I think I can see her now circulating among the wives of the prominent pioneers. (N. B. She is listening as I dictate this).

I have had a very satisfactory holiday on the whole, getting my afternoons entirely free, and often a day free, when Edith

* Austin Fox, distinguished lawyer in New York—class of 1869, Harvard.

and I would row off and take lunch somewhere on the Sound.

Did I tell you that I am writing a sketch of Cromwell for *Scribner's*? It is to be about the length of my Rough Riders, appearing in six numbers, and then in book form, and I get $5,000 for it and 15% on the book.

I envy you Bayreuth. In a perfectly dumb way I have always admired Wagner and I should like greatly to see his operas in their own place.

Give my best love to Nannie and all.

Ever yours,
THEODORE ROOSEVELT.

STATE OF NEW YORK
EXECUTIVE CHAMBER
ALBANY

At Oyster Bay, N. Y.,
August 28, 1899.

Mr. H. C. Lodge, c/o J. S. Morgan & Co., Bankers, London, England.

Dear Cabot:—I was overjoyed with your last letter. I have wished often this summer that I could have been abroad with you. However, I have thoroughly enjoyed being at home. In fact, I do not believe any other man has ever had as good a time as Governor of New York. I am not, thank Heaven, under the least illusion as to the permanence of my position; for both my good qualities and my defects—including in the last, the habit, to which you have once or twice unfeelingly alluded, of expressing a great variety of opinions on a great variety of subjects, and, formerly, at least, with some intemperance of expression—will tend to make my official life short. I should like to be re-elected Governor, but I do not expect it, and I should be quite willing to barter the certainty of it for all possibilities of the future. As for the Vice Presidency, I do not think there is anything in that. But in any event, I shall do just as you advise—that is, let it take care of itself.

Meanwhile, I am having a splendid time, and I really have for the moment a strong hold on the people of the State. Edith and I spent eight days going around to the Pioneer picnics, county fairs, etc., and I really think she enjoyed it as much as I did. We ended by a visit to the President at Platts-burgh. He was, as always, most pleasant. My relations with Platt are as cordial as ever, and the machine, as a whole, is a good deal impressed by the way I am received around the State. So that as far as I can see no trouble threatens in the immediate future. On September 23rd, I am to open the cam-paign in Ohio, where I am sorry to say the anti-Hanna crowd seem worse than lukewarm. I am also to speak in Maryland, where the contest is very hard, and the result in doubt. I do both at the President's request, in addition to the request of the local people. In New York I am very anxious to have us carry the Assembly. Whether we shall succeed or not I do not know.

Root is doing very well. He has called for a number of additional regiments, and the mere fact of having done so will help matters in the Philippines. I believe they will all be needed there. Of course, I still feel very doubtful about Otis personally, but I earnestly hope that the President is right— that no great difficulty will be found in pacifying the islands after the dry season begins.

Wood is continuing to do splendid work in Santiago, but thinks the whole policy of managing the island needs revision. He writes me at length and I am going to show his letters to Root from time to time as I get the chance, in addition to show-ing them to you.

The beloved Speck is here fresh from Samoa, where he has worked to good purpose with our man Tripp. He is going back to Germany in a fortnight. I wish to Heavens he would instill a little common sense into the Kaiser!

Give my best love to Nannie and the boys. Edith is very well. We spent about six hours in our row boat yesterday. At present she is very stiff from having ridden Texas. I accom-panied her on the surrey horse, a large amiable mare, with no conception whatever of a saddle horse's functions, steering about the same way that the surrey itself does.

Ever yours,
THEODORE ROOSEVELT.

STATE OF NEW YORK
EXECUTIVE CHAMBER
ALBANY

At Oyster Bay, N. Y.,
Sept. 11th, 1899.

Hon. H. C. Lodge, c/o J. S. Morgan & Co., Bankers, London, England.

Dear Cabot:—I suppose this will be my last letter to you while you are on the other side, although I am not certain just when you get back. I am still in the midst of the county fairs. It has been very tiresome, and in some way, a bore; but on the other hand, I have been glad to meet the men who make up the back bone of the bulk of the republican party in this State—the old style American countrymen. I am greatly impressed with the strong, rugged, simple nature of the great majority of these men. They are healthy, they are powerful, they are emphatically good material out of which to make a strong, self-poised republic. Did I write you of my delight at meeting one Hiram Tower, his wife and his seventeen children? I have had very few uncomfortable incidents and think my trips have on the whole done good. The only trouble at all has come where one county has felt jealous because I went to another in as much as I could not possibly go to them all; or where there has been hostility on the part of outsiders to the men in control of a given fair. It is a dreadful task to try to keep the republican party united here. Aside from the deep seated causes of division between the two wings, which shade off into the irrational and unscrupulous machine men on the one hand and the quite as irrational and unscrupulous independents on the other, there are the bitter factional fights and splits caused by mere personal vindictiveness and sore-headedness on the part of some men. Moreover, while the great bulk of the scoundrels in any job are democrats, it is exceedingly difficult to prevent just enough dabbling in scoundrelism by republicans to give the independents a chance to say that both parties are equally bad. As for the antics of the independents, they are of course past belief. At present, Tammany is in disfavor, thanks to the Ramapo water steal, and a little bit of some of the work done by the Mazet Committee. Many of the Independents want Van Wyck legislated out of office, while others blandly declare that in any event they desire to run their own candidates, and would just as soon accept Tammany help as republican help. It is a dangerous thing to legislate a man out of office, for it is easy to create sympathy for him, and I am not certain what is the wise and proper thing to do in the premises. I wish that Senator Platt who has an extraordinary mastery over all the leaders, great and small, of the Organization itself, not only in the city, but in the thoroughly healthy country communities, could gauge public opinion better. As it is, I am at a great loss to know what to devise, or what to consent to here in New York. I think I told you that I am to speak in Maryland and in Ohio this Fall. They have never told me the date I am to speak in Massachusetts. I have written on to find out. Senator Beveridge of Indiana was out here yesterday. He has just come back from the Philippines. His views on public matters are almost exactly yours and mine. I want you to meet him.

We shall go up to Albany about the first of October, but I hate to leave Oyster Bay, and shall come back here whenever I get the chance, so as to get a little exercise. Our rowing trips have been the greatest pleasure to us this summer, and we have succeeded in teaching every child, bar Quentin, to swim.

Faithfully yours,

THEODORE ROOSEVELT.

STATE OF NEW YORK
EXECUTIVE CHAMBER
ALBANY

October 20th, 1899.

Hon. H. C. Lodge, 31 Beacon Street, Boston, Mass.

Dear Cabot:—I have just gotten your letter while on my way to Cincinnati. I am greatly concerned at the news about your mother. I will go to Bigelow's, but will you tell George Lyman, etc., that I go there at your request so that I may see more of you. I hesitate to write you about other matters when you are so anxious about your mother. Do give her my warmest love.

I didn't read what Schurz said; I don't care what that prattling foreigner shrieks or prattles in this crisis, and I would no more read his speeches than I would read the editorials of the *Evening Post*, unless for some reason it was necessary to answer them. The leather-tongued Warner has been denouncing me. I had a good meeting and hit straight at Tammany. Of course I am having a rather hard time as I have got a heavy cold and this travelling about is perfectly infernal.

With best love to Nannie and again telling you what I know you know how deeply concerned I am about your mother and about your anxiety, I am,

As ever yours,

THEODORE ROOSEVELT.

THE UNION LEAGUE CLUB
NEW YORK

Dear Cabot,   Oct. 25th, '99.

After sending you that Oregon letter yesterday I suddenly thought you might regard it as a sympton of desire on my part to get into the Presidential campaign. Heaven forbid! I wrote the writer at once that of course McKinley was inevitable, and that I was not in the race in any way or shape. I sent it to you because I thought the remarks about the "1909" business all right.

McLean will be beaten in Ohio, I believe; I am on my way to help McComas who I fear has little chance.

I do hope your dear mother is improving. Yours, T. R.

Private.   BOSTON, MASS.,
Dear Theodore:—   Oct. 25, 1899.

I have your two letters, and before this reaches you you will have a letter from Bigelow himself conveying his invitation more formally than through me. My chief reason for wanting you there is because you are nearer to me and I can see something of you. I think I can square it with George Lyman, although he has got it very much on his mind having you, but I feel as if I had the first claim.

As to the letter from Wood, which you enclose, I see no reason to change my opinion but that your attitude has been, and is, the correct one. There are plenty of men who would like to get up a fight with McKinley and use you for that purpose, but I do not at present see any advantage to you in such a course. I will talk it over with you fully when we meet. Simon, of course, I know, and he is all that Wood says, so far as astuteness and capacity go. More than that I am unable to say in regard to him, but in any event this is a matter to be treated with great caution, and certainly nothing should be done until after election; but I repeat that I see no good reason as yet to change your original attitude which I think you very wisely took.

My mother seems about the same—not better and I think not worse—but she is very feeble. She may rally, as she has great vitality and constitution, and the fact that she has not grown worse since I wrote you is encouraging.

Let me know when to expect you so that I can meet you at the train.

I am sorry you have a bad cold, and I wish you did not have to take all these distant journeys; they are very wearing.

Always sincerely yours,
H. C. LODGE.

STATE OF NEW YORK
EXECUTIVE CHAMBER
ALBANY

December 2, 1899.

Hon. H. C. Lodge, Senate Chamber, Washington, D. C.

Dear Cabot:—Today I gave Edith the little blue watch and she was perfectly delighted with it. I have never seen her like a present so much. She is perfectly well as are all the children.

I wish to Heaven I could see you and talk with you, for I have had very ugly times here politically recently!

What an admirable report Root has made. He was a genuine Godsend to the administration.

Give my warm love to Nannie.

Always yours,
T. R.

UNITED STATES SENATE
WASHINGTON, D. C.

Personal.

My dear Theodore:—   Dec. 7, 1899.

Many thanks for your note of the 2nd. I am very glad that Edith liked the watch. I think myself it is extremely pretty, and I do not believe that two persons of more refined taste could have been discovered than those who chose it.

I have been meaning to write to you ever since I came to Washington, but there has been a rush of business and I have put off doing so from day to day. Your interests and your future have been constantly in my mind. The general impression of course is that you would be very foolish to take the Vice-Presidency, although I have never failed to convince the two or three people with whom I have talked fully about it. My own opinion has not changed. I can put it most tersely by saying that if I were a candidate for the Presidency I would take the Vice-Presidency in a minute at this juncture. Of course I may be all wrong, and I am not going in the least to push my opinion on you. I did not hesitate to urge you to take the Assistant Secretaryship of the Navy, or the Police Commissionership of New York, but this is a very different matter. When a man is candidate for the Presidency, no friend, however close, has the right to urge him to follow a course in the slightest degree against his own judgment. In such a very momentous matter a man himself must be sole judge. Your own inclination is against it, and very likely it is correct, for I have great faith in your instincts about yourself. The opinion of most of your friends points probably the same way. You can have it if you want it by simply saying so. There is no doubt on that point, but under these circumstances I shall not urge you to take it, or indeed to say anything further about it, and I am sure that you will stay where you are. You are in a splendid situation in any event so far as the future is concerned, and whatever you do or decide will satisfy me, and I shall work along the line you prefer to follow just as vigorously and zealously as if you were pursuing some other which I might think more favorable. I feel very sanguine about your future, and you are quite certain to be reelected, which is the next step, and beyond which there is no need of our looking at present.

I have been thinking about you in connection with the State Police bill, and could see that you had a somewhat awkward situation to handle, but it is quite clear to my mind, from what I read in the newspapers, and from what Root said to me, that although the measure is theoretically sound it would be most unwise to press it. I should say that you had no course open to you in the interests of the party in the State except to stop it. Of course on this matter you are a thousand times better judge than I am, and I merely throw out this observation for what it is worth.

I suppose also that you will have some trouble over the re-doubtable Lou Payne, but I do not think this will be a serious case. You have the State with you against Mr. Payne by a very large majority.

I see that Dooley has been making game of you, and as he once devoted a paper to me I naturally take pleasure in the misfortunes of my friends, although I am bound to say that I felt that, when I was made the subject of a Dooley paper, I had advanced far on the high road of fame.

The session promises to be interesting. We are going to get a first rate money bill, and I hope some good legislation on Puerto Rico and Hawaii. The Senate, with a large Republican majority, is a very comfortable place.

With best love to Edith and the children,

Always yours, H. C. Lodge.

STATE OF NEW YORK
EXECUTIVE CHAMBER
ALBANY

Dec. 11th, 1899.

Dear Cabot:—

I have yours of the 7th inst. In the first place, do you not think that Beveridge would be a good man on the Committee on Foreign Relations? He seems to be sound on those matters.

Now, about the Vice Presidency. It seems to me that the chance of my being a presidential candidate is too small to warrant very serious consideration at present. To have been a good Colonel, a good Governor and a good Assistant Secretary of the Navy is not enough to last four years. If McKinley were to die tomorrow I would be one of the men seriously *considered* as his successor—I mean that and just no more. But four years hence the Spanish War will be in the very remote past and what I have done as Governor will not be very recent. Nobody can tell who will be up by that time. Of course, I should like to feel that I would still be in the running, but I do not regard it as sufficiently probable to be worth receiving very much weight.

There therefore remains the question of what each office is by itself. The Vice Presidency is a most honorable office, but for a young man there is not much to do. It is infinitely better than many other positions, but it hardly seems to me as good as being Governor of this State, which is a pretty important State. Then while it is very unlikely that I could be President, there is a chance of my being something else—Governor General of the Philippines, or a Cabinet Officer, or perchance in the remote future, Senator. Mind you, I do not think that any of these things are likely, but at least there is sufficient chance to warrant my taking them seriously, while I do not think the chance for the presidency *is* sufficient to warrant our taking it seriously. If I am Vice President I am "planted" for four years. Here I can turn around. Platt told me definitely that of course he was for me for a renomination—that everybody was—and though we shall have a good deal of friction from time to time, I do not believe it very likely that he will come to a definite break with me, because I like him personally, I always tell him the truth, and I genuinely endeavor to help him, if I can, with proper regard for the interest of the State and party.

The upshot of it is that it seems to me that I had better stay where I am. The great argument on the other side is, as I have said before, your judgment, which on the whole I have found better than my own. Some of the Western men are wild to have me go on to strengthen the ticket, but it scarcely seems to me that the ticket needs strengthening. Root would be an admirable man.

Give my best love to Nannie.

Ever yours,
THEODORE ROOSEVELT.

UNITED STATES SENATE
WASHINGTON, D. C.

Personal.

Dec. 13, 1899.

My dear Theodore :—

Beveridge is a very bright fellow, well informed and sound in his views. I like him very much, but he arrived here with a very imperfect idea of the rights of seniority in the Senate, and with a large idea of what he ought to have. He expected to get the chairmanship of the Philippine Committee which is going to be one of the biggest committees in the Senate, and which they have forced me to take much against my will for I sacrifice a great deal of personal comfort to do it, and he wanted in addition a place on Foreign Relations. I thought I was unusually lucky to get on Foreign Relations after I had been four years in the Senate, during which time I was not on any committee that ever met. We have had many applications for the one vacancy on Foreign Relations, and it has gone to Wolcott who had the longest service. The Committee put Beveridge on the Committee on the Philippines—which I think he is fortunate to get and where I think he ought to be. Personally I am very glad to have him there.

The Vice-Presidency I consider a settled question, since you feel as you do, though I do not take the same view of your prospects that you do, but if Root goes on to the ticket it leaves a vacancy in the Cabinet which would just suit you, and is better for you than the Vice-Presidency would be. If I were you I would keep on the lookout and I think there would be a fair opportunity of getting it. You have stood aside for McKinley, and were wise in doing so I think, and you will also stand aside for Root, and I do not see why these actions should not have due credit given to them. Meantime, as you say, you are very well where you are despite the many perils that surround the Governorship of New York, and there is always the chance that there may come an opening in the Senate. There is nothing that I can do at this moment to forward your interests since you decide not to take the Vice-Presidency, but I am always here on the look-out, as you well know.

Give my best love to Edith.

Always yours, H. C. LODGE.

STATE OF NEW YORK
EXECUTIVE CHAMBER
ALBANY

Dear Cabot:—   Dec. 14th, 1899.

Many thanks for yours of the 13th. Of all things I should like to be Secretary of War, if Root should decide to take the Vice Presidency.

By the way, I want to congratulate you on the triumph in Boston. That was first rate.

Yes, I saw Dooley's article and enjoyed it immensely. It is really exceedingly bright. How he does get at any joint in the harness!

What an awful time the English are having in the Transvaal. I should think they would feel pretty melancholy.

Is there any chance whatever of my catching a glimpse of you? Are you going to be in New York at all?

Ever yours, T. R.

UNITED STATES SENATE
WASHINGTON, D. C.

Personal.

Dear Theodore :—　　　　　　　　　　Dec. 16, 1899.

Thanks for your note of the 14th. The victory won in Boston was a very great and important one. I hardly dared to hope for it, but there was some division in the Democratic party which helped, and then the Republican vote of Boston turned out, which it rarely does, and elected Mr. Hart. His term is for two years, and it is a shattering blow to the Democratic party to lose control of Boston. Hart is a most excellent man, sound and sensible, who has been Mayor before and will give us a thoroughly good administration.

I should say that England was having a bad time in the Transvaal, and the papers this morning give an account of a worse repulse than they have yet had at all. This time it has fallen on Buller. The fact is that they have been whipping hill tribes and Dervishes so long that they have forgotten how white men fight and underestimate their antagonist. They also overlook the fact, which always weighs enormously with me in judging anything of this sort, that history for three hundred years had shown that there were no tougher or more stubborn fighters on the face of the earth than Dutchmen and Huguenots. I doubt if there are any people who have exhibited a greater capacity for holding up under defeat and resisting odds than the men of these two stocks, and yet everyone I saw in London last summer talked perfectly lightly about it, as if they had nothing to do but fight one or two short actions and then walk into Pretoria. The fundamental trouble, in my judgment, is with the head of the War Office. I saw Lord Wolseley in London, met him at dinner and had a long talk with him. He seemed to me a most charming and agreeable man, but if I ever saw anyone whom I should set down as lacking in effectiveness and as a fighter he was that man. I do not believe that he and his particular following can manage this war, and I said so last summer after I had seen him. They have deliberately set aside Roberts, and they do not employ Kitchener, who struck me when I met him, as one of the finest types of the effective fighter that I have ever met.

I wish I could see you and talk all these things over, for they are very interesting.

We must look out for that Secretaryship of War if things go right. It would be the place of all others for you, and I do not see why it could not be brought about.

I have now got the Philippines in my especial charge, and I have been much gratified by the manner in which the Committee insisted that I should take the place.

I hope you noticed the manner in which we knocked Pettigrew's* resolution out the other morning. It seems to us a good opportunity to give him a blow between the eyes at the start and we did it to perfection.

I do not see any present chance of my getting to New York. I am very busy here with my new committee, and as Gus and Constance are coming on for the holidays I cannot leave home, but if I can arrange sometime later to meet you in New York I will certainly do so.

Always yours, H. C. LODGE.

UNITED STATES SENATE
WASHINGTON, D. C.

Private and Confidential.

[December 19th? 1899.]

Dear Theodore:

I have just had a talk with Platt. He said that he was anxious that you should succeed in your ambition and be a Presidential candidate, and taking the usual view he had therefore advised you against the V. P. as not likely to be beneficial. This was voluntary and I am satisfied that he is for you for the future. But so far as the V. P. is concerned his views are changing, if not changed, by nothing I said but by the drift of events. I did not press my views upon him but let him talk and was much surprised by all he said. 1st.—There is not going to be a vacancy in War Dept., (do not breathe a word of this). 2nd.—There are several New York candidates for the

---

* Richard F. Pettigrew, a Senator from South Dakota.

V. P. None quite to his mind, I think, and doubtful if they could win. If any one of them does win it will be awkward for us. This is my own opinion thrown in. Platt told me that he was coming to see you Saturday and would then talk over with you your own affairs and the V. P. He agreed with me that you had merely to say the word to have the V. P., so you see I am no dreamer on that point. Now think this well over. I am not going to urge you, but things are so shaping themselves that the V. P. is becoming stronger and more desirable for you than I had thought possible. Do not say a word of what I have written *to anyone*. It is all in the deadest confidence. *Above all* do not let Platt suspect in the remotest way that I have written you or that you had the faintest idea that he was going to talk to you about your own affairs. "Your fingers on your lips" as Hamlet says. Love to Edith. Tell her of course.

Yrs., H. C. LODGE.

UNITED STATES SENATE
WASHINGTON, D. C.

Personal.

Dec. 22, 1899.

Dear Theodore :—

I read last night with great interest and pleasure your first Cromwell number. I liked especially the first part in which you treat with great force and vigor, as it seems to me, the general situation of Europe and of European opinion at that time. The point that the great rebellion was the beginning of the new time and not the end of the old seemed to me especially well taken. When you revise the book you ought to correct your quotation from Macauley. It is not "general of the Lord," but "The servant of the Lord."

I hope you will tell me what manner of interview you had with Platt after you see him tomorrow.

Always yours, H. C. LODGE.

STATE OF NEW YORK
EXECUTIVE CHAMBER
ALBANY

Dec. 26th, 1899.

Dear Cabot :—

I thank you for yours of the 22nd. I seem to have a genius for getting familiar quotations a little wrong. I will correct the one you refer to at once.

By the way, I wish you would look at my article on Expansion and Peace in the *Independent* of Dec. 21st.

Rather to my surprise Platt only spoke a word or two to me, simply saying he had not changed his belief—that I ought not to take the Vice Presidency. However, I am to see him again Thursday morning, and I will report to you in full afterwards.

Always yours,
THEODORE ROOSEVELT.

STATE OF NEW YORK
EXECUTIVE CHAMBER
ALBANY

Dec. 29th, 1899.

Dear Cabot :—

I had a long talk with Platt and Odell yesterday. In the first place, we have come to a very satisfactory agreement in State matters. I mean satisfactory in view of the extraordinary complications of our New York politics, the wide divergency of interests and the endless trouble produced by the corruptionists on the one hand, and the vain, self-seeking and visionary reformers on the other. Platt does not want me to fight Payne and feels pretty bitterly about it, but here I could not compromise and I refused to alter my position. However, as I suppose the Democrats will support Payne, or at least the great majority of them, the attitude of the Republican machine means that I will not get him out. At any rate I shall cease to be responsible for him. Otherwise we are free of most of the rocks. I do not see many ahead. I am not able to do exactly as I should like in all things, but really it is astonishing how large the number is in which I am able to manage matters on a nearly ideal basis. But the worry and effort is more than you would believe.

As to the Vice Presidency, Platt told me that you and Chandler wanted me nominated; that some of the far western Senators wanted me because they thought I would strengthen the ticket in their States; but that the general opinion was that it would not be a wise move for me personally, as I should be simply shelved as Vice President and could do nothing, for if I did anything I would attract suspicion and antagonism. Lucius Littauer had been examining me about the Vice Presidency, telling me that all the western Congressmen who spoke of me and who professed much friendship for me were against my taking the nomination for Vice President for the reasons given above. All my western friends keep writing me to the same effect. I do not think I have had a letter from any of them advising me to take the nomination for Vice President, and I have had scores urging me not to take it.

I almost think I must run down to Washington for a couple of days to see you.

Give my warm love to Nannie.

Ever yours,
THEODORE ROOSEVELT.

UNITED STATES SENATE
WASHINGTON, D. C.

Confidential.

Dear Theodore :—   Dec. 29, 1899.

Thanks for your note of the 26th. Platt told me that Root would not be Vice-President because the President wished him to remain in his Cabinet. Yesterday I heard, practically at first hand from the White House, that it was substantially agreed that Root was to be Vice-President. After such contradictions I am not surprised that Platt said nothing much to you about the Vice-Presidency but advised you not to take it. He certainly gave me to understand that his views were tending in the other direction. Under these circumstances I do not know what to say. Of course if Root is to have the Vice-Presidency that would open a much better place for you if we could bring it about, of which I would not despair. I will talk further with Platt when he comes back.   Always yours,   H. C. LODGE.

STATE OF NEW YORK
EXECUTIVE CHAMBER
ALBANY

Dec. 30th, 1899.

Hon. H. C. Lodge, Senate Chamber, Washington, D. C.

My dear Cabot:—I hasten to write you because of a most unexpected bit of information. I find that after Platt's return from Washington he *did* tell a couple of New York politicians that I would undoubtedly have to accept the Vice Presidency; that events were shaping themselves so that this was inevitable. He gave me no hint of this, taking exactly the opposite view, and I do not understand what was up, or for the matter of that what is up now, but I send you this for your own private information.

Always yours,
THEODORE ROOSEVELT.

1900

STATE OF NEW YORK
EXECUTIVE CHAMBER
ALBANY

Jany. 2nd, 1900.

Dear Cabot:—

Of course, I wrote to Platt at once and was only too glad of the chance to do anything I could for Coolidge.

I have had a lot of ugly problems recently and now and then I feel like throwing up my hands, but I never do, and as I have managed to worry along somehow through the rocks so far, I shall try my best to continue to do so. But oh Heavens, what a complicated business New York political life is!

Best love to Nannie.   Ever yours,
THEODORE ROOSEVELT.

UNITED STATES SENATE
WASHINGTON, D. C.

Confidential.

Dear Theodore :—   Jan. 2, 1900.

Thanks for your letter of the 29th. I am glad that things, on the whole, are in such good shape, but I can easily understand what difficulties there are in your path. Your course is also right about Payne, but it is easy to see, even at this distance, what a trouble it must have been to you.

As to the Vice-Presidency I dare say everybody else is right; they probably are, and I am wrong. At all events it is pretty clear that the New York people are not disposed to go in for it and agree with you in regard to it. That certainly is conclusive.

I wish you would come down here and pass a couple of days. Why will you not run over any time for Sunday? It will do you good, and give us an opportunity to have a talk. We shall always have room for you here.

Always yours, H. C. LODGE.

UNITED STATES SENATE
WASHINGTON, D. C.

Personal.

Dear Theodore :—   Jan. 6, 1900.

À propos of the attack which the gentle Godkin is making on us in his reminiscences I enclose an article from the Boston Journal, which you might like to see.

Always yours, H. C. LODGE.

UNITED STATES SENATE
WASHINGTON, D. C.

Personal.

Dear Theodore :—   Jan. 10, 1900.

Thanks for your letter of the 8th. I should never have known Godkin had been making attacks on us had it not been for the articles which I saw in the Boston *Herald* and this article in the *Journal*.

The fight is on here about the Philippines, and although my committee has no legislation in prospect it seems to have plenty of work to do in the way of debate with the enemy.

Always yours,   H. C. LODGE.

STATE OF NEW YORK
EXECUTIVE CHAMBER
ALBANY

Jany. 16th, 1900.

Hon. H. C. Lodge, Senate Chamber, Washington, D. C.

Dear Cabot:—I never wrote you to say how much I liked your answer to Mason.* I thought what you said about England's attitude toward us during the Spanish war particularly good.

As you may possibly have seen, I am having my own times just at present.

Always yours,
THEODORE ROOSEVELT.

UNITED STATES SENATE
WASHINGTON, D. C.

Personal.

Dear Theodore :—   Jan. 18, 1900.

Thank you for your note of the 16th. I am glad that you like what I said to Mason. I send you by this mail my remarks made on amending my colleague's resolution, which I wish you would look over. He wanted full enquiry, and I was determined that he should have it. I think one or two points, especially at the end, will please you.

I observe you are having some difficulties, but I cannot but believe that you will carry the Payne fight through all right.

Always yours,   H. C. LODGE.

* Senator William Mason of Illinois.

STATE OF NEW YORK
EXECUTIVE CHAMBER
ALBANY

Dear Cabot:—   Jany. 22nd, 1900.

Another note of congratulation. Your Webster speech* was splendid. There has been but one opinion concerning it.

I saw George Lyman, and Henry Payne of Wisconsin has just passed the night with me; while on Saturday Platt for the first time stated to me very strongly that he believed I ought to take the Vice Presidency both for National and for State reasons. I believe Platt rather likes me, though I render him uncomfortable by some of the things I do. He would have cheerfully taken Root for the Vice Presidency, but he fears now that unless I take it nobody will be made Vice President from New York, and that this would be a pity. Payne was as always thoroughly sensible and rather humorous. He took the view that I would be exceedingly fortunate to get through one term as Governor of New York without having irretrievably ruined myself for the future and I had no reason to tempt Providence for a second term, if an honorable opening occurred anywhere else.

As you know, the thing I should really like to do would be to be the first civil Governor General of the Philippines. I believe I could do that job, and it is a job emphatically worth doing. I feel that being Vice President would cut me off definitely from all chance of doing it; whereas in my second term as Governor, were I offered the Philippines, I could resign and accept it.

I am getting so anxious to see you that I do not know but I will have to run down. On the other hand, it does not seem possible for me to get away. I am having a very ugly and uncomfortable time over Payne.† It was wholly impossible for me to take any course save what I did. Like the population of Poker Flat I only venture to draw the line against individuals whose immorality is professional; but in Mr. Payne's case it *is* professional. We have his own sworn testimony to

* Made at the unveiling of the statue of Daniel Webster in Washington.
† "Lou" Payne.

the effect that up to the time he was appointed he was a lobbyist who made no money aside from what he got from corporations for taking care of their interests at Albany—not by appearing before Committees, but by what he called his "personal influence" with members. There were judgments amounting to some forty thousand dollars filed against him when he took his present position; but being a frugal man, out of his seven thousand dollars a year salary he has saved enough to enable him to borrow nearly half a million dollars from a Trust Company, the directors of which are also the directors of an insurance company which is under his supervision—this aside from the money he has borrowed elsewhere. As Insurance Superintendent he last year rendered such disinterested aid to Mr. Whitney* when Mr. Whitney's Metropolitan Railroad was in danger of being made to pay a tax to the State, etc., etc., that in a burst of similar disinterested enthusiasm Mr. Whitney lends him off hand a hundred thousand dollars (which by the way he forgetfully charges to "construction accounts") and this at a time when owing to the tightness of the money market Whitney was fighting for his life against his Wall Street rivals.

In a really civilized community Mr. Payne would not be kept in for a moment, and I do not know a single decent republican who favors his being kept. But the machine is afraid of him and dares not take sides. They did not think I had any chance of winning against him, but I have now come very close. The democrats will be almost unanimous against me, of course, but I have at least two-thirds of the republican Senators, and unless the opposition bolt the caucus (which of course they will do if paid sufficiently high) I will win. Altogether it is a very ugly and unpleasant muss.

Always yours,

THEODORE ROOSEVELT.

* Hon. W. C. Whitney, former Secretary of the Navy.

UNITED STATES SENATE
WASHINGTON, D. C.

Personal.

My dear Theodore :—   Jan. 25, 1900.

I have just received your letter of the 22nd. I am glad you like my Webster speech. I will send you a full copy as soon as it is in print.

I am going to have a talk with the President and a very frank talk as soon as possible about both the Vice Presidency and the Philippines. You know the direction in which I should like to see you go, but if you want to go to the Philippines my one desire is that you should have what you want. I have great faith in your own instinct as to what you prefer, and there is no question that there is great work to be done in the islands, although I should rather see you take the chance of something bigger at home. I am inclined to think that the Vice Presidency would be an open road in either direction, but I can tell you more after I have talked with the President. I heard in a curious way the other day that the President intended to send you as Governor General of the Philippines but that you knew nothing about it. Of course I have said nothing to anyone and shall not, but I am going to follow up this trail.

I think you are going to win out handsomely on Payne, and I read your description of him, and of the standard of morals you endeavored to live up to with great amusement.

Always yours, H. C. LODGE.

UNITED STATES SENATE
WASHINGTON, D. C.

Private and Confidential.

Dear Theodore :—   Jan. 27, 1900.

I had yesterday afternoon a long talk with the President. I asked him point blank whether he was thinking of sending you as Governor-General of the Philippines. He said not at present;

that he had talked over the matter with President Schurman*
and had told him what he would now tell me, that when civil
government was established there under act of Congress, or
otherwise, and a Governor-General was authorized, he thought
that you were the ideal man to be the first pioneer Governor in
those islands, that there was no one whom he thought so well
fitted for that great work, but that the war was still going on,
and that he did not think it wise at present to divide the military and civil power, that it would not be fair to you to send
you out there as Civil Governor until this situation had altered
and the Civil Governor could have control of everything. The
force of this I of course saw myself and admitted; in fact, I
have not believed from all I could learn that it was wise at
present to appoint a Civil Governor. It will come along, however, before very long, and I cannot see why the Vice Presidency would not be as good a bridge as any other. I talked
with him also about the Vice Presidency. He is evidently perfectly content to have you on the ticket with him, and realizes
that if your name is brought forward you would be nominated
with a rush. I think now I know the whole situation, and that
you do too. I am clear in the opinion that the time has come
when you should make up your mind whether to refuse to be
the candidate for Vice President and run again for Governor
of New York, or let your name be brought forward for the
second place on the national ticket and remain quiescent in
regard to it—which of course would be taken as a willingness
to accept it and is all that would be necessary, in my opinion.
I wish you would write me what course you decide to follow.
I am not going to urge you one way or the other, but I think
the trend of events is steadily making your acceptance more
desirable. You have, however, better means of knowing than
I, and I have great confidence in your instinct in the matter.
If you do not take the Vice-Presidency New York will have
lost it. This Platt does not want to have happen, and the attitude of the organization, which has now come around to desire
you to take it, is something to be considered.

I should say you had won very handsomely in the **Payne**

* J. G. Schurman, President of the U. S. Philippine Commission.

case, and your canal report is evidently a great success. Nonetheless I think the Vice Presidency the better road to the future, as well as the safer one.

Always yours, H. C. LODGE.

STATE OF NEW YORK.
EXECUTIVE CHAMBER
ALBANY

January 30th, 1900.

Senator H. C. Lodge, Washington, D. C.

Dear Cabot: I have just received your letter and it has given me much food for thought. I shall have to see Senator Platt before I can say anything. There is an amusing, new complication in the fact that Woodruff* may have already gotten all the delegates from New York, so that Platt cannot get them away from him, in which case Platt will certainly not want me to stand. Moreover, if Woodruff is to be the Governor, that may again cause a grave question whether I ought to stand, as it is by no means certain that he could carry the State. Woodruff is a most good humored, friendly fellow, wild to have me nominate him for Vice President, which I suppose for my sins I might have to do (not if *I* can help it), and he is amusingly and absolutely certain that nothing can prevent his nomination. He is a great worker, and he has had rather a remarkable success in getting nominations and handling the machine here, and he is absolutely confident that he can get the Vice Presidency. He had a long and frank talk with me the other day, though I told him I could not speak as frankly in return. He explained that he did not want the Governorship; that he had seen Black cut his own throat from ear to ear, and seen me keep the machine from cutting its throat (and mine too) by main force, and at the constant peril of a break which would have been just as fatal and which could only be averted by the incessant exercise of resolution and sleepless judgment; and that he did not want the Governorship, while he did very much want the Vice Presi-

* Hon. Timothy Woodruff.

dency, chiefly because he had plenty of money and could entertain, and he knew he could act as Presiding Officer of the Senate. The money question is a serious one with me. As you know, my means are very moderate, and as my children have grown up and their education has become more and more a matter of pressing importance, I have felt a very keen regret that I did not have some money making occupation, for I am never certain when it may be necessary for me to try to sell Sagamore and completely alter my whole style of life. As Governor, I am comparatively well paid, having not only a salary but a house which is practically kept up during the winter, and thanks to the fact that the idiots of the magazines now wish to pay me very large prices for writing, on account of my temporary notoriety, I was enabled to save handsomely last year and will be enabled to do so again this year. But great pressure would come upon me if I went in as Vice President. I could only live simply. Of course, I could not begin to entertain as Morton and Hobart have; and even to live simply as a Vice President would have to live would be a serious drain upon me, and would cause me continual anxiety about money. If the place held out a chance of doing really good work, I should not mind this, for I must try to carry out my scheme of life, and as I am not to leave the children money, I am in honor bound to leave them a record of honorable achievement; but of course the chance for a Vice President to do much of anything is infinitesimal. I suppose I should have leisure to take up my historical work again, but that is about all. If the Vice Presidency led to the Governor Generalship of the Philippines, then the question would be entirely altered, but I have a very uncomfortable feeling that there will be a strong although entirely unreasonable feeling against my resigning. Of course, there should not be, as the succession is arranged in the Secretaryship of State.

I am extremely pleased at the conversation you report with the President. President Schurman had spoken to me about his intention to speak to the President concerning the Governor Generalship, but I had not thought over the matter one way or the other in connection with him and had not the slightest idea whether he had carried out his intention. It is quite needless to say that I absolutely agree with the theory that until the war is over, we want to have the military authority not merely supreme but alone. It would never do to have a divided authority, and it would not be worth while for a really good man to go out there with divided authority. In public life it seems to me the blue ribbon part is of very small value. The point is to get hold of some job really worth doing and then to do it well. The Governor Generalship of the Philippines, especially the first Generalship, would be exactly such a piece of work. I should approach it with a very serious sense, not only of its importance, but of its difficulty; but as far as I can see among those who are likely to be considered as candidates, I would be quite as apt to do well as any.

As soon as I can I will see Senator Platt and then will let you know.

It would be idle for me to thank you, old man. As I have said before, if I began to thank you I should have to take up so much time that there would be very little time left for anything else. You are the only man whom, in all my life, I have met who has repeatedly and in every way done for me what I could not do for myself, and what nobody else could do, and done it in a way that merely makes me glad to be under the obligation to you. I have never been able to do, and never shall be able to do, anything in return, I suppose; but that is part of the irony of life in this world.

I am glad you like the canal report. I came to the conclusion that the position had to be taken boldly. I doubt if anything comes of it at the moment; but it will ultimately.

As for the Payne matter, seemingly I have won out; by dint of combining inflexible determination with extreme good nature, and resolutely refusing the advice of Godkin, Parkhurst and of the various small-fry Chapmans, Villards, etc., who wanted me to quarrel with the machine, in which case I should have had about six votes out of fifty in the Senate. Of course, these gentlemen are not only unwise but dishonest. Their opponents are too fond of calling them impracticable and omitting their dishonesty. Heaven knows they *are* impracticable; but they are also eaten up by vanity, hypocrisy, mendacity and

mean envy. In fact, they combine with great nicety the qualities of the knave and the qualities of the fool.

How I have gone over them! Whatever comes hereafter it
is a great pleasure to feel how I have trodden them down.

And on the other hand, I have made the machine act with
absolute decency and have never yielded one hair's breadth to
it on a question of morality or principle. I can say quite conscientiously that during my term the Governorship of New
York has been managed on as high a plane as the Governorship
of Massachusetts!

What a terrible time the English are having! There is no
question that the Boers outfight them. I am heartily ashamed
of Mason, Hale and the other men of their stamp who show the
particularly mean attribute of jumping on England when she is
down. But of course those who have been entirely against their
own nation cannot be expected to have any sense of propriety
in dealing with another nation which was friendly during the
war with Spain.

With best love to Nannie.

Ever yours,

THEODORE ROOSEVELT.

UNITED STATES SENATE
WASHINGTON, D. C.

Private and Confidential.

Dear Theodore: Feb. 2, 1900.

I have your letter of the 29th. I had a long talk with Senator
Platt yesterday about you, and also talked with President
Schurman. Platt is going to see you Saturday morning and
talk with you further in regard to it. If it was a question of
your taking the Vice Presidency for itself I should beg you most
earnestly not to do it. My belief in your taking it arises from
my conviction that it is the true stepping stone for you either
toward the Presidency or the Governor Generalship of the Philippines. I think it is the best road to the former, but the Presi-

dency is always uncertain. I believe it is to be an almost absolutely sure step to the latter, and when I expressed my views to Schurman he saw at once the force of my position. Unless we fail at the next election—of which I see no serious danger as yet—a Governor General will be appointed to the Philippines under an act of Congress, but that is not likely to come to pass inside of two years, and probably not until somewhat later. If you are on the ground you will have the right to say that that is the position you want and it could not be refused to the Vice President, and with the existing law as to the succession to the Presidency there is no good reason why the Vice President should not resign if there was a sufficiently strong reason for his doing so. In this case that reason would exist, and it would be clear to everybody that nothing would so impress the Asiatic mind, and nothing would so satisfy this country, as sending you the second officer of the government to be the first Governor General of our new possessions. It would give the office the importance which it deserves, and would then always remain, and would impress the inhabitants of the Philippines as nothing else could do. On this point I feel very confident, although, of course, no man can read the future. I understand your objections perfectly to the place [the Vice-Presidency]. I see the importance of the question of money, but you must remember that if Morton and Hobart lived in a certain way, Stevenson lived in three rooms at a hotel, and there is a reasonable medium which you could follow with perfect dignity and propriety without going beyond your income. The Vice President, as you know, has eight thousand a year, and I certainly should be the last to suggest to you ever overrunning your income, and I see no necessity for it if you took the place. There can be no question about the President's intention for he stated it not only to me but to Schurman, and Schurman has promised to press it upon him again so as to have it all very clear.

Now you know the whole of my views in regard to it. I honestly think the trend of events is such as to make it almost impossible to decline the Vice Presidency. As for Woodruff having the delegates, the day you say you will be a candidate, with the support and approval of Mr. Platt, Woodruff could not get a delegate in the State. If New York offers Woodruff as the Vice President the Vice Presidency will go elsewhere, and New York does not want to lose it, and if I am not much mistaken they will insist on your taking it.

As for what I do for you, you know very well I do it because it is one of the greatest pleasures and interests in my life.

You have won very handsomely in the Payne matter, and have held the organization together while you did it, which is no small feat, but how many times can you be sure of repeating it? As Mr. Platt said yesterday you have no enemies now who would interfere with your great strength as a Vice Presidential candidate at the polls in New York, but, he added, that no man can tell how long it would be before any Governor of New York would find himself surrounded by a large crop of very dangerous enemies.

I think we shall manage to keep our neutrality, and that the government will be kept from doing anything in the way of meddling in the Transvaal war. There is a very general and solid sense of the fact that however much we sympathize with the Boers the downfall of the British Empire is something which no rational American could regard as anything but a misfortune to the United States.

We had a lively morning with Pettigrew in the Senate day before yesterday. I sent you a *Record* with the debate in full. If you can get a few minutes it will amuse you to read it. Not having served in the war I could not apply to him the epithet which I think belongs to him, but I was glad to have two old soldiers like Hawley and Sewall do it. From them it came with perfect propriety, especially as Sewall has a son in the Philippines. The Philippine question is going to be the great issue of the election, which is another reason that is going to make men more and more turn to you for the second place on the ticket.

Always yours,   H. C. LODGE.

Dear Cabot:—   February 2nd, 1900.

The publication in the *Sun* has rather forced matters. I have been going over it with Edith and with one or two men here, and some hundreds of men have been going over it with me by letter and telegram, or in person. With the utmost reluctance I have come to a conclusion that is against your judgment. I know that you looking at matters from the outside have a clearer vision than I have; yet in this case I think it is obscured by your personal friendship for and belief in me and in what you regard as my future career. As you know I feel that to consider the Presidency in any way as a possibility would be foolish. American politics are kaleidoscopic, and long before the next five years are out, the kaleidoscope is certain to have been many times shaken and some new men to have turned up. The only thing for me to do is to do exactly as I have always done; and that is, when there is a chance of attempting a bit of work worth the trial, to attempt it. You got me the chance to be Civil Service Commissioner and Assistant Secretary of the Navy, and it was by your advice that I went into the police department. All three jobs were worth doing and I did them reasonably to my own satisfaction. Now the thing to decide at the moment is whether I shall try for the Governorship again, or accept the Vice Presidency, if offered. I have been pretty successful as Governor. As I wrote you, with the Payne business settled as it has been, I have got the departmental work of the State on a really high plane of execution. I have committed myself to a great policy in reference to the canals. There is ample work left for me to do in another term,—work that will need all my energy and capacity—in short, work well worth any man's doing. I understand perfectly that in New York with the Republican party shading on the one hand into corrupt politicians, and on the other hand, into a group of impracticables of the Godkin-Parkhurst type who are essentially quite as dishonest, the task of getting results is one of incredible difficulty, and the danger of being wrecked very great, and this without regard to one's own capacities. For instance, if the machine were very strong and could get the complete upper hand, they would undoubtedly like to throw me over, while the *Evening Post* style of independent always tends to be so angered at my securing good results along lines which he does not understand, that he will join Tammany to try to destroy me, as he did when I ran before. But this is simply the inevitable risk in such a State as this. It is not possible to count on a political career in New York as it is in Massachusetts, and the only thing to do is to face the fact, do good work while the chance lasts, and show good humor when, as inevitably must happen, the luck turns, and for no fault of one's own, one is thrown out. But in the Vice Presidency I could do nothing. I am a comparatively young man and I like to work. I do not like to be a figurehead. It would not entertain me to preside in the Senate. I should be in a cold shiver of rage at inability to answer hounds like Pettigrew and the scarcely more admirable Mason and Hale. I could not *do* anything; and yet I would be seeing continually things that I would like to do, and very possibly would like to do differently from the way in which they were being done. Finally the personal element comes in. Though I am a little better off than the *Sun* correspondent believes, I have not sufficient means to run the social side of the Vice Presidency as it ought to be run. I should have to live very simply, and would be always in the position of "poor man at a frolic." I would not give a snap of my fingers for this if I went into the Cabinet or as a Senator, or was doing a real bit of work; but I should want to consider it when the office is in fact merely a show office. So, old man, I am going to declare decisively that I want to be Governor and do not want to be Vice President. Publicly I shall only say I don't want to be Vice P. Edith bids me to say that she hopes you will forgive me!

Ever yours,

THEODORE ROOSEVELT.

STATE OF NEW YORK
EXECUTIVE CHAMBER
ALBANY

Feby. 3rd, 1900.

Hon. H. C. Lodge, Senate Chamber, Washington, D. C.

Dear Cabot:—Now this letter is to be strictly secret.

I have found out one reason why Senator Platt wants me nominated for the Vice Presidency. He is, I am convinced, genuinely friendly, and indeed I think I may say really fond of me, and is personally satisfied with the way I have conducted politics; but the big monied men with whom he is in close touch and whose campaign contributions have certainly been no inconsiderable factor in his strength, have been pressing him very strongly to get me put in the Vice Presidency, so as to get me out of the State. It was the big insurance companies, possessing enormous wealth, that gave Payne his formidable strength, and they to a man want me out. The great corporations affected by the franchise tax have also been at the Senator. In fact, all the high monied interests that make campaign contributions of large size and feel that they should have favors in return, are extremely anxious to get me out of the State. I find that they have been at Platt for the last two or three months and he has finally begun to yield to them and to take their view. Outside of that the feeling here is very strong indeed against my going. In fact, all of my friends in the State would feel that I was deserting them, and are simply unable to understand my considering it. I appreciate entirely the danger of this position, but after all I suppose there is no work without an attendant risk, and it does not seem to me that I am ready to leave a real piece of work for a position in which there is not any work at all and where I really do not think there is anything for me to do and no reputation to make.

I earnestly hope the Philippine business can wait a couple of years.

Ever yours,

THEODORE ROOSEVELT.

UNITED STATES SENATE
WASHINGTON, D. C.

Personal.

My dear Theodore: Feb. 5, 1900.

I have your letters of the 2nd and 3rd, and you know me too
well to suppose that I am going to find any fault because you
have decided against my opinion. I think you are a great loss
to the ticket, and I think the Vice Presidency is the better path
to better and more important things, but of all this you must be
the final judge and you are quite as likely to be right as I am,
in fact I have great faith in your own instincts and whenever
the time comes to help you in any other direction of course I
shall take hold just the same. I wish I could think of somebody to go on the ticket which would add strength to it. I fear
our friend Woodruff will not do.

Always yours, H. C. LODGE.

STATE OF NEW YORK
EXECUTIVE CHAMBER
ALBANY

Dear Old Cabot:—   Feby. 9th, 1900.

Edith was so much touched by your letter that I must write
you just a line about it myself. Of course, I should jump at the
Senate if there was a possibility of getting there. I think that
a Senator occupies on the whole the most useful and most honorable position to be found in any civilized government, and I
should never think twice about the money in such a position as
that. But of course Senator Platt will be a candidate for re-
election and equally of course I shall support him. So the Senatorship is out of the question. As for the Vice Presidency, the
"possibilities" which your prejudiced eyes see in my career are
remote improbabilities, and I had better take the position, if
offered, which gives the chance to do immediate work of use.

Best love to Nannie.   Ever yours,

THEODORE ROOSEVELT.

STATE OF NEW YORK
EXECUTIVE CHAMBER
ALBANY

March 8th, 1900.

Dear Cabot:

Even before speaking of your great Philippine address, I must tell you how moved I was by what you wrote of your dear mother; the tears came to my eyes; you know we both loved her dearly, and she loved us because she knew next to herself and Nannie you had no people in the world who cared for you quite as we do.

As for your speech, I hardly know how to say what I feel about it lest I should seem to speak in strained terms. It is not only the greatest speech you have made, and by far the greatest speech made on the subject by anyone; it is also, I honestly believe, one of the really great speeches of our history; a speech that will rank with the speeches of the great leaders on the great topics and at the great crises; as when Fisher Ames spoke on the Jay Treaty or when Webster expounded the Constitution as it had grown to be.

I long to see you, and I look forward eagerly to my visit to Washington in May.

Yours ever,   T. R.

STATE OF NEW YORK
EXECUTIVE CHAMBER
ALBANY

March 12th, 1900.

Hon. H. C. Lodge, Senate Chamber, Washington, D. C.

Dear Cabot:—As soon as I had read the first sentences of your speech I realized that you had made your great hit. I am delighted at it.

I am having ugly times here at present. Among all my woes the most vivid at the moment is the Ramapo water job. This was sneaked through a few years ago by a combination of Republicans who controlled the legislature and Democrats who controlled the city government. We ought to draw its fangs at this session of the legislature; but for the first time this year I have seen what the papers so often talk about;

that is, the alliance between the Republican and Democratic machine leaders for personal and pecuniary objects. Some of Mr. Croker's lieutenants and possibly Mr. Croker, and some of those who have the ear of Senator Platt and are in the inner ring of the Republican machine, are pecuniarily interested in the defeat of any anti-Ramapo legislation. They have tried to influence me in every way. They want to try that perfectly cheap trick of making believe to do something, and not doing it; that is, they propose to pass the bill (which is and ought to be permissive in form) and put its execution in the hands of those who they know favor Ramapo. Comptroller Coler* is the only man surely against it and they want to cut him out of the bill; and they try to influence me by saying that he may be my successful opponent for the Governorship on the Democratic ticket if I now build him up. Very possibly they are right about this, but it is just one of those cases where we cannot afford to take such a possibility into account; and as a matter of fact, they are now building him up in the most effective fashion by convincing the people at large that both machines are down on him because he is for the people's interest. I am taking measures to see that he is left in. They also want to pass the bill so late that the Mayor can veto it after the legislature has adjourned, and thereby to shift the responsibility on him. As a matter of fact, whatever they do as a sham will be recognized as such and will hurt them accordingly. But with their queer shortsightedness in great matters like this, they fail to understand the interest of the people. There has been an effort made to prevent my becoming active in the matter by holding up my Forest, Fish & Game Commission, which I have headed with Austin Wadsworth. However, I of course cannot afford to have my Commission confirmed on any such terms. Heavens, how thankful I shall be when the session of the legislature is over; and still more thankful when sometime early in May I get down to see you!

Warm love to Nannie. Ever yours,

THEODORE ROOSEVELT.

* Bird Coler.

UNITED STATES SENATE
WASHINGTON, D. C.

Personal.

March 14, 1900.

Dear Theodore :—

Thanks for your letter of the 12th. It is a very kind and great compliment to me to think that you have such a high opinion of my speech. It seems to have produced a real impression.

I see all the difficulties of that Ramapo water job. It must be a most trying situation. Of course your Forest and Game Commission, good as it is, is wholly secondary to such a question as that, and I do not see that you have any choice except to do what you are doing, stand up as hard as you can against it. I should think you *would* want the Legislature to adjourn.

We are in the throes of a desperate struggle over the Puerto Rican bill. Some Western newspapers have undertaken to bully Congress from wise and proper legislation, and it looks very much as if they would succeed, for they have stampeded a certain number of Senators. The position is a trying one, but I keep on hoping that we shall work it out all right.

Always yours,   H. C. LODGE.

STATE OF NEW YORK
EXECUTIVE CHAMBER
ALBANY

March 14th, 1900.

Dear Cabot :—

You and Davis did yourselves proud on the Nicaragua Canal treaty. Give that good Minnesota gentleman my love. You probably saw that I took some interest in the treaty in its original form.

Just at the moment I seem to have things rather my way here. I finally got the organization all straight on the Ramapo business, but it took blood to do it, and of course, I have some of the extremely irreconcilable fellows on the other side to reckon with yet.

I have heard two or three times from Edith, but she has not reached Havana yet. Meanwhile I am combining the functions of a statesman with those of a mother in Israel.

Ever yours,
THEODORE ROOSEVELT.

STATE OF NEW YORK
EXECUTIVE CHAMBER
ALBANY

Dear Cabot :—   March 16th, 1900.

I send you herewith a letter from Rev. Dr. Lyman Abbott. On this Porto Rico question I am bound to say that the chief sentiment seems to be much the way Dr. Abbott puts it. I have not answered him because I shall keep out of the matter until I know more about it; and not give in then unless you say so!

Ever yours,
THEODORE ROOSEVELT.

UNITED STATES SENATE
WASHINGTON, D. C.

Personal.

My dear Theodore :—   March 19, 1900.

I understand the feeling about Puerto Rico, but I think it is largely sentimental and not based upon facts. I send you a copy of a letter I wrote to a constituent of mine in Massachusetts which will give you what I have to say in regard to it. I hope we shall find some solution of it here. My impression is that when the bill is passed all the excitement will die out. At the same time there is much excitement now, and if I were you I would not get into it or say anything about it. There is no reason that you should, and there is a great deal of feeling on both sides.

Ever yours,   H. C. LODGE.

STATE OF NEW YORK
EXECUTIVE CHAMBER
ALBANY

April 9th, 1900.

Dear Cabot :—

I shall be down to spend two or three days with Anna the 9th of May. Then I shall be able to go over everything with you at length. It looks to me as though you had come out of the Porto Rico business all right. The naval business is splendid.

What a perfectly extraordinary affair this Dewey outburst is! As regards the man himself, while it does not diminish my regard for him because of what he has done in the past, it cannot help but alter my views of him now. Upon my word, I think Bryan would be preferable to a man who in his desire for the presidency says he will take the nomination from any party; that he does not care what the policies of any party are; and that he has no principles which he desires to enunciate. Of course among right thinking people there can be but one verdict upon it, and I cannot help but believe that he will be laughed out of court. Still the unthinking may under the glamor of his naval glory support him, and the educated jacks who especially delight to call themselves "thinkers" here in the East are actually coming out in his favor, because they hate the republican party and do not want to go back to Bryan. What a crew they are! Of course just such a thing was done in '48 and though Taylor turned out admirably and moreover never, like Dewey, made a fool of himself, yet the way the nomination was made, and the reasons, were absurd.

Well, the second legislative session is through. I do not know whether you saw a little *résumé* I put forth about its work. I have succeeded beyond my expectations in this office. The party is stronger because of my administration. Everything has been as clean as a hound's tooth, as I said it should be. The business of the State is managed with entire honesty and entire efficiency. During the two sessions of the legislature not a bad bill has become a law, and very many excellent measures, some of them of most far reaching importance, have been put upon the statute books.

As for my own future, it is by no means clear. I still feel very strongly that there would be nothing in the Vice Presidency for me. The McKinley men in the West rather want me to take it because they think I would help McKinley; and the machine men, and above all, the big corporation men of the William C. Whitney, Thomas Ryan, Anthony N. Brady and C. P. Huntington stripe are especially anxious to have me gotten out of New York somehow. In default of any other way, they would like to kick me upstairs. Lou Payne of course is an influential man, a past master in wire pulling, and he will be a center around which all the disaffected will rally; and then I have had to go against the feeling of the communities where I get the effective bulk of my support by advocating the canal bill. This bill is of vital consequence to New York's future, and it represents a policy in which two-thirds of New Yorkers believe, but the remaining one-third consists of Republicans from the strong Republican counties away from the big cities. The people of the big cities are for it, but they are mostly against me anyhow. The honest voters of the country districts which do not border on the canal are against it, and they are my supporters alike at the primaries and at the polls. Senator Platt was as active as I was in getting the measure through; but of course, I am in office and I am the man with whom they will feel discontented—(not that the measure is really through, but merely a provision for a survey). This may have a bad effect upon me, although of course it may not. I think every one is satisfied, or at least everyone outside of the *Tribune* office and the lunatic mugwump circles, that I have made everything possible out of this position and the average farmer, and the plain man in the ranks of the Republican party generally has absolute confidence in my honesty, and knows that I am really trying to represent the people and to do what is best for them. This gives me a great strength and renders it unlikely that the Machine will turn me down; and still the Machine probably could if it wished to; and it might wish to, unless it thought that the election would be so close that I could not with safety be thrown overboard; because undoubtedly so to throw me

over would cost tens of thousands of votes. On the other
hand, the anti-expansionist and lunatic goo-goo crowds hate
me with an entire and perfect hatred, and will do all they can
to beat me at the polls. So that my future is anything but clear.
However, I really care astonishingly little. The great thing
has been to succeed these two years, and that I can really say
I have done. I have had a first class·run for my money. I
have given an efficient, upright administration, and have put
public affairs on a higher plane than I have ever before seen
them in this State; and I have done everything that one man
could do towards lifting the party up and putting it in proper
shape.

Excuse this long letter about my own small parochial affairs,
but I wanted you to know the whole business.

With love to Nannie.   Ever yours,

THEODORE ROOSEVELT.

UNITED STATES SENATE
WASHINGTON, D. C.

Personal.

Dear Theodore: April 11, 1900.

Thanks for your letter of the 9th. I think we have come
through the Puerto Rican matter very well. The naval business is all right if we can hold the proper price for armor in
the Senate.

The Dewey business is simply sad to me and pitiful. I do
not think he has the remotest chance of being nominated for
the Presidency, but perhaps he will fall and take the Vice
Presidency with Bryan. It is too bad to see a man who has
really done a great thing coming down to that.

I read your little summary with care, and I thought you
made a very good showing indeed. I have been intending to
chaff you when I saw you about your saying the Senate had
behaved splendidly by confirming all your nominations, but
when I think of my own sinful record in voting against Presi-

dential nominations in the Senate I came to the conclusion I would say nothing, except that if they did confirm all your nominations it is much in their favor. All that has been done seems to be good. There are other things, I know, you would like to do, but we have all learned to be patient.

I have not changed in the least as to the Vice Presidency. On the contrary I see so many possible dangers in New York that I should like more than ever to get you out of those troubled waters with a view to your future, but I am not going to say anything more to you, for you know what I think, and I defer entirely to your judgment which is likely to be better than mine, for you understand the Governorship and its dangers better than I do.

I doubt if you have much trouble with the Canal bill, and I think you will run very strong for the Governorship. The hatred of the goo-goo crowds never hurt anybody yet and is not going to hurt you. After all is said and done you have accomplished some great work, and that is the main thing, although my thoughts go more to your future than to your past just now.

It will be a perfect delight to see you on the 9th.

With best regards,

Always yours, H. C. LODGE.

UNITED STATES SENATE
WASHINGTON, D. C.

Personal.

Dear Theodore :   April 16, 1900.

I have your letter of the 13th and the one from Root, which I have read with interest. I had a talk with the President the other day in which he said that he had talked with you in New York and much as he should like to have you on the ticket he had been convinced by what you said and that he was inclined to think that your running for Governor might help the ticket more than in any other way. He was very nice about the whole thing. If you go to that Convention, however, as a delegate, as I see stated in the newspapers, you will be nominated, as the situation looks today, and if you are nominated in that Convention you will be unable to refuse. The party will take the ground that they have done a great deal for you and always stood behind you, and that now that they want a service of you you must give it. If you persist in refusing in the presence of the Convention which nominates you I am very much afraid it will hurt in future, and there are lots of good men who are strongly for you now who will not like it. I have been worrying about this ever since I saw that you were to go as a delegate. If some candidate for the Vice-Presidency should be absolutely decided upon before the Convention meets then it will be all right for you to go, but of this I see no prospect. We shall go there, I think, unsettled as to the candidate for the Vice-Presidency, and if you are present they will nominate you and nothing can stop it, and in my judgment you will be forced to accept. If you stay away with your absolute declination, which you have already put out, I do not think you will be nominated. Root is not right about the leading men of the party here. That may be the case of the two or three members of the Cabinet, but the general feeling is that you are the one man for the Vice-Presidency among those who are looking solely for the interests of the party at large.

Think this thing over, for I assure you there is great danger in it and as you have made up your mind to stick to the Governorship I want you to carry out your own plans, which may very well be much better than I thought possible originally. We shall have time, however, to talk this over when you come on.

I know of course that it is too late for you not to be chosen a delegate, but it will be easy enough for you to find at the last moment that you cannot go to the Convention and let an alternate take your place. Always yours, H. C. LODGE.

STATE OF NEW YORK
EXECUTIVE CHAMBER
ALBANY

April 17, 1900.

Hon. H. C. Lodge, U. S. Senate, Washington, D. C.

Dear Cabot:—It has been already suggested to me that I ought not to go to the convention, but I believe that I would be looked upon as rather a coward if I didn't go. I think we can have the Vice-President matter all fixed up in advance.

Meanwhile, we have a possible riot at Croton Dam where the riotous Italians have begun by assassinating one of the National Guard. As a matter of fact, I think that one of the contractors decidedly oppressed the employees, but of course now that the latter have taken to violence we have got to put them down and shall do it at any cost, and the result may be that I won't be desired as the Vice-Presidential candidate in June. However, I will see you in May and we will go over everything.

I am having a horrid time with my thirty-day bills. I don't mind those that are all bad or those that are all good, but there is a large intermediate class which offer great difficulties.

Always yours,

THEODORE ROOSEVELT.

UNITED STATES SENATE
WASHINGTON, D. C.

Personal.

Dear Theodore:

April 19, 1900.

I have received your letter of the 17th. I cannot conceive of anybody thinking you a coward in not going to the Convention. If the Vice-Presidency is fixed beforehand of course all would be well. I wrote you as I did because I think it would be very likely to turn out in the way I mentioned, and I did not want you to think that with my views I was encouraging you to get into a position where you would be forced to take the Vice-Presidency.

I can imagine how annoying your trouble with the bills must be.

I am looking forward to seeing you in May when we can talk everything over.

Always yours, H. C. LODGE.

STATE OF NEW YORK
EXECUTIVE CHAMBER
ALBANY

April 23d, 1900.

Dear Cabot:—

I send you the inclosed as a sample of the literally hundreds of letters that I am receiving. All my friends in the West seem to be hostile to my taking the Vice-Presidential nomination.

By the way, I did *not* say that I would not under any circumstances accept the Vice-Presidency. I have been careful to put it exactly as you advised.

Always yours,

THEODORE ROOSEVELT

P. S.—Since writing the above the letter from Proctor came which I also send to you. I find also that Silas Wright refused the nomination of Vice-President on the ticket with Polk after he had been nominated, came back and ran for Governor and was elected by a larger majority than that by which Polk carried the State.

I think that one feature of the present situation is overlooked, viz.: that if I am now nominated for Vice-President, it will be impossible to get it out of the heads of a number of people that the machine had forced me into it for their own sinister purpose and that I had yielded from weakness, as they know I do not want the position of Vice-President.

UNITED STATES SENATE
WASHINGTON, D. C.

Personal.

April 25, 1900.

My dear Theodore:

I have your letter of the 23rd. The western people here, so far as I can see, all want you to take the nomination. I am not going to try to advise you in any way, as you know, but I am still of the opinion that if you go to the Convention you will be nominated. I am equally of the opinion that if you should refuse the nomination when the party made such a claim upon you it would hurt your future prospects nationally. The point made that people will think you have been pushed into the Vice-Presidency by the machine in New York is, if you will pardon my saying so, very local. How widely this idea is spread in the State itself I do not know; but it certainly does not exist outside of the State. Proctor may be quite right in his opinion. I do not set up to be a prophet as to the future but I only attempt to exercise my best judgment. It is to be remembered moreover, that Proctor is out of the Administration and it seems to me from the two letters you send me as if you were being advised by persons hostile to McKinley, who were not over anxious to see the ticket strengthened or to see a man on it whom they are bound to support enthusiastically. I may be wrong about this, but the tone of the Indiana letter seems to me to point very much that way.

I think that by absolutely declining and remaining away from the Convention you might escape the nomination, but even that is doubtful. At any rate you would be in a position to refuse it, but if you go to the Convention I cannot change my mind as to the effect a refusal there would have on your fortunes.

I have forgotten the incident of Silas Wright but let me call your attention to the fact that he was never President, whereas Van Buren was.

Always yours,

H. C. LODGE.

UNITED STATES SENATE
WASHINGTON, D. C.

Confidential.

Dear Theodore :   June 5, 1900.

I am always good at volunteering advice and as you know my habit you won't mind. This Ice Trust is a piece of very great political luck for us in view of the attack that is constantly made on us as the party of trusts. I think its political importance can hardly be over-estimated. Now my suggestion can be put in a word. Be very cautious about what you do in regard to Van Wyck. Do not run any risk of converting a knave into a martyr. You know the situation better than I do but I could not resist sending you this word of anxiety. The Ice Trust will not only play a part in the campaign throughout the country but I have a strong impression that it will form the only great issue in New York. New York always prefers its own issues, and I am sure it will take a much greater interest in this than in the Philippines or the Gold Standard. It is a terrible load for the Democrats to carry both locally and nationally and we must make no mistake in dealing with it.

I saw Mr. Youngs yesterday and you may feel perfectly at ease on that matter. He has told you before this what Hanna and I said.

I wish you could have heard Carter this morning dress Pettigrew down. It was really a very handsome piece of rough invective.

We are squeezing things through tonight, and I hope we shall adjourn tomorrow.

Always yours,   H. C. Lodge.

STATE OF NEW YORK
EXECUTIVE CHAMBER
ALBANY

Dear Cabot :—   June 9th, 1900.

I have just received your letter of the 5th on my return from Concord and Groton. You have exactly my view of the matter. The ice trust is a Heaven sent piece of business for us. Our people have short memories, and ice is not of much account in November, but I cannot help thinking that this will count seriously, and it takes the pith right out of them on the one great issue which they thought they had. But haste and over-severity on my part may undo all the good effects. It is not an easy situation, because failure to act may look as if I were condoning their wickedness. Still I think I shall be able to steer through it. I have had awful times myself recently. Senator Platt is not in a pleasant frame of mind with me, chiefly because of the franchise tax. He told me last night that he thought it would lose me so many votes as to jeopardize my election. I told him that it would not lose me anywhere near the number of votes we would lose on account of the appointment of Hazel,* and that if the corporations began to ride ugly that I should give them the roughest handling that they had yet had. I had said incidentally that while they undoubtedly had great influence in conventions and could affect my renomination that I did not think they could affect my election at all.

By the way, will you look at the last *Century* where I have an article on Latitude and Longitude in Reform and see if you do not think it represents about the ideas upon which you and I have acted.

Ever yours,

THEODORE ROOSEVELT.

WESTERN UNION TELEGRAPH COMPANY

HINGHAM, MASS., June 20, 1900.

Hon. Henry Cabot Lodge, Hotel Stratford, Philadelphia.

Referring to Plunkett telephone, the Convention is evidently for Roosevelt and that I wire you cordially approve withholding my name and uniting on him if Massachusetts delegation approve. Unreservedly concur in any action the Massachusetts delegation think best.

JOHN D. LONG.†

* John R. Hazel had just been appointed U. S. Judge, Western District of New York. It was he who administered the oath of office to President Roosevelt at Buffalo after the death of President McKinley.

† He was strongly suggested for Vice-President by Administration forces.

STATE OF NEW YORK
EXECUTIVE CHAMBER
ALBANY

At Oyster Bay,

Hon. Henry Cabot Lodge, Nahant, Mass.   June 25, 1900.

Dear Cabot: The enclosed explains itself. I think from every standpoint that the appointment of Daly will be a master stroke. I know the little fellow and he is a corker. I should be only too glad to have him as an officer under me.

Well, old man, I am completely reconciled and I believe it all for the best as regards my own personal interests and it is a great load of personal anxiety off me. Instead of having to fight single-handed against the trusts and corporations I now must take pot luck with the whole ticket and my anxiety on behalf of the nation is so great that I can say with all honesty there is none left. As regards my own personal election on one thing you may rest assured, I am most deeply sensible of the honor conferred upon me by the way the nomination came. I shall do my best to deserve it and not to disappoint those who trusted me and think well of me. I should be a conceited fool if I was discontented with the nomination when it came in such a fashion, and according to my lights I shall endeavor to act not only fearlessly and with integrity but with good judgment. Edith is becoming somewhat reconciled.

Nannie's letter was just dear. Give her my warm love and say to her I do wish she could have seen my hour of triumph.

As for you, old trump, I shall never forget how, as I mounted the platform, you met me with a face of almost agonized anxiety and put your head down on the table as I began to speak, and, as I turned for a glass of water in the middle of the speech, you whispered with a face of delight that I was doing splendidly. It certainly is odd to look back sixteen years when you and I sat in the Blaine convention on the beaten side while the mugwumps foretold our utter ruin, and then in this convention, over which you presided to think how you recognized me to second McKinley's nomination and afterwards declared* me myself nominated in the second place on the ticket.

Give my love to Bay and John.

Faithfully yours,   THEODORE ROOSEVELT.

* I was permanent chairman of the Convention.

Confidential.   NAHANT, MASS.,
                                                     June 29, 1900.
Dear Theodore :—

I have read your letter of June 25th, and I do not suppose
that you will read this answer until you return from the West,
but I want you to read it over as there are many things I want
to say to you.

Mr. Hoar and myself are so overwhelmed with applications
for our West Point appointment that we have decided to have
a competitive examination. There seemed no other fair way
to settle it. There has been a tremendous pressure put on for
Daly, but there are other excellent candidates, among them a
young fellow from the Western part of the State who was in
the fight at El Caney, and for whom I cannot help feeling a
great deal of interest. A competitive examination is, on the
whole, the fairest way.

I want you to make one speech in Boston during this campaign, sometime in October if possible, and I want you in
making your arrangements to count this in. It will be a personal favor to me to have you do it, and the State is counting
on you. It will be the great meeting of our campaign here.
You name your own day and we will make everything conform
to it.

Another thing that I should like very much to have you do
if you can. You are going to make several tours in the West
and elsewhere. Curtis Guild would like very much to go with
you on one or more of these trips, and I suppose, of course,
you will have to have one or more assistants in speaking. You
could not get a better man. He served through the war, and
although he was not fortunate enough to be at Santiago his
record both in the United States and in Cuba was most excellent and really distinguished. He is an admirable speaker, as
you know, fit for any occasion or any audience. He is a charming companion and the kind of man you would like to have
with you. He was beaten last year for Lieutenant-Governor.
Things have gone rather wrong with him, and it would be an
immense pleasure to him if you would take him with you.
I have no doubt you can arrange it, and I am sure you will if
it is possible.

I have got to go out to Canton with my committee to notify the President of his nomination on July 12th, the same day on which Wolcott notifies you. This is a cheerful little journey to take in the middle of July, but if all goes well I mean to pay myself for it by running down to New York on my way home and passing the night at Oyster Bay with you. I shall arrange, if it is humanly possible, to leave Cleveland the night of the 12th, and that will bring me to New York sometime during the 13th, so that I can come to Oyster Bay that afternoon. We could then talk over many things.

Meantime there are some few things which I want to say now. As you well know I have never had the slightest doubt that for your future the Vice Presidency was the best thing but I loyally submitted to your decision last winter. Now it has come, and in a manner which was perfectly irresistible. Any man might be proud to take that great nomination coming as it did from the heart of the convention. I am sure it is for the best, although I do not pretend to say that the office in itself is suited to you and to your habits, but for the future it is, in my judgment, invaluable. It takes you out of the cut-throat politics of New York, where I am sure they would have destroyed your prospects, if you had remained two years longer, and it gives you a position in the eyes of the country second only to that of the President. All my views are fixed upon the future, and it is in regard to that that I want you to be very careful. You probably realize all I am about to say just as well as I do, but still there is no harm in my saying it. The President, being the President, can take but a slight part in the campaign. It would not be becoming or possible for him to make speeches as he did in 1896. You will, therefore, be the central figure of the active campaign. Our enemies are going to make this a feature of their attack. I enclose a cartoon from the Boston *Herald*—one of the meanest of our foes—which shows what I mean, and there have been dozens of others like it. Now we know that there is no foundation for such a thing as this, but nothing finds lodgment in the human mind so easily as jealousy. We must not permit the President, or any of his friends, who are, of course, in control of the campaign, to imagine that we want to absorb the leadership and the glory. I want you to appear everywhere as the champion of the party, and above all as the champion of the President. That is, on every occasion I want you to appear, as you did at the Convention, simply as a leading advocate for McKinley and to make this clear in everything you say. Fortunately his policies on the great questions are our policies. He is doing admirably so far as I can see in all directions, and especially in the difficulties in China, and I am anxious that your advocacy of him should appear in everything you say. My purpose in this is to secure by every righteous means the confidence and support for you of the President and of all his large following. This is going to be of immense importance to us four years hence, and that is why I desire that you should appear, not only during the campaign but after the election, as the President's next friend, just as Hobart was. There is today no one who could stand against you for a moment for the nomination for the Presidency, but no one can tell what will happen in four years. I believe myself that by judicious conduct we can have it just as surely within our grasp four years hence as it would be today, but we should make no mistakes.

This is a long lecture, but I have had it on my mind to say ever since the Convention, because my thoughts are running so steadily to your future.

I have thought a great many times of the dramatic meaning of my declaring you the nominee for Vice President. It is one of the things that it is very pleasant to think about, although I doubt if anyone but you and I thought of it, which, perhaps, makes it all the pleasanter.

I am surprised at the manner in which you noticed my expression when you took the platform. I was so anxious that I bowed my head over the table when you began, and I did not know that you saw it. It was all right, however, for you never spoke better in your life, and what you said could not have been improved.

I do not want you to become too vain, and so I enclose herewith a view taken of you by William Lloyd Garrison and

Edward Atkinson. I should also like to call your attention to the fact that the Springfield *Republican* said the day after the nomination, "that the Republican party was now given over to the corrupt materialism of Hanna, the cynical political ethics of Lodge, and the swashbuckler fervor of Roosevelt," so there we are, all three in a bunch.

I see that the Anti-Imperialists are going to have a great meeting in New York and perhaps start a new ticket. They are vocal, but I do not think they have many votes.

Give my best love to Edith. I am sure that she will soon come to see that it is all for the best.

Always yours, H. C. LODGE.

Personal.   NAHANT, MASS.,
                                            July 5, 1900.
Dear Theodore :—

I enclose a letter from George Lawrence, the Congressman from our Western District, who is one of the best fellows in the world, and also my answer. If you could arrange on any off day to slip over from Albany to North Adams you would have a great meeting and do a great deal of good. I should love to have you do it and should come up there and speak with you any day you could come, but of course my one special request is to have you for the meeting in Boston. I could not give up Boston for North Adams, and I do not like to ask you to do too much. Think it over, however, and do the best you can.

Always yours, H. C. LODGE.

Personal.   NAHANT, MASS.,
                                            Aug. 2, 1900.
Dear Theodore :—

Do not forget your promise to me to make one speech in Boston. It is very important to us to have that one meeting, and I want you to bear it in mind when making your arrangements. I suppose, of course, that it will be when you return from the West, and the sooner you can fix the date the better.

I am glad to see that you are taking a comparative rest. I

have just returned from Tuckanuck where I have been resting absolutely for two weeks and which did me a great deal of good.

I have just read in the Boston *Herald* a long interview with Godkin, which you will probably see. It is quite astonishing the way in which you and I seem to weigh on his mind. He is unable to leave us out of anything and his agony of impotent hatred is pleasant to witness. It is very fitting that he should support Bryan.

Give our best love to Edith.

Always yours, H. C. LODGE.

OYSTER BAY,
August 3, 1900.

Hon. Henry Cabot Lodge, Nahant, Mass.

Dear Cabot: Won't you write at once to Hanna? It is going to be a matter of very great difficulty to get them to let me get back from the West in time to make the Boston speech. Their primary plan absolutely ruled out any speeches in New York, not bringing me back until the 30th of October, and then to do this they had to rule out the Pacific slope. I have had a disagreeable time with Proctor. He has been insistent that I should speak in Vermont. Manley also insistent that I should speak in Maine, but he was entirely considerate whereas Proctor was not. I am getting a little rest, but very little, for I have some work every day and my throat is still in bad shape, so that I look forward to my two months campaign with anything but pleasure. Won't you wire Hanna as well as write him.

Always yours,
THEODORE ROOSEVELT.

Personal.

NAHANT, MASS.,
Aug. 6, 1900.

Dear Theodore :—

I have your letter of the 3rd, and will, of course, write to Hanna, but I suppose he will absolutely refuse to let you come to Massachusetts as our State is so safe. It will be a terrible disappointment to them here, where I told them you had promised me you would come; still I will do the best I can with Hanna and you must back me up. I am much more disturbed to hear that your throat is troubling you, and it is evident from the tone of your letter that you have been under a severe strain, which is as I feared. You have got a hard trip before you, and of course you must spare yourself as much as you can. I am very glad Curtis Guild is going with you, because he is not only a good speaker but he is thoroughly sympathetic and will be devoted to you and do everything he can to help you and relieve you. I saw him yesterday and he is perfectly delighted that it is all arranged for him to go with you on your trip. You must help me all you can to get Hanna to give me a date, but I am afraid it is going to be rather a close fit if you do not get back until the 30th.

Give my love to Edith.

Always yours,   H. C. Lodge.

OYSTER BAY,
August 7, 1900.

Hon. H. C. Lodge, Nahant, Mass.

Dear Cabot: I saw Hanna yesterday, and he was very positive about my not going to Boston. He said what is, of course, perfectly true that I could not go to one tenth of the places where my presence might be of the greatest help, and that to take forty-eight hours away to go to a perfectly sure State he regarded as not right. He and Proctor have wanted me to go to Vermont and Maine this August and I have refused on the ground, which is perfectly true, that by the most careful economy of my strength, or rather my throat, I will probably still be unable to do the work I ought to do in the doubtful states, and I surely ought not to do needless work.

Now, would it be possible to come to one of your Spring dinners instead? This time I could promise absolutely to go to any dinner you wanted me to in the Spring. As I understand it, you really don't want me in the campaign, but just to have me in Massachusetts.

It has been impossible to get any real rest. I do get half a day off continually, and row or ride, but my mail is a very

great burden, and what with my work as Governor and the
innumerable people with very bad or very good motives who
insist on seeing me, I am on the jump all the time; but I won't
mind anything if I can get through the two months and do
decent work in the campaign.

Always yours,
THEODORE ROOSEVELT.

Personal.   NAHANT, MASS.,
Dear Theodore :—   Aug. 11, 1900.

I have received your letter of Aug. 7th. I think Mr. Hanna
must have changed his mind, for I had a talk with him about
it on Thursday, the 9th, and told him that we did not want
you to come on until after your return from the West, and
then we wanted simply one night for Boston. I do not know
what they mean about 48 hours. You can leave New York at
one o'clock, get on and make your speech and be back the next
morning. Hanna said there was no reason in the world why
you should not take one of the nights out of your New York
fortnight and come to Boston. Mr. Bliss, who was with him,
said you ought to make one speech in New England. It is altogether different from Vermont and Maine, for these come before your Western trip. Mr. Hanna said distinctly if you would
name one night after you got home for Boston he would approve
it entirely, and I wish you would do so. It is perfectly true that
we are a safe State, but a good deal is expected of us and we
ought to have one big meeting before the election. You know
I would not urge you to do anything which I did not consider
of real importance, or anything which would put the least strain
upon your health, but if you are going to be able to make some
speeches in New York it is as easy to come to Boston as to
many places in your own State. As Hanna and Bliss gave it
their entire approval I hope you will arrange for a night for us
after your return.

I am sorry that you are not getting more rest, for I know
how much you have to go through.

Always yours, H. C. LODGE.

Personal.

NAHANT, MASS.,
Aug. 18, 1900.

Dear Theodore :—

Thanks for your note. I am glad you are going to show Hanna my letter, and I wish among the multiplicity of your affairs you would remember and fix the day for Boston. It is important to us to know in good season, and if you do not determine it before you go away I fear that your New York people will make a great fight on giving us even one evening, but it really is important to us here. We are going to carry the State all right, of course, in any event. That is so well known that there is great apathy, and as we have a possibility of gaining two Districts it is extremely important to rouse out the vote. Your coming would do more for us in that direction than anything else.

I start in in Maine on Wednesday. I fear we shall be disappointed in the majorities both there and in Vermont. I cannot quite make up my mind as to the right interpretation of the apathy which is very apparent. As I see it here it exists on both sides, and I am inclined to think the same is true of the country. If it means that the country has made up its mind and is going to elect McKinley as a matter of course and therefore does not care to be bothered with an exciting campaign very good, but if it means that the Republicans are over confident, or for any other reason are not going to exert themselves to get every vote out, then we may get beaten in some of the doubtful States, because the Democrats always come out better than we do. Your trip in the West will throw a good deal of light upon that. Curtis Guild is perfectly delighted at the prospect of going with you, and I do not believe you could have chosen a better companion.
Always yours, H. C. LODGE.

OYSTER BAY,
August 22, 1900.

Hon. Henry Cabot Lodge, Nahant, Mass.

Dear Cabot: First, let me congratulate you and Nannie on the marriage.* It took us completely by surprise so that our wedding present may take a little time in following.

* Marriage of my older son George Cabot Lodge to Miss Elizabeth Davis, daughter of Judge John Davis.

Now about your letter. I shall see Odell on Friday and try to get him to fix definitely when I can go to Boston. I shall have difficulty I know because the situation here in New York is not satisfactory. The apathy of which you speak is very marked here. There is not the slightest enthusiasm for Bryan but there is no enthusiasm for us and there seems to be no fear of Bryan. The wage worker is no longer interested in free silver and can not be frightened by the discussion of it.

Faithfully yours,

THEODORE ROOSEVELT.

OYSTER BAY, N. Y.,
Aug. 27th, 1900.

Hon. H. C. Lodge, Nahant, Mass.

Dear Cabot:—Odell says you shall have a night for the Boston speech. He has not yet fixed the dates of my speaking here. Will you therefore write him telling him what nights are convenient for you and arrange with him what the date shall be?

Henry Payne writes me a rather discouraging letter from the West where he says the apathy is as great as here. Odell is to be nominated for Governor, and it is unnecessary to say I shall do everything I can to help carry him through. Platt and the Machine generally have spent the last two months in making it just as difficult for me as possible to get the Republican independents to support the ticket.

With best love to Nannie.

Always yours,

THEODORE ROOSEVELT.

OYSTER BAY, N. Y.,
Aug. 28th, 1900.

Hon. H. C. Lodge, Nahant, Mass.

Dear Cabot: Bay really has a touch of genius in him, and we cannot hold genius to the lines to which we hold more commonplace people. Edith has just written Nannie to find out where to send our wedding present.

As I have just written you, Odell has cordially agreed that I make a speech in Boston, but you must write to him and keep him up to the mark so that he will not suddenly fill all my dates.

Platt and the Machine have hampered us greatly by their action, and unless there is a sweeping change in public sentiment, it will be a close, though I believe a victorious fight in this State. So far I think it is not overconfidence but downright apathy and indifference that we have to fear.

Ever yours,
THEODORE ROOSEVELT.

Personal.   NAHANT, MASS.,
                                                 Aug. 30, 1900.
Dear Theodore :—

Thank you for your notes of the 27th and 28th. I will write to Odell as you suggest. It is very important that we should have the date fixed as soon as possible because it will be the great meeting of our campaign.

Thank you for your kind words about Bay. Whatever his manner of getting married he has made a most fortunate choice, in my opinion, and I hope it will develop him.

I have noticed with surprise the things that Platt has been saying and I cannot imagine why he does it as there seems to be no purpose to serve. It looks as if he was a good deal shaken and was taking pleasure in being merely mischievous. I think very well of Odell, as you know; in fact I have always had a very high opinion of him, and under the circumstances it seems to me he is a very strong man for Governor. I had rather thought that Coler's nomination would be the best thing for us in view of the hostility of Tammany, but I am not at all sure that his defeat may not work as well. Coler would have drawn, I suppose, a certain number of Independent and uncertain Republican votes which no man picked out by Croker can do. I think his defeat will tend to solidify our party and help Odell. The apathy and indifference are hard to understand.

I have been trying to analyze them and determine on what they rest. It seems to me that the principal cause lies in the fact that people are busy and prosperous, and with the easy going temper so characteristic of Americans decline to admit to themselves or to think that there is the slightest danger of changing the conditions under which they are now doing well. The Gold Democrats here are going to vote about as they did before and any that return to Bryan will, so far as my observation goes, be replaced by men who voted for Palmer and Buckner and will now vote for McKinley. We must look for a pretty severe falling off in both Vermont and Maine. How much I cannot even guess. It may well be that the apathy arises from the fact that the people know perfectly well what they are about and are going to turn out and beat Bryan when the time comes. Upon this the Vermont and Maine elections will throw some light. I have spoken in Maine and had a very great meeting, as big as I have ever seen at Old Orchard, over 6,000 people, which seemed to me to promise well, for I am quite an old story to them and have no exceptional drawing qualities. If I were to venture a prediction it would be this: I think we shall carry in the East all that we carried before by reduced majorities. I think we shall make very large gains West of the Mississippi and in the inter-mountain states, and have very much the same fight in the Middle West that we did in '96 with much the same result. The states which I think are in danger are Indiana, Maryland and West Virginia. As I have watched the campaign I have come to the conclusion that the net result will be that we shall get as many, and probably more, electoral votes than we did before with smaller popular majorities in the East where they were perfectly abnormal in '96, which will tend to reduce the total popular majority. After it is all over we can see how bad a prophet I am.

I am to speak in New York on the 14th at the Riding Academy, and thence I go to Colorado to help Wolcott. I hope I may be there when you strike the State on your great swing around the circle.

Always yours, H. C. LODGE.

WESTERN UNION TELEGRAPH COMPANY

Dated Elgin, Ill., Oct. 6, 1900.

To Hon. H. C. Lodge, Nahant, Mass.

In view of scoundrelly statement George Fred Williams* I suggest you immediately dare him to tell all he knows stating there is not a detail of trip which cannot be given widest publicity. You might as well call the bluff.

THEODORE ROOSEVELT.

Personal.   NAHANT, MASS.,
                                                        Oct. 8, 1900.

Dear Theodore :—

I received your telegram yesterday and I hope you got my answer saying that I had denied what Williams said at once, invited him to tell anything he thought he knew, and informed him that we were not to be blackmailed into silence. I confess to an emotion of surprise that you should have thought it possible I should have allowed such a statement to go unnoticed. Williams' interview appeared in the *Evening Globe* on Friday. My reply appeared Saturday morning in the *Journal, Herald, Advertiser* and *Globe.* I send you clippings from the *Herald* and *Journal.* You will see that it was complete, and by the headlines that it was not hidden. If there is anything more that I can say let me know and I will say it, but the appearance is here that I have driven Mr. Williams into a complete retreat. I suppose the Associated Press, as usual, sent out his statement and omitted to send my denial. That appears to be the way they usually treat me.

I will send this letter to Mr. Youngs so that he can make sure of its reaching you, and when you get it if you will send me a

* I joined Roosevelt at Cheyenne and spoke with him during his trip through Colorado. After speaking constantly from the train we spoke in Denver and thoroughly worn out drove out to Senator Wolcott's place at Wolhurst where we passed the night. The next day we began at Colorado Springs, then went to Victor where we had a stormy time and were mobbed; we finished at Cripple Creek. Mr. Williams put out a story that we were drunk at Wolcott's house and apparently the next day and that this was the cause of the disorder at Victor. At Wolhurst we were a very tired company and after a simple supper went at once to bed. Mr. Williams's story was entirely false and a pure fabrication. My wife and niece were with us on the trip.

line to say whether you are satisfied or not I shall be very much obliged.

Here in the East I think everything is looking well. I do not like the reports from Indiana but otherwise I see nothing but assurances of victory.

I was disgusted to see the account of your experience after attending church in Chicago, but I am certain that these tactics, which they appear to be adopting everywhere, will only hurt them and swell our majority. You are having a terribly hard time but doing work of immense value. My thoughts are with you constantly and I am very anxious about you. Your journey and what you have said I find to have had a most excellent effect here.

With best regards,

Always yours, H. C. LODGE.

SPRING VALLEY, KY.,
Oct. 14th, 1900.
Dear Cabot:—

I have your letter of the 8th. You did exactly right. All the newspaper correspondents joined in a round robin which was published in the Chicago *Times-Herald*, and other Chicago papers of Oct. 7th. If it has not been published in Boston I would suggest getting a copy of the Chicago *Times-Herald* of Oct. 7th and having it published there. It smashes Mr. Williams in fine shape.

I think we shall carry Indiana. I have waded into brother Bryan pretty heavily and he is beginning to feel sore. What a thorough paced hypocrite and demagogue he is, and what a small man!

Ever yours,

THEODORE ROOSEVELT.

OYSTER BAY, N. Y.,
Nov. 9th, 1900.
Hon. H. C. Lodge, Boston, Mass.

Dear Cabot:—Just a line to say how glad I was to get your telegram. I have any amount to tell you about the canvass. If political conditions were normal in the South, Bryanism

would have received scarcely a score of votes in the electoral
college. Well, I am delighted to have been on the national
ticket in this great historic contest, for after McKinley and
Hanna, I feel that I did as much as any one in bringing about
the result—though after all it was Bryan himself who did most.

Do tell Nannie that I have got to give her full information
about certain of my ardent backers, the Mulhalls of Oklahoma
Territory. The members of the family whom I know are
Colonel Mulhall, his son and two daughters, one of whom is
named Miss Bossie. There are also several gentlemen friends
with sporting proclivities, occasional homicidal tastes and
immense resourcefulness in every emergency. No ordinary
novelist would venture to portray such types, because he
would regard them as hopelessly exaggerated. They have a
large and very prosperous ranch some sixty miles from Oklahoma City, and they all came in to see me at the regimental
reunion last July, together with a dozen of the Mulhall cowboys. The Colonel is a solidly built person with chin whiskers
and an iron jaw. One daughter drove the buckboard; the
other rode a horse man fashion, the latter being Miss Bossie.
She took her part with the cowboys in a steer roping contest
in the afternoon, and afterwards together with the rest of her
family, dined with me in evening dress, not particularly different from that of more conventional regions. They have
many greyhounds and wanted me to come out for a wolf
hunt, which I could not do, so Miss Bossie sent me a stuffed
wolf as a mascot. During my campaign I came upon the
entire family at St. Louis where they had come in to race some
of their horses. They were democrats but were backing Mc-
Kinley chiefly because I was on the ticket. They were all very
glad to see me, but especially the Colonel and Miss Bossie,
both of whom had bet heavily upon me, Miss Bossie telling
me that unless I won I must never venture to come near their
ranch, as she had bet all her ponies and race horses on the
result. She has written Edith to congratulate her and the
Colonel has wired me.

I hope you noticed how I called down Croker, Van Wyck
and Devery when there threatened to be trouble in New York.

I was glad that Croker gave me the chance through his man Devery.

Harry Davis has written us such a characteristic note of congratulation upon our victory over what he calls the "combined idiocy and evil of the country."

Ever yours,

THEODORE ROOSEVELT.

UNITED STATES SENATE
WASHINGTON, D. C.

Personal.

Dear Theodore :—   Nov. 28, 1900.

I send you under another cover an oration which my friend Mr. Stephen O'Meara of the Boston *Journal* delivered last Fourth of July. I want you to do me the favor to read it over, for it is admirably written and preaches a doctrine in which you and I very cordially believe. I think it also is to be said that it preaches it in a fine manner and in exceptionally good English. Mr. O'Meara has been for years one of your most thorough and cordial supporters. He now controls the *Journal,* and if you could write him a line about his oration I know it would gratify him extremely. I hate to bother you with things like this, but it is really worth reading.

Always yours, H. C. LODGE.

STATE OF NEW YORK
EXECUTIVE CHAMBER
ALBANY

December 5, 1900.

Hon. H. C. Lodge, Senate Chamber, Washington, D. C.

Dear Cabot:—I have yours of the 28th. I have written O'Meara with great pleasure. That was really a splendid address.

Is there any way I can help about the Foreign Relations Committee?

Ever yours, T. R.

UNITED STATES SENATE
WASHINGTON, D. C.

Personal.

Dec. 7, 1900.

Dear Theodore:—

Thanks for your note of the 5th. I am very glad you wrote to O'Meara.

I am afraid there is nothing you can do about the Foreign Relations Committee. Everybody wants me to have it on both sides of the Senate, in the Committee, and I think throughout the press. I have had letters and articles from Minnesota in regard to it and from other parts of the country, but there Cullom stands in the way, and unless he can be induced to get out of the way there will be difficulties.

I am sorry you cannot come here on the 12th, but I understand perfectly your reasons. Glad to hear from Platt that you are coming after all.

Always yours, H. C. L.

STATE OF NEW YORK
EXECUTIVE CHAMBER
ALBANY

Dec. 17th, 1900.

Hon. H. C. Lodge, Senate Chamber, Washington, D. C.

*Dear Cabot:—*I think both the French pieces simply delicious. What paper outside of France would solemnly accept "Doubtful" as the name of a presidential candidate!

I need not say how greatly I enjoyed both the Senatorial dinner and the symposium upstairs afterwards.

In great haste,

Faithfully yours,

THEODORE ROOSEVELT.

1901

UNITED STATES SENATE
WASHINGTON, D. C.

Personal.

Dear Theodore :—

Feb. 6, 1901.

Delighted to get a line from you and to know what you have been doing. The papers have been filled with all sorts of despatches about you, mostly fakes, invented, I suppose, in Denver. The fakes I could willingly have spared, for it annoyed me that they could not let you alone when you were off for a holiday. I think you must have had a delightful time, and it was just the thing for you to do.

About the speaking, I shall be very glad to consult with you, but I think it would be wise for you to go to Boston to the Home Market Club. The President himself went one year, and I can see no possible objection to your going. As you refused last autumn I fear it would cause a great deal of feeling if you did not go now. I told them I thought any time after the 15th of March would be safe. Telegraph me your decision on this.

We have had a crowded and busy session, and I personally have been worked to death, as I have had to take over the work of the Foreign Relations in addition to other things. I do not see any prospect of my getting the chairmanship, although I do the work. Apparently Cullom* is going to insist on his seniority, and that will mean that Frye† will be forced to take it.

I have just returned from Chicago, where I went to make an address on John Marshall before the Bar Association. I had a very appreciative audience.

We are to meet and dine with you when you get here, and, of course, we should have liked to have Edith come here, but Anna said she had written her you would go nowhere but to the Depews, so we were compelled to give it up. However,

* Shelby M. Cullom, a Senator from Illinois.
† He was the senior Republican on the Committee but would not consent to be Chairman.

you will be here sometime after the 4th and I shall then have
an opportunity to see you and talk things over.

With best regards,

Always yours, H. C. Lodge.

UNITED STATES SENATE
WASHINGTON, D. C.

Personal.

Feb. 23, 1901.

Dear Theodore :—

I got your letter and answered it and addressed my letter to
the place where your letter was dated, but not being sure
whether it was Coloron Mountain or Colbran it may possibly
have miscarried (no reflection on your handwriting intended—
merely my ignorance of geography). As I asked you in it to
telegraph me in regard to the Home Market Club, which I
was anxious to have you accept, and have heard nothing from
you I fear my letter was lost. There was nothing in it except
the Home Market Club that was of much importance, but I
wanted you to know that I was very glad to hear from you and
replied immediately. It is a great disappointment to me that we
cannot have both you and Edith to break bread under our roof
before Edith goes back, but as Anna told me that Edith has
written that she would go nowhere except to Senator Depew's
Nannie and I were perforce compelled to give up any plans
we had. You will be here, however, sometime longer, as there
will be an extra session of the Senate in any event, and we can
have an opportunity then to talk.

I got your telegram, also, saying "all right about Wood."
I did not know exactly what you meant, as he had been confirmed some days before and it *was* all right. I was a little
puzzled as you did not ask any questions, but simply made
the statement.

I shall be glad indeed to see you. We are in a perfect crush
here in these last days and all of us driven to death. I think
that Cuba—where the situation looks to me very ugly—is
likely to force an extra session, and I differ from most people
in feeling that the President is fully justified in his determina-

tion to have Congress share with him the Cuban responsibility. I want an extra session as little as anybody, but I think
the President is right. We may find some way out of it but I
do not as yet see the way. Always yours, H. C. LODGE.

                                        SAGAMORE HILL,
                        OYSTER BAY, LONG ISLAND, N. Y.,
Dear Cabot:—   Feb. 26th, 1901.

Your "Coloron" letter never arrived—not unnaturally.
Now, I don't want to speak at the Home Market Club or anywhere else at present, if I can help it; chiefly for the excellent
reason that I have nothing whatever to say. Before going
into any speeches I want to have a long talk with you; and I
do *not* want to speak at all unless I feel I have some message
to deliver.

It was exasperating to learn, not only that those ridiculous
stories about my hunting trip had been published but that
they had coolly attributed them to my "press agent"; not a
newspaper man was within 40, and as a matter of fact probably
not within 90 miles of where I was at any time during my hunt.

Tell Bay I like his Greek Galley very much. Tell Nannie I
shall send her a cougar skin. Yours ever, T. R.

                              OYSTER BAY, N. Y.,
                              March 27th, 1901.
Hon. H. C. Lodge, Senate Chamber, Washington, D. C.

*Dear Cabot:—*Some friends of mine who have been at the
German field maneuvers last year were greatly impressed with
the evident intention of the German military classes to take
a fall out of us when the opportunity offers. I find that the
Germans regard our failure to go forward in building up the
navy this year as a sign that our spasm of preparation, as they
think it, has come to an end; that we shall sink back, so that
in a few years they will be in a position to take some step in

the West Indies or South America which will make us either put up or shut up on the Monroe doctrine; they counting upon their ability to trounce us if we try the former horn of the dilemma. They believe that the action taken, and especially the words spoken, in the Senate and House last year have tended very much to cool England's feeling toward us and count upon England standing to one side if the fight occurs. I have good reason to believe that they will back England very strongly in energetic protests if we abrogate the Clayton-Bulwer treaty, or attempt to build the canal on our own hook. Now my own view, if I had the power, would be that we should tell Great Britain that we wanted to be friendly and would like a treaty that would keep their self respect as well as ours, but yet which would permit us to handle the canal as outlined by the amended treaty of last year. If this is impossible I would then abrogate the Clayton-Bulwer treaty anyhow. But I would not take the last step unless I had counted the cost and unless I was prepared to back up words by deeds, to keep on building the navy and to make our army such that we could send out a formidable expeditionary force of small size. The Germans at present I know count with absolute confidence upon our inability to assemble an army of thirty thousand men which would be in any way a match for a German army of the same size.

I think Lord Lansdowne's position is both mischievous and ridiculous, but I also think we should be exceedingly cautious about embroiling ourselves with England, from whom we have not the least little particle of danger to fear in any way or shape; while the only power which may be a menace to us in anything like the immediate future is Germany. Before we abrogate the Clayton-Bulwer treaty we want to be sure of the position we intend taking should Germany and England combine against us. Of course such a combination would be one of the utmost folly for England, because she is certain to have her paws burned, while the nuts would go to Germany. But the last two years have shown that British statesmen are capable of committing the wildest follies; while the attitude of the entire Bryanite party, plus creatures like Mason in our own party, and the Godkin-Parkhurst-Atkinson type of mendacious mugwump, shows the same thing in us. In short, I wish to see us act upon the old frontier principles "Don't bluster, don't flourish your revolver and never draw unless you intend to shoot."

Love to Nannie.

Ever yours,

THEODORE ROOSEVELT.

SAGAMORE HILL,
March 29th, '01.

Dear Cabot,

I am to open the Buffalo Exposition in due form on May 20th. It will be a great occasion, one worthy of your attendance and speech. Do come. We shall then appear together, and our two speeches reverberate through time together!

Seriously, it is worth your coming.

Yours,

THEODORE ROOSEVELT.

UNITED STATES SENATE
WASHINGTON, D. C.

Personal.

Dear Theodore :—

March 30, 1901.

I have your letter of the 27th, and it is needless to say how profoundly I agree with all that you write, and how much the same thoughts have been occupying my own mind. If we cannot make a treaty with England which will pass the Senate next December nothing in the world, in my opinion, will be able to stop the passage of the canal bill. We shall be obliged to meet the question squarely and abrogate the treaty. I am extremely sorry that this seems probable. I have hoped against hope that we could get rid of the Clayton-Bulwer Treaty by amicable negotiations, but the stupidity of England seems to stand in the way of everything. I had a long talk with John Hay in regard to this the other morning, and then he sent me Lansdowne's despatch with the request that I should give him my views in regard to future arrangements.

I enclose you a copy of what I wrote him as you may be interested in seeing it, and it gives in a condensed form my general views in regard to it. As to Germany, I have heard the same reports that you have; in fact that sort of rumor has been in the air for a good while. I have myself very grave doubts as to their undertaking to attack us. It would be a pretty dangerous undertaking under any circumstances, but at the same time it is well within the range of possibilities, and the German Emperor has moments when he is wild enough to do anything. If it comes at all it will come through some attempt in South America, probably in Brazil. Mahan, you know, takes the view that we should not undertake to keep Europe out of South America below the Caribbean Sea, that Northern South America and Central America are enough for us to protect. I confess that I do not agree with this view at all, and yet I see the difficulties of enforcing the Monroe Doctrine in Southern Brazil, for example, and in getting our people to understand the importance of doing so at such a distant point. Our only safety is in being thoroughly prepared. I think so far as the Army goes we are pretty well off. The last reorganization bill gives us as many men as the country will stand, and, what is more important, gives us a system capable of quick expansion. But the navy is the vital point. We must go on and build up the navy as rapidly as possible. I am sorry there should have been even the slightest break in this last winter, but I feel confident that it will be renewed at the next session. We must do all we can to get strong recommendations from the administration for a further increase of the navy next December, and we must make a big fight for new ships. You and I agree absolutely as to the importance of this. If we have a strong and well equipped navy I do not believe Germany will attack us. At the same time there is a fundamental danger which arises from our rapid growth economically. We are putting a terrible pressure on Europe, and this situation may produce war at any time. The economic forces will not be the ostensible cause of trouble, but they will be the real cause, and no one can tell where the break will come. Practically speaking the essential thing now is to urge the building of the Navy, and I hope we can get the President to make a recommendation in his next message.

As to Germany backing up England in case we abrogate the treaty, I do not see exactly what she could do. She is no party to the Clayton-Bulwer Treaty, and has no concern in it. Nor do I believe that she is ready to make trouble at this moment. That the English should undertake to go to war about the canal seems impossible, although, I admit, they have done a good many impossible things lately. If, however, there is any danger of that kind, now is the time to take the step, for England is too exhausted by the African war to enter on any new struggle, and Germany has all she can handle in China at the present moment.

The Buffalo people have just been here, and I suppose that I shall have to accept, although I feel somewhat at a loss to know what to say on such an occasion. Nevertheless, it is rather an important function, and as you are going to be there, and want me to come, I think I will try it.

With best regards,

Always sincerely yours,

H. C. LODGE.

OYSTER BAY, N. Y.,
April 4th, 1901.

Hon. H. C. Lodge, Senate Chamber, Washington, D. C.

Dear Cabot:—I have been looking up Charles 11th and Condé. I think they fell off toward the end of their lives, whereas Sheridan grew; but I do not think that Sheridan ever grew to be as great as the Frenchman was in his first campaigns against the Spaniards and Imperialists, or the Swede in his first campaigns against the Russians, Poles and Saxons.

Ask Nannie if she has ever read "The Semi-Attached Couple"? It is to me an amusing and interesting picture of "le highlif" seventy years ago.

I am very glad to hear you may go to Buffalo.

Always yours,

THEODORE ROOSEVELT.

UNITED STATES SENATE
WASHINGTON, D. C.

Personal.

Dear Theodore :—   April 8, 1901.

I have your letter of the 4th. Your judgment may be right
about Charles 11th and Condé, but I cannot quite agree to it
in regard to the latter's earlier campaigns. However, you are
a far better judge than I.

Nannie said she read the "Semi-Attached Couple," as I did,
many years ago, and it was a very good story. There was another which appeared about the same time, I believe, which
we also read, called "The Semi-Detached House."

I have no doubt I shall enjoy Buffalo very much, except that
I have no idea what to say there. I shall see you before that,
however, at Boston at the Home Market Club.

Everything here is quiet as ever.

Always yours,   H. C. LODGE.

OYSTER BAY, N. Y.,
April 10th, 1901.

Hon. H. C. Lodge, Senate Chamber, Washington, D. C.

Dear Cabot :—I have your letter of the 8th inst. I am *so* glad
that you do not know what you are going to say at Buffalo!
I have not the slightest idea what to say myself, and am having most painful work grinding out something for the Home
Market Club on the 30th. I suppose that really I ought to
have been adamantine and refused to speak, because this is a
slack water time and there is not very much to say. However,
I am in for it and shall do my best.

Yesterday I had a most comic experience. I received a nice
letter from Pritchett, the President of the Massachusetts Insti-
tute of Technology, enclosing a copy of what I took to be his
opening address when inaugurated. I opened the pamphlet at
random and immediately became absorbed in the sentiments
expressed. They seemed to me to contain truths which above
all others we need to insist upon when dealing with educated

men, with graduates and undergraduates of higher institutions of learning. So much was I struck with it that I sat down and wrote him a line of appreciation, telling him I thought his address without exception the best thing of the kind I had ever read. I handed it to my Secretary to post, and just as he had left the house I turned to the beginning of the address and found it was by you, and not by Pritchett. Then I had a quarter of a mile sprint after my Secretary (which reflected credit on a person who in age and bodily habit is growing to have an unpleasant resemblance to the late lamented Mr. Tracy Tupman) and recovered the letter before it was sent.

Ever yours,
THEODORE ROOSEVELT.

UNITED STATES SENATE
WASHINGTON, D. C.

Personal.

Dear Theodore :—
April 13, 1901.

I have your letter of the 10th. I was very much amused by the Pritchett incident, and very much flattered. I do not know when I have had a more genuine compliment. The curious thing was that, although I had not seen Pritchett for six months, in his speech he took exactly the line that I had taken in my speech as that which ought to be taken, and justified at once all that I had said about him. He did not put it, of course, in the same way that I did, but the spirit was the same. Everything works for the best sometimes, and the fact that you had to make a run to catch your secretary, I have no doubt will do your figure good.

The Board of Visitors to the Naval Observatory have been here, and Professor Pickering came in to see me. He is very hostile to the naval control, like most of the astronomers, but he told me that President Harper had heard from you, and that when the Board met later in New York they were going to ask you to meet with them and give them your views. I told him I thought that you, like myself, knew very little about the purely scientific work, but that you had very decided opinions, owing to your experience in the Department, as to the manner of administration. If they do ask you to meet them I hope you will go, because I think you can say with great force what I said, as we agree on the general proposition. The case, in a few words, is this: For many years the scientific work of the Observatory has not been what it ought to be. This has been partly owing to the variation which always comes in the abilities of different professors at different periods, and partly from the fact that some of the Superintendents have been carelessly selected and were not officers with any scientific training at all. But the main difficulty of late years has been the incessant effort of the astronomers outside to take the Observatory away from the Navy Department. This has made it the subject of contest, and has kept up a feeling of uncertainty and created factional divisions in the forces at the Observatory. Under these circumstances, the work has suffered. The astronomers, of course, put their argument on the ground that they want the National Observatory to do better work, which is very proper, but the real object of the astronomers is to get control of the institution. Now I am very clear that nothing will be gained by shifting the Observatory to another Department, and while it is in the Navy Department, it is perfectly clear to me, that a naval officer, properly selected, ought to be the Superintendent. On these points from the talks we have had I am sure you and I agree. To detach it from the Navy Department and put it under another, or to leave it simply as an independent institution by itself, would destroy all responsibility and would lead to the extravagance which has marked so many of the scientific government institutions. I doubt very much, also, whether such a change would really improve the work. Now the Board, under the law, has really no right to concern itself with the question of administration. They have the power, and I think it is their duty, to advise the line of work which should be followed, and then the Superintendent and the astronomers can follow this line and better results will be obtained than is now the case, but if the Board goes in to change the executive administration and break down the naval control they will bring on a fight in Congress that is likely to endure for some time, and during which all prospect of improvement in the work of the Observatory will be lost, because the Navy on the one hand, and the astronomers on the other, will be constantly fighting each other and not attending to science. This, I think, would be a misfortune, and the way to get an improvement in the work of the Observatory is for the Board of Visitors to do as I have suggested. I hope you will have an opportunity to meet the Board and put these points to them, which, from your knowledge as Assistant Secretary, would have great weight.

As to Buffalo, I do not know what I shall say, but I think I shall probably develop some of the things which I mean to say to the Home Market Club as to the responsibilities which our increasing commerce brings us, and I hope the line will not interfere with you.

With best regards,

Always yours, H. C. LODGE.

Personal.   NAHANT, MASS.,
Dear Theodore :—   June 17, 1901.

Our speeches at Buffalo seem to have made quite a sensation and aroused all the discussion we could have possibly hoped. I received the other day, from our Consul at Glasgow, a long and withering editorial in the Glasgow *Herald*. George Meyer sent me Smalley's despatch in the *Times*, which you may have seen, in which he pitches into us in great style. Perhaps you saw the long and rather friendly article from the *Novoe Vremya*. The extracts from the German papers you have, of course, seen. The *Evening Post* really did us a great service by its savage assault, chiefly directed against me, which set the discussion going. I think we have fully attained our object and have made Germany aware that we are watching her.

The Secretary of State has got the matter much at heart. I had a long talk with him before I left Washington and he has done all that can be done, but he cannot seem to impress upon our excellent friend Long the necessity of having a man-of-war down there. Hay says, very justly, that La Guayra is the most important point in the world just now for a powerful ship of the American navy. With great difficulty and much urging we have succeeded in getting Long to send the *May-flower*, which seems very insufficient but still it is something.

We hope to get off on the 3d of July.

Give our best love to Edith.

Always yours,   H. C. LODGE.

OYSTER BAY, N. Y.,
June 19th, 1901.

Hon. H. C. Lodge, Nahant, Mass.

Dear Cabot:—I see in the papers that the President is not going on to Commencement. Under those circumstances ought I to come on or not? I have been inclined to think that I ought to so as not to give any excuse for talk to the effect that I was feeling angered, or was indifferent. Will you let me know what you think, as if I am not going I ought to write at once?

By the way, Yale is to give me an LL.D. on her two hundredth anniversary next October.

With best love to all,   Ever yours,

THEODORE ROOSEVELT.

OYSTER BAY, N. Y.,
June 19th, 1901.

Hon. H. C. Lodge, Nahant, Mass.

My Dear Cabot:—No, I did not see a single foreign comment on our speeches. I wonder if I could get hold of that dispatch in the *Times* and of the comments in the German papers? Smalley is a copper-riveted idiot any way. However, in point of dullness of apprehension I fear he does not differ materially from his English masters. I am rather astounded that they should fail to understand that we were not thinking of them at all. On the whole I am friendly to England. I do not at all believe in being over-effusive or in forgetting that fundamentally we are two different nations; but yet the fact remains, in the first place, that we are closer in feeling to her than to any other nation; and in the second place, that probably her interest and ours will run on rather parallel lines in the future. Moreover, as far as England is concerned I do not care a rap whether she subscribes to the Monroe doctrine or not, because she is the one power with which any quarrel on that doctrine would be absolutely certain to result to our immediate advantage. She could take the Philippines and Porto Rico, but they would be a very poor offset for the loss of Canada. 'I should regard a war with England as a calamity because of its future results to both powers and especially to England; but its immediate effect would be beneficial to the United States. The German Consul General at New York was out here at Laura's after we had made our Buffalo speeches, and I had a long talk with him. He evidently wanted to see me because he was on the eve of his departure for Germany to see the Kaiser. I told him exactly what I should tell anyone; that I was anxious to keep on friendly relations with Germany—indeed I might say peculiarly anxious, for I have a hearty and genuine liking for the Germans both individually and as a nation; that I did not want any exclusive trade privileges as against Germany with South America save as they might come legitimately by reciprocity treaties, and that I was delighted to see South America kept open commercially to Germany and to the United States on an equal footing; that if a big German speaking community in a South American state could not stand misgovernment, and set up for itself, there would be in that fact by itself nothing to which I should object; but that I did not desire to see the United States gain any territory in South America itself, and that as far as I was concerned I would do all in my power to have the United States take the attitude that no European nation, Germany or any other, should gain a foot of soil in any shape or way in South America, or establish a protectorate under any disguise over any South American country.

I had heard that the *Evening Post* had been sailing into us. I am inclined to think that it did us a genuine favor.

Ever yours,

THEODORE ROOSEVELT.

OYSTER BAY, N. Y.,
June 22nd, 1901.

Hon. H. C. Lodge, Nahant, Mass.

Dear Cabot:—Your letter settled it and I have decided to come on. I wish I could go to Nahant, but many months ago I promised Frank Lowell to stay with him, and I have just declined to go down to Beverly on Tuesday night with George Lyman, and also going down to Taunton with Frank Lowell himself for Wednesday night on the plea that I have got to leave Boston early Thursday morning. I wrote George Lyman that while I could not go to Beverly, if after commencement he would arrange for you and me and Murray Crane, just us four with no one else, to dine somewhere in town, I should be delighted, and you could go down to Nahant immediately afterwards. I suppose it would be my only chance to talk things over with you. I have a good deal that I should really like to consult you about, although after all there is nothing of importance that will not keep until next fall.

All the Colorado State authorities wrote me inviting me to address them on the quarter centennial of their coming to Statehood, August 2–3, and I accepted because I was afraid that after having declined to address the legislature last winter, it would look churlish on my part to refuse them again. Moreover, it enabled me to escape the pressing request that I should make a Republican speech for the Republicans of that State, about which Wolcott had been so insistent, and which I thought extremely unwise this year. Ever yours,

THEODORE ROOSEVELT.

Personal.

NAHANT, MASS.,
June 27, 1901.

Dear Theodore:—

I enclose the clippings you said you wanted to see. George Meyer sent me the Smalley letter, and the article from the Glasgow *Herald*, which is a perfectly stupid thing, was sent me by the Consul. The Russian article is really interesting.

I was very glad we had that talk last night. George Lyman,

who is heart and soul absorbed in your interests, has had it on his mind to say to you what he did about those men in Philadelphia, where their presence troubled him a great deal. I know that you will not mind his talking so frankly about them, for it arises simply from his anxiety for you. I was especially struck with your summing up of the situation, for it corresponded exactly with my own. We are very apt to think alike on many subjects, and I was pleased to see that we had come to the same conclusion. I do not think there is anything to be done at present, except to keep a lookout. I see the dangers just as you see them, but there can be no doubt that at this moment nothing could be better than your prospects. The real danger is the unknown quantity of the next three years.

If you do get a chance to write me a line while I am gone address it in care of J. S. Morgan & Company, London.

Give our best love to Edith.

Always yours,   H. C. LODGE.

OYSTER BAY, N. Y.,
June 29th, 1901.

Hon. H. C. Lodge, Nahant, Mass.

Dear Cabot:—Smalley's letter was not enclosed, but the Glasgow *Herald* article and the very interesting quotation from that St. Petersburg paper were both in. They are extremely interesting. I return them both.

I shall write you from time to time. Both from Michigan and Illinois I am receiving what might be called conditional offers of friendship, but fortunately from men of tact who do not want anything done at the moment. The *Evening Post* is in a perfectly crazy campaign against me for Odell.

Ever yours,

THEODORE ROOSEVELT.

OYSTER BAY, N. Y.,
Aug. 20th, 1901.

Hon. H. C. Lodge, c/o J. S. Morgan & Co., Bankers, London,
England.

Dear Cabot:—I may be a mere prophet of evil, but I do not anticipate any good out of the belated action in the Sampson-Schley case. The trouble is that Sampson originally absolutely right had elaborately done the wrong thing again and again; and that their superiors have committed the fatal error of striking soft. It has just been one of the cases where the effort to weave in and out around the trouble has proved a failure. Either the President and Secretary ought to have stood by Schley straight out from the beginning, or if they shared the belief of ninety-five percent of the navy, including all the best officers, they should have hit him hard at the very beginning. In the course they have pursued they have elaborately combined all possible disadvantages. As regards the Board, Dewey, I suppose, will take the lead. The popular feeling is overwhelmingly for Schley, and I think that Dewey now cares very little for the navy people, or for the real interest of the navy. In consequence I thoroughly believe that he will yield to the popular clamor and to his feeling against the administration and whitewash Schley. Of course, he may be true to his old naval traditions, in which case he will be very severe upon him. But I do not regard the outlook as promising.

My fortnight's trip west was to attend the quarter centennial celebration of statehood in Colorado at Colorado Springs. I have been greatly astonished at the feeling displayed for me, not only in Colorado and Kansas, but in Missouri and even in Illinois. All the Colorado people, and all their leaders are a unit, and are perfectly straight out in their declarations. In Kansas and Missouri there have been genuine popular movements started on my behalf, and, if there is any real strength at all in the movement for me, those two States will be in it. In Illinois, at the moment the bulk of the leaders on both sides are heartily for me, and all took particular pains to call upon me and assure me of the fact. I could not understand their action at first; but it appears that just at this time the Illinois people genuinely want me, and therefore the politicians feel they can strengthen themselves by coming out for me. However, I do not feel that the play of the forces is by any means as simple in Illinois as in Kansas and Colorado, and I am not prepared to say how much substance there is in the movement for me. The trip was a revelation to me. I know with what extreme caution one must accept what one hears on such a trip. But the men who spoke to me were not nobodies. They were national committeemen, chairmen of state committees, Congressmen, and the like. Many of them spoke with as little reserve and as much emphasis as you and Murray Crane and George Lyman that night at dinner. I told them all that they must be prepared to have New York against me. To some this came as a surprise, but most of them had already discovered it.

Did I ever tell you that just before I left for the west when I met Platt, he volunteered the statement that he should support me for the presidential nomination when the time came? I do not put much confidence in this, because I think he is growing very feeble and will be ousted definitely from his leadership during the next three years by Odell; and because he and Odell down at bottom are politicians of the same stripe who have more in common than either can ever really have with me. Platt's reason for announcing that he would support me was that I had always behaved in a strictly honorable manner towards him, and though I had often not done what he wished, I had never lied to him or deceived him. Of course, Odell has; but equally of course in the last resort Odell will often do things for him which Platt would not even ask me to do, and Platt knows this perfectly well, and I am rather inclined to think that when he acts in cold blood he will probably remember this as the decisive factor.

I write you this so that you may know exactly how things stand. I hope I need not say that I do not write because my nomination seems at all likely. Looked at dispassionately it is of course very nearly out of the question that a man can be nominated with his own State against him, and it is practically certain that my State will be against me. But at the moment there is undoubtedly a feeling for me, especially in the west, and to a certain extent also in New England and in those parts of the south where there is a genuine Republican party, of so strong a character that it must be taken into consideration. as a factor of possible weight in the nomination.

Give my warm love to Nannie and to Bay and his wife and Henry Adams.

Ever yours,
THEODORE ROOSEVELT.

BUFFALO, N. Y.,
Sept. 9th, 1901.

Dear Cabot:—

I answered your cable to Hotel Brighton, Paris, and hope it reached you. There is no use in telling you of the stunned amazement of the people over the attempted assassination of the President. You know all about it, because you know your own feelings. I was with Senator Proctor in Vermont at the time, and at first the news seemed literally incredible. You and I have lived too long, and have seen human nature from too many different sides, to be astounded at ordinary folly or ordinary wickedness; but it did not seem possible that just at this time, in just this country, and in the case of this particular President, any human being could be so infamous a scoundrel, so crazy a fool as to attempt to assassinate him. It was in the most naked way an assault not on power, not on wealth, but simply and solely upon free government, government by the common people, because it *was* government, and because, though in the highest sense a free and representative government, it yet stood for order as well as for liberty. McKinley is a man hardly even of moderate means. He is about as well off say as a division superintendent of the New York Central railroad. He lives in a little house at Canton just as such a division superintendent who had retired would live in a little house in Auburn or some other small New York city or big country town. He comes from the typical hard-working farmer stock of our country. In every instinct and feeling he is closely in touch with, and the absolute representative of, the men who make up the immense bulk of our Nation—the small merchants, clerks, farmers and mechanics who formed the backbone of the patriotic party under Washington in the Revolution; of the Republican Party under Lincoln at the time of the Civil War. His one great anxiety while President has been to keep in touch with this body of people and to give expression to their desires and sentiments. He has been so successful that within a year he has been re-elected by an overwhelming majority, a majority including the bulk of the wageworkers and the very great bulk of the farmers. He has been to a high degree accessible to everyone. At his home anyone could see him just as easily as anyone else could be seen. All that was necessary was, if he was engaged, to wait until his engagement was over. More than almost any public man I have ever met, he has avoided exciting personal enmities. I have never heard him denounce or assail any man or any body of men. There is in the country at this time the most widespread confidence in and satisfaction with his policies. The occasion chosen by the assassin was one when the President was meeting great masses of his fellow-citizens in accordance with the old American idea of the relations between the President and the people. That there might be no measure of Judas-like infamy lacking, the dog approached him under pretense of shaking hands.

Under these conditions of National prosperity, of popular content, of democratic simplicity and of the absolutely representative character of the President, it does seem utterly impossible to fathom the mind of the man who would do such a deed. Moreover, the surgeons who have in all probability saved the President's life, have thereby saved the life of his assailant. If he is only indicted for assault with intent to kill, and behaves well while in jail, he will be a free man seven years hence, and this, after having committed a crime against free government, a thousand times worse than any murder of a private individual could be. Of course I feel as I always have felt, that we should war with relentless efficiency not only against anarchists, but against all active and passive sympathizers with anarchists. Moreover, every scoundrel

like Hearst and his satellites who for whatever purposes appeals
to evil human passion, has made himself accessory before
the fact to every crime of this nature, and every soft fool
who extends a maudlin sympathy to criminals has done like-
wise. Hearst and Altgeld, and to an only less degree, Tolstoy
and the feeble apostles of Tolstoy, like Ernest Howard Crosby
and William Dean Howells, who unite in petitions for the
pardon of anarchists, have a heavy share in the burden of
responsibility for crimes of this kind.

As soon as I heard the news I came straight to Buffalo. My
position was of course most delicate, but I felt that the only
course to follow was that which was natural, and that the
natural thing was to come at once to Buffalo, where I might
see how the President was getting on; and to stay here until
he was on the high road to recovery. As soon as I had seen
and talked at length with the doctors, I cabled you. After
my talk with them I became very confident of the President's
recovery. I found that they would have felt this entire confidence if it had been an ordinary case of some stranger in a
hospital, and that it was only the magnitude of the stake that
caused their anxiety. Long before you receive this letter I
believe the last particle of danger will have vanished; nor do
I anticipate even a long convalescence. The President's
splendid inherited strength, the temperate life he had led, and
his singularly calm and equable temper of mind all count immensely in his favor.

Of course, I have stayed absolutely quiet here, seeing a
great deal of Root, of whom I am very fond.

In Vermont, and just previously in Minnesota and Illinois,
I had a most interesting time. In each state I was received with
wild enthusiasm, and the Governor of Illinois and Senator
Knute Nelson in Minnesota and Senator Proctor in Vermont
at the dinners to me proceeded to nominate me for President. I
understand entirely that in the case of a promise where no
consideration passes from the party on the other side, the promise is in no wise binding, and simply expresses present intentions. If I had been able I should have liked to defer the
expressions of feeling for some time to come, because in the

next three years all may change utterly, and indeed probably will change; but just at present Illinois and Minnesota, like Vermont, are heartily for me, because there is a genuine popular sentiment for me. As yet, Odell has no hold whatever outside of New York. Fairbanks has gone to Illinois, Minnesota and Kansas, and in every place the leaders had told him they could not support him, because they were going to support me, as that was what the popular feeling demanded. All of this may absolutely change, and I do not want you to think that I attach any special importance to it; but I wanted you to know exactly how things stood. I am going to speak in the campaign both in Ohio and in Iowa. In New York Odell is absolutely in the saddle at the moment.

Give my warm love to Nannie and to all.

Ever yours,

THEODORE ROOSEVELT.

PARIS,
Sept. 12th, 1901.

Dear Theodore :

You have done many and many a kind thing for me but never a kinder than sending me in the midst of all your anxiety and strain that cable. It was almost impossible to get news here when we wanted it most. The miserable [Paris] *Herald* which will publish a yacht race bulletin every five minutes would give only one despatch some 15 hours late in the day. We could get nothing and your cable was the first authentic thing. Porter* had nothing and it gave him great relief. I also had it wired to Storer† so you see your benefaction touched more than one.

The news now is so reassuring that I feel that I can write. What a hideous attempt at murder it was ! What a marvelous escape it seems to be !

In addition to the sorrow and anxiety which every American felt, in addition to the personal regard for the President which is strong from many years of association, I was deeply affected

* Gen. Horace Porter, American Ambassador.
† Bellamy Storer, Minister to Belgium.

by thoughts of you. There is no one thing I want so much, as you well know, as to see you President, chosen, as I feel sure you are to be, by the vote of the people. It wrung my heart to think of your coming to the great place through an assassination, for I knew how terribly that idea must be haunting you and how it must weigh upon you. Then I was worried for fear that you were not properly guarded, altho' reason told me that every precaution would be taken and I could hardly keep from cabling you to have proper guards. I suppose the President's recovery is now pretty sure and that I may dismiss these anxieties but I do not like to think of the terrible strain this last week must have been to you. I could not be of any earthly use I know but I have fretted severely that I was so many thousand miles away from you at such a moment. For heaven's sake take care of yourself. You have had a trying summer with all your anxiety about the children which I trust is now allayed and then you have had to bear this great tension. Do be careful in all ways. I am longing to see you just to assure myself of your well being. Something pleasanter.

In the midst of life we are in death and conversely comedy is always rubbing elbows with tragedy, like the porter in Macbeth. Read the following which I cut from *La Patrie*—

"La présidence de M. Roosevelt, vice-président, pendant la maladie, ou bien en attendant l'élection du nouveau président si M. MacKinley devait mourir, ne semble pas être très populaire. M. Roosevelt est un peu le Chamberlain de l'Amérique du Nord. Son *jingoisme* est considéré comme dangereux pour les États-Unis. Il est colossalement riche et trop mêlé à toutes les spéculations financières de New York pour avoir les sympathies de la foule."

The first part is the ordinary trash of the *Evening Post,* but the last sentence is what is new and delightful. Bacon says that foreign nations are a present posterity and if posterity regards you as a member of Morgan syndicates it will be very queer.

La Patrie is a worthless, boulevard, anti-everything sheet, but the *Temps* is a serious paper and had a long and well informed article about our constitutional arrangements and about you. It managed to say one or two amusing things however and used one phrase which I am sure will delight Edith. It said that you were "un puissant chasseur devant l'Éternel." How queer it sounds in French. George Lyman who is here and has been worrying about you too came up from Italy in the train with a German. They fell into conversation and the German asked George if he knew you and me (I mention this because it tickled my vanity); whether I was not to be Secretary of State when you were President; if we were not two very dangerous men and haters of Germany.—To all of which George responded appropriately. Then the German said that he thought you must be very dangerous because he understood that last winter you had killed *1800* (!) "mountain cats." So you see how fame spreads. Let me have a line to tell me of your well being and how Edith and the children are. If you answer me at once it will reach me (care J. S. Morgan, London) before we sail October 5th. Nannie sends her best love to Edith and mine goes with it. We have thought a great deal of her in these last days. Nannie's best love to you too and John's.

Ever yours, H. C. Lodge.

Private.   Paris,
Dear Theodore :   Sept. 19th, 1901.

I do not mean to burden you with letters but I cannot refrain from thanking you from the bottom of my heart for your letter of the 9th from Buffalo. It was so good of you to write to me at such a moment in the midst of such strain and anxiety and I value your doing so more than I can say. All you write about McKinley, his representative character and his nearness to the people is profoundly true. But the scoundrel who murdered him is not the weak man of unbalanced mind brooding over an imaginary wrong like Bellingham, or Lawrence, or Guiteau, a sporadic type known at all periods of history; he is the legitimate result of an organized body formed among other things for the murder of the representatives of government, law and order. These men are the enemies of govern-

ment, society and patriotism. We should fight them as we
would fight any other armed enemy. I hope and believe that
we shall pass stringent legislation against them, and for the
restriction of immigration; break up these gangs in Paterson
and elsewhere and have a law making it a capital offense to
attempt to injure or kill the President or Vice President. All
sorts of reports as to the Cabinet are in the newspapers here,
the one this morning being that Hay is going to stay. I am
sure I hope so for then you will have both him and Root. The
newspapers here were rather adrift about you and what you
represented at first and the Department of Foreign Affairs
sent me word that they would like some statement as to the
facts of your life and your political views. On the promise that
I should not appear in any way I furnished them with a statement and they, controlling their press as they do, have used it
with excellent effect. Friendly from the beginning the tone of
the press is now not only kindly and appreciative but well informed. I am to meet M. de Pressense, the editor of the *Temps,*
which is an official organ, at breakfast on Monday and I shall
be able perhaps to give him some useful information. The
sympathy here was very marked and not only by the flags,
bound with crape, everywhere but in the tone of the people.
I think I shall have some things to tell you of interest bearing
on reciprocity from what I have learned here and in Russia.

I had a pleasant note from Lord Lansdowne a day or two
ago anent the treaty and I have strong hopes that we shall get
one which you can lay before Congress in December and which
we can promptly ratify. Then the canal bill can be passed at
once and we must be careful that the choice of route is left to
the President. We must not tie you down to Nicaragua for I
am strongly inclined to think that Panama is best.

We are so distressed about the children. Poor Alice and poor
little Quentin. It is cruel to think that baby should have suffered so. What a terrible trial for Edith and then to have the
great national calamity come. Give her our dearest love. You
and yours are ever in our thoughts. Do take care of yourself
and keep well guarded. Just at this moment there are weak
minds inflamed by the "event" and, therefore, dangerous. By

the way, Amen to what you say of Hearst and the *Journal*—it is an efficient cause in breeding anarchists and murder. Once more dear Theodore take care of yourself. I am not surprised at what you say of Vermont, Illinois, etc. And now it is good to feel that you have all this strong sentiment behind you, independent of the event, and I am longing to be at home, longing to see you and Edith.

Ever yrs, H. C. LODGE.

EXECUTIVE MANSION
WASHINGTON, D. C.

Dear Cabot :—   September 23, 1901.

I must just send you a line, hoping it will catch you before you leave, for naturally you have been in my thoughts almost every hour of the last fortnight. It is a dreadful thing to come into the Presidency this way; but it would be a far worse thing to be morbid about it. Here is the task, and I have got to do it to the best of my ability; and that is all there is about it. I believe you will approve of what I have done and of the way I have handled myself so far. It is only a beginning but it is better to make a good beginning than a bad.

I shall not try to give you even in barest outline the history of the last two weeks, and still less to talk of the policies that press for immediate consideration. I hope you can make it convenient to come and see me soon after your return.

I had a very nice talk with Murray Crane. Give my love to Nannie and all.

Ever yours,
THEODORE ROOSEVELT.

EAST POINT
NAHANT

Private.

Dear Theodore :   Oct. 17th, 1901.

We talked of so many things* that I have been employed ever since in thinking it all over and getting everything coordinated in my own mind. Where you are concerned, I am, as

---

* I went to Washington immediately on my arrival from Europe and stayed with the President at the White House.

you well know, anxious and critical and never so much so as
at this moment. After careful reflection on all that has happened in these momentous weeks, I cannot see that you have
made a single mistake. You have done admirably, splendidly,
and I am building greatly on your message which struck me
as sound and fine throughout. By the way, one verbal suggestion—I feel doubtful about the phrase "Judas-like." Is it
too rhetorical for a President's message? I am not certain
either way, but I doubt about it and I wish you would take
Edith's opinion on it and on my suggestion.

I saw Wolcott in New York. He is laid up with a touch of
gout and the Dr. says cannot travel for a week or ten days.
He will then come to Washington to see you. He asked me to
explain his delay. Be assured you have no more loyal friend
than he. You will also see another good friend in Don Cameron* on Oct. 24 or thereabouts. Mrs. C. is anxious that you
should persuade him to return to the Senate. I should be glad
if he would. The "average" man especially the man of business is with you and is satisfied and confident. They will be
with you on the Southern question. You are very right there,
but as we agreed in talk, *all* questions of patronage must be
kept in abeyance and must wait until the English treaty (and
if it is coming the Danube treaty also) is out of the way. Such
an attitude will help the treaty I know. I hope Morgan proved
amenable. Your seeing all these Senators and especially asking them to lunch is most wise and effective. Daniel† is the
key of that special position. The more I think of it the better
I like the paragraphs of the Message on reciprocity. I hope
you will keep it just as it is. It is a difficult question and you
have handled it perfectly to my thinking.

Love to Edith.

Ever yrs, H. C. LODGE.

* James Donald Cameron of Pennsylvania. He left the Senate in 1897.
† Senator John W. Daniel of Virginia.

EAST POINT

Private.   NAHANT

Dear Theodore: Oct. 19th, 1901.

Needless to say everyone here, literally everyone, is with you heart and soul on the Booker Washington matter. Needless for me to say how utterly right I think you are. But I confess the Southern outbreak is to me melancholy and disappointing. I am always hoping that they will learn and broaden, and then comes a thing like this showing the narrow stolidity and imperiousness which are so disheartening. But they surely will learn and we must go on hoping.

Love to Edith.

Ever yrs,   H. C. LODGE.

Private.   NAHANT,

Dear Theodore: Oct. 24th, 1901.

By the way, you seem to have had a fine time and a great reception at Yale which is as it should be and very satisfactory. I am very glad you went on all accounts and especially because you will not have another opportunity to leave Washington for sometime and it was well to break at once any association of ideas with the President's going away to a celebration of any sort.

Bert Peirce* was here this afternoon just back from Russia. As soon as he gets his oldest boy established at school he is going on to Washington and I hope you will see him and give him an opportunity to tell you something about opportunities for American trade in Russia, for what he has to say is worth hearing and considering. I am most anxious that he should have Cridler's place as you suggested, for he is a first class man and will be most valuable in the Department and a real addition to your force. I believe I forgot to tell you that he was with Hitchcock† when the latter was at St. Petersburg and I wish you would ask Hitchcock his opinion of Peirce.

* H. H. D. Peirce, youngest son of Prof. Benjamin Peirce of Harvard. He had been for some years Secretary of Embassy in St. Petersburg.
† E. A. Hitchcock, Secretary of the Interior.

I received your letter of Oct. 19th for which many thanks. I am glad that you have a good Republican for the Virginia judgeship and although I like Harry Tucker, I hoped that you would have. You understand of course that I could not refuse the request of certain men to bring the matter like this to your attention and I fear that I shall have many such cases but I do it officially. When, and not often I hope, I have anything where I have a strong personal interest as in the case of Peirce, I shall present it differently.

I am delighted to hear what Morgan said. If we can now secure Daniel the treaty will go through rapidly and easily I feel sure. Wolcott said to me in New York that he wanted only good men and that it would be a real favor to him if you would point out anything wrong with anybody past or present. I know that he wants to suggest only good men. In that connection let me say that I do not know how well informed Stuart is about other matters but I am quite sure that he is mistaken about Teller and that you want to be very careful with that eminent Senator. I saw Hale in Boston where he had been taken ill which prevented his going to Washington and I was greatly pleased by his tone. He spoke of all you had done with high approval and said it was the duty of us all to support you strongly. I am glad that he is feeling that way for whatever reason and I will tell you more of what he said when we meet.

Poor Ted. I am very sorry for his accident, but luckily it is not a serious break and at his age will soon knit. I can imagine that Edith finds some compensation in his being off the field for the rest of the season. Constance had him to lunch when she was at Groton and I judge that they struck up quite a friendship.

I wouldn't appoint anyone in Colorado until you have talked with Wolcott himself. He is going back there I am glad to say to take up the fight for the party.

Best love from Nannie.

Ever yrs, H. C. LODGE.

Personal.

WHITE HOUSE
WASHINGTON

Dear Cabot :—   October 28, 1901.

Before receiving your second letter I had found out that Pruden* strongly objected to going.

You will be amused to know that the Peirce-Cridler matter, about which I had decided in a conversation with John Hay before seeing you, has excited the ferocious onslaught of Penrose, Elkins, Platt, Hall and others for whom Cridler has acted as office broker, all of them insisting that I am turning him out and appointing a kinsman of yours in spite of his pre-eminent fitness. I find President McKinley had already told Hay that Cridler would have to go.

The Booker T. Washington incident was to me so much a matter of course that I regarded its sole importance as consisting in the view it gave one of the continued existence of that combination of Bourbon intellect and intolerant truculence of spirit, through much of the South, which brought on the Civil War. If these creatures had any sense they would understand that they can't bluff me. They can't even make me abandon my policy of appointing decent men to office in their own localities.

Love to Nannie.

Faithfully yours,

THEODORE ROOSEVELT.

Hale has written Long that he is against *any* increase of the navy.

Private.

EAST POINT
NAHANT

Dear Theodore :   Nov. 1st, 1901.

Thanks for your letter of Oct. 28th. I am very glad that Pruden is to stay where he is. He is an invaluable man and a good one too. I had the impression that it was his wish to go into the Army but I see now what the truth was.

I have been much amused by the Cridler business. I knew President McKinley meant to get rid of him and you told me

* For many years a clerk at the White House.

that you had determined to do the same thing and so I spoke of Peirce to you as I should have done to President McKinley. At first some of the papers of the mugwump variety thought that they had caught me in a bit of spoils work. Then Scott attacked me and announced that Cridler had looked out for openings for West Virginia and the whole press went over to my side as a judicious patriot. The names of Cridler's backers had an interesting effect.

You take exactly the view of the Booker Washington incident that I did and of course I knew that all they said would not deflect you one hair in your policy. Indeed in that respect it has strengthened your hands.

What you tell me of Hale's letter to Long is disheartening but not wholly surprising. I had not talked with him about the Navy and his tone about you was as I wrote you most cordial and friendly. When you see him I would be the soul of good nature and let him know firmly you are bent on your policy. If he stands out we must beat him. He has his committee in hand owing to the Democrats but if you get Mc-Millan* who carries great weight and Hanna, both of the committee, with you we can prevail over him as we have done before. In the House the committee will be with you all right. There Cannon is the foe of the Navy. It would be well for you to try to soften him by an Oriental politeness and I think much can be done. But I want you to see Moody in this connection. He is naturally with us and he has more influence with Cannon than anyone and if he backs the Naval committee they will win easily.

MacVeagh† writes me that he has been talking to Cullom and that he reported to you about it. He has made more headway than anyone else altho' I doubt his effecting anything. You know of course that the Chairmanship of Foreign Relations is the only thing I desire. I believe too that I could be of more service to you and your administration there than anywhere else or than anyone else. If Cullom opens the subject you can of course say properly that you earnestly hope he will retain

* James McMillan, a Senator from Michigan.
† Wayne MacVeagh of Pennsylvania.

Interstate Commerce but I had rather give up every place I have and all prospects of the Chairmanship I want so much than have you for my sake say or do anything which could embarrass you in the faintest degree with any Senator. My fortunes and opportunities are of mighty little consequence compared to the success of your administration and a friendly Senate is one of the elements of success. I am with you in all events. Other Senators are the ones to look after. Kohlsaat could do more with Cullom than anyone provided my name was not brought in. I think MacVeagh may write him.

I shall make a speech a week from tomorrow. I have discussed reciprocity on the line of your Message and have told the exact truth about the treaty difficulties. I hope that it may do good. I have gone my entire strength on the Navy. I hope you will like what I have said. I shall send you the speech and ask you to read it.

Best love always to Edith.

Ever yrs, H. C. L.

Personal.

WHITE HOUSE
WASHINGTON

Dear Cabot:—   November 5, 1901.

I will speak to the Secretary of the Navy at once.

I have been talking to Cullom, impressing upon him the great importance of the interstate business. If the corporation legislation were given to his committee, I think he would stay, but he is afraid the Judiciary Committee will seize it.

Faithfully yours,

THEODORE ROOSEVELT.

U. S. SENATE CHAMBER
WASHINGTON, D. C.

Dear Theodore: Dec. 3d, 1901.

The Message was fine—all I expected which is saying a great deal and I am very proud of your first utterance as President. I have never seen an annual Message followed with so much interest and attention in the Senate and I am told it was even more marked in the House.

I heard nothing but strong commendation and satisfaction expressed by everyone on our side.

Nannie went up and listened to it all, a tribute to you I assure you. Congress is very friendly, and all looks well for good work.

I shall try to get off tomorrow for a ride, but if it proves impossible I will telephone to the White House.

Ever yrs,   H. C. L.

U. S. SENATE CHAMBER
WASHINGTON, D. C.
Dec. 13th, 1901.

Dear Theodore:

I had been counting on a ride with you this afternoon but this confounded cold and laryngitis which I have been struggling with all the week came on with renewed force last night and altho' better this morning I am going to keep housed today and try to get rid of it. I hope I shall be all right tomorrow and able to ride with you in the afternoon if so be as you want me.

Meantime I have steered the treaty into calm waters by getting an agreement to vote on Monday which is the essential point. I have gone over the lists and we are safe for a more than ample two thirds. This will be doing well for before the holidays.

The House will not get the Philippine bill* over to us until Thursday so we cannot touch it until after the recess, but I have had my committee together and we are ready for it.

Yrs,   H. C. L.

1902

U. S. SENATE CHAMBER
WASHINGTON, D. C.
February, 1902.

Dear Theodore:

Will you ride in this drizzling rain or walk? Just as you please if you will let me know. Walking may be less wet—

* At that time I was Chairman of the Committee on the Philippines and a member of the Committee on Foreign Relations.

riding better sport if the horses do not balk too much. Have just come in out of the wet—hence my question.

Yrs, H. C. L.

Root says walk! I'll call at 4.00.   T. R.

U. S. SENATE CHAMBER
WASHINGTON, D. C.

Dear Theodore: March 24th, 1902.

There is to be a celebration of Edw. Everett Hale's 80th birthday, in Boston next week. Mr. Hoar is to preside. It would please them both immensely if you would write a letter to Mr. Hoar to be read at the meeting in praise of Dr. Hale. No man as you know deserves it more. His life has been noble and beneficent so I hope you will write. He has of course his weaknesses. He is an admirer of yours of many years standing. He even thought you remarkable and of great promise when you were in college!!!

Ever yrs, H. C. L.

U. S. SENATE CHAMBER
WASHINGTON, D. C.

Dear Theodore: April, 1902.

The Senate has adjourned over so I shall be free tomorrow and am longing for a ride in the afternoon. Let me know if you are going and will pick me up and when.

Make it as early as you can for we have to dine at seven you know in order to go to the theater.

Yrs, H. C. L.

First class! I'll call for you at 3:45.*   T. R.

U. S. SENATE CHAMBER
WASHINGTON, D. C.

Dear Theodore: May 19th, 1902.

Thanks for the photograph. It is an amazingly good snap picture of a horse running at a jump. One of the best I have

---

* I give this wholly unimportant note and the similar one of February from the many which exist because they recall the life outdoors and the walks and rides which played so large a part in our hard-worked days at that period and bring to me memories which are among the best possessions the years have left me.

ever seen and with the autograph will serve to recall some happy days passing all too fast. Dolliver* made a very fine speech today. The best I ever heard him make. It was a very powerful argument admirably put. When you see him say a word about it.

Love to Edith.   Ever yrs, H. C. LODGE.

U. S. SENATE CHAMBER
WASHINGTON, D. C.
May 20, 1902.

Dear Theodore:

I will come tomorrow eve. the 21st with pleasure.

Judge Gray † writes me that he would like much to see you but that he cannot yet scale the White House stairs and that of course if you are good enough to come and see him he will be at your service at any time you appoint.

Yrs, H. C. LODGE.

WHITE HOUSE
May 26, 1902.

Dear Nannie:

Surely you and Cabot have the right, above all my other friends, to feel a sense of personal proprietorship in whatever of right thinking there may be in this message; for you two are present in all I have said or done in public life.‡

Yours, T. R.

U. S. SENATE CHAMBER
WASHINGTON, D. C.
May 30, 1902.

Dear Theodore:

I have just finished reading your speech aloud to Nannie. We are both delighted. To us both it seems wholly admirable

---

* Jonathan Prentiss Dolliver, a Senator from Iowa.

† Justice Horace Gray of the Supreme Court. He was very ill at the time.

‡ This was written in a handsomely bound copy of his first message to Congress, December 3rd, 1901; the time occupied in binding accounts for the delay between delivering the message and sending the book.

and one of the best speeches you ever made alike in form and substance. It is everything it should be—in nothing finer than the quietness of the tone. Never was Emerson's "force of understatement" better displayed. It will be very effective and go home to the heart and head of the country.

Nannie sends her best love.

That speech was really a great piece of work.

I am glad to see too that your conception of the situation and mine do not differ essentially!

Ever yrs, H. C. L.

Dear Cabot: June 4, 1902.

By the way, I think it will rejoice your heart to know that Governor Brodie of Arizona (late Lieutenant-Colonel of the Rough Riders) is going to appoint Ben Daniels (late one-eared hero of that organization) as warden of the Arizona Penitentiary. When I told this to John Hay he remarked (with brutal absence of feeling) that he believed the proverb ran, "Set a Rough Rider to catch a thief!"

Love to Nannie.

Ever yours,

THEODORE ROOSEVELT.

NAHANT, MASS.,
June 5th, 1902.

Dear Theodore:

I hear on my return here that Judge Gray is so much more weak that he has resigned. I do not know whether it is true but if it is I want of course to talk with you before you decide. I have not bothered you because I thought it would not come for some time but I have thought it over a great deal.

Love from Nannie.

Ever yrs, H. C. LODGE.

Personal.   OYSTER BAY, N. Y.,
                                                      July 10, 1902.
Dear Cabot:

I have received your letter. We were overjoyed by the arrival of your young namesake.* I wrote to Bay that we were so glad to know that Bessie was doing well.

Now as to Holmes†: If it becomes necessary you can show him this letter. First of all, I wish to go over the reasons why I am in his favor. He possesses the high character and the high reputation both of which should if possible attach to any man who is to go upon the highest court of the entire civilized world. His father's name entitles the son to honor; and if the father had been an utterly unknown man the son would nevertheless now have won the highest honor. The position of Chief Justice of Massachusetts is in itself a guarantee of the highest professional standing. Moreover, Judge Holmes has behind him the kind of career and possesses the kind of personality which make a good American proud of him as a representative of our country. He has been a most gallant soldier, a most able and upright public servant, and in public and private life alike a citizen whom we like to think of as typical of the American character at its best. The labor decisions which have been criticized by some of the big railroad men and other members of large corporations constitute to my mind a strong point in Judge Holmes' favor. The ablest lawyers and greatest judges are men whose past has naturally brought them into close relationship with the wealthiest and most powerful clients, and I am glad when I can find a judge who has been able to preserve his aloofness of mind so as to keep his broad humanity of feeling and his sympathy for the class from which he has not drawn his clients. I think it eminently desirable that our Supreme Court should show in unmistakable fashion their entire sympathy with all proper effort to secure the most favorable possible consideration for the men who most need that consideration.

Finally, Judge Holmes' whole mental attitude, as shown for instance by his great Phi Beta Kappa speech at Harvard is

* My older grandson.
† Oliver Wendell Holmes, then Chief Justice of Massachusetts.

such that I should naturally expect him to be in favor of those principles in which I so earnestly believe.

Now a word as to the other side. It may seem to be, but it is not really, a small matter that his speech on Marshall should be unworthy of the subject, and above all should show a total incapacity to grasp what Marshall did. In the ordinary and low sense which we attach to the words "partisan" and "politician," a judge of the Supreme Court should be neither. But in the higher sense, in the proper sense, he is not in my judgment fitted for the position unless he is a party man, a constructive statesman,* constantly keeping in mind his adherence to the principles and policies under which this nation has been built up and in accordance with which it must go on; and keeping in mind also his relations with his fellow statesmen who in other branches of the government are striving in cooperation with him to advance the ends of government. Marshall rendered such invaluable service because he was a statesman of the national type, like Adams who appointed him, like Washington whose mantle fell upon him. Taney was a curse to our national life because he belonged to the wrong party and faithfully carried out the criminal and foolish views of the party which stood for such a construction of the Constitution as would have rendered it impossible even to preserve the national life. The Supreme Court of the sixties was good exactly in so far as its members fitly represented the spirit of Lincoln.

This is true at the present day. The majority of the present Court who have, although without satisfactory unanimity, upheld the policies of President McKinley and the Republican party in Congress, have rendered a great service to mankind and to this nation. The minority—a minority so large as to lack but one vote of being a majority—have stood for such reactionary folly as would have hampered well-nigh hopelessly this people in doing efficient and honorable work for the national welfare, and for the welfare of the islands themselves,

* No man is fit to be in the Supreme Court if he is not a constitutional lawyer, in the sense that Marshall was; a constitutional statesman believing in great party principles, and willing to continue the Constitution so that the nation can develop on the broadest lines.

in Porto Rico and the Philippines. No doubt they have possessed excellent motives and without doubt they are men of excellent personal character; but this no more excuses them than the same conditions excused the various upright and honorable men who took part in the wicked folly of secession in 1860 and 1861.

Now I should like to know that Judge Holmes was in entire sympathy with our views, that is with your views and mine and Judge Gray's, for instance, just as we know that ex-Attorney General Knowlton is, before I would feel justified in appointing him. Judge Gray has been one of the most valuable members of the Court. I should hold myself as guilty of an irreparable wrong to the nation if I should put in his place any man who was not absolutely sane and sound on the great national policies for which we stand in public life.

Faithfully yours,
THEODORE ROOSEVELT.

P. S.—Judge Gray's letter of resignation to take effect upon the appointment of his successor, or as I may otherwise desire, has just come, so that I should know about Judge Holmes as soon as possible. How would it do, if he seems to be all right, to have him come down here and spend a night with me, and then I could make the announcement on the day that he left, after we have talked together?

Personal.   NAHANT, MASS.,
To the President:—   July 11, 1902.

You will perhaps remember the Reverend Mr. Stuntz who came home from the Philippines and made such a strong report in favor of all we were doing there, which gratified the Secretary of War very much and which was published last winter. We intended to have him before the Committee as a witness, but the list was so long that his name was not reached. He stood by us when we needed such testimony and all he said was very much appreciated at the time. I send you his letter simply to let you see what he says about the Legislature,

in regard to which I am afraid you thought me a little impracticable. It indicates simply that there are observers there of
long experience who are deeply interested in our management of
the Philippines who feel grave doubts as to the legislative experiment. That we must try the experiment sooner or later
I have no doubt, but I do feel that it is of the utmost importance to move very slowly. In all history no Asiatic people
have established a representative government until Japan
tried it, and their experiment has not been a very brilliant
success. It is for this reason that I hesitate so much about
having it in the bill* and am so anxious to go very slowly in
setting it up.

I have the honor to be, with the highest respect,

Sincerely yours,   H. C. LODGE.

Personal.   NAHANT, MASS.,
                                             July 28th, 1902.
Dear Theodore:

I have just perused the letter of the "Committee of Supervision" addressed to you. It really deserves only a line from
Mr. Cortelyou to say that he will bring it to your attention.
But I cannot help admiring the audacity of the portentous
conceit of the whole thing especially in view of the fact that
the N. E. Anti-Imperialist League of which they are all members has just announced that it will contribute money to the
extent of its abilities to elect Democratic Congressmen everywhere. I suppose they represent themselves. Certainly they
represent no one else and I do not believe that they will be a
very effective adjunct to the Democratic party. But you can
rest easy for they are prepared to help you out and supervise
everything for you or with you. They treat you very well in
their patronizing way but as usual the roles of villains in the
piece are reserved for Root and myself. How queer they are!
You evidently have very wicked partners.

Love to Edith.

Yrs,   H. C. L.

* The organic Act for the Philippines.

Personal.   OYSTER BAY, N. Y.,
                                             July 30, 1902.
Dear Cabot:

The foolish letter* of Adams, Schürz, and Welsh was simply
acknowledged by my secretary. My present intention is to
take no further notice of it. They do not give a specific instance, although they say they could give several. It is of
course an unpardonable bit of folly and impertinence on their
part to speak as they do. If they gave me a definite case I
should look it up; but I am in no way bound to ask them what
the definite particulars are of cases which they allege that they
have, when they do not choose to volunteer the information.
If I had to write a general answer to their letter, I would either
simply send them a copy of my Arlington speech or else take
off their individual hides. The latter would be what I should
like to do, but I hardly think it is worth while dignifying them.
There is one consideration, however: I should like to keep this
anti-imperialist issue to the fore in the congressional campaigns, for if it is made the main issue we can certainly beat
the Democrats out of their boots. For this reason I have
thought it possible it might be well to take some notice of it.
I doubt, however, whether they are important enough to keep
the public gaze fixed upon them.

                         Faithfully yours,
                            THEODORE ROOSEVELT.

There has been a ferocious *Catholic*—instead of A. P. A.—
outbreak against Taft! It is on behalf of the friars.† I earnestly desire that you speak in New York State this fall.

                                             NAHANT, MASS.,
                                             July 30th, 1902.
Dear Theodore:

Delighted to get yours of the 29th and to know that you are
coming here. We shall of course meet you at Newport. I assume that here you just want a quiet day and I shall have no
function or reception whatever because if a beginning is made
on such things there is no end. It must be something or noth-

---

* Relating, I assume from what follows, to the Philippines.
† Spanish friars in the Philippines.

ing. If there is any one (or more) whom you want to see for any reason whatever let me know and I will arrange to have them here.

It is too bad that Edith cannot come. We should so like to see her and have her under our roof here.

We have a room for Mr. Cortelyou whom we shall be delighted to see and if you have others in your suite let me know so that I can make provision for them elsewhere. As I understand you will come from Newport here on Sunday and spend Monday.

I see comments on some interview attributed to me anent the Anti-Imperialist's letter. I gave none. All I said was that I had nothing to say and should discuss the Philippines on the stump. This for your information as apparently some obliging reporter has compiled a statement for me.

Love to Edith.

Yrs, H. C. L.

Personal.   OYSTER BAY, N. Y.,
                                              August 7, 1902.
Dear Cabot:

All your various communications will receive due heed. There is an awful muss over the District Commissionership which I shall explain to you when we meet.

I am sending to you, for your private information, a copy of a letter of mine to Commissioner Ware, because I am decidedly pleased with the showing my regiment makes in the official figures of the relative losses suffered, and number of pensions applied for, by the various regiments who served before Santiago.

Faithfully yours,
THEODORE ROOSEVELT.
Enclosure.

Is it convenient for you and Nannie to meet me at Newport at the christening* and then have me on Sunday evening go with you (in my car!) to Nahant?

* Roosevelt was to be a godfather, and my wife godmother, of Theodore, youngest son of Winthrop Chanler.

NAHANT, MASS.,
Aug. 9th, 1902.

Dear Theodore:

Yours of the 7th has just come. I am sorry there is a muss over the Dist. Commissioner and as I do not know what the trouble is of course cannot say anything. You understand that I recommended West, as I do very heartily, because I have known him a long time, like him and am certain that he is honest, able and loyal. He is a very superior man to any of the Commissioners in my experience except Macfarland and has I should think the best of local and political support as well as universal newspaper backing.

I send you by this mail the letters about Cameron Forbes* which you asked him to get. I want you as a favor to me and in justice to him to read them over. I confess I was amazed by them. I have never seen such a set of endorsements. They come from the very strongest business men from Seattle to Boston. He insisted on separating those who knew his work from those who only knew him. He is honest all through. He can get any amount of political letters but said you had not asked for them. I really think he is exceptionally fitted for the work and ambition alone takes him to it. He has now gone to his ranch. He was afraid that you might think him over impatient on account of his asking to see you. But I told him not to disturb himself on that point. The fact is, he has had some big business offers open until October and he does not want to take them because he wants public work and yet he does not like to throw them over because he does not wish to be idle. I told him not to be nervous or restless, that the matter could not be decided now and that he must wait with philosophy.

We shall meet you at Newport and come up with you. I assume that under this arrangement you will *not* go to Newport Monday the 25th but will stay here quietly thro' the day and go up to Boston late in the afternoon. I would of course greatly prefer that you should pass Monday night

* W. Cameron Forbes of Boston, afterward Commissoner and Governor-General of the Philippines.

here but I think you will have to show yourself in Boston. It would not do not to and they expect you late on Monday.

I read your letter about your regiment with great interest. It is really a very fine record all round and the low percentage of pensions is very much to their honor.

As a statistician however even that low percentage interests me for it completes the disposition of the regiment. In office— in jail—pensioned—dead in their boots—I believe that will account for them all. Excuse this jibe. I seriously think it is a most remarkable and honorable record. You have a right to be proud of it.

I have so many things to say to you and to talk over that if I run on I shall never finish and so I shall wait until we meet.

Best love to Edith.

Ever yrs, H. C. Lodge.

Personal.

To the President :—

NAHANT, MASS.,
Aug. 9th, 1902.

I send herewith letters in relation to Cameron Forbes. He has divided them himself into those of gentlemen who have known his work and other letters from persons who have simply known him and about him. He has also enclosed all the envelopes in which the letters originally came and I forward everything just as it came to me. I confess I was astonished at the letters which have been voluntarily given to him. They form one of the most remarkable endorsements I have ever seen. They come as you will notice from very leading men in all parts of the country. I should regard it as a personal favor if you would take the trouble to look over these letters for I do not see how any man could be more highly commended and on better authority for the post which he seeks. Mr. Forbes told me that you had asked him to get letters from business men and he did so. He is able to get political and senatorial letters from Iowa, Nebraska, Wyoming and one or two other Western States but will not do so unless you wish it. I really think he is a very strong man and that is why I ask you to look at the letters which you asked him to procure.

I remain, Sir, with the highest respect,

Faithfully yours, H. C. LODGE.

Personal.   OYSTER BAY, N. Y.,
                                              August 11, 1902.
Dear Cabot:

I guess I shall appoint Forbes, but I do not like even to express an opinion now, for I dare not make up my mind until I get the whole list before me.

I have been chuckling over your account of the disposition of the regiment, and Edith will be equally amused.

Of course I shall stay Monday with you at Nahant; but do you really think I have got to go to Boston on Monday evening? Remember that I have spoken in Boston on Commencement Day, and I very earnestly desire to avoid speaking again, if it is possible.

Friday I spent the night camping out for the benefit of Kermit, Archie and a small cousin. They all had a thrilling time enjoying the discomforts, and were compensated by hearing a fox bark and later seeing it. As there was an 8-mile row in the evening and an 8-mile row the next morning back, and very little intervening sleep, I was able to accept the ending of the trip with philosophy.

I have had a very nice letter from Hoar, and shall announce Judge Holmes' appointment today.

Faithfully yours,

THEODORE ROOSEVELT.

P. S.—I do not want to go to Boston at all. If I do go couldn't I speak before the Social Settlement people? They have been bothering me to talk to them for sometime. I hail the chance on these trips to talk to some special body on some special subject, for it is a terrific strain to have to meet the same kind of an audience and to make the same kind of a speech again and again.

NAHANT, MASS.,
Aug. 17th, 1902.

Dear Theodore:

I got back last night from McMillan's* funeral—a melancholy journey, and found your telegram and letter which I answered as best I could by wire. When you see Cortelyou's telegram you will understand why I replied as I did from Detroit.

It is too bad that you have to go to Boston and you may be sure that we do not want you to. But the first schedule having provided for it they got their minds set and it would not have done to change afterwards. I know what a strain the conventional wayside speech is but you need not talk more than 5 minutes in either Lynn or Boston. It is really to show yourself and no more.

Glad to hear what you say about Forbes but shall not mention it. He must take his chance of course.

As for Holmes I have never known a nomination received in the Press with such a chorus of praise—here and everywhere. McComas† who has read H's books and decisions speaks of him in the highest terms. So did the Senators at Detroit; —all seem pleased.

I am looking forward as you may imagine to seeing you. I shall be with you throughout your trip in the State both going and coming.

Love to Edith.

Ever yrs, H. C. LODGE.

SOMERSET CLUB
BOSTON

En route to New York,
Aug. 20th, 1902.

Dear Theodore:

Yours of the 19th reached me this morning just as I was leaving Nahant. I think on the whole it is as well not to take in Mr. Bloomfield on this trip. The Governor agrees with me as we have tried for obvious reasons to make everything

* Senator McMillan, to whom we were all greatly attached.
† L. E. McComas, a Senator from Maryland.

purely official. I know however the attraction which Mr. Bloomfield and his enterprise* and their like have for you and they all gravitate to you like iron filings to a magnet—which is not a little queer when I consider you and them. But I am far from disapproving. On the contrary. They will all vote for you and in the aggregate they are many. So I approve because I want you elected in case I should be defeated for the Senate. So that I may have the Cabinet to fall back upon —State Dept. preferred.

I had a note from Holmes telling me what he had written you. The very first rate man who is to succeed him as Chief Justice has put the idea in his head that if he remains C. Justice it will be interpreted that he does not want the Supreme Bench. I wrote him that he would be confirmed unanimously, that unless you desired to appoint him in the recess, which was not usual in appointments to the Supreme Court, the proper and dignified and natural thing for him to do was to remain Chief Justice [of the Supreme Court of Massachusetts] until his name had gone into the Senate and was confirmed. No one, I wrote him, would interpret it as meaning that he did not want to be Associate Justice [of the Supreme Court of the United States] for everyone knew that he would accept and that his name would not go in otherwise. Therefore, I said, be at peace and do not resign the C. Justiceship until you are nominated to the Senate and confirmed or until you receive a recess appointment which latter event is not likely to occur. I trust sire that this advice founded on truth and wisdom will meet your approbation.

We are looking forward to meeting you at Newport.†

Best love to Edith.

Ever yrs, H. C. Lodge.

* Settlement work.

† After going to the christening at Newport the President came as he had planned to my house at Nahant, stayed a day or two, made a speech in my own little town and then we went across the State to see the school at Northfield, returning thence to Fitchburg where another speech and reception. Then I was taken ill and obliged to return home. The President went to Springfield, thence to Pittsfield and on the way to Lethbridge his carriage was run into by a trolley car and was upset and his guard was killed. It was a very serious accident and a narrow escape for the President.

NAHANT, MASS.,
Sept. 3d, 1902.

Dear Theodore:

I hate a quitter and I felt a good deal like one yesterday. Nevertheless I was wise to go home for I have come round all right here and another long day in the cars I am afraid might have made me worse which I did not want in view of the Portland speech which I think it is important to make.

You remember my speaking of Ballard and his articles in connection with the charge of suppression in the Philippines. He sends me one about you which I think good. Also a specimen of his regular work. He is industrious and useful.

The more I think of that Duchess of Marlboro' business the more disgusted I am.

The Gov. and Dalton* seem to have given you a great reception. I wish I could have been there.

Sincerely yrs, H. C. LODGE.

Personal.   NAHANT, MASS.,
                                             Sept. 22nd, 1902.
Dear Theodore:

I take advantage of Edith's kindness to send you a private word on matters political. I have been digging about trying to get at the situation. I think I know it here. I do not like it. Trusts, thanks to you, we can manage. Tariff reductions for trusts we can meet in agreement as you met it so well Saturday—admirable speech. Trust and Free Trade papers don't like it. Others do. But it is right.

Tariff revision we can discuss. I do not fear it.

But the rise in the price of coal † we cannot argue with. It hurts people and they say (this is literal) "We don't care whether you are to blame or not. Coal is going up and the party in power must be punished." The colder the days get the more people want coal and the more they will have to pay if the strike goes on. By the first week in November if the strike does not stop and coal begins to go down we shall have

* Dalton, Mass., the home of Governor—afterward Senator—Crane.
† Due to a general strike in the anthracite coal fields.

an overturn. I am no alarmist but the indications now on this alarm me. I care nothing for the rest. Despite Henderson and the tariff and the trusts I believe we should hold the House and come out all right if it was not for the rising price per ton of coal which we cannot answer because it produces an unreasoning sentiment. Now I do not write this to bother you needlessly but to tell you the very great danger in this region and to ask if there is no pressure to bring to bear on those operators to make some small concession—a small one would do now. We have powerful friends in business. The administration is strong. Can nothing be done—*not in public* of course, I know that is out of the question, but by pressing the operators? It seems to me the crying need of the moment. I am ineffective in such matters as coal barons, but I will go anywhere, do anything I can. There are others far better than I whom you can call on. There is still time, plenty of time, to deal with it.

Take care of yourself.

You know so much more than I about the coal situation that you can give me light.

God bless you.

Yrs, H. C. LODGE.

Private.   NAHANT, MASS.,
Dear Theodore: Sept. 25th, 1902.

I felt great distress and not a little anxiety when I read the sudden news of your operation which was not dispelled by the newspaper reports but was relieved by Mr. Cortelyou's thoughtful kindness in sending me a special message.

I am so sorry for the pain and suffering and for the trouble I know you felt in disappointing so many people. The country is full of sympathy and at the same time extremely glad that the travelling has stopped.

I know I urged the tours or at least advised them and yet I have been miserably anxious all the time you were on the road and that is, I suppose, the same reason why everyone is so pleased to have you safe in Washington. All you have said and done has been of great good and service to the party and to sound policies but I think you have covered the ground and given the lead pretty thoroughly. You need not feel troubled on that score. You have helped the campaign wonderfully and are stronger than ever yourself in the real affection of the people.

Had I known you were ill I should not have sent you that depressed letter about the coal strike, but as it is in your hands I can only say the strike is uppermost in my mind and all I said in the letter I am more convinced of than ever. Therefore I poured it out to you. The worst is I cannot see what to do. We are running straight on to what may become an overwhelming demand that the government take the mines—which would be an awful step and we are being driven forward chiefly by the insensate folly as it seems to me of the operators.

I wish I could see a way out. The Attorney General* knows all those men and I know no one keener or bolder than he. Can he do nothing with them personally?

Gus carried a handsome majority of delegates last night. He has won † against great odds, all by himself by sheer energy, pertinacity and really unusual organizing capacity.

Foss‡ running on Billy Russell's old platform of free trade in everything Massachusetts buys and protection for all she makes has beaten Adams by a narrow margin. I have never seen anything like it. He is now, he says, going to attack our platform in the State Convention and substitute his own. He is mad with pride and vanity apparently. A large number of "business men" seem to be for him as he has made several— 10 or more—millions in speculation in stocks.

I sometimes think that "the business man in politics" is too often one who has no business to be there.

Odell seems to have downed Platt, but they endorsed you all right I observe.

Constance is slowly mending.

* Philander C. Knox—afterwards Senator from Pennsylvania.
† Enough delegates to nominate him for Congress.
‡ Eugene N. Foss.

Will you tell Mr. Cortelyou how grateful I am to him for the telegrams.

Give my best love to Edith.

Ever yrs, H. C. Lodge.

WHITE HOUSE
WASHINGTON

Dear Cabot: September 25, 1902.

It is exasperating to be laid up with this infernal leg trouble,* but thank fortune I was able to make my speech on the trusts and on the tariff. I am greatly relieved to hear that Constance is getting better. My leg was attended to just in time, but I think it will be all right now, though I am not allowed to put it to the floor even for a moment. At present my chief regret is that Washington is not nearer Nahant so that I might see you.

Ever yours, T. R.

Private.   NAHANT, MASS.,
Dear Theodore: Sept. 27th, 1902.

I was delighted to get a line from you but not a little troubled to learn that the condition of your leg was so near the danger line and worse than I had supposed. You are I know taking good care of it but there cannot be too much care and quiet. I shall remain profoundly anxious until I know that all is well.

The coal business here is getting rapidly worse. School houses are closing for lack of fuel. Prices are enormous and rising—much higher here on account of our distance from the mines than in the middle States and it is fast getting to the point where coal cannot be had at all at any price.

If no settlement is reached it means political disaster in New England and especially in this State. We shall lose the three close districts which will give the Democrats five, and Gus and George Lawrence will both be in serious peril. Our vote on the Governor will fall to the danger point. The demand that the

* The result of his accident.

Government take the coal fields is rising louder all the time. It is a perilous cry. When cold weather comes it will be far worse. You have no power or authority of course—that is the worst of it. Is there anything we can appear to do? Is there any form of pressure we can put on the operators who are driving on to ruin? The Unions are just as obstinate but the rising public wrath makes for them and they stand all the firmer. You must get very tired of my talk about this for I end with no practical suggestion. But the matter is pressing us so hard here that I cannot refrain from telling you our troubles. Why, sane, sensible, conservative men are urging us to declare in our platform that the coal fields must be taken! We shall not do it of course but it is a bad sign. I hope this condition is peculiar to N. England but there is no doubt of the situation here.

Best love to Edith.

Ever yrs, H. C. L.

WHITE HOUSE
WASHINGTON

Dear Cabot: September 27, 1902.

First, let me say how pleased I was to know that Gussie had practically won his nomination. I forgot to mention it before because everything had been swallowed up in the anxiety about Constance.

Now as to what you say about the situation.* I entirely agree with you that it is alarming, and chiefly from the cause you mention. There is a further cause. Now that there is complaint of high prices at home, people are being very much worried at the way in which articles are sold at a lower price abroad than they are sold here. The fact is undoubted. It is of course due to the further fact that in every business the surplus is disposed of at below the regular prices. The popular way of expressing the fact is that the trusts sell goods lower abroad than at home, because of the way they are pampered by the tariff; yet the type example being used, for instance,

---

* The coal strike.

in Kansas is the price of a pair of American shoes in Kansas and in London respectively; and of course there is no shoe trust. This is a tariff question pure and simple, and has no relation whatever to the trusts. Yet I think it has a good deal of a hold on the popular mind. Moreover, in the Northwest there is a good deal of formless and vague uneasiness about the trusts in favor of tariff revision.

But the real concrete trouble is in connection with the coal strike. The tariff of course has nothing whatever to do with the matter, as there is no tariff on anthracite coal. The coal operators are not combined so as to enable us legally to call them a trust; and if they were, all that we could do would be to proceed against them under the law against trusts, and whatever might be the effect as between them and the consumers in ordinary times, such a proceeding would damage, slightly at least, both them and the working miners, and would therefore have no possible effect of a favorable nature upon the present strike even if it were not improper to take it. There is literally nothing, so far as I have yet been able to find out, which the national government has any power to do in the matter. Nor can I even imagine any remedial measure of immediate benefit that could be taken in Congress. That it would be a good thing to have national control, or at least supervision, over these big coal corporations, I am sure; but that would simply have to come as an incident of the general movement to exercise control over such corporations.

All this is aside from the immediate political effect. The same unreasoning feeling which made the farmer in Kansas hold the government responsible because he himself had tried in vain to carry on an impossible agriculture in the arid regions, will now make the people hold the government responsible if they do not get enough coal. I have been in consultation with Quay, on the one hand, and with Sargent* on the other, as to what I can do, each of them having been in touch, both with representatives of the operators and with Mitchell.† One of the great troubles in dealing with the operators is that their

---

* Head of the Railroad Engineers.
† John Mitchell, head of the coal miners' Union.

avowed determination in connection with the present matter
is to do away with what they regard as the damage done to
them by submitting to interference for political reasons in
1900. From the outset they have said that they are never
going to submit again to having their laborers given a triumph
over them for political purposes, as Senator Hanna secured
the triumph in 1900. They are now repeating with great
bitterness that they do not intend to allow Quay to bully them
into making any concession for his political ends, any more
than they would allow Hanna to do it for his. I shall soon see
Quay again, and I may see Hanna. I shall see Sargent and
Wright.* Unfortunately, the strength of my public position
before the country is also its weakness. I am genuinely independent of the big monied men in all matters where I think
the interests of the public are concerned, and probably I am
the first President of recent times of whom this could be
truthfully said. I think it right and desirable that this should
be true of the President. But where I do not grant any favors
to these big monied men which I do not think the country
requires that they should have, it is out of the question for
me to expect them to grant favors to me in return. I treat
them precisely as I treat other citizens; that is, I consider
their interests so far as my duty requires and so far as I think
the needs of the country warrant. In return, they will support me, in so far as they are actuated purely by public spirit,
simply accordingly as they think I am or am not doing
well; and so far as they are actuated solely by their private
interests they will support me only on points where they think
it is to their interest to do so. The sum of this is that I can
make no private or special appeal to them, and I am at my
wits' end how to proceed. I shall consult Root in the matter.

Ever yours,

THEODORE ROOSEVELT.

P. S.—I shall make no more tours this year, and no speeches
until after election; then only three or four special ones in
November. I have delivered my message, and hope you will
like what I said about the tariff.

* Carroll D. Wright, Commissioner of Labor.

Personal.

September 30, 1902.

Dear Cabot:

After a second operation my leg seems really to be on the high road to recovery though there are features I do not enjoy —the dressing for instance.

After consultation with Root, Knox, Murray Crane and others on the one side, and after previous consultation with Senator Quay, Sargent and others from their standpoint, I have been inclined to think that there was a chance of my doing something anyhow. I have not yet worked the matter out perfectly clearly in my mind, but yesterday Root went on to see Morgan and explain to him that in three or four days I should take some action, probably by inviting the operators' to come to see me and requesting in good faith an effort on their part to come to an agreement, by arbitration or otherwise, with the miners. Thus I shall have a free hand to do what I deem best. I may be unable to do anything now, but I may tell them that I shall advise action along the lines I have explained in my speeches but of a much more radical type in reference to their business unless they wake up. I am also, however, to see the representatives of the coal miners. At any rate I am thoroughly awake and will do what I can.

Faithfully yours,

THEODORE ROOSEVELT.

Private.

[NAHANT, MASS.,]
Oct. 1st, 1902.

Dear Theodore:

I received your letter of the 27th day before yesterday but an all day trip to Alice Hay's wedding yesterday has delayed my answer. I agree of course with all you say. I look at the situation just as you do. I know only too well that you have no power by law to do anything. But the appearance of trying to do something will help wonderfully. It will prevent people's saying that the government takes no interest in the matter.

The newspaper reports that you have been conferring with Root and Knox and Moody and Crane about it have already done good. The popular feeling is becoming so intense that I cannot help hoping that we may be able to make a break. The tariff *per se* I do not fear but the coal strike is a hopeless antagonist.

Apart from that everything here is in fine shape. The party is thoroughly united and in good form. Mr. Hoar's resolution about you in our platform is eloquent and beautiful, very different from most convention resolutions. It will please you I know. The rest of the platform—(largely written by the undersigned) you will approve. It is straight-forward and not timid.

The recounts make no change in Gus's district. He has 76 out of the 130 delegates and will be nominated on Thursday. If elected as I think he will be he will be of value to you, to the party and to ever yours.

Constance improves a little but it is very slow. I have a continual anxiety about you not to be relieved until you are again out and about. I know you are taking every precaution.

Best love to Edith.

Ever yrs, H. C. Lodge.

Personal.   Nahant, Mass.,
Dear Theodore: Oct. 5th, 1902.

Your note of the 30th came and I was greatly relieved by the line about your leg. I am so glad to know that it is really getting well but what a painful trying thing it has been. It must have caused you a great deal of suffering.

I was deeply disappointed by the result of the conference and felt so strongly that when I spoke yesterday I did not dare to do more than heartily to commend your course and urge united support of yourself which everybody believes in here. If I had let myself go I should have said some things about the operators which would have been pretty bitter. I am thoroughly glad that you called the conference even though it has failed for the moment. Your action is universally approved and what you said was fine. You made no mistake. The general feeling clearly is that Mitchell made a fair proposition and that the operators are chiefly to blame. But the merits are lost sight of in the one primary desire to get coal. If people can get coal their sympathy for the miners will not control them. The operators who seem to me to have behaved as badly as possible made only one point that if they had proper protection they could supply coal. In some instances I think they have had that chance and failed. But it ought to be proved to the country either that they can or cannot supply coal if given proper protection. In either event the strike would break. Gov. Stone ought to be made to give them a protection which all the country can see is sufficient. I do not know that this is possible but it is the only way to remove their one ground of resistance. The feeling against the operators is growing very keen indeed. I fear that they are incapable of yielding to it. You know infinitely more than I. Only one thing is absolutely clear. The country is with *you* and will be with you in future measures and if you give the people coal no one can ever stand against you. The matter has not yet become political but if the strike continues until election no one can say how much harm it will do us.

Ever yrs,   H. C. L.

Personal.

October 7, 1902.

Dear Cabot:

I have your note of the 5th instant, with enclosures. I am feeling my way step by step trying to get a solution of the coal matter. Most of my correspondents wish me to try something violent and impossible. A minor but a very influential part desire that I send troops at once without a shadow of warrant into the coal districts, or that I bring suit against the labor organization; the others demand that I bring suit against the operators, or that I under the law of eminent domain, or for the purpose of protecting the public health, seize their property, or appoint a receiver, or do something else that is wholly impossible. My great concern is, of course, to break the famine; but I must not be drawn into any violent step which would bring reaction and disaster afterward.

Ever yours,

THEODORE ROOSEVELT.

WESTERN UNION TELEGRAPH COMPANY

Received at Nahant, Oct. 7, 1902.
Dated Washington, D. C.

To Hon. H. C. Lodge, Nahant.

I have just given the following to the press.

On Monday Oct. the 6th Hon. Carroll D. Wright Commissioner of Labor went to Philadelphia and gave to Mr. John Mitchell the following from the President. If Mr. Mitchell will procure the immediate return to work of the miners in the anthracite regions the President will at once appoint a commissioner to investigate thoroughly into all the matters at issue between the operators and miners and will do all within his power to obtain a settlement of those questions in accordance with the report of the Commissioner. Mr. Mitchell has taken this matter under consideration but the President has not yet been advised of any decision.

GEORGE B. CORTELYOU,

Secy.

Private.   [NAHANT, MASS.,]

Dear Theodore: Oct. 11th, 1902.*

My best thanks for your letter of the seventh. Everything you have said and done has been wholly admirable and you have not made a mistake. Although the conference failed the failure does not in the least affect the fact that your action was eminently wise and has strengthened you beyond words with the people. I am so filled with anger against those operators that I have not dared to trust myself to speak of them in public. Such insolence and arrogance coupled with such stupidity I

* Written before the above telegram was received.

have never seen. I firmly believe Morgan is behind them. He is playing with fire. The Socialistic feeling is growing apace and the demand that the government take the mines—one of the greatest disasters that could befall us. I am not surprised that you are overwhelmed with suggestions of impossible plans such as you describe. You can only keep up the pressure—trust to public opinion and wait on events just as you are doing. The pressure is getting so strong as I watch it in the papers and hear it all about me that I cannot but believe a break will come simply from the acuteness of the strain altho' I should be at a loss to say how. If the strike should end before election we should do very well here in Congressmen. Apart from the strike, conditions are good and locally coming our way. If the strike continues until election no man can say how much it will hurt us. Mr. Shaw* made a most admirable and most telling speech the other night in Boston. It delighted everybody. I hope and pray that all this strain and anxiety is not hurting you physically and that your leg is getting right again.

Love to Edith.

Ever yrs, H. C. Lodge.

WHITE HOUSE
WASHINGTON

Personal.

Dear Cabot: October 17, 1902.

On the suggestion of Foulke I shall write you one incident while it is fresh on my mind, in connection with this coal strike. The wild advice I have received in reference to it is really extraordinary. I must show you a letter from Stuyvesant Fish which is as startling of its kind as anything I have ever read. Also another from good Dr. Van Dyke which is to the effect that if federal troops are sent into the district they should enforce altruism at the bayonet's point on the operators.

The crisis came at the last moment. Between the hours

* Leslie M. Shaw, Secretary of the Treasury.

of 10 P.M. and 1 A.M. I had Perkins and Bacon* on here, on
behalf of Morgan, but really representing the operators.
Neither Morgan nor anyone else had been able to do much
with those wooden-headed gentry, and Bacon and Perkins
were literally almost crazy. The operators had limited me
down, by a fool proviso, to five different types of men, including
"an eminent sociologist."

This was a ridiculous proviso because I could have appointed
bad men in every case and yet kept to its letter; and they ought
to have given me a free hand. The miners, on the other hand,
wanted me to appoint at least two extra members myself,
or in some fashion to get Bishop Spalding (whom I myself
wanted), and a labor union man on the Commission. I regarded their contention as perfectly reasonable, and so informed Bacon and Perkins and the operators. The operators
refused point blank to have another man added, and Bacon
and Perkins came on nearly wild to say that they had full
power to treat on behalf of the operators, but that no extra
man should be added. Finally it developed that what they
meant was that no extra man should be added if he was a
representative of organized labor; and argue as I could,
nothing would make them change; although they grew more
and more hysterical, and not merely admitted, but insisted,
that the failure to agree meant probable violence and possible
social war. It took me about two hours before I at last grasped
the fact that the mighty brains of these captains of industry
had formulated the theory that they would rather have anarchy
than tweedledum, but that if I would use the word tweedledee
they would hail it as meaning peace. In other words, that they
had not the slightest objection to my appointing a labor man
as "an eminent sociologist," and adding Bishop Spalding on
my own account, but they preferred to see the Red Commune
come than to have me make Bishop Spalding or anyone else
the "eminent sociologist" and add the labor man. I instantly
told them that I had not the slightest objection whatever to

* Robert Bacon, then a member of the firm of J. P. Morgan & Co., afterward
appointed Assistant Secretary of State, and later Secretary of State, by Roosevelt.

doing an absurd thing when it was necessary to meet the objection of an absurd mind on some vital point, and that I would cheerfully appoint my labor man as the "eminent sociologist." It was almost impossible for me to appreciate the instant and tremendous relief this gave them. They saw nothing offensive in my !anguage and nothing ridiculous in the proposition, and Pierpont Morgan and Baer, when called up by telephone, eagerly ratified the absurdity! And accordingly, at this utterly unimportant price, we bid fair to come out,of as dangerous a situation as I ever dealt with.

Love to Nannie.

Ever yours,

THEODORE ROOSEVELT.

P. S.—In secrecy, Stuyvesant Fish's proposition was that the bituminous miners were entitled to get all the benefit they could out of the stoppage of the anthracite coal supply, and that with "all due respect to my humanitarian motives," he must protest on behalf of the operators, miners and carriers engaged in the bituminous coal trade against any effort of mine to secure a settlement which would interfere with the legitimate extension of their business! The only analogy I could think of would be a protest by the undertakers against the improper activity of the Government quarantine officers in preventing the admittance of Asiatic cholera to our shores.

As for the multitude of creatures who want me to "seize the coal barons by the throat," on the one hand, or, on the other hand, to "stamp out the lawlessness of the trades unions" by the instant display of force under penalty of being considered a demagogue—why, I couldn't begin to enumerate them.

T. R.

Personal.   NAHANT, MASS.,
                                                   Oct. 20, 1902.
Dear Theodore:

It was very good of you to find time in the midst of all your great cares to write me your letter of the 17th. It is putting it very mildly to say that I have enjoyed every word of it, and I have read it more than once. There is really something splendid in the perfect willingness of these great business minds to have a representative of organized labor, provided only that he is called a sociologist. It certainly was a small price to pay to get a settlement, and no human being has the slightest objection to it, though I have been extremely amused by the efforts of some of the editors to show why your labor man was a sociologist. The business man dealing with a large political question is really a painful sight. It does seem to me that business men, with a few exceptions, are worse when they come to deal with politics than men of any other class. As for the Stuyvesant Fish idea it is colossal. It defies comment. It is also an example of the business man. I can hardly find words to tell you though how fine I think your action has been and what wisdom, power and ability you seem to me to have displayed. It is a very great public service you have rendered, and I rejoice in it more than I can express. It has had a great effect already in this state. The tide turned in our favor as soon as the settlement was known. I was speaking in the Western part of the State and I could see the change go on, as the spirits of our people went up, and I think we have every reason to believe that we shall elect our Governor by a good large majority, and elect twelve Congressmen, all by reduced majorities, but still with a gain of three seats. I may be over sanguine, but that is the way it looks to me now. Bates* is making an admirable campaign. His speeches are strong and manly, and he has displayed a grasp of both State and National questions that I hardly anticipated. I am very well satisfied with the outlook here. Moody wrote me depressing accounts of Illinois and Wisconsin, but I cannot help hoping that the settlement of the coal strike will help us there as it has done here. In any event the popularity which it has brought to you has surpassed anything I have seen. There never was the least doubt about your nomination, but I consider that your success in this settlement has made your calling and election equally sure.

Now I am going to trespass on your time with a matter here. This is the treaty with Newfoundland.

* John L. Bates, then Lieutenant Governor—afterward Governor—of Massachusetts.

I am very anxious to see some arrangement made with New-foundland. I think in the broadest view it is very important for us to detach Newfoundland from Canada by some such arrangement, and I hope it can be done. I wrote this to Mr. Hay, but I told him at the same time that it would be im-possible for us to sustain the treaty unless it was reasonably satisfactory to the Gloucester people. I urged him to send for the Collector of the Port, who is a very intelligent man, and consult with him, as Moody was away. Moody knows the situation thoroughly and understands Gloucester. I suppose by this time he has returned. I have sent to Mr. Hay some of the objections made by the Collector of Gloucester to the proposals of Sir Robert Bond. They can, I hope, be met and overcome. I urged Mr. Hay by telegraph not to sign the treaty before election. The mere knowledge that the treaty had been signed might turn Gloucester against us and cost us the Con-gressional District. The fishing interests in this State, of which Gloucester is the principal seat, are very sensitive and very suspicious of any arrangement with Canada and New-foundland. The fisheries though not large in the whole volume of Massachusetts industries nevertheless represent a good many millions, but they represent more than that, for the fisher-men are a most important resource in time of war. Gloucester sent more men into the Navy during the Spanish War in pro-portion to its size than any city in the country, and more absolutely than any city except New York and Boston. Ad-miral Higginson told me that they were superior men and in three months most of them were petty officers. Some 450 men went into the Navy of the United States for the war from that one little town and every one was a first class seaman. There-fore, we have to stand by the fishermen. Mr. Hoar and I could not sustain a treaty to which there was serious objection. I am very anxious if possible to bring about some treaty which they will accept, even if they did not approve of all the clauses, but we must be very careful of our steps, and it would have been most unwise to have signed the treaty just before election.

Always yours,   H. C. LODGE.

Personal.   NAHANT, MASS.,
Dear Theodore: Oct. 27, 1902.

I have your line of the 24th. I have heard from Hay about the treaty and am going to write him today more fully in regard to it. If Moody could stay here a day or two after election we might be able to arrange it. I want to save the treaty, as you well know, but as I wrote you, the fishermen are not easy to deal with and are very sensitive and suspicious. We should endanger the treaty if we did not make every effort to get them in line beforehand.

I think we shall elect Bates, but I cannot tell how much the majority will be reduced. The big corporations, who expect to have matters before the Legislature, are undoubtedly doing all they can for Gaston,* and there is a certain amount of breaking away from Bates among the so-called better element. I am anxious, though I feel sure of electing him, but I do not want him cut down too far. The Districts, I think, are looking very well, but there is an uncertainty in the atmosphere which worries me. If you had not settled the coal strike we should have been washed out.

We are thinking of you a great deal today,† as you know, and I have sent you a word by wire to tell you of our good wishes.

I am working very hard, speaking every night, and this week I expect two or three times a night. Our strongest appeal to the Republicans is to stand by you, and that is why the Districts look better than the Governorship.

Always sincerely yours,

H. C. LODGE.

Personal.   NAHANT, MASS.,
Dear Theodore: Nov. 3, 1902.

I am glad you received the little book safely. Everything in it, of course, was old to you, but I wanted you to have it in book-form.

* Col. William A. Gaston, Democratic nominee for Governor this year and in 1903. He and Roosevelt had been classmates.
† His birthday.

You say that you are finishing your message, which reminds me of a very important matter, to wit, Immigration. The House passed a most excellent bill, as you probably know, revising the entire immigration law and putting in the illiteracy test. It came to the Senate, our Committee went through it with the utmost care and have reported it favorably. It is now on the Senate calendar. We ought to get it through at this short session without fail. It is the best chance we have had to secure this important legislation. I wish very much you would put in a strong paragraph in your message urging the passage of the bill now so nearly completed, and I will try to get Penrose to take it up as soon as we meet.

We are on the eve of election. My judgment on the facts as they come to me (and I have been in every part of the State, not having worked so hard or made so many speeches for years) is that we shall elect our Governor by a greatly reduced majority, and on the face of things we ought to have 12 Congressmen. Three of the Districts are very close and we may not do so well. There is a very strong feeling against Bates personally, wholly unreasoning and proceeding on the profound idea of a certain element which you well know "that he is not our kind." I do not find any such drift against the Congressmen. I must confess though that there is an uncertainty about the political atmosphere which worries me. This is an anxiety not supported by facts, but I have it nevertheless. It is possible, I fear, that we may have a bad break, although I do not anticipate it. We have made a good fight and done everything we could and we ought to win to the extent I have stated, although of course, the majorities will be reduced, which is of no earthly consequence if we hold our own in Congressional seats. We now have 10 Congressmen out of 13, so if we get 12 out of 14 it will be a handsome gain, and 11 out of 14 would give us one additional Republican seat.

Always sincerely yours,
H. C. LODGE.

WHITE HOUSE
WASHINGTON

Personal.

Dear Cabot :   November 6, 1902.

I think on the whole we can congratulate ourselves on the result. The West did better than the East, but that is because in the East the reaction from the tremendous anti-Bryan majorities has come.

Give my love to Constance and my heartiest congratulations to Gussie.*

I was immensely amused with the card you sent me.

Love to Nannie.

Faithfully yours,

THEODORE ROOSEVELT.

* He had been elected to Congress.